Praise for *Interim Governments*

"*Key to the success of any nation-building mission is the government that can oversee the transition from conflict years, the international community has become increasingly engaged in justice some occasions providing such transitional regimes. Karen Guttieri and Jessica Piombo have assembled a first-rate group of authors to examine this phenomenon from both historical and functional perspectives. Their conclusions will sometimes surprise—for instance, that imposed nondemocratic regimes have proven more enduring than democratic ones—and always inform. Interim Governments is thus to be welcomed as an important addition to our understanding of how efforts at state building, democratization, and post-conflict reconstruction actually play out.*"
> —James Dobbins, Director of the International Security and Defense Policy Center at the RAND Corporation, and lead author of *The Beginner's Guide to Nation Building*

"*Interim Governments raises many important questions and provides solid answers. Constructive definitions are offered and brought to life in lively and balanced case studies, showing which elements are unique and what lessons are most transferable to other situations. This text is timely, fills a subject space that needs to be addressed, and will prove to be a valuable tool to practitioners, trainers, and academics.*"
> —Frederick D. Barton, Center for Strategic and International Studies

"*This is a well-conceived, well-executed project that is sensibly organized and timely. With thematic coherence among the chapters, which are written to a uniformly high standard, the analysis is fresh, even in areas that have received considerable attention elsewhere.*"
> —Richard Caplan, University of Oxford

"*This volume offers a unique set of insights into the study of interim governments. When surveying the number of countries that are currently experiencing or may soon experience some form of interim government, the relevance of this study becomes obvious. It is particularly critical for policymakers in intergovernmental organizations and governments to understand the political, governmental, social, and security complexities associated with supporting or standing up a post-conflict interim government.*"
> —Jeff Fischer, independent consultant specializing in elections and conflict

"*Protagonists in today's deeply divided societies, wracked by war, often and usually eventually arrive at the realization that politics—not poisonous violence—is the least costly and most desirable way to redress their differences. When they do, the findings and lessons in this volume on interim governments should well serve as a guide on how to make the difficult and inevitably turbulent transitions from war to peace. Rigorous and engaging, this book will set the standard for the study of interim regimes for years to come.*"
> —Timothy D. Sisk, University of Denver

"*There are few transitions as fraught with danger as the transitions from autocracy to democracy or from civil war to civil peace. Combine them, as is often the case, and the dangers multiply. The editors and authors of this wide-ranging and insightful volume are superb guides to the analytical and policy challenges these transitions entail. Both scholars and policymakers are well-advised to pay attention to the thoughtful chapters gathered here.*"
> —Michael W. Doyle, Columbia University, and former UN assistant secretary-general

Interim Governments

Interim Governments

Institutional Bridges
to Peace and Democracy?

Edited by

Karen Guttieri *and* **Jessica Piombo**

UNITED STATES INSTITUTE OF PEACE PRESS
Washington, D.C.

UNITED STATES INSTITUTE OF PEACE
1200 17th Street NW, Suite 200
Washington, DC 20036-3011
www.usip.org

First published 2007

Printed in the United States of America

The paper used in this publication meets the minimum requirements of American National Standards for Information Science—Permanence of Paper for Printed Library Materials, ANSI Z39.48-1984.

Library of Congress Cataloging-in-Publication Data

Interim governments : Institutional Bridges to Peace and Democracy? / edited by Karen Guttieri and Jessica Piombo.
   p. cm.
Includes bibliographical references and index.
ISBN 978-1-60127-017-7 (hard cover : alk. paper)
1. Interim governments. 2. Peace-building. 3. Democratization.
I. Guttieri, Karen, 1964– II. Piombo, Jessica.
JC496.I58 2007
 321'.08—dc22
 2007032945

To all the bridge builders
who work and sacrifice for peace

Contents

Illustrations

Foreword

Interim Governments: Institutional Bridges to Peace and Democracy? is a significant and timely contribution to the increasingly important study of transitional regimes. With a broad spectrum of countries currently under or likely soon to be under some form of interim government, the centrality of the volume's subject to ongoing scholarly and policy debates about nation building and post-conflict reconstruction is readily evident. After all, a firm understanding of transitional experiences in societies that have recently emerged from conflict is vital for defining best practices in the present, particularly within today's context of regional upheavals and international activism. It is also vital for ensuring successful transitions in the future—that is, for strengthening efforts to institutionalize security and democratic governance in all post-conflict societies.

Although peace and democracy are the stated objectives of virtually every present-day transitional regime, tellingly, editors Karen Guttieri and Jessica Piombo have framed the volume's subtitle as a question rather than fact. Do interim governments reliably serve as bridges to peace and democracy, particularly as the international community becomes increasingly engaged in shaping and even administering transitional regimes? The volume explores many meaningful aspects of this question: how have interim models changed since the end of the Cold War; how does international involvement in the transitional process transform the balance of power among domestic elites; how does an interim regime affect the nature of the posttransition government? The fundamental question posed in the title gets to the volume's core, helping the contributors focus on pragmatic, practical, and pressing issues of transitional governance.

To help navigate these questions and attendant political, governmental, social, and security issues, Guttieri and Piombo enlisted a team of world-class scholars from the fields of comparative politics and international relations. Productively organized around three main sections—theories, case studies, and conclusions—the volume presents penetrating theories and wide-ranging empirical findings in a coherent and integrated fashion. The five theory-based chapters each offer keen insight into the latest thinking on transitional governance, offering many stimulating and useful prescriptions, such as encouraging self-rule, promoting agents of change, and engaging minorities. The nine case-study chapters—which either individually or comparatively examine the transitional experience of countries ranging from Afghanistan to Liberia—each provide insights into the broad challenges faced by interim regimes, such as local spoilers, endemic corruption, and budgetary and resource constraints.

While I will leave it to the reader to discover how the volume's many questions are explored and/or answered, I trust the editors and contributors will appreciate my highlighting two salient themes. Although each transitional government is unique in context, form, and structure, the first theme is a common one: legitimacy, governance, and security are inextricably intertwined aspects of stabilization; they are mutually reinforcing elements essential to the success of any transitional regime. As is so starkly evident in present-day Iraq, without meaningful security, good governance and the provision of public services are difficult to attain; without public legitimacy, meaningful security and the rule of law are threatened; and without good governance, legitimacy and public acceptance are lost. Somewhere within this precarious triangular construct sits the role of economic development, which is equally critical to achieving a long-term, successful transition.

While these elements form the core of any transition plan and are touched on throughout this volume, one additional element needs consideration: the role of personality. The personal qualities of interim leaders not only sway the interactions and decisionmaking of key actors in transitions, they also influence the legitimacy and functionality of any government structure—interim or not. As a corollary to this factor, the leadership style of local politicians can greatly affect public perceptions and attitudes. Just as a weak leader can undermine an effective government or transition process, so too can a strong leader help a country heal and evolve. Although these are highly subjective matters not easily measured nor frequently cited as significant variables in comparative politics or international relations, they are wild card factors that warrant serious study.

The volume's second salient theme is that the role of the international community in interim governing structures has a significant bearing on the legitimacy of the transitional and posttransitional regimes—and, by extension, on the security, governance, and economic development of the country. As Guttieri and Piombo argue, the identity of those international agencies forming and administrating governments is strongly related to the overall legitimacy of resulting regimes. Further, they observe that the very idea of internationalized interim administrations "harks back to an imperial era, the [bitter] memory of which for many around the world is still fresh." Although this observation about past grievances is not elaborated, the idea of historical memory and perception is highly significant and warrants consideration as another subjective element contributing to a transition's success or failure. In short, internationalized interim regimes are not formed or administered in a vacuum. When creating, implementing, and overseeing transitional regimes, the international community in general—and the United States in particular—must be acutely aware of this fact. Their administrative actions in one country can have a dramatic effect on perceptions elsewhere, and thus have broad implications and unintended consequences for future internationalized transitional regimes and nation-building missions, even in distant parts of the globe.

Interim Governments is only the most recent in a long line of important and timely volumes on peacemaking and nation building in USIP's publication catalog. Just within the past year, the Institute has published, among many other volumes, *Friends Indeed? The United Nations, Groups of Friends, and the Resolution of Conflict*, by Teresa Whitfield; *Human Rights and Conflict: Exploring the Links between Rights, Law, and Peacebuilding*, edited by Julie Mertus and Jeffrey Helsing; *Council Unbound: The Growth of UN Decision Making on Conflict and Postconflict Issues after the Cold War*, by Michael J. Matheson; *Leashing the Dogs of War: Conflict Management in a Divided World*, edited by Chester Crocker, Fen Osler Hampson, and Pamela Aall; and *Constructing Justice and Security after War*, edited by Charles T. Call.

Although transitional regimes are by intent meant to be temporary, their presence on the international scene will undoubtedly remain a constant as long as violence and conflict plague the world. But should decisionmakers and policy implementors pay heed to the thoughtful, astute, and telling observations and conclusions contained herein, perhaps there will be less need to ask whether interim governments are reliable bridges to peace and democracy.

Richard H. Solomon, President
United States Institute of Peace

Part One

Theoretical Considerations

1

Issues and Debates in Transitional Rule

Karen Guttieri and Jessica Piombo

Nothing is harder to manage, more risky in the undertaking, or more doubtful of success than to set up as the introducer of a new order.
—**Niccolò Machiavelli,** *The Prince*

Introduction

Transitional regimes—also called interim governments—bridge old and new orders of rule. Interim governance occurs at a hinge in history, a central point upon which future national—and at times international—stability depends. This historical moment is laden with contradiction and uncertainty. Interim governments, although historically significant, are meant to be fleeting and indeterminate, but at times an "interim" government lasts for more than a decade, or it transitions to a series of "temporary" governments rather than a stable, permanent, domestic regime.

Despite the domestic character and significance of governance transitions, the assembly and maintenance of interim structures has increasingly become an international project. The United Nations and other international organizations have taken on significant roles in state building to create or strengthen governing regimes.[1] The United States in particular has made considerable investments in regime change, to the point of placing stability, security, transition, and reconstruction activities on the same footing as major combat

---

The opinions in this chapter are those of the authors, who are writing in their personal capacities and not as representatives of the government of the United States or of the institutions with which they are affiliated. None of these ideas represent an official position of the U.S. government.

1. Francis Fukuyama, *State-Building: Governance and World Order in the 21st Century* (Ithaca, N.Y.: Cornell University Press, 2004), ix. "Nation building," by contrast, implies creation of the shared bonds of history and culture (99).

operations. This marks a major development in the evolution of the mission the U.S. government has set for itself in international affairs and the rebuilding of war-torn countries.[2]

The often-stated goals of external actors in state building are peace and democracy. The logic behind state-building efforts in Afghanistan, Iraq, and elsewhere is that durable regimes are vital to a lasting peace. An emphasis upon the particular character of new or strengthened regimes arose with normative consensus on (and empirical evidence about) the desirability of democracy, characterized by political processes that are participatory, open, and competitive; elections that are free and fair; and chief executives who are openly selected and subject to checks on their power.[3] However, despite a very strong correlation between peace and democracy, there remains some uncertainty about democracy's role. Anocracies, governments that exhibit a mix of democratic and autocratic features, are particularly prone to instability, including armed conflict or overthrow.[4] Democratization often brings with it inherent risks of opening the space for political contestation in already violently conflicted societies.

One of the contradictions in this process rests in the awkward attempt to create a sovereign state by suspending sovereignty. Most recent state-building attempts entail removing a state's ability to govern itself in order to construct a new, sovereign state from without. However, there are two additional contradictions inherent in this externally driven process. First, the very institutions that are created through external interventions can undermine the attempt to replace those imposed institutions with indigenously grown ones. Second, the very notion of suspending sovereignty in order to restore it is problematic and harks back to an imperial era, the memory of which for many around the world is still fresh.

Niccolò Machiavelli long ago noted other difficulties in establishing a new order. To do so creates sure enemies among those who profited under the old order and unsure friends among those who would support the new. Uncertainty derives in part from the unfamiliarity of a new system and in part from familiarity with the old. The residual legitimacy of the previous

2. U.S. Department of Defense, Under Secretary of Defense (Policy), "Military Support for Stability, Security, Transition, and Reconstruction (SSTR) Operations" (November 28, 2005, no. 3000.05). The text defines stability operations as including both "military and civilian activities." National Security Presidential Directive 44 followed on December 7, 2005, and endorsed the DoD directive.

3. Varying representations of these traits are characteristic of a polity score rated as a democracy (6 to 10). Monty G. Marshall and Ted Robert Gurr, *Peace and Conflict 2005* (College Park, Md.: Center for International Development and Conflict Management, University of Maryland, 2005). Freedom of organization and expression, including press freedoms, are often cited as requirements for full realization of democracy. See also Larry Diamond, *Developing Democracy: Toward Consolidation* (Baltimore: Johns Hopkins University Press, 1999).

4. Monty G. Marshall and Ted Robert Gurr, *Peace and Conflict 2003* (College Park, Md.: Center for International Development and Conflict Management, University of Maryland, 2003).

regime, including legal and administrative structures, can be a barrier to cooperation for those who live in "fear of opponents who have the law on their side."[5] The difficulty of establishing a new order is magnified for innovators who cannot "stand on their own feet," are unable to use force on their own, and must rely on others. This is just the situation implied in international administration.

Interim rule is thus significant, precarious, and changing in potentially problematic ways. Yet too little is known about the factors that make for success and failure in transition, in particular with respect to the explicit goals of peace and democracy and the implicit goal of strengthening effective sovereignty.

Our project aims to identify the rationale, form, and effects of contemporary interim regimes. We define an interim regime as an organization that rules a polity during the period between the fall of the ancien régime and the initiation of the next regime. The transitional period begins when the old regime falls—when it disintegrates, is torn apart from within, is overthrown by an invading force—and it ends when a new, supposedly "permanent" regime takes over. One of the key aspects in the functioning and effects of transitional regimes involves the issue of who initiates, sets the rules for, and then manages the transitional process.

In the first section of this chapter we review the relationship between theory and practice. This exercise unpacks the assumptions of the dominant, institutional frameworks and situates us at a juncture in history in which the division between domestic and international politics has become extremely thin. The term *international community* now refers to an agent of political transformation, not just a creature of it. Often a reference to the most powerful states, the international community is now a major actor, commonly involved in the day-to-day process of reconstituting governments thanks to the developments in peacekeeping and democratization that we discuss in the pages that follow. The heavy footprint of the international community affects the legitimacy of the resultant governments, which in turn affects stability, governance, and democratization.

We focus this institutional lens upon the paths of transitional regimes from around the world in a larger study, for which this chapter provides a conceptual framework. Looking at interim governments in Afghanistan, Bosnia, Cambodia, the Democratic Republic of the Congo (DRC), East Timor, El Salvador, Guatemala, Indonesia, Iraq, Kosovo, and Liberia, we seek lessons for both theory and practice. What was the rationale for the chosen interim structure? Are these structures composed of domestic or international components, or do they represent elite pacts or popular will? What are

---

5. Niccolò Machiavelli, *The Prince*, trans. Robert M. Adams, 2nd ed. (New York: W.W. Norton, 1992, 1977).

the legitimacy issues associated with these choices? What are the consequences for the extension of state control, the management of resources, the development of civil society, and the staying power of the new order?

The Evolution of Transitional Rule

Temporary regimes in dozens of countries across the globe have come and gone through the postwar and post–Cold War eras.[6] Some of these were more fleeting than others. These cases differed not only in longevity but also in causes and consequences. The post–World War II transitions in Germany and Japan are well-known examples of external roles in state reconstruction and democratization. These transitions revealed a key trade-off between stability and renewal: deep purges also created gaps in local governance capacity. The defeat of fascism and the subsequent dismantling of colonial structures throughout Asia and Africa also augured a "second wave" of mid-twentieth-century democratization, transitions that took place in an era of significant international intervention. In these early transitions, the role of external actors, from start to finish, was *the* significant factor in many of the processes.

Following this wave of transition immediately after World War II, the onset of the Cold War was characterized by East-West competition over the nature of political order in newly independent states, resulting in relative regime stability as each camp propped up supportive regimes around the globe. The next significant wave of regime change did not occur until the 1980s and early 1990s, in what is now called the "third wave."[7] In contrast to the significant role played by international actors during the postwar second wave of democratization, the third wave transitions were largely spurred by internal factors. Where influential, the international community affected the timing and sometimes the course of the transition, but often in an indirect manner and frequently as only one aspect of a much larger process. Scholars used terms like "demonstration effects" and "snowballing" to describe the influence of international events on what were, by far, primarily domestically determined processes related to the collapse of communism and the fall of domestic dictators.[8] In the initial phase of the third wave transitions, domestic power structures may have been discredited, yet they still often functioned, and domestic elites initiated the transition.

---

6. A partial list of postwar sites of transitional regimes includes the following: Afghanistan, Angola, Argentina, Bangladesh, Bosnia, Cambodia, Central African Republic, Chile, Congo, Croatia, East Timor, Ecuador, El Salvador, Eritrea, Ethiopia, Fiji, German Democratic Republic, Ghana, Greece, Guatemala, Haiti, Kosovo, Liberia, Mozambique, Namibia, Nicaragua, Nigeria, Papua, Peru, Romania, Rwanda, Serbia, Sierra Leone, Somalia, South Africa, South Korea, Tajikistan, Thailand, Uganda, and Venezuela.

7. Samuel Huntington, *The Third Wave: Democratization in the Late Twentieth Century* (Norman, Okla.: University of Oklahoma Press, 1993).

8. Ibid.

By the late 1990s and early 2000s, however, the role of the international community increased. Great powers and international institutions—no longer stymied by Cold War rivalry—took on expanded and more direct roles in the creation and maintenance of interim governments. Foreign invasion, rather than changes in the balance of power between domestic rulers and opposition, produced notable transitions. In many other cases, devastating civil wars tore apart and destroyed the legitimacy of domestic power structures that could mediate the transition from war to peace. As the nature of regime collapse evolved, the role of the international community increased. In the wake of this destruction and domestic power vacuum, great powers and international institutions took on an expanded and more direct role in the creation and maintenance of interim governments. Advocates of humanitarian intervention applauded military interventions to end civilian suffering and to promote democracy, while critics called humanitarian intervention "an extension of a de facto international imperial power over the 'failed state' part of the world."[9]

Theoretical Developments: International and Comparative Politics

Post-conflict democracy building currently represents a leading edge in democratization studies.[10] We contend that internationally created interim regimes constitute a distinct evolution in the practice of transitional governance.[11] We seek to consider the variants of this form in relation to other models of transitional rule. Here, we trace the evolution of this new model of interim government, identify the issues and debates that set this model apart from preexisting models of interim governments, and assess the implications for the consolidation of post-conflict peace, stability, and governance.

U.S. state-building projects in Afghanistan and Iraq and a dozen years of increasingly ambitious UN efforts have inspired many studies.[12] While some scholars have focused on the causes of state collapse and the consequences of international efforts to end civil wars[13]—and others on democratization or marketization[14]—most have been interested in peace, usually

---

9. Fukuyama, *State-Building*, 97.
10. Marc Plattner, "Introduction: Building Democracy After Conflict," *Journal of Democracy* 16, no. 1 (January 2005): 5–8.
11. Richard Caplan argues that the international administration of war-torn polities is related to, but different from, military occupation, the UN trusteeship model, and traditional peacekeeping. See Richard Caplan, *International Governance of War-Torn Territories: Rule and Reconstruction* (Oxford: Oxford University Press, 2005).
12. RAND quickly published a review of post–World War II U.S. nation-building efforts. James Dobbins et al., *America's Role in Nation Building: From Germany to Iraq* (Santa Monica, Arlington, and Pittsburgh: RAND, 2003).
13. Kalevi J. Holsti, *The State, War, and the State of War* (Cambridge and New York: Cambridge University Press, 1996) on the former; and Stephen John Stedman, Donald Rothchild, and Elizabeth M. Cousins, eds., *Ending Civil Wars: The Implementation of Peace Agreements* (Boulder and London: Lynne Rienner Publishers, 2002) on the latter.
14. Roland Paris, *At War's End* (Cambridge and New York: Cambridge University Press, 2004) and Mark Peceny, *Democracy at the Point of Bayonets* (University Park: Pennsylvania State University Press, 1999).

defined by the absence of a return to war. But they have differed over the means to get there, whether through security guarantees, power-sharing pacts, transitional authorities, or local or national elections.[15]

Indeed, in most of these works, comparativist and international relations (IR) scholars have created literatures that tend to talk past one another. Although this is perhaps reflective of the different sources of change in the various waves of democratization, the traditional IR theory tool kit offers limited resources to deal with the practical problems of state building. Meanwhile, comparativists tend to focus so much on domestic political institutions and processes that they overlook the extent of external influences.

A long-standing IR focus on systemic influences on state behavior provided little insight into the development of effective domestic governance.[16] Pragmatic institution builders of academe pay tribute to this tradition, as when James Fearon and David Laitin argue in favor of aligning state-building missions with great power interests.[17] However, even these authors recognize the need to build domestic instruments of political order. External actors make war to create change to suit national interest.[18]

Meanwhile, another stream in IR did focus on the character of the states themselves; in particular, it looked at democratic institutional mechanisms for conflict resolution and civil society checks on the state.[19] Unfortunately, the evidence on *new* democracies is sobering: democratizing states are actually more prone to conflict than their authoritarian and established-democracy counterparts.[20] Because of this dynamic, some scholars argue explicitly for a go-slow approach that focuses on sequencing—in particular, institution-

---

15. See, among others, Michael W. Doyle, "War Making and Peace Making: The United Nations' Post–Cold War Record," in *Turbulent Peace*, ed. Chester A. Crocker, Fen Osler Hampson, and Pamela Aall (Washington, D.C.: United States Institute of Peace, 1996, 2001), 529–560; and David A. Lake and Donald Rothchild, "Containing Fear: The Origins and Management of Ethnic Conflict," *International Security* 21, no. 2 (Autumn 1996): 41–75.

16. Works such as *War and Change in World Politics* and *After Victory*, for example, are more concerned with hegemonic war and the construction of global order than with domestic strife and state building. Robert Gilpin, *War and Change in World Politics* (Cambridge: Cambridge University Press, 1981); and G. John Ikenberry, *After Victory* (Princeton: Princeton University Press, 2001).

17. James Fearon and David Laitin, "Neotrusteeship and the Problem of Weak States," *International Security* 28, no. 4 (2004): 5–43. Fearon and Laitin are interested in solving the problem of recruitment for difficult missions. They advocate a full breach with the already weakened norm of recruiting impartial, nonsuperpower nations to lead peacekeeping missions.

18. John M. Owen IV, "The Foreign Imposition of Domestic Institutions," *International Organization* 56, no. 2 (2002): 375–409.

19. In 1989, Francis Fukuyama published an influential article that fit this stream and also seemed to legitimate the American model of governance and the drive to export democracy. Francis Fukuyama, "The End of History?" *The National Interest* 16 (Summer 1989): 3–16.

20. Edward D. Mansfield and Jack L. Snyder, "Democratization and the Danger of War," *International Security* 20, no. 1 (1995): 5–38; Edward D. Mansfield and Jack L. Snyder, "Democratic Transitions, Institutional Strength, and War," *International Organization* 56, no. 2 (2002): 297–337.

alization before democratization.[21] Yet the days are now past when arguments for authoritarian transition might be acceptable.

Democracy has become widely understood to be a behavioral standard in the society of states; as UN secretary-general Kofi Annan said in 2000, "The principle of democracy is now universally recognized."[22] Authoritarian regimes find it increasingly difficult to justify their existence in terms of effectiveness of governance or economic growth. Regardless of their performance in office, unless authoritarian rulers can claim legitimacy based on democratic elections, they come under pressure to liberalize. As a result, we have seen an increase in what Andreas Schedler labels *electoral autocracies:* autocratic regimes that govern with a veneer of electoral legitimacy.[23]

As part of this evolution in the norms of legitimate rule, countries have increased their emphasis on democracy promotion. Democracy promotion is not a new excuse for intervention by one state into the affairs of another, but international audiences seem to have grown more sympathetic to such arguments. As Mark Peceny observes, U.S. promotion of democracy dates at least to the liberation of Cuba in the Spanish-American War and has become "a crucial part of what it means for the United States to be leader of the free world."[24]

Because of the international acceptance of democracy as the only form of legitimate rule,[25] and the impact this consensus has had on both regime change and state building, the constructivist approach now seems to be the most useful lens that IR theory provides through which to analyze the multilayered process of state building. The ability to redefine interest and even identity is vital to the process of constructing political order.[26] However, what

---

21. Paris, *At War's End.*

22. "Kofi Annan's Closing Remarks to the Ministerial," Warsaw, Poland, June 27, 2000. Article 21 of the 1948 Universal Declaration of Human Rights proclaims the right to participatory governance, including periodic elections. See UN General Assembly Resolution 217A (III), December 10, 1948, www.un.org/Overview/rights.html. Several initiatives by regional organizations reinforce this concept. For example, the European Union accepts only democracies as new members. In the 1990s, the Organization of African Unity identified democracy as a standard of "good governance"; the Organization of American States declared coups against democracy to be illegitimate. For discussion on democracy as a norm, see Michael McFaul, "Democracy Promotion as a World Value," *Washington Quarterly* 28, no. 1 (2004–5): 147–163. A definition of norms is available in Ann Florini, "The Evolution of International Norms," *International Studies Quarterly* 40 (1996): 363–389. A theoretical discussion of norms is provided in Jurgen Habermas, *Between Facts and Norms: Contributions to a Discourse Theory of Law and Democracy* (Cambridge, Mass.: MIT Press, 1998).

23. Andreas Schedler, ed., *Electoral Authoritarianism: The Dynamics of Unfree Competition* (Boulder and London: Lynne Rienner Publishers, 2006).

24. Peceny, *Democracy at the Point of Bayonets,* 218.

25. Yossi Shain and Juan Linz, eds., *Between States: Interim Governments and Democratic Transitions* (New York: Cambridge University Press, 1995).

26. Here we borrow from John Ruggie's comment on what separates constructivism from realist and liberal approaches. John Ruggie, *Constructing the World Polity* (London and New York: Routledge, 1998).

remains is to identify the circumstances under which these changes are likely to occur and to lead to positive outcomes for the polity.

While IR scholars focus on these macro-level factors, comparativists retain a helpful focus on democratization and governance within states. Most theories of democratization have been interested in the transition from authoritarian rule and the consolidation of democracy.[27] Authors in this tradition examine issues of political culture and democracy; levels of economic development and their impact on the likelihood of transition and ability to sustain democracy; class composition and democracy; and the role of elite pacting in transitions from authoritarian rule.[28] Comparativists tend to examine primarily domestic factors and to assume that the state itself remains a functioning and viable entity throughout the transitional period. A more internationalized variant of the democratization literature examines the role of international assistance in promoting democratic transitions, yet it still falls short of assessing the long-term effects of international assistance on the viability and persistence of democratic regimes.[29]

The issue of temporary transitional regimes and interim governments has barely been touched in the field of comparative politics, with one significant exception. To date, the seminal work on interim government remains *Between States*, the volume edited by Yossi Shain and Juan Linz and published in 1995.[30] In this work, the editors and their case-study authors developed four models of interim governments: (1) revolutionary, (2) power sharing, (3) incumbent caretaker, and (4) international administrations. The revolutionary model is initiated from outside the regime and includes, as Andrew J.

---

27. Most theories of democratization follow in the footsteps of the "transitology" school, exemplified by the works of Larry Diamond, Marc Plattner, Philippe Schmitter, Terry Lynn Carl, Guillermo O'Donnell, and the hundreds of scholars whose works depart from the frameworks established by these authors.

28. For the seminal early work on political culture, see Gabriel Almond and Sydney Verba, *The Civic Culture: Political Attitudes and Democracy in Five Nations* (New York: Sage Publications, [1963], 1989); for the modern adaptation, see Robert Putnam, *Making Democracy Work: Civic Traditions in Modern Italy* (Princeton: Princeton University Press, 1994). On class requisites and economic development, see Barrington Moore, "The Democratic Route to Modern Society," in *Social Origins of Dictatorship and Democracy: Lord and Peasant in the Making of the Modern World* (Boston: Beacon Press, 1962), 413–432; and Seymour Martin Lipset, "Some Social Requisites of Democracy: Economic Development and Political Legitimacy," *American Political Science Review* 53, no. 1 (March 1959): 69–105. For analyses of elite pacting, see the seminal work by Guillermo O'Donnell and Philippe Schmitter, *Transitions from Authoritarian Rule: Tentative Conclusions about Uncertain Democracies* (Baltimore: Johns Hopkins University Press, 1986). For a review and critique of all these theories, which ultimately proposes that the nature of the outgoing regime is the critical factor in the transition, see Barbara Geddes, "What Do We Know About Democratization After Twenty Years?" *Annual Review of Political Science* 2 (1999): 115–144.

29. See, for example: Krishna Kumar, ed., *Postconflict Elections, Democratization and International Assistance* (Boulder and London: Lynne Rienner Publishers, 1998); Kevin J. Middlebrook, ed., *Electoral Observation and Democratic Transitions in Latin America* (La Jolla: University of California–San Diego, 1998); John Abbink and Gerti Hesseling, eds., *Electoral Observation and Democratization in Africa* (London and New York: Palgrave MacMillan, 2000).

30. Shain and Linz, *Between States.*

Enterline and J. Michael Greig note in this present volume, overthrow by either external or internal agents. Examples include France in 1944, Cuba in the 1950s, Ethiopia in the 1970s, Algeria in 1962, and Nicaragua in 1979.

The other three models imply more engagement of the ancien régime. In the power-sharing model, the regime compromises with opposition forces when it is weakened or collapses. Examples offered include Poland in 1989, Nigeria in 1993, South Africa in 1990–93, and Czechoslovakia's "Velvet Revolution" in 1989. In the caretaker model, incumbents initiate the transition when the costs of repression outweigh the risks of transition. Examples include South Africa in 1993–94 and Spain in 1976. In the international model, incumbent regimes accept external facilitation when long-standing domestic rivalries make it impossible to find a domestic-led solution. Examples include Afghanistan in 1991 and 2002, Namibia in 1989, and Cambodia in 1993.

Control and legitimacy vary in the Shain and Linz transition models. Revolutionary forces controlling transitions may enjoy legitimacy through popular participation but lack the benefits of legality that Machiavelli noted as a consideration. Violent disputes between moderate and radical elements of the new regime, and violent score settling with elements of the old regime, are dangers of revolutionary transitions. Competing revolutionary agendas tend to outweigh promises of democracy promotion, making the prospects for democratic development judged to be poorest after revolutions.

In contrast, a power-sharing government controlled by an outgoing administration derives its legitimacy from a bargain. However, the bargain may be tenuous in light of shifts in power between the opposition and the incumbents and the ability of the incumbents to enforce reforms without provoking a backlash. The prospects for democratization are somewhat better, but some obstacles persist. The old regime enjoys residual legitimacy and resource advantages that may work against reform, while opposition constituencies may become frustrated with negotiations and a slow pace of change.

Caretaker transitions typically appoint a formal, independent body that provides legalistic rather than democratic legitimacy. Caretaker transitions also wrestle with balancing public demands for retribution and the incumbents' desire for amnesty. This transition model appears to enjoy the best prospects for democratization, according to Shain and Linz, if incumbents display a genuine commitment or are so discredited that it is possible to build anew without violent upheaval.

In the international model posited in *Between States,* the United Nations—representing the international community—confers legitimacy and oversees the process, but in doing so it must overcome mistrust among long-standing domestic rivals. The linkages between this international model and the external overthrow of the revolutionary model are not fully considered in *Between States,* and the prospects for democratization are depicted as indeterminate.

We should note that even in this earlier work, the assembled authors focused on how the different institutional forms affected prospects for democratization, and their cases were motivated and populated by cases of postcommunist transitions to democracy. This focus was current with the disciplinary agenda of comparative politics at the time. A decade on, however, the nature of the transitional governments in and of themselves needs to come under the microscope. Significant developments in the practice of regime change include the starting and ending states and even the agents of change. A variety of forms of internationalized transitional administrations in particular prompt us to revisit the Shain and Linz framework ten years later. All the cases explored in this volume entail some degree of external involvement, and this in itself is a remarkable feature of the recent era.

New Directions

We argue that the nature of these new administrations is distinctly different from the international model set forth in *Between States* and early comparative literature on democratic transitions. First, the role of the international community is vastly more powerful now than it was in the early studies. External authorities have, in some cases, assumed *sovereignty*, in the sense of territorial control, and *governance*, in the sense of political administration. They have occupied in order to pacify and democratize so that they might produce "a political order that will fit into the world order they have in mind."[31] The expanded authority is evident in the power to declare a country war torn and therefore in need of repair.

Second, in terms of starting states, the international community has recognized that in many countries torn apart by internal strife, the urgent need to reconstruct institutions of governance cannot be met by domestic forces: there are often no domestic structures that can run the transitional government, at least in the initial phases. Therefore, the interim governments that now occur in the context of postwar transitions tend to be initiated and often managed by external actors. In the initiation phase of the earlier transitional regimes—particularly those described in the transitology school and by Shain and Linz—domestic power structures may have been discredited, yet they still often functioned, and domestic elites initiated the transition. Even the international model advanced by Shain and Linz was administered through domestic, rather than international, agents.

Third, the early models explicitly eliminated analyses of international takeovers. In fact, Shain and Linz, when discussing their international adminis-

---

31. Robert Jackson, "International Engagement in War-Torn Countries," *Global Governance* 10 (2004): 21–36.

tration model, specifically recommend *against* the intrusive engineering by external actors that became common after 1995. They argue that this type of administration was not appropriate for transitions that occurred in the context of state disintegration or violent civil war in which the domestic government was completely discredited.[32] *Between States* does not present a model of transitional governance for situations in which no government structure existed, for example, due to collapse in a civil war (as in Somalia, the DRC, and elsewhere). And it does not address situations in which the government structure collapsed after invasion by a foreign power that nonetheless wanted an international mandate to establish a new regime (Afghanistan and Iraq) or negotiated entry of an outside military force to protect secessionists (arguably, East Timor and Kosovo). And yet, since 1995, we have seen increased occurrence of this very requirement, to create government from scratch.

In transitional administrations in the wake of civil war and state collapse, much more is at stake than simply the quality of democracy in the resulting regimes. In many instances, the very nature, legitimacy, functioning, and viability of post-conflict state structures are at stake. For example, states like Somalia seem to be stuck with a series of virtually permanent "transitional governments" that cannot even govern the capital city. Other countries like Afghanistan have gone beyond the "transitional government" phase, yet the resultant central government can barely project force beyond the capital city.

In response to such recent developments, the innovations in transitional administration have been profound. At the same time, the more traditional, domestic-driven transitional administrations still exist, although they too seem influenced by international norms and have evolved in terms of their effectiveness in creating stable and legitimate post-conflict regimes.

Our project therefore assesses numerous cases of recent interim regimes, arranging the studies to reveal insights about how the various regimes affect domestic order, legitimacy, and good governance. These are features commonly described as vital to postwar stabilization and reconstruction and, by extension, to international peace and security. In terms of the first, the fact that international engagement is not homogenous leads us to ask a set of questions: Does the identity of the external facilitator affect the legitimacy of the interim government? Does the process of selecting an interim government affect the durability of the regime? How does the establishment of direct transitional authority, for example, provide necessary stability? Under what circumstances is external pressure productive or counterproductive, and how

---

32. In chapter four of *Between States*—"The International Government Model Revisited"—Shain and Berat argue that "from the experience of Namibia and Cambodia, we see that a 'failed state,' to use Heldman and Ratner's terminology, is unsuited to the model. The most important factor for the success of the model is the viability of an incumbent regime which has committed itself, because of domestic and international pressure, to effecting a democratic regime change via cooperation with its rivals" (74–75).

do we measure it? Regarding the issue of *good governance,* are there benefits of an internationally created and managed interim government for the creation of a domestic, democratic government that has enough state capacity to provide at least the internationally accepted minimum of public goods?

In probing these new directions—each of the cases in this volume explores these questions—our work builds directly on the work of Michael Doyle, Marina Ottaway, Bethany Lacina, and others. We find in Doyle's work an exemplary approach that takes domestic environmental conditions into account for external transitional administrators.[33] He observes that from case to case, competitors for postwar rule vary in number, coherence, and hostility to one another. He then provides prescriptions based upon his assumption that these domestic factors influence the nature of external intervention. External actors are more likely to be needed in circumstances in which the factional conflicts are particularly divisive and incoherent, but when the factions are more reconciled, as in El Salvador, Namibia, and Tajikistan, less intrusive transitional authority is needed. In that event, external actors provide transparency, continuing coordination mechanisms, and technical assistance in elections and police training that build capacity.

A situation in which factions are coherent and hostile, as in Cambodia, mandates a stronger role for the international community; international actors must settle conflict between combatants that are still capable of fighting while administering the transition to a peaceful order. The continuing potential for factions to spoil a peace accord limits the leverage of the international regime that must keep all factions placated. Although Doyle sees variance in the demand for external intervention, the problem remains to recruit outsiders willing and able to supply it.

Doyle's work does not simply make useful distinctions among post-conflict environments; one can also extend his analysis of UN administrations to generate models of international transitional regimes. Doyle and Sambanis assess the evolution of UN interventions and distinguish between those with solely monitoring and facilitation functions, supervisory authority, executive authority, and administrative authority.[34] Monitoring and facilitation missions support a domestically created and administered transitional regime; the international authorities have no mandate or authorization to actually take on any governance functions. When the United Nations has administrative authority, it also monitors and assists a caretaker interim regime; domestic institutions hold full leg-

---

33. Doyle et al., "War Making and Peace Making," in Hampson, Crocker, and Aall, eds., *Turbulent Peace,* 550–551.

34. Michael W. Doyle and Nicholas Sambanis, *United Nations Peace Operations: Making War and Building Peace* (Princeton and Oxford: Princeton University Press, 2006), 324–325. Jarat Chopra and Richard Caplan offer other versions of this typology. Jarat Chopra, *The Politics of Peace-Maintenance* (Boulder, Colo.: Lynne Rienner Publishers, 1998); and Caplan, *International Governance of War-Torn Territories.*

islative authority. Unlike the pure monitoring missions, however, the administrative missions have the authority to intervene to assist in a flailing domestic administration.[35] Increasing in international influence, UN missions with executive authority vest executive authority in the UN agencies, while the United Nations and fledgling domestic institutions share legislative authority. In the most internationalized of these, under the supervisory authority missions, the UN transitional authorities wield full legislative, executive, and administrative authority.

In essence, Doyle and Sambanis are expanding on the forms of international administrations provided by Shain and Linz, as depicted in figure 1.1. In this figure, we have substituted "international actors" for Doyle's "UN administrations," allowing for the fact that these transitional bodies could be composed of a much broader range of actors than Doyle and Sambanis assess. The functions of these transitional bodies, however, are likely to approximate the distinction among advisory, executive, and supervisory authority that the authors lay out. In these three types of international administrations, the first encapsulates the model as originally conceived by Shain and Lynn Berat, while the second and third represent the incorporation of the fully internationalized model, in which international actors take on actual functions of governance and move beyond a merely supportive role.

Yet, despite Doyle and Sambanis's elaboration of the forms of international administration, their analysis provides little insight into the viability of the interim government structures themselves. On this topic, Ottaway and Lacina explicitly consider the costs and benefits of working with extant power structures.[36] The authors compare "local transitional governments" with "power sharing" and "international administrations."[37] They provide their deepest insights on the matter of outcomes. Like an external shock to the political system, an international administrative authority ought to be able to create deep changes, yet these often fall short. In Afghanistan, an international coalition working together with local insurgents overthrew the Taliban regime and set about remaking the nation. However, warlords proved adept at manipulating the *loya jirga* (lit., "grand council," a traditional Afghan governing assembly) process to consolidate their influence. The "local transitional government" approach is less costly in lives and treasure, argue

---

35. Doyle and Sambanis, *United Nations Peace Operations.*

36. Marina Ottaway and Bethany Lacina, "International Interventions and Imperialism: Lessons from the 1990s," *SAIS Review* 23, no. 2 (Summer–Fall 2003): 71–92. See appendixes two and three for depictions of the Doyle and Ottaway-Lacina models.

37. Although the authors lump them together, we view the *reinstallation* of democratically elected leaders who had been deposed—for example, in Haiti and Sierra Leone—as a very different project than reliance on a caretaker or power-sharing government. Another difficulty with the Ottaway-Lacina framework is the separation of internal and external rule, when we tend to see some sort of indigenous interim regime set up alongside international administrations.

Figure 1.1   Fully Internationalized Interim Governments

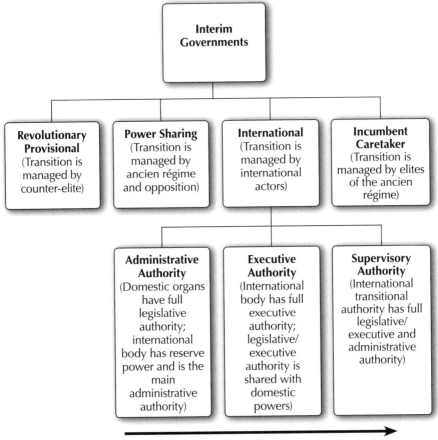

Direction of International Authority

Source: The authors are indebted to Aurel Croissant, who developed the first iteration of this figure based on his adaptations from Shain and Linz (1995) and Doyle (2003, 551–553).

Ottaway and Lacina, but it is also less likely to truly shift existing power structures. For example, despite a massive commitment of troops and other resources to the United Nations Transitional Authority in Cambodia (UNTAC), efforts to preserve functioning state institutions gave the advantage to the incumbent, Hun Sen. A key lesson of *Between States* relates to the wisdom of preserving the viability of the incumbent regime. Specifically, the value of preserving the incumbent regime must be weighed against the possibility of antidemocratic practices, such as those that occurred in Cambodia.

The alternative, in which the international actors decide rather than advise, has its own problems. Exercising authority without judicial review for long periods of time not only risks creating a culture of dependency but also jeopardizes the establishment of a stable rule of law and respect for human rights.

In Bosnia, for example, the Office of the High Representative (OHR) has exercised increasing authority; it removed eleven officials and public servants and imposed sixteen laws at the state and entity levels between December 2004 and October 2005.[38] In response, the Council of Europe initiated an inquiry—known as the Venice Commission—into the compatibility of OHR practices with human rights standards. The commission argued that, although the OHR's use of such powers was beneficial to the governance of Bosnia, without respect for due process and judicial control, the practice betrayed the democratic principles the OHR was attempting to inculcate.[39] Similar issues of accountability have been raised with regard to the powers of the United Nations Interim Mission in Kosovo (UNMIK).[40]

Although it seems helpful to differentiate according to the degree to which the outside actors utilized existing administrative and political structures, important questions remain: how do the interim administrative structures channel political conflict, and what are the consequences for the legitimacy and the governing capacity of the resulting regimes? To answer these questions, our project picks up where Shain and Linz, Doyle and Sambanis, and Ottaway and Lacina left off. We begin this process by raising a number of themes in the nature of war, peace, and transitional governance that we believe have changed since 1995. In the following sections, we discuss the major issues and debates in the field of conflict and reconstruction studies that relate to the issue of interim and transitional regimes, focusing on the nature of conflict and conditions of change; the norms of sovereignty and intervention; elections as mechanisms to create political order; and the outcome of transitional regimes. In the case studies of this volume, the authors probe the effects these issues have on post-conflict transitions, particularly the viability of post-conflict structures of governance.

Internal Conflict and International Peacekeeping

The nature of conflict itself affects the nature of the transitional regime. Although most conflicts since World War II have been within states, the United Nations was initially reluctant to violate sovereignty in order to address them. In the early 1990s, however, more peacekeeping missions began to deal with internal strife. Regional organizations, coalitions of the

---

38. Human Rights Watch, "Human Rights Overview: Bosnia and Herzegovina," hrw.org/english/docs/2006/01/18/bosher12238.htm.
39. Council of Europe European Commission for Democracy Through Law (Venice Commission), "Opinion on the Constitutional Situation in Bosnia and Herzegovina and the Powers of the High Representative," 62nd Plenary Session, 2005 (CDL-PV(2005)001), www.venice.coe.int/docs/2005/CDL-PV(2005)001-e.asp.
40. Ombudsperson Institution in Kosovo, "Fifth Annual Report Addressed to the Special Representative of the Secretary-General of the United Nations" (2004–05), www.ombudspersonkosovo.org.

willing, and individual nations also began to develop peacekeeping and peacemaking capabilities, with or without explicit UN authorization.[41]

Resolving civil war situations is inherently different from resolving inter-state wars and often requires a heavier involvement of the international community. When conflict breaks out between states, combatants can retire behind the state boundaries to heal. Civil war combatants have to live side-by-side with one another and the victims of their violence. The role of the state in relation to society also sets internal conflicts apart. A state defeated in international conflict might lose legitimacy in the eyes of its society; a state that was itself a combatant in an internal war has deeper legitimacy issues, assuming that the state has remained intact.

Often, however, the degree of state disintegration and delegitimation has progressed to the point where no internal organization can take over government functions. In this case, the international community has increasingly borne the brunt of actual governance. Beginning with the intervention in Cambodia in 1993, the international community began to assume wide-ranging administrative roles. These roles were expanded in some international administrations, as in Kosovo and East Timor, to include basic policing, the provision of social services and other public goods, and legislation. Making reference to the colonial administration of the late nineteenth and early twentieth centuries, some observers call this approach "trusteeship."[42] Some distinguishing features of this approach include the following:

- International and domestic governance structures mix together. Internationals advocate "capacity building" and/or "participatory governance."
- Whenever possible, intervention or rule is legitimated externally by a UN mandate.
- External peacekeeping troops and possibly civilian police are deployed.
- External agents may seek to advance the national interests of contributing states, but they do not seek long-term occupation or annexation of the territory in question.

Most of the interim governments examined in our project were forged in violent environments. Deep divides, whether based on ethnicity, religion, or

---

41. Alex Bellamy and Paul D. Williams, "Who's Keeping the Peace?" *International Security* 29, no. 4 (2005): 157–195. Prior to the intervention into Liberia by the Economic Community of West African States Monitoring Group in 1990, and NATO's entry into the Kosovo conflict in 1999, invitations or UN Security Council mandates were required to involve international agents in state-building projects.

42. Stanley Hoffman, "On the War," *New York Review of Books* 48, no. 17 (2001), www.nybooks.com/articles/14660; Mats Berdal and Richard Caplan, "The Politics of International Administration," *Global Governance* 10 (2004): 1–5; and Fearon and Laitin, "Neotrusteeship." This notion evokes "a paternal mode of human conduct," as opposed to a contract into which parties enter willfully. See William Bain, *Between Anarchy and Society: Trusteeship and the Obligations of Power* (Oxford: Oxford University Press, 2003).

territory, characterize most of these cases. Some of the struggles took the form of independence movements (East Timor and Kosovo), while others were irredentist conflicts (the Bosnian Serbs). The remainder focused on fights for state control. All the cases highlight the conditions of the settlement and the process of disarmament, demobilization, and reintegration as playing an important role in the interim structures that followed.

Changing Norms of Sovereignty

Unsurprisingly, along with the changes described above, norms governing when and how extensively the international community can and should *legitimately* intervene have developed. The concept underlying peace enforcement missions directly conflicts with the norm of the inviolability of state sovereignty (Article 2.7 of the UN Charter), which for decades had discouraged the international community from interference in the domestic politics of another state. Once the norms of sovereignty had begun to be eroded by the creation of peace-enforcement missions, it was a short step for the international community to begin to take over the nuts and bolts of governance rather than to act merely as an external guarantor.

Developments in international norms of sovereignty create a new context for the legitimation of the use of force. Advocacy of "popular sovereignty" resting in the people rather than a ruling regime figured prominently in the United Nations Commission on Global Governance report and was expanded in *The Responsibility to Protect*.[43] This concept is now enshrined in the outcome statement of the 2005 UN World Summit.[44] International intervention undertaken in the name of popular sovereignty commits itself to ensuring that it actually establishes popular sovereignty as an outcome of the intervention.

In a reverse shift, the responsibility to protect introduces a new paternalism that overrides the notion of indigenous rights to rule. In Cambodia, Kosovo, and East Timor, the international community has been described as having "suspended" sovereignty according to a model based on post–World War I League of Nations mandates and UN trusteeships.[45] In both events, victors in war created the conditions for a governance regime in states that they considered not yet prepared for self-rule. Yet the United Nations is not a trustee ruling on behalf of a sovereign in exile (as in the international law of

---

43. UN Commission on Global Governance, *Our Global Neighborhood* (London: Oxford University Press, 1995); and International Commission on Intervention and State Sovereignty et al., *The Responsibility to Protect: Report of the International Commission on Intervention and State Sovereignty* (Ottawa: International Development Research Centre, 2001).

44. United Nations, "World Summit Fact Sheet 14–16 September" (New York: United Nations, 2005).

45. Alexandros Yannis, "The Concept of Suspended Sovereignty in International Law and Its Implications in International Politics," *European Journal of International Law* 13, no. 5 (2002): 1037–1052.

occupation), nor does it rule on behalf of the local population.[46] Rather, the United Nations rules "on behalf of the peoples of the world in accordance with the UN Charter."[47] This situation is substantively distinct from the ways that transitional regimes had been initiated in the past when, as noted previously, domestic elites initiated the transition and indigenous power structures functioned (in one form or another) during the transitional period of even the international administrations.

Now, not only is the international community much more directly and extensively involved in the day-to-day management of the post-conflict regime but its involvement is also considered *legitimate*, sometimes even obligatory. To ignore a country that has no capacity to self-govern, due to years of civil war or the removal of its ruling structures by another state's forces, is now considered illegitimate and morally objectionable.[48]

The Role of Elections

Electoral assistance is a prominent form of external aid to democratic transitions. This often involves technical assistance, such as aid with logistics, training, voter education, and computing. Outside actors might observe or even adjudicate in the event of election disputes. In the more substantive forms of electoral assistance, outsiders may actually administer and supervise elections, as in Cambodia, Eastern Slavonia, Bosnia, East Timor, and Kosovo.[49] Assistance packages are created for each situation in accordance with the technical needs, the level of experience of indigenous authorities, and the benefit of having an external third-party presence in order to enhance the legitimacy of the process.

If elections are meant to legitimate the transitional order, one must immediately question the nature of the electoral mandate. Whether or not there is an internal demand for an electoral process, and whether this process is then seen as legitimate, vastly affects both the process and the outcome of elections

---

46. On the international law of occupation, see Eyal Benvenisti, *The International Law of Occupation* (Princeton: Princeton University Press, 1993); Eyal Benvenisti, *The International Law of Occupation*, pb. ed. (Princeton: Princeton University Press, 2004); and Karen Guttieri, "Symptom of the Moment: A Juridical Gap for U.S. Occupation Forces," *International Insights* 13, special issue (1997).

47. Yannis, "The Concept of Suspended Sovereignty," 1048. With sovereignty suspended in this way, Yannis suggests our inquiry turn to the rights and obligations of the United Nations.

48. International Commission et al., *The Responsibility to Protect*.

49. For a review of two seminal works in this field, see Gideon Rose, "Democracy Promotion and American Foreign Policy: A Review Essay," *International Security* 25, no. 3 (Winter 2000/1): 186–203; Jennifer McCoy, Larry Garber, and Robert Pastor, "Pollwatching and Peacemaking," *Journal of Democracy* 2, no. 3 (Fall 1991): 2–14; Thomas Carothers, "The Observers Observed," *Journal of Democracy* 8, no. 3 (July 1997): 32–47; Robert Pastor, "Mediating Elections," *Journal of Democracy* 9, no. 1 (January 1998): 154–163; and Andrew Reynolds and Jorgen Elklit, "The Impact of Electoral Administration on the Legitimacy of Emerging Democracies," *Journal of Commonwealth and Comparative Politics* (July 2002): 86–119.

as transitional instruments. Accordingly, variations in election mandates are noteworthy for their impact on both transitional processes and outcomes.

Alternative views on the value of elections after war imply different requirements for their quality with respect to inclusiveness. Is there a trade-off, for example, between the inclusiveness of popular elections and the stability of an elite pact? Proportional representation (PR) systems are often preferred because they enhance inclusion and decrease the difference between vote share and seat share, both of which increase legitimacy. Proportional and similar systems can also help to defuse the zero-sum nature of electoral contests that more majoritarian electoral systems can create and, therefore, are seen as better for conflict prevention than their majoritarian counterparts.[50] These systems, however, can be undermined when, as often happens, they include a number of set-aside seats that are filled by executive appointment. Concentration of power at the national tier or weak federal systems can further undermine the potential for PR systems to function inclusively.[51] They are also better mechanisms to guarantee the transition than to create effective governance, because they tend to deliver fractured legislatures that have difficulty achieving policy outcomes. Majoritarian systems are less inclusive and more prone to zero-sum outcomes, but they also deliver more unified and less fractured governments.[52] The trade-off comes down to determining the benefits of inclusiveness versus effective governance: power sharing is often necessary to secure a peace agreement and to convince all the parties to buy into the new system, but it can also hobble the resultant government.[53]

Another view is that elections are held more for the benefit of the international audience than for the domestic one. In Iraq, for example, some have argued that the rapid push for elections was done as a way for the United States to legitimate the use of force to its own domestic and international audiences.[54] In these cases, the population does not need to accept the election as legitimate in order to achieve its purpose. When elections are held more for the international audience than for the citizens of the transitional administration, the structure and timing of elections is therefore likely to differ.

---

50. Ben Reilly and Andrew Reynolds, *Electoral Systems and Conflict in Divided Societies* (Washington, D.C.: National Academy Press, 1999).

51. Jessica Piombo, "Political Institutions, Social Demographics and the Decline of Ethnic Mobilization in South Africa," *Party Politics* 11, no. 4 (July 2005): 447–470. Piombo also has a book forthcoming on this topic.

52. See Arend Lijphart, *Patterns of Democracy: Government Forms and Performance in Thirty-Six Countries* (New Haven. Conn.: Yale University Press, 1999).

53. For more on this dynamic, see the chapter in this volume by Donald Rothchild.

54. Peceny, *Democracy at the Point of Bayonets*. See also Karen Guttieri, "Elections in Iraq: Managing Expectations," *Strategic Insights* 4, no. 2 (2005).

Finally, the timing and conduct of elections after conflict are topics of significant debate and extremely critical to the entire transitional process.[55] Transferring sovereignty back to local authorities requires some mechanism by which to select these authorities. Often, international actors choose to organize elections in order to increase legitimacy among the domestic audience. However, elections can be held too early in the process to allow new political forces to coalesce into coherent parties capable of running election campaigns, therefore ensuring that only previously organized political agents will secure office. Not all the important political forces in a country may be ready to operate as political parties if elections are held too quickly; this is especially critical for political organizations because they must be capable of mounting viable election campaigns. They may not know *how* to run and manage a campaign; they may not have been able to establish party structures at the grassroots level around the country; and they may simply not have had enough time to recruit experienced and qualified candidates.

Whether or not the obstacles to the formation of political organizations can be overcome, other problems also arise when elections are held too early. If elections are held soon after the transition from hostilities, there may not be sufficient security for the electoral administration to organize the elections and for political parties to campaign freely. With insufficient lead time, voter education programs are likely to have reached just a small portion of the potential electorate, so many people may not understand the electoral process and what (or whom) they are voting for. Others point out that the electoral process needs to follow, not precede, demilitarization.[56]

The consensus here is that holding flawed elections is worse than having no elections. For example, the 1992 elections in Angola were premature and a step in the wrong direction, according to many observers. The reason was that the two principal combatants had not yet disarmed and demobilized, which left open the "exit" option for the loser in the presidential race. Therefore, by the time the votes were counted, Jonas Savimbi's União Nacional para a Independência Total de Angola (UNITA) movement claimed that the election had been rigged, refused to accept the loss, and returned Angola to war. These events "traumatized the country," reports Ottaway. "They taught the population that elections can lead to greater violence; that they are a less effective source of power than weapons; and that the people's choice is ultimately meaningless because leaders do not respect it."[57]

Holding elections early may also lead to the organization of sectarian or other low-level, rather than national, forces, since these associations already

---

55. See, for example, Terrence Lyons, *Demilitarizing Politics: Election on the Uncertain Road to Peace* (Boulder and London: Lynne Rienner Publishers, 2005), and Kumar, *Postconflict Elections.*

56. See both Lyons, *Demilitarizing Politics,* and Kumar, *Postconflict Elections,* for more on these points.

57. Marina Ottaway, "Angola's Failed Elections," in Kumar, *Postconflict Elections,* 150.

have some form of association on the ground. This can lead to the elevation of ethnic, religious, tribal, or other nonideological political activities. In Bosnia, rushed elections empowered hard-liners and cast a doubt on the universal desirability of quick democratization. As Fareed Zakaria states, "There *can* be such a thing as too much democracy."[58] Alternatively, if sectarian factions were not well organized previously, early—even if flawed—elections may be desirable before divisions harden.

For these reasons, Thomas Carothers has argued that the contribution of elections is overplayed, because often participation in states undergoing transition goes no deeper than the act of voting, and government accountability remains weak.[59] Elections are unlikely to overcome long-standing disaffection between citizens and elites when structural factors like sociocultural divisions or economic cleavages are beneath it. The situation in Iraq would seem to support Carothers's viewpoint. On January 30, 2005—many months after a "transfer of sovereignty" from the occupation forces to Iraqis themselves—the people of Iraq participated in their first open election in fifty years. In the lead-up to the vote, U.S. secretary of defense Donald Rumsfeld argued that holding elections in Iraq was an important development for the Iraqi people and for the external forces occupying the country. Elections would transfer sovereignty back to Iraqis, provide them with a sense of ownership, and therefore reduce the reasons for insurgency. When the voting for a transitional National Assembly occurred, Iraqi voters were confused about the election itself, and the elections were boycotted by a key component of the electorate.[60] In December 2005, there was greater participation in the vote for Iraq's parliament, but voters chose along strictly factional lines. As a result, the impact of elections on the incipient civil war in Iraq has been limited at best.

In contrast to these pessimistic predictions, other observers argue that even flawed elections are a step in the right direction. The reason is that the exercise of administering elections provides valuable experience to the new authorities and, over time, strengthens their ability to operate. In this line of reasoning, elections are important not only for building participation but also for strengthening government accountability. Carrie L. Manning has asserted that even if the elections are not entirely free and fair, the simple act of organizing elections and voting in them begins to train citizens how to behave in democratic polities. Once these behaviors become more ingrained,

---

58. Fareed Zakaria, *The Future of Freedom* (New York: W.W. Norton, 2003).
59. Thomas Carothers, "The End of the Transition Paradigm," *Journal of Democracy* 13, no. 1 (2002): 5–21.
60. Guttieri, "Elections in Iraq."

then the elections can become more genuine and issues of electoral fraud can be addressed.[61]

The impact of elections remains an open debate, and there is no clear evidence pointing in one direction or the other. For these reasons, each of our case studies investigate the effects of holding elections as transitional mechanisms.

The Outcome of Transitional Regimes

When Shain and Linz published *Between States,* the definition of success was very clear: "the assumption of power of a freely elected government."[62] That definition suited a transition from authoritarian rule in which the state and its monopoly on the legitimate use of force were unlikely to be in question. In the current era it has become more difficult to determine and measure when a transitional period has ended. This is what may have changed most from the earlier to the later cases of interim governance, because international intervention complicates the issue. We suggest that a transitional period has ended when a new or reconstituted, permanent, domestic government is able to wield *effective internal sovereignty.* By effective internal sovereignty we mean the dissolution of the interim structures and the *resumption of law and order functions* by the domestic regime.

Several locations lie along this route. The formal transition of power occurs with the founding elections, and this is the point at which Shain and Linz concluded that a transitional period had ended. We prefer to extend the analysis through to the *effective* or *genuine* transfer of power, which is when the domestic government is capable of creating and enforcing law and order. When the rule of law is reestablished (recreating the Rechtsstaat, or constitutional state), and when it is enforced by a domestic government, the interim period is over. If the "new" regime is able to enforce law and order only with the support of external powers, then the interim period may not genuinely have concluded.

When external military forces are engaged in the transition, the standards for success are multiplied. The post-conflict government must acquire a monopoly on force that extends across the nation. In some cases it must demonstrate an ability to hold its own territory without outside help. Meanwhile, the external actors have different interests and roles during a transitional period and hence different standards for success.

In the wake of civil conflict, transitional regimes confront the dual problems of extending state authority throughout the territory and bringing military forces under a unified civilian command. Extending state authority to

---

61. Carrie L. Manning, "Post-conflict Statebuilding and Comparativist Theories of Political Change" (paper presented at the annual meeting of the International Studies Association, Hilton Hawaiian Village, Honolulu, March 3, 2005).

62. Shain and Linz, *Between States.*

the peripheral areas of the country's territory has been a problem facing states since the end of colonialism in the 1950s, a situation made worse by the stasis imposed by the Cold War's support of the juridical aspects of statehood over the empirical.[63] States that had no capacity to govern or to meet even the minimal monopoly on the legitimate use of force as laid out by Max Weber certainly cannot carry out any of the more expansive functions common to the modern welfare state.[64] Basic control of territory, subduing internal rivals such as warlords and other non-state-sanctioned power holders, eludes recently installed governments from Afghanistan to Somalia.

The problems facing a newly installed regime encompass all the issues of extending state authority, yet contemporary international norms—more compelling during international intervention—preclude new governments from co-opting, repressing, or eliminating tribal authorities, religious leaders, or other competing sources of power.[65] Additionally, these new governments must reintegrate various sectors of society that were affected by internal conflict.

Disarming and demobilizing rival authorities, which often are also formal combatants in a civil war situation, constitutes a problem both for extending state authority and for establishing unified civilian rule. Coordination between external civilian and military actors adds more dimensions. To illustrate, the attempts by an external civilian power to create integrated structures in Kosovo were hampered because the NATO military force had earlier accepted Serb security and parallel structures.

The issue of eliminating internal rivals has become more complicated in international interventions. Often these tensions assume center periphery and ethnic overtones, which renders efforts to eliminate or co-opt them both difficult and against current international law. In Afghanistan, the United States empowered warlords to fight against the Taliban and, in the early stages of transitional rule, worked with these groups in a form of indirect governance. Once authority transitioned back to an indigenous organization, Hamid Karzai's central government had to contend with these regional warlords in the periphery. Even the external civilian Coalition Provisional Authority (CPA) in Baghdad at times competed against U.S. military division commander powers in the periphery.

The potential legitimacy issues associated with internationally imposed interim regimes further complicate the matter of extending state authority and demobilizing internal rivals. A transitional regime laden with outside

---

63. Robert H. Jackson and Carl G. Rosberg, "Why Africa's Weak States Persist: The Empirical and Juridical in Statehood," *World Politics* 35, no. 1 (1982): 1–24.

64. Cf. Peter Evans, "States," in *Embedded Autonomy: States and Industrial Transformation* (Princeton: Princeton University Press, 1998), 43–73; and Fukuyama, *State-Building*.

65. Mohammed Ayoob, "State Making, State Breaking, and State Failure," in Hampson, Crocker, and Aall, eds., *Turbulent Peace*, 127–142.

actors may lack the legitimacy to convince citizens to obey it instead of local powers, because the latter may often be perceived by residents as *more legitimate.* They may even go so far as to reject their own leaders who cooperate with outsiders. For example, when Bosnian-Serb leader Biljana Plavsic fired a hard-liner in her cabinet in 1997, she was perceived as turning on her own and for some time after needed NATO to provide her with physical protection.[66]

Iraq illustrates yet another possibility—a legitimacy-efficacy conundrum. In an American military poll taken in February 2005, Iraqis in Baghdad and elsewhere were asked, "How would you rate your confidence in . . . ?" More respondents declared confidence in the armed national opposition to improve the situation in Iraq than expressed confidence in the U.S. military. Fortunately, their top choice was the formal indigenous structure of the Iraqi National Guard.[67] Despite these findings, polls indicated at the same time an Iraqi desire for U.S. forces to remain until the government can assume more control. The external forces, while not viewed as legitimate, nonetheless were viewed as necessary supplements to the domestic force.

Project Overview and Initial Conclusions

Early drafts of this chapter served as a conceptual guide for a series of case studies, whose authors were asked to address a set of questions that relate to two main areas: how these internationally governed transitional regimes affect, first, post-conflict domestic order and legitimacy and, second, good governance. In turn, the first part of the volume is composed of theoretical chapters that introduce many of the issues later taken up in the empirical chapters. These theoretical chapters lay out different dimensions of the issues under debate, and all ultimately raise the question of how much change really occurs in transitional periods. That is, can fundamental power relations be altered?

In the first part of the volume, Antonio Donini's chapter provides a valuable discussion on the top-down processes of post-conflict reconstruction and gaps that emerge with it between the top and bottom: between international and local communities, and again between national and local groups. Arguing that it is more important to build a viable social contract than to

---

66. Kimberly Zisk Marten, *Enforcing the Peace* (New York: Columbia University Press, 2004).

67. In this poll, 20 percent expressed "a great deal/quite a lot" of confidence in the armed opposition, only 15 percent gave this rating to the U.S. forces, and 76 percent gave it to the Iraqi National Guard. Seventy-six percent replied "not very much/none at all" regarding confidence in the U.S. military. The largest "don't know" number went to the armed opposition, at 29 percent. See Michael E. O'Hanlon and Nina Kamp, *Iraq Index* (Washington, D.C.: Brookings Institution), www.brookings.edu/iraqindex. The poll was taken on February 2, 2005; 90 percent of the sample came from Baghdad, and the remaining 10 percent from Mahmoudiya, Istiqlal, and Taji. The margin of error is ±3 percent.

build an electoral democracy, Donini advocates a more inclusive approach. Elite bargains and interim governments that focus on the macro-institutions of the state often leave the conditions of daily life untouched and do little to address the security concerns that motivated people to support insurgencies in the first place.

Carrie Manning focuses on elite manipulation of transitional processes despite a seeming rupture in governance and authority. Manning's contribution takes on the idea that there are critical junctures during which power relationships are substantially renegotiated. In Steven Krasner's theory of punctuated equilibrium, institutions no longer structure politics during periods of rapid change or during periods of institutional suspension, in which power relations can be radically renegotiated. Manning, however, shows that even in these periods of rapid and massive change, institutions still structure politics. Even if newly implanted, as in a power-sharing arrangement or a temporary government, they still influence the process. Thus, the punctuation of the equilibrium is really not all that abrupt, and authority often remains in the hands of those who were powerful before the transition began.

Donald Rothchild's chapter focuses on power-sharing systems as tools of conflict management, finding that often these are actually counterproductive for peace and effective governance in the long term. Power-sharing agreements are fragile. Guarantees by external actors can rarely overcome the insecurity produced by power-sharing agreements that suffer internally from information and credible commitment dilemmas. These arrangements build new cycles of insecurity even if they were designed as mechanisms to reassure weaker parties.

Andrew J. Enterline and J. Michael Greig offer a completely different type and level of analysis. Their methodology is quantitative, and their argument centers on the macro level: they examine how externally imposed governments affect democracy and stability. Arguing that external imposition is a form of revolutionary change, the authors investigate the causes of political instability in externally imposed polities. Their analysis comes up with several interesting findings: imposed democracies initially create increased political instability when compared with imposed nondemocracies; economic development in externally imposed democracies often creates increased discontent and incidences of instability, rather than less; and in ethnically diverse countries, imposed nondemocracies are more stable than imposed democracies. Enterline and Greig note that the commitment of the foreign power imposing a polity is a key factor in stability: the longer the occupier remains in the country, and the more resources it commits (especially to strengthen the security apparatus), the better the chances for a lasting peace.

The second part of the volume turns to case studies selected to present a variety of interim governments that range from the traditional, mostly domestically organized transitional regimes to fully internationalized ones. Each of the cases under investigation experienced a different degree of domestic and international control in their interim governments, ranging from the primarily domestically managed transitional governments in Guatemala, El Salvador, Indonesia, and Liberia to the completely internationally run interim governments in East Timor, Iraq, and Kosovo. The various cases illustrate important differences in the form of the interim regime. Through this mix of experiences, the cases provide a sample of a broad range of transitional governance arrangements that are currently in practice, enabling a comparison of their longer-term effects.

In investigating the transitional governments in these countries, we posed a set of questions predicated on the fact that international engagement is not homogenous:

- Does the identity of the external facilitator affect the legitimacy of the interim government, and does the process of selecting an interim government affect the durability of the regime?
- How does the establishment of direct transitional authority, for example, provide necessary stability?
- Under what circumstances is external pressure productive or counterproductive, and how do we measure it?
- Regarding the issue of good governance, are there benefits of an internationally created and managed interim government for the creation of a domestic, democratic government that has enough state capacity to provide at least the internationally accepted minimum of public goods?
- How do the choices of an interim administration affect the quality of regime that results once the interim period has ended?
- Is democracy always the outcome, and how does the type of interim regime affect the nature of the post-transition government?
- Do some structures, such as caretaker or internationally mandated opposition-led structures, face greater likelihood of protracted or "stunted" transitions?

Finally, we asked our case study authors to address how the nature of the international authorities constituting the transitional regimes affects the domestic acceptance of these regimes. This relationship will have a direct affect on virtually all the issues with which we are concerned. Many observers have noted that one of the problems in the first two Iraqi interim regimes was that they were seen to be either direct American occupation authorities or puppets of the occupying forces.

Larry Diamond argues that if transitional regimes have international legitimacy, then they are more likely also to receive domestic acceptance:

"When there is broad international engagement and legitimacy, people within the post-conflict country are less likely to see it as the imperial project of one country or set of countries. All else being equal, international legitimacy tends to generate greater domestic legitimacy, or at least acceptance, for the intervention."[68] We posit, however, that this is an empirical question rather than a theoretical statement, and therefore one of the issues that the following papers raises revolves around investigating the relationship between the identity of those creating and running transitional regimes and the legitimacy of resulting governments.

Posed in this way, these questions create a natural bridge between comparative politics and international relations. Few areas of inquiry bridge the traditional divide between these two fields more than the study of post-conflict stabilization and reconstruction, and within this, the issue of transitional regimes. When designing transitional regimes, the arrangements necessary to help create a stable, peaceful, and democratic political order hinge directly on the nature of the conflict, the interests and capacities of international actors, and the strengths and capacities of the various parties to the conflict at the time of the intervention.

Some contextual features of the cases are particularly noteworthy. The interim governments examined in our project were largely forged in violent environments. In almost every case the context is one of deep ethnic or sectoral division. Independence movements marked some conflicts (East Timor, Kosovo), irredentism characterized others (Bosnian Serbs), and competition for control of the state characterized the remainder of the cases (including the postinvasion competition among Iraqis).[69] In other cases (Guatemala, El Salvador, and Indonesia), authoritarian regimes gave way in the face of domestic opposition. El Salvador and Guatemala confronted strong rebel

---

68. Diamond, "Lessons from Iraq," 15.

69. Kosovo's independence movement led to international intervention, Bosnia's war seemed at once internal and interstate, and factions within Liberia and the DRC fought over control of the state. Other countries, such as Afghanistan and Iraq, experienced interim governments following foreign invasion and, in the case of Iraq, external occupation. After Indonesian-supported militia in East Timor committed widely condemned atrocities, Indonesia relinquished control. This permitted a robust Australian peacekeeping force to arrive unopposed to guard over the United Nations' administration of East Timor's independence. Civil wars in El Salvador, Guatemala, Cambodia, Bosnia, Liberia, Burundi, and the DRC were addressed by internationally brokered—and to varying degrees internationally implemented—peace accords. These cases in particular, then, highlight the conditions of the settlement as playing an important role in the interim structure that followed. Bosnia's war was waged among robustly organized armed forces supported by outside powers. Although the devastation of modern organized combat was severe in Bosnia's case, the organizational structure provided leverage for disarmament, demobilization, and reintegration efforts. In the case of Kosovo in 1999, a NATO bombing campaign against Serbia led to withdrawal of Serbian support to militia forces committing abuses, as in East Timor, against the majority dissident population. As in East Timor, a robust but permissive entry set the stage for a highly articulated UN bureaucratic administration.

movements, while international actors pushed military-dominated regimes toward more inclusive government.

The cases vary in the way the previous regimes ended. In Indonesia, the dictator Soeharto and his chosen agent of the interim, B. J. Habibie, both understood the scope of their domestic and international legitimacy crisis. They accepted that the authoritarian regime was no longer viable, but they also appreciated that the opposition was not sufficiently robust to take over or even yet to share in the governance structure. In Afghanistan, when outside powers aided insurgents against the Taliban regime, there was no hurting stalemate, peace accord, or capitulation. The victors viewed themselves as being entitled to the spoils of the state after war. Only now, however, other interested parties—that is, international, national, and non-governmental agencies—inhabited their field of play. Despite victory, the U.S. invasion to topple Saddam Hussein's regime in Iraq created a power vacuum. President George W. Bush himself has called the U.S. quick capture of Baghdad a "catastrophic success."[70] When the occupation proved weak, resistance and internal competition among Iraqis came to the fore. The war itself proved less costly in lives than in the years of occupation and stabilization that followed.

William D. Stanley's comparative study of transitions in El Salvador and Guatemala provides an example of the classic interim government model in which military regimes confront legitimacy crises. In both cases, the international community provided guidance and management at crucial junctures in the transitional process, as during a critical period of voter registration in El Salvador.

Michael S. Malley provides Indonesia as a case study of an incumbent-caretaker model of transition from authoritarian rule. The East Asian financial crisis of 1997 and the global currency crisis that accompanied it undermined the Soeharto regime's hold on power. As liberalization snowballed into a full-blown transition, Soeharto stepped down in favor of a domestically appointed and managed caretaker government. As in Stanley's examples, rivalries within the armed forces critically shaped the resultant transitional processes. The incumbent, confronting a weak opposition and a divided military, controlled the transition, ensuring, in a theme similar to that in Manning's chapter, that he would remain a powerful actor in the post-transition phase.

Devon Curtis's chapter on Burundi and the DRC presents two cases of externally facilitated peace agreements that led to domestic power-sharing interim governments. The larger international community was unwilling to get involved to any significant degree, leaving the peace processes to be

---

70. Nancy Gibbs and John F. Dickerson, "Inside the Mind of George W. Bush," *Time* 164, no. 10 (2004).

pushed forward by regional actors and organizations. Domestic actors managed the interim governments, but external actors made critical decisions about who could participate in the talks leading to the creation of the temporary regimes and who would lead those transitional governments once created. Curtis shows that an elite focus on power-sharing bargains creates a sharp disconnect between the elite-centered transitional government and the citizens on the ground. Together, these dynamics create domestic legitimacy problems. In this analysis, Curtis matches the insights of both Donini and Manning, fleshing them out with rich empirical detail.

In his chapter on Liberia, E. Philip Morgan brings out the insight that internationally governed transitional governments have difficulties gaining legitimacy on the ground, even if the United Nations and other international actors consider the government viable. Like Curtis, Morgan stresses the trade-offs in populating an interim government: should they include combatants and therefore potentially create a government with questionable legitimacy on the ground, or should they exclude combatants and therefore leave potential spoilers out of the peace process? Morgan introduces a new dimension into the analysis by addressing the role of economics. Just as victors may fight over spoils rather than focus on governance, the international community may also gain leverage by creating domestic institutions with significant international oversight and/or control of the economy to retain influence even in domestic processes.

Aurel Croissant compares the transitional processes in Cambodia and East Timor. In both of these cases, the international community plays a more direct and involved role than in any of the prior chapters. Echoing Donini, Croissant makes the fundamental point that sustainable peacebuilding and transition from authoritarianism to fully institutionalized liberal democracy require more than ending civil strife. Croissant argues that there is a delicate balance among creating an effective and impartial international regime, incorporating locals to increase ownership, and preparing citizens to resume control. He presents Cambodia as a cautionary tale about pushing democratization on a war-torn country too quickly, without any change in underlying power structures. In these insights Croissant brings together the arguments of Manning and Enterline and Greig. Reconstruction takes at least a decade, and democracy can be created prematurely.

In the range of the fully internationalized interim administrations, our chapters cover Afghanistan (the least internationalized of this variant), Bosnia, Kosovo, and Iraq, although the conditions leading to the need for a fully internationalized interim administration differ among cases. Lenard J. Cohen's assessment of the regime in Kosovo provides a case of the full neo-trusteeship type of administration in the wake of civil war and the absence of agreement on the future status of territory. UNMIK, the international administration, assumed virtually all governance functions—security, economy, services—for more than ten years. UNMIK also demonstrates some of the drawbacks of the international administration model, such as being hampered by organizational rivalries and difficulties in coordinating the large number of organizations operating under the UNMIK umbrella. The ambiguity of Kosovo's future status—as an independent state, part of Serbia, or something in between—adds to the burden of transition. Violent events in 2004 sparked a renewed effort by the international community to move simultaneously toward achieving international standards, such as minority protections, and some form of enhanced sovereignty, if not full statehood.

Writing on Bosnia, Mark Baskin brings out the dilemmas created when local transitional administrations share power with international actors: the problems of negotiating cumbersome power-sharing arrangements between the indigenous actors are compounded when power is shared, yet again, with the international actors. Baskin argues that by remaining aloof and continuing to characterize itself as only a facilitator, the United Nations misses a critical role to force greater coordination and cooperation. This also means that in Bosnia, the responsibility for transformation continues to rest with the affected society.

Thomas H. Johnson's chapter on Afghanistan illustrates a common theme in the volume: even in a situation where there is no clear "victor's justice," the groups that are strong at the cessation of conflict write the rules of the game to skew it in their favor for the long term. Paralleling Curtis and Morgan, who demonstrated how the composition of the participants in peace talks influences the viability of the interim administration, Johnson emphasizes that the Bonn Agreement was not a peace agreement because the losers were not at the table; only the winners of Operation Enduring Freedom participated in the process. This left the transitional and permanent regimes with spoiler problems that hamper the ability of the Kabul government to extend control outside the limits of the capital city.

Writing on Iraq, Christina Caan, Beth Cole, Paul Hughes, and Daniel P. Serwer bring the insider's perspective to an analysis of interim government under insecure conditions administered by an international agent (the United States) that had never intended to run an occupation government. Their analysis of Iraq continually brings out the theme of an "iron triad" of legitimacy, governance, and security; interim governments need all three in order to create any form of government that can rule without challenge. Every time the coalition forces made an improvement in legitimacy, governance, or service provision, the failing security situation would create problems for the continuance of those improvements, further sapping the legitimacy of the forces.

This chapter brings out strongly the idea that international legitimacy does not create domestic legitimacy and that domestic legitimacy is easily lost. Partly because they were not elected from below and partly because the

Iraqis felt no sense of ownership in the process, transitional institutions there lost legitimacy. Accordingly, this chapter brings the volume back full circle to Donini's insights that a failure to bring about positive peace can actually threaten even the minimalist concept of securing the negative peace.

A few of the more important findings from these studies are as follows:

- Despite an apparent window for vast change, the groups that are powerful at the end of the conflict phase tend to be the ones that remain powerful into the post-conflict phase. Even in these periods of rapid and massive change, institutions still structure politics. These institutions may have been newly implanted, as in a power-sharing arrangement or a temporary government, but they nonetheless still influence the process.

- Internationally run transitions tend to create the largest disconnects between the elite and the masses. Negotiations to build cooperation among former aggressors commonly focus on elite power sharing, and governance programs tend to focus on getting the macro-level institutions in place. This often creates a government out of touch with the realities of life for common people and the security issues they face (Afghanistan, Bosnia, Donini). However, even in the domestically run transition in Indonesia, the elites were so concerned about buying off potential secessionists that they neglected to address intercommunal violence.

- Elite-driven power-sharing arrangements and transitional governments have difficulty extending their powers. The lack of power and the preoccupation with an elite division of power seem to have prevented many of these governments from creating governance capacity and transparency. The governments that have experienced the best records on this front are the ones designed and driven more by internal than external powers (Burundi, DRC, Donini, Manning).

- The international community can play a critical, though limited, role even in interim regimes that are domestic affairs (El Salvador, DRC). However, imposed nondemocracies appear to be more stable than imposed democracies (Enterline and Greig). The commitment of the foreign power that is imposing a polity is a key factor in stability: the longer the occupier remains in the country and the more resources it commits (especially to strengthen the security apparatus), the better the chances for a lasting peace.

- In most cases, implementing peace agreements and a transitional government without a coercive enforcement capability has longer-term negative effects. In some, it allows combatants to remain outside the transitional process, remaining potential spoilers. In others, the failure to establish civil order creates legitimacy crises for outsiders and the locals taking over for them (Iraq, Kosovo).

- The international community is developing a new tool, evidenced in Liberia, of withholding economic sovereignty once political sovereignty is returned to domestic forces. The results and effectiveness of this tactic have yet to be fully realized (Morgan).

- Domestic contenders will exploit gaps at the seams of external authorities when they are divided among multiple agencies, including civilian and military components (Bosnia, Kosovo).

- There is a difficult tension between organizing an international regime to completely run a country and attempting to prepare that country to resume sovereign governance (Bosnia, Cambodia, East Timor, Iraq). Ambiguity over sovereignty adds to the burden of transition (Kosovo).

In sum, this project follows in the footsteps of many who have begun to merge the insights of comparative politics with international relations and to apply new approaches to the study of conflict resolution and transitional regimes. Together, this diverse body of work has already begun to modify the model proposed by Shain and Linz, yet the task still remains to draw the various works together into a comprehensive attempt to analyze the new interventionism in transitional regimes. We explore various aspects of the newly emerging range of interim regimes, focusing on issues of legitimacy, conflict management, and how international involvement affects the balance of power among domestic elites. Ultimately, we are interested in exploring how transitional regimes affect political stability and good governance in the reconstruction phase and beyond.

Overall, the chapters provide an overview of the various forms of interim governance, with particular emphasis on their effects on longer-term legitimacy, stability, and governance. The cases that experienced primarily domestic-led interim regimes help to clarify when the influences of the international community become critical, while the more internationally managed interim regimes display the unique mix of challenges and opportunities that these regimes face. Creating domestic legitimacy through external trusteeship (as in Iraq and Kosovo, for example) proves to be quite problematic and is a theme that surfaces in many of the cases in the volume. The collected works submit that the interventionism of the international community, especially its commitment to state building, raises fundamental issues of legitimation, restructuring, conflict resolution, and how all this relates to building the micro-foundations of government. Through these works we hope to lay the groundwork for future efforts to monitor and assess the conditions and programs that enable transitional governments to create stable and legitimate systems of governance in post-conflict and transitional societies.

2

Knocking on Heaven's Door

Meeting Social Expectations in Post-conflict Transitions

Antonio Donini

Editors' Note

Antonio Donini's chapter contributes a valuable perspective on the themes of legitimacy and stability by focusing on the disconnects between elites and grass roots. Donini reminds us that during top-down processes of post-conflict reconstruction, a gap emerges between the top and the bottom: between international and local actors, and again between national and local groups. Transitions are not linear processes, he argues, and while formal transitions may ensure a negative peace (that is, a cessation of conflict), securing a positive peace (understood as human security) is an entirely different story. This is because of what Donini calls a "perceptions gap": plans and actions of the center are often perceived differently in the periphery. The perceptions gap can create not only dangerous misunderstandings and feelings of marginalization but also transitional governments that do little to ease the security concerns that motivated people to support insurgencies in the first place.

When the international community comes in with the standard reconstruction package—to create national security, to form a democracy, and to build state institutions—it not only fails to assess what people on the ground feel that they need, but it also fails to include the people in discussions on their own future. This can create disconnects in legitimacy and perceptions of effectiveness that can undermine a transitional process. Therefore, a healthy center-periphery dynamic is a central ingredient to successful transitions; a disconnect between the two would have negative effects on durable peace.

Donini makes these arguments through an analysis of the rhetoric of rights: countries must have a respect for rights before democracy can be built. By this, Donini means that rights are respected when there is a social contract in place. Democracy is

different from "rights" and, in fact, "might (of the majority) does not make right."
Elections and formal democracy often do little to ensure that people are included, that
significant groups are not marginalized, and that potential spoilers are made to feel
their concerns are reflected in the government. Arguing that the emphasis on electoral
democracy should be replaced with a focus on creating a viable social contract between
the state and citizens, Donini points to the fact that elite bargains and interim govern-
ments that focus on the macro institutions of the state often leave the conditions of
daily life untouched. Because the international community is so focused on getting
the prescription right—holding elections, building state institutions, and standing up
national armies—it misses the fundamental point that before any of these objectives
can be reached, the society must have respect for rights. In order to create a durable
peace and governments with domestic legitimacy, then, views from the bottom must
be included from the initial stages of reconstruction and transition.

■ ■ ■

In order to be effective, externally assisted transition processes in countries recovering from conflict must address the perceptions, expectations,
and realities of ordinary people and communities at the local level. This
seems an obvious proposition, yet far too often there are serious disconnects between the "views from above" of the transitional government and
the international community that supports it, and the views and aspirations of communities and citizens who have most to gain from a durable
peace. While there is a growing and varied literature on the political and
institutional aspects of transitional situations and the role of international
actors therein,[1] the "view from below" is largely terra incognita.[2] International analysts and academics have tended to focus on what happens in
the capitals of countries recovering from conflict and—to a lesser extent—
on how the capital affects the periphery (or not). They rarely consider the
indigenous processes of social transformation that may be happening
where the tarmac ends or where there is no road. Ignoring the views from
below is not only unwise, it is also likely to result in costlier and less
durable transitions.

In this chapter I will discuss the importance of societal perceptions, the
shortcomings of current imposed-transition formulas, and prescriptions for

The comments of Karen Guttieri, Jessica Piombo, and Norah Niland on earlier drafts of this
chapter are gratefully acknowledged.

1. See, for example, Stephen John Stedman, Donald Rothchild, and Elizabeth Cousens, eds.,
   Ending Civil Wars: The Implementation of Peace Agreements (Boulder, Colo.: Lynne Rienner,
   2002), and G. John Ikenberry, *After Victory: Institutions, Strategic Restraint and the Rebuilding of
   Order after Major Wars* (Princeton: Princeton University Press, 2001).
2. Among the very few exceptions, see Jarat Chopra, "Building State Failure in East Timor,"
   Development and Change 33, no. 5 (2002): 979–1000, and Jarat Chopra and Tanja Hohe,
   "Participatory Intervention," *Global Governance* 10, no. 3 (2004): 289–303.

bridging the perceptions gap. I will show that a healthy center-periphery dynamic is a central ingredient to successful transitions. Conversely, center-periphery disconnects can have lasting and negative effects on the prospects of durable peace. My starting point is that the plans and actions of the center—the processes set in motion by external actors and the government that they are supporting—are perceived very differently in the periphery. Often, these plans and actions are far removed from the expectations and realities of local people and communities. They arise from altogether different realities and worldviews. Moreover, the nature of power relationships, local coping mechanisms, and other grassroots socioeconomic processes may bear little relationship to the "grand plan" the center and the outsiders may be promoting. This can lead to dangerous disconnects or forms of dualism in social transformation, which need to be better understood from both theoretical and very practical perspectives.

This chapter has two main sections. In the first section, I offer some general reflections on the nature of transitional processes and the objectives that are pursued ("we the peoples" versus the "temple of states"). In the second section, I investigate why it matters to understand the perceptions of local communities ("the view from below") and offer some conclusions and areas for future research. Section two will draw on fieldwork conducted by Tufts University in early 2005 in three transitional situations—Afghanistan, Kosovo, and Sierra Leone[3]—as well as on other recent experiences.

"We the Peoples" versus the "Temple of States"

Like the Roman god Janus, the international conflict resolution system has two faces. The first is the hard-nosed face of realpolitik and of transient political compromise made on that altar of the temple of states, the UN Security Council. The second is the benevolent face of the UN Charter, of the Universal Declaration, and of the promise of a better life for "we the peoples." Conflict resolution and peacebuilding look at the first face. Humanitarian action and the promotion of human rights look at the second for guidance. Each face sometimes has to suffer the grimaces of the other. In a sense, both faces are physiological to the international community, at least in its present dispensation. Messing around with the physiognomy of gods is always a dangerous proposition: states are wont to pay tribute to the god of universal ideals, but their practice, when they are in conflict resolution mode, always puts politics at the fore.

---

3. Antonio Donini et al., *Mapping the Security Environment: Understanding the Perceptions of Local Communities, Peace Support Operations and Assistance Agencies* (report commissioned by the UK NGO-Military Contact Group (NMCG), and published by the Feinstein International Center, Tufts University, June 2005), fic.tufts.edu.

This same dichotomy—between the aspirations of citizens and the transition agenda of a fledgling state apparatus striving for legitimacy and sovereignty—repeats itself in most countries recovering from crisis and conflict. It often results in an uneasy balance, if not open tension, between the rights of citizens—including their fundamental right to participate in the shaping of their own institutions of governance at the central and local levels—and the macro-level imperatives of state building.

How national and international actors intervene and affect this dynamic constitutes a key variable that can make the difference between durable peace with justice and a fragile peace that may spiral out of control. This dynamic can be best understood in center-periphery terms, that is, in terms intriguingly reminiscent of classical dependency theory.[4] The processes of "world ordering" in societies recovering from conflict, especially when an internationally approved military and civilian force is present, result in obvious linkages of dependency between the political and economic decision-making centers of the northern metropolises and the fragile recovering national state in the periphery. As in dependency theory, the center of the periphery—the capital and main urban centers of the country in transition—is subsumed into power and management relationships originating from the "metropolitan" centers abroad. In a sense, it becomes part of the center. Whether sovereignty is formally suspended or not, the global networks of force, governance, and aid create explicit and implicit forms of "occupation" that, de facto, incorporate the capital and its subordinated dependencies into the grand plan for peace and reconstruction.

Thus, we have seen the emergence of the United Nations' "kingdom of East Timor,"[5] the U.S. principality of the Green Zone in Iraq, the assorted bunkerized baronies and fiefdoms of UN peace support operations and aid agencies in Afghanistan and elsewhere. The expatriate presence, with its corollaries of conspicuous consumption and distortion of local markets, is generally large and visible in the capital and in a handful of subnational centers. These visible forms of "occupation" are usefully complemented by the less visible: top-down forms of governance, management styles, and exogenous values; types of personal behavior of expatriate personnel; and, of course, high levels of financial assistance. These all serve to incorporate the leadership and elites of the capital and the main urban centers of the recovering country into a network of power, patron-client, and economic relationships that are functional to the world-ordering agenda. Aid agencies, in particular non-governmental organizations (NGOs), which are already powerful agents

---

4. While the works of Raul Prebisch, Immanuel Wallerstein, André Gunder Frank, and their epigones focused primarily on economic dependency, their arguments are well worth extending to the political and conflict-resolution spheres.

5. Jarat Chopra, "The UN's Kingdom of East Timor," *Survival* 42, no. 3 (September 2000): 27–39.

of governance, if not of government, in northern societies, become the "force multipliers" and the "peaceful weapons of the new world order" aimed at expanding the center's reach into the periphery.[6]

How deep down into society does the center-periphery relationship extend? This is where we have to depart from traditional dependency theory. In fact, dualism—a category of analysis that "dependistas" normally rejected—comes in handy to clarify what often happens below the surface.[7] In many situations—East Timor, Afghanistan, and Liberia come to mind—the processes and structures put in place by the internationally supported peace plan come into opposition or tension with existing local structures of social organization.[8] These could be traditional community or tribal structures or new institutions that may have emerged from the conflict (for example, warlords) or from the breakdown of law and order (for example, drug lords).

Sometimes the centrally mandated institutions of governance coexist with the local entities, while at other times friction, if not open conflict, arises. The tension can manifest itself at the village level or higher up the center-periphery chain at the district or provincial levels. The point here is the double disconnect that emerges between the centrally mandated processes—normally endowed with strong de jure legitimacy—and the local structures—regardless of their local legitimacy—on the one hand and the perceptions, expectations, and aspirations of communities and citizens on the other. Two (sometimes more) parallel realities may coexist: the thin veneer of the top-down processes of conflict resolution, rehabilitation, and, often, modernization, and the more or less hidden or visible community-based or warlord-imposed structures on the ground. The extent to which the central "grand plan" is able to successfully address this dualism is likely to make the difference between durable peace and continuing conflict, armed or otherwise, on the ground.

---

6. For each of these points, see, in turn, David Kennedy, *The Dark Sides of Virtue. Reassessing International Humanitarianism* (Princeton: Princeton University Press, 2004), xviii; Colin Powell, "Remarks to the National Foreign Policy Conference for Leaders of U.S. NGOs," (speech, U.S. Department of State, Washington, D.C., October 26, 2001), www.yale.edu/lawweb/avalon/sept_11/powell_brief31.htm; and Michael Hardt and Antonio Negri, *Empire* (Cambridge and London: Harvard University Press, 2000), 36. Cooley and Ron note that NGOs increasingly tend to act "like a business" or "like a government" or both: Alexander Cooley and James Ron, "The NGO Scramble. Organizational Insecurity and the Political Economy of Transnational Action," *International Security* 27, no. 1 (Summer 2002): 5–39.

7. For a critique of dualism, see Andre Gunder Frank, *Capitalism and Underdevelopment in Latin America* (New York: Monthly Review Press 1967, rev. ed. 1969, and London: Penguin Books, 1971). Interestingly, toward the end of his life, Frank softened his position on dualism, noting the emergence of a new dualism between those who can and those who cannot participate in a worldwide division of labor.

8. For a particularly well-documented case study of this dynamic, see Stephen Ellis, *The Mask of Anarchy: The Destruction of Liberia and the Religious Dimension of an African Civil War* (New York: New York University Press, 1999).

According to conventional wisdom, if the right tools are applied in transitional situations to the right mechanisms and in the right sequence, the international community can orchestrate or support a peace process that transforms the "external legitimacy" provided through an internationally brokered peace agreement into an internal legitimacy for fledgling governmental authorities. The package usually implies a mix of tools including an externally supported peace mission, an interim or transitional government, the drafting of a constitution, and internationally supervised elections. As part of the solution, the process is expected, of course, to generate a "peace dividend," usually in the form of a massive injection of funds for residual humanitarian assistance, capacity development, and reconstruction.

The goals of outside intervention are commonly expressed in terms of negative and positive peace or of enhancing human security.[9] "Negative peace" describes the absence of active armed conflict. "Positive peace" is a much broader concept that encompasses economic and social well-being as well as cultural identity. Positive peace implies a minimum of physical security, of course, but it also implies a situation in which the structural conditions that gave rise to the conflict are being addressed and in which the local people have a sense of empowerment, participation, and accountability. Similarly, the security of individuals and communities can be defined narrowly in terms of "physical security" or more broadly as "human security"—a concept that connotes a much wider range of rights and aspirations. Although there is no agreed-upon definition of human security, the term is generally understood to imply a broadening of traditional state-centric concepts of security to include greater focus on individuals, addressing threats to their survival and ensuring the conditions necessary for the fulfillment of the entire gamut of rights. It means, in short, "protecting and empowering people" so that their safety and well-being are not subordinated to "state security agendas."[10]

As they trundle down the center-periphery axis, the peace- and nation-building agendas may well result in "negative peace" if we define the term as "the absence of war," or at least the containment of conflict within acceptable limits. Does this approach promote "positive peace" and democracy for the citizenry? And if it does, is it formal democracy of the "vote-and-forget" variety or real democracy that corresponds to the aspirations of citi-

---

9. For the original definitions of positive and negative peace, see Johann Galtung, "Violence, Peace and Peace Research," *Journal of Peace Research* VI, no. 3 (1969): 167–191. The Tufts study (see note 3 above) adopted the positive/negative peace/human-security conceptual framework.

10. Sadako Ogata and Johan Cels, "Human Security—Protecting and Empowering the People," *Global Governance* 9, no. 3 (July–September 2003): 273–282. See also the 1994 Human Development Report of the United Nations Development Programme (UNDP), the first major policy publication to expand the traditional concept of security from state to individual security: *Human Development Report 1994: New Dimensions of Human Security,* hdr.undp. org/reports/global/1994/en/.

zens for justice, human security, and a say in how their affairs are run? And if not the latter, what changes are required in the international community's recipe book?

The empirical evidence of negative peace strategies leading to improved human security is mixed at best. There are a few cases in which linear regime transitions produced democracy and stability (Namibia, Mozambique, South Africa, East Timor). These are cases in which a solid peace agreement was in place and no actors were either willing or able to spoil the peace. In other cases, although the formal transition process has run its course, there is little evidence that the outcome has been just or has significantly advanced the rights of citizens (Cambodia, Bosnia, Kosovo). In others still, some of the ingredients for a just and peaceful political order are in position, but major and stubborn square pegs are refusing to fit into round holes (Afghanistan, the DRC, Iraq, Palestine). It is these more intractable cases—which are characterized by their lack of democratic tradition, contested environment, volatile security, and major policy dilemmas for external actors—that deserve a closer look.

Transition in these cases is hardly linear. Different geographical areas and segments of society can go forward or slide backward at the same time. Disconnects can arise between the center and the periphery and between the formal peace process—which may advance—and the reality of governance and security experienced by the citizenry—which may stagnate or even deteriorate. The situation of minorities may not improve. The formal peace process, often confined to the capital, may leave the provinces untouched. This is particularly the case in countries where there is no "democratic" tradition or electoral culture. Warlordism and criminalized economies may continue to hold sway. Issues of accountability for past or continuing human rights violations are unlikely to be addressed for fear of derailing the peace process. A culture of impunity may continue to thrive.

Because the international community puts so much emphasis on building democracy in these top-down processes, the entire project of constructing a durable peace has really become a process of creating a formal democratic political system. This leads us to a more fundamental question: *Is* democracy the right vessel for promoting peace with justice? Or is it yet another case of "the West knows best"? Indeed, some would argue that the international community has been more adept at imposing solutions (with which it is familiar) from without rather than supporting processes (usually unfamiliar) that should be generated from within.

Recent experience from situations as disparate as Northern Ireland, Somalia, Afghanistan, Chechnya, eastern DRC, and perhaps Iraq would seem to indicate that in hotly contested environments where minorities or subnational power holders do not obey the "capital rule," majoritarian, winner-take-all democracy is not necessarily the answer. Might (of the majority) does not make right. The promotion of human security requires not simply inclusive, as opposed to majoritarian, democracy but also the actual protection of fundamental rights, not just their formal recognition. The protection of rights is a sine qua non for a just peace and the emergence of authorities who are legitimate in the eyes of citizens; democracy is a useful add-on. Recently, the same issue has been raised in the context of the Palestinian question: would the human rights of Palestinians and Israelis be better protected and advanced in the context of an Israel-Palestine entity where all citizens would have equal rights rather than in a nonviable Palestinian state? Rights are vital to creating a just peace. Indeed, democracy cannot work without respect for rights. Elections, for example, will work only if security and a rule of law are in place. The law must be upheld by, and also guarantee the rights of, communities, minorities, and other marginalized or disenfranchised groups (demobilized soldiers, for example) capable of unraveling peace processes. In other words, elections require a positive peace to serve democracy.

Obviously, evidence that something is being done to redress the abuses of the past is an important additional element likely to encourage groups and communities that may be suspicious of a capital-driven process to support it. But perhaps the most important preconditions are understanding the perspectives of local people and giving them a sense that they have a stake in the transition process, a point that Andrew Natsios has called the "ownership principle."[11] For this to happen, people's views must be taken seriously and opportunities to participate in shaping and running local institutions must be found. These institutions must make sense in terms of the local beliefs about how legitimacy is constructed. Otherwise, those selected or elected may have strong external legitimacy but be perceived as illegitimate by the community.

This idea of local conceptions of legitimacy, which dates back to Max Weber, seems to be lost in the "democracy now" mantra of the international community. The regrettable result is that local groups and communities are seldom consulted, with the consequence that local expectations and perceptions may bear little relevance to actual realities. Because perceptions can often shape realities, understanding the perceptions from below and factoring them into the transition process is an important prerequisite for success.

In sum, meeting these rights-based preconditions does not necessarily require holding elections as we know them. What *is* required is an acceptable social contract, grounded in local realities and modes of legitimation, that links the citizens to their local institutions of governance and the state and that is clearly understood by all. Ideally, the contract would also build on local or traditional practices of justice and conflict resolution. The *shuras*

---

11. Andrew Natsios, "The Nine Principles of Reconstruction and Development," *Parameters* (Autumn 2005): 4–20.

(councils) in Afghanistan and the *gaçaca* hearings in Rwanda are good, if imperfect, examples of such traditional systems. Yet whether or not it builds on tradition, the social contract must have teeth in order to be able to demonstrate that all citizens are equal vis-à-vis the law and have recourse to a judicial system (not necessarily a "modern" one) that works. This implies that accountability at all levels should be high on the nation-building agenda. If not, the social contract will not be credible.

Unlike "democracy," which tends to be an abstraction, the *problématique* of rights is immediately understood by citizens—whether it is the right to life or to an opinion or the right to send girls to school or to protect crops from an abusive commander.

What does this mean concretely for peace processes and for the external actors that support them? It means that for such processes to have more chances of success, the international community needs to move away from linear center-periphery approaches that are essentially top-down—where the priorities of national and international actors tend to focus on what happens in the capital—to more inclusive and participatory processes that take into account what is happening in the society. A better balance must be struck between the demands of the state, which obviously needs to reestablish itself and to provide a framework for the transition, and the needs of "we the peoples" who want to see evidence that things are changing for the better. This requires support for bottom-up approaches as well as much more attention to understanding the dynamics of peacebuilding at the local and community levels.

The View from Below

Recent research on perceptions of local communities in countries recovering from conflict and their relationship to externally mandated interventions confirms the existence of this major perceptions gap.[12]

Center-Periphery Dislocations

In Afghanistan, the formal calendar of the peace process has been more or less respected, but it has done little to advance the rights of citizens or to improve their socioeconomic plight. While the adoption of the new constitution is a step forward, it is merely "a piece of paper," as the outgoing UN special representative of the secretary-general remarked, that has done

---

12. In addition to the Tufts study and the articles by Chopra and Hohe quoted above, which cover similar ground, there have been several studies of perceptions of local populations in contested environments: see, for example, Andreas Wigger, "Encountering Perceptions in Parts of the Muslim World and Their Impact on the ICRC's Ability to Be Effective," *International Review of the Red Cross* 87, no. 858 (June 2005): 343–365.

nothing for minorities and citizens on the ground.[13] Formally, at least, women have been included in the democratic process and have been elected to parliament, but there has been little or no change in the reality of their plight at the village and community levels. Communities had high expectations of a peace dividend, but their perception, which does not always correspond to the reality, is that "nothing" has been done and that the government and the overall aid effort are fundamentally corrupt.

The extent of disenfranchisement is proportional to the distance—geographical, cultural, or political—from the capital. A number of recent studies have shown that the top priority for Afghans is security, and the key determinant for security is the control that warlords and feudal, drug, and other abusive local power holders exercise over the citizenry at the local level, outside the capital.[14] The formal peace process has done little to address the current behavior of such abusive authorities—in many cases, they were warlords who had been defeated by the Taliban and who were reinstated as useful allies courtesy of the post-9/11 coalition intervention—or the heinous crimes and human rights violations committed by them and their various predecessors.

In fact, a deliberate trade-off was accepted early on: it was decided at the time of the Bonn Agreement that the peace process required the inclusion of the warlords (but not the defeated Taliban). Thus, in order not to derail the peace process, issues of impunity and accountability for past abuses would have to wait. Spoilers, in other words, earned influence in the new national state institutions by virtue of their capacity and potential willingness to unleash violence. "Justice is a luxury . . . we must not lose peace for justice" said then Afghan Interim Authority chairman Hamid Karzai.[15]

Until very recently, therefore, neither the United Nations nor U.S. authorities felt the need to meaningfully address the issue of justice or to support the transitional authority in confronting the warlords. Thus, the emerging central government remained completely separated from the realities of life as experienced by most people outside the capital. The disconnect is even further compounded by the continuing conflict and the fact that in large swaths of the country the only visible development is the flourishing criminalized

---

13. Special Representative Lakhdar Brahimi called the constitution "a new source of hope" for Afghans, but he warned that it was the responsibility of Afghans, both government and people, to make it a genuine reality. Press briefing by Manoel de Almeida e Silva, spokesman for the special representative of the secretary-general on Afghanistan, January 4, 2004, www.un.org/apps/news/infocusnews.asp?NewsID=643&sID=1.

14. See the surveys of popular perceptions in issues of rights and security done in 2004 by the Afghan Human Rights Research and Advocacy Consortium (www.afghanadvocacy.org) and in early 2005 by the Afghan Independent Human Rights Commission (www.aihrc.org.af).

15. Hamid Karzai, interview by Lyse Doucet, *Hard Talk*, BBC, June 14, 2002. On the *problématique* of human rights in Afghanistan, see Norah Niland, "Rights, Rhetoric and Reality: A Snapshot from Afghanistan," in *The UN Human Rights and Post Conflict Situations*, ed. Nigel White and Dirk Klaasen (Manchester: Manchester University Press, 2005).

economy, linked to the resumption of the large-scale opium production the Taliban had effectively eliminated. It is no surprise, then, that away from the artificial ambiance of the capital, with its pollution, traffic jams, and boom-town–aid-town appearance, Afghans feel disenchanted.

In these circumstances, the 2005 parliamentary elections, in a country with no democratic or electoral culture, did not significantly change the parameters of the disenchantment. A first-past-the-post system does little to protect minorities from discrimination or abuse. Elections simply reinforce the perception that the international community is more interested in the illusion rather than the reality of a stable peace: a thin wet cloth on fires that continue to simmer. As in other crisis situations, the cloth may keep the fire in check for a while, but unless the forces fueling the fire are dealt with, short-term gain may turn into long-term pain. Arguably, the Taliban and the warlords are there for the long haul. As one captured Taliban commander put it, "You Americans have clocks. We have time."[16]

Conceptions of Peace and Security

An intriguing finding of the Tufts University study, which was based on extensive interviews and focus group meetings with individuals and communities at all levels of society in the three countries covered—Afghanistan, Kosovo, and Sierra Leone—was the extent to which outsiders (peace support operations and assistance agencies) and insiders (local communities) differed in their understanding of the meanings of such concepts as "peace" and "security." For the former, physical security—protection of themselves and their activities from physical harm—was very much on their agenda. For the latter, even in areas considered relatively insecure from the perspective of the outsiders, peace and security were defined in terms of human security.

Afghan citizens interviewed for the study had a much wider understanding of "security" than physical protection and safety alone. Security is a multilayered concept in which the socioeconomic and human rights considerations—human security—play a key, if not preponderant, role. Typically, the focus group discussions with communities would start by identifying physical security issues, usually with an acknowledgment that there had been some improvement in recent months. This would be followed by debate within the group about the "elements" of peace. After some preliminary scratching of the surface, issues of employment and access to services and welfare would come to the fore. In sum, in the relatively secure physical environment of areas where the focus groups and interviews were held, the absence of armed conflict was *an* important consideration, but the absence of

---

16. Quoted by Lt. Gen. Karl W. Eikenberry, commanding general, Combined Forces Command, Afghanistan, at a lecture at Harvard University's John F. Kennedy School of Government, May 5, 2006.

stable and secure livelihoods was *the* fundamental determinant in the security perceptions of local communities.

Employment as a component of peace and security came up repeatedly, particularly among the most disadvantaged. An illiterate shopkeeper in Kabul gave the clearest formulation when he stated, unknowingly paraphrasing Lenin, "Peace is jobs and electricity." Often, as soon as one participant mentioned employment, the others chimed in with their own definitions. As a farmer from the Paghman district (Kabul Province) put it, "Now we have security but no jobs—so the peace is not complete."

Peace is much more than the absence of war, the interviewees in the three countries are saying. Positive peace—employment, education, health, electricity, and a better life; in other words, the fulfillment of human security needs—is high on their agenda. They are also quick to define what is preventing positive peace from being achieved: a corrupt police force, criminality, and a pervasive sense that unless the warlords and/or corrupt elements are reined in and the violations of the past are addressed, chaos could well ensue. In the three situations, communities were grateful for the military intervention that brought open warfare to an end.

The Tufts study, as others before it, also shows the importance that individuals attach to justice: redress for violations of the past and disarming and neutralizing the men with guns are high on everyone's agenda. What they seem to expect are processes of social transformation that result in more transparent and accountable forms of local governance. In Afghanistan, many of those interviewed had participated in the presidential elections, and some spoke of President Karzai with respect; nevertheless, the workings of the government in Kabul and the perspectives of "parliamentary democracy" seemed arcane and far removed from their very real human security concerns.

Similar concerns were expressed in Kosovo and Sierra Leone. There was a clear sense that for communities, the overall security situation had improved. This had allowed communities to shift their sights, progressively, from physical-security issues—freedom from fear and violence—to a range of human-security concerns. As for the outsiders, their progression on the axis was notably slower. This reflects both the nature of their work and the real-time security concerns resulting from attacks against aid workers and other foreigners (in Afghanistan). It also reflects a certain sluggishness in adapting to a situation that presented many post-conflict aspects *and* continuing uncertainties—for example, what would happen when the foreign militaries left (all three situations)?

The perceptions and cognitive gap were present to some extent in all three situations, but they were much more starkly palpable in Afghanistan. Some of the outsiders, in particular aid workers, had a relatively good understanding of what was happening beyond the Kabul "bubble"; they made a point, despite the obvious security risks, of remaining in touch with projects and activities on the ground. Others seemed to be living in a "virtual" Afghanistan: foreigners talking mainly to their look-alikes, shuttling between heavily fortified compounds, and hardly interacting with Afghans other than those who spoke their language or shared their values. Between the bunkerized and the dispossessed, the gap could not have been more extreme.

In one sense, the foreign militaries fared better than the aid agencies. Civil-military relationships are key to force protection, and some of the militaries had rather systematic techniques for interaction and intelligence gathering (about which, unsurprisingly, they were reluctant to talk). As for the UN missions in the three countries visited, one sensed that, as in other transition situations, their subculture suffered from an "asocial alienation" rooted in "diplomatic habit, relating institution to institution or at most talking to a minority elite."[17]

The implications of this disconnect between the formality of the peace and nation-building processes and the perceptions of the locals are obviously wide ranging. As in other countries—East Timor, Liberia, Kosovo, and Sierra Leone, for example—the social mores that govern power relationships in Afghanistan at the local and community levels have little in common with the processes masterminded at the central level by those who wield power in Kabul and by their external patrons. Clan, tribe, warlord, and traditional *khans* (village chiefs, usually landlords) hold the reality of power. Unless indigenous mechanisms can be nurtured to guarantee a minimum of rule of law, transparency, and accountability, elections orchestrated from above will not empower individuals and communities at the end of the center-periphery chain. In addition to being costly, elections may in fact reinforce ingrained and abusive power structures. As two careful observers of such processes point out, relying on elections as "the sum total of popular participation in building a state simply replicates the utter disconnect between the people and the government, laying the foundations for institutions to fail again."[18] Nurturing participation at the grassroots level is a key challenge for maximizing the chances of success in transitional situations. So far there is little evidence that the international community understands the challenge or is prepared to rise to the occasion.

Do Local Views Matter?

The inability to nurture participation and to nurture the emergence of reasonably effective and accountable institutions of governance at the local level has been a major failure in recent transitional situations. International organizations, such as the UNDP and the World Bank, have tried several

17. Chopra and Hohe, "Participatory Intervention," 290.
18. Ibid., 292.

routes in countries in and recovering from crisis; their attempts are often plagued by both disrespect for local aspirations and agency turf wars. The norm has been to create top-down "Westphalian" constructions, focusing primarily on pushing Western rationality down the center-periphery governance pike, with scant attention to outcome.

At the same time, these organizations have also experimented with a social engineering route, bequeathing equally mixed if not misguided results. In Afghanistan during the Taliban era, for example, UNDP launched the PEACE project.[19] This ambitious endeavor was predicated on the establishment of local *shuras* to interface with the external actors and to decide upon and manage small-scale rehabilitation initiatives. These councils were intended as participatory entities of governance at the subdistrict level. While the project was to some degree successful in mobilizing local participation around discrete projects, its social engineering aspects proved more problematic. The issue was that they tended to displace existing structures, the remnants of the existing state administration and/or local traditional decision-making mechanisms. The *shuras* were thus functional to the externally orchestrated project rather than the expression of an indigenous aspiration (and they tended to wax and wane with the availability of project funds). Moreover, they did not address issues of discrimination and marginalization, including the role of women and girls.

In East Timor, the issue of local administration was plagued by turf battles and incompatible top-down and bottom-up approaches championed, respectively, by the United Nations Transitional Administration in East Timor (UNTAET) and the World Bank. The former embodied an "absolutist form of authority, but succeeded in excluding the local population from the equation."[20] The latter, through the Community Empowerment and Local Governance Project (CEP), pursued a more innovative approach to empower village councils by bringing decision making to the community level, such as on issues related to the destination of development funds, providing the basis for a nascent form of self-administration to emerge. But the World Bank project was only partly successful, both because of the clash between it and the hierarchical institutional culture of UNTAET and because the ambitious CEP approach underestimated the cultural sensitivities and complexities involved in empowering ordinary villagers—particularly women—in a very traditional environment. Nevertheless, it constitutes a valuable experience from which much can be learned in terms of promoting participatory forms of governance.[21]

Gaining a better understanding of local realities and worldviews of people at the periphery, especially when they are undergoing rapid trans-

---

19. The acronym stands for poverty eradication and community empowerment.
20. Chopra, "Building State Failure in East Timor," 979.
21. Chopra and Hohe, "Participatory Intervention," 289–303.

formations in their social environments, seems like an obvious precondition to developing participatory forms of governance and management of externally provided resources. There are at least three immediate reasons why such methods are not more widespread. First, gaining this understanding can be an arduous and sometimes lengthy practice, and in periods of rapid collapse or state disintegration, the international community either may not be willing or may not have the luxury to spend this time. Second, pursuing forms of participation based on local realities obviates the cookie-cutter approach that the top-down processes enable: the international community cannot just pick a plan from the bookshelf and employ it from one country to another. Obviously, changing these patterns is a matter of convenience, expediency, and will.

The final reason is deeper, however. Not all traditional and local practices are internationally acceptable, and one should be careful not to mythologize the local. People may be poor, but their social relationships and local coping practices can be exceptionally complex and often unjust. Some of this complexity may include odious social practices, abusive behavior, and rampant discrimination. One group's coping mechanism might involve raiding another group's cattle. Survival may entail exploiting bonded labor, selling girls as brides, cultivating opium poppies, dabbling in criminalized economic activity, and the like. Traditional patron-client relationships or the presence of abusive warlords may represent huge obstacles to the participation of local people in the shaping of their institutions of governance and, ultimately, their future.

The answer to the dilemma posed in this last point is to emphasize that working locally does not mean condoning abusive or odious practices. Agents of social change must be careful to maintain some distance and "cognitive respect."[22] This means that one must take with the uttermost seriousness the ways in which others define their reality. It does not mean that one has to remain morally neutral when it comes to working in a participatory manner on this reality. One must work quietly, and somewhat disbelievingly, using the universalist template as a broad road map.

The issue of how to reconcile the lofty universalist principles enshrined in the UN Charter and the Universal Declaration of Human Rights with local realities, beliefs, and aspirations is an old one. Historically, development actors—both the knights in shining armor of rapid modernization and the mendicant orders of small-scale participatory development—have avoided or ignored the discourse of rights, including, ironically, the vocabulary of economic and social rights.[23] Increasingly, however, the rights,

---

22. Peter L. Berger, *Pyramids of Sacrifice: Political Ethics and Social Change* (London: Basic Books, 1974), 134.

23. For a summary of the debate, see Peter Uvin, *Human Rights and Development* (Bloomfield, Conn.: Kumarian Press, 2004), especially 47ff.

conflict-resolution, and development communities have been forced to work closer together, including through the emergence of new "rights-friendly" approaches to humanitarian and development action.[24] While the complexity of the issues that need to be addressed at the local level should not be underestimated, the injection of a rights *problématique* in the development of strategies for local participation can only be positive in the long run.

Nothing, however, replaces a sophisticated understanding of local realities, of social dynamics, and of peoples' aspirations. This is the precondition for a successful externally guided intervention. Just to give one example, in Afghanistan the Tribal Liaison Office (TLO), a small local NGO that works on civil society and participation issues, has been relatively successful in making inroads for civic education in the most difficult and tribalized areas of the eastern part of the country. Being from the same tribal terrain, the TLO staff have been able to work directly with tribal structures and have, for instance, given the tribal "police" some basic training, including on human rights issues. Additionally, the staff convinced tribal leaders that it was in their interest to allow their womenfolk to vote in the presidential and parliamentary elections. This is slow and painstaking work, but work that is immediately understandable from within local structures. The gamble is that, over time, the worldview will evolve that this is more effective and durable than the top-down, one-size-fits-all modernization approach.

In sum, the thrust of the argument of this chapter is that externally aided social processes will ultimately hit the sandbanks of good intentions if they are not grounded in the perceptions and aspirations of individuals and communities at the grassroots level. Locals understand "rights" intuitively, and they have an innate comprehension of what is just and unjust; they don't necessarily understand "democracy"—hence, the importance of addressing rights issues before, or at least at the same time as, the formal democratic process. This makes a strong case for a "peace-with-justice" agenda. Peace first and human rights later is a recipe for failure.

In terms of how current externally supported peace operations are constituted, the prescriptive changes required are quite obvious:

1. Usually, supporting human rights at the local level and addressing past abuses are low on the agenda. They have to be given much higher prominence from the very beginning, including in the enabling UN Security Council resolutions. The temptation for trade-offs between a process of reckoning on the one hand and stability on the other must be resisted because trade-offs give abusive authorities the wrong signal. The message that abuses will no longer be tolerated must be

---

24. Ibid., 122. For a case study on how aid agencies in Afghanistan tackled human rights issues, see Niland, "Rights, Rhetoric and Reality."

clear, and concrete visible steps must be taken to show that measures against impunity will be enforced.

2.   Local participation is key. While the establishment of legitimate and transparent state structures at the central level should remain a priority, equal billing must be given to support for local institutions of governance, building where appropriate on existing or traditional institutions. It should also be recognized that the state is not necessarily the vessel for legitimate and transparent institutions of governance at the local level (from Afghanistan to Somaliland, there are many examples of "stateless" institutions that function in a reasonably representative manner, enjoy legitimacy in the eyes of the local population, and are technically situated outside the state framework).[25]

3.   The international community must accept that building democracy takes time. It must be prepared to support fragile peace processes for the long haul. Formal democracy—that is, elections—should not be an end in itself. The establishment or reestablishment of a functioning social contract between the citizens and the state, from the local to the national level, should take priority. Elections make sense solely when an effective framework that guarantees basic rights—a modicum of rule of law and security for citizens—is in place.

4.   Social transformation at the local level in countries recovering from conflict is a seriously underresearched area. Grand recovery and reconstruction plans are drawn up, resourced, and (sometimes) implemented without much ground-truthing of the perceptions and expectations of the local citizenry. This is a worrisome, if rarely admitted, reality. Feeling the pulse of the population and factoring in their expectations is not rocket science.[26] Yet, doing so implies fundamental changes in the ways in which outsiders, and the power elites they support, operate.

Predictions in matters of transitions and peacebuilding are notoriously difficult, given the wide variety of situations and the variables that influence them. The shape of peace agreements, the form and functions of internationally mandated missions, and the urgency of delivering a perceptible peace dividend have rightly received the attention of scholars and policymakers. Other pieces in the transition puzzle have received scant attention, as I have shown in the preceding pages. The tension between the de jure and the de facto legitimacy of institutions of governance at the subnational level is one underresearched area from which key lessons for durable peace can be

---

25. See Scott Pegg, *International Society and the De Facto State* (Brookfield, Vt.: Ashgate, 1998).
26. A methodology for doing this is presented in annex 3 of the Tufts study.

learned.[27] (Carrie Manning's chapter in this volume represents an important step in the process of exploring this tension.) The effects of transitional processes on peoples' rights is another. One can posit that legitimacy, peoples' rights, and popular representation through a transparent process adapted to local circumstances and traditions are the key ingredients in a sustainable peace process. These three elements form the basis for a viable social contract that links the citizenry to its local institutions of governance and upwards to the state. If the contract builds on local traditions of governance and resolution of conflict, it will be easily internalized by all concerned. Mechanisms for upward and downward accountability, including accountability of aid agencies to beneficiaries, can help to consolidate the social contract. "Democracy" on its own, especially if it is of the formal electoral variety, is unlikely to do the trick.

Processes of social change are far from linear. While the international community is intent on reconstructing the state in countries recovering from conflict in its own Westphalian image, the complexities of power and economic and social relationships at the subnational level are likely to remain largely untouched by its top-down Weberian conception. The local population will feel, rightly, excluded from the nation-building equation. The formal trappings of democracy, disconnected as they are from the concerns of citizens and communities and the daily realities of poverty, hardship, and, often, abuse, will hardly constitute a valid mobilizing myth strong enough to give a sense of meaning to their engagement in the transition process.[28]

Moreover, if the peace dividend fails to materialize, "democracy" will be seen as little more than a cargo cult. Anthropologists and development sociologists have been teaching us for decades that social transformation will fail unless "it is illuminated from within."[29]

Perhaps the time has come for nation builders to heed this warning too.

---

27. See Chopra and Hohe, "Participatory Intervention," 289–303.

28. Berger, *Pyramids of Sacrifice*, 216. On the concept of mobilizing myth as applied to development and related international activities, see Craig Murphy and Enrico Augelli, "International Institutions, Decolonization and Development," *International Political Science Review* 14, no. 1 (1993): 71–85.

29. Berger, *Pyramids of Sacrifice*, 216.

3

Interim Governments and the Construction of Political Elites

Carrie Manning

Editors' Note

Moving from a consideration of bottom-up to top-down processes, Carrie Manning discusses the impact of transitional governance on the elites: Is there a tabula rasa period, or is there elite continuity despite an internationally administered interim regime? How much room for genuine change does an interim period provide, or does it simply allow elites to maneuver themselves to remain in power despite a seeming rupture in governance and authority?

Manning argues that the process of transition, which the international community seems to think will open up politics enough for the locus of power to shift away from established power holders, really just entrenches those actors and groups who are organized enough at the point of transition to play influential roles in the transitional processes. She tackles this issue from the perspective of elite turnover: the actors who are able to get themselves into the interim regimes—whether because they have the ear of the international community or because they are thugs who have the potential to wield violence—will be able to turn this participation to their advantage.

Manning's chapter raises an intriguing dimension in the process of stabilization and interim governments: how does authority move in the transition from one order to another? Viewed in this light, Manning's contribution becomes part of an emerging literature that started in the field on power sharing and now appears in her research, taking on the idea that there are critical junctures during which power relationships are substantially renegotiated. Steven Krasner's theory of punctuated equilibrium holds that during periods of rapid change, institutions no longer structure politics. During these periods of institutional suspension, power relations can be radically renegotiated. Manning shows, however, that authority often remains in the hands of those who were powerful before the transition began.

Introduction

The institution of an interim government is a strategy frequently used by external actors when charged with restoring political order in the wake of conflict or state collapse. It is appealing as a temporary stopgap measure that addresses pressing needs but that holds final decisions about the allocation of political power in abeyance. Yet interim governments may well have a lasting impact on politics, not least because the establishment of an interim government is in part a process of constructing political elites. The rules and procedures for determining who will play what role in the interim government, for deciding the structure and powers of the interim government, and for outlining the provisions made for the relationship between international and national authorities—or between interim government and citizens—all have an impact not only on the complexion of the interim government itself but also on the longer-term distribution of power and authority within the political system.

Decisions made with the short term in mind will affect the tactical and strategic calculations of existing and aspiring political actors. They will determine what resource allocations (financial, human capital, political capital) and skill sets are most advantageous for those seeking political power. They influence the beliefs of elites, aspiring elites, and citizens about the purpose and scope of government in the country. They set the parameters for acceptable political interaction, and they create winners and losers—that is, those with a stake in the political system and those with a stake in changing that system. To be sure, the rules of the game established under an interim government may be changed by writing a new constitution or reforming legislation. It is more difficult, however, to disempower those who have been given power and authority under interim rules. Indeed, it is precisely this group that is likely to write the permanent rules. Interim governments, then, may be short in duration but cast a long shadow into the future.

This chapter seeks to shed light on two questions: How do postwar interim governments contribute to the construction of political elites? And how does this process of elite construction affect the chances for post-conflict stability and good governance over both the short term and the longer term?

By "construction of political elites," I mean essentially the recruitment and socialization of politicians. This includes (1) choosing who rules by selection or exclusion of individuals and organizations for political leadership roles; (2) creating incentives that shape tactics and strategies which elites and aspiring elites will use to gain or retain power; and (3) shaping beliefs about the scope and purpose of government and about the limits of acceptable behavior within the political system. In short, the construction of elites has to do with determining who gets and retains power and how they do it. The process of elite construction in turn may affect ordinary citizens' identity and voting behavior, perceptions of the legitimacy of the political system, and, more broadly, the ability of the system to sustainably process political conflict.

Many factors, of course, will influence the nature of political elites and their relationships with one another in the new political system. A sizeable literature already exists on issues related to the sources and intensity of conflict,[1] the involvement of international and regional actors,[2] and the impact of institutional design, especially power sharing.[3] The character of interim government is itself shaped by these variables. However, interim government structures exert influence on the nature of politics in the longer term first by affecting who gets early access to the levers of the state and then by influencing the expectations and strategies of these elites as they seek to hold onto power over the transition to permanent governing arrangements.

The cases for this chapter were selected on the basis of two criteria. First, it includes only those cases of interim government in which wholly new governments were convened as part of the transition from war to peace, rather than those cases in which existing state structures and wartime incumbents remained in power and ancillary commissions were set up to support the peace process. Thus, cases such as Mozambique, El Salvador, Croatia, and Angola (1992 and 1997) are excluded.[4] Second, I consider no cases in which the scope of external authority left no significant role for local political actors at all.

---

1. Roy Licklider, "The Consequences of Negotiated Settlements in Civil Wars, 1945–1993," *American Political Science Review* 89, no. 3 (September 1995): 681–690; James D. Fearon and David D. Laitin, "Ethnicity, Insurgency, and Civil War," *American Political Science Review* 97, no. 1 (February 2003): 75–81; and William Zartman, *Ripe for Resolution: Conflict and Intervention in Africa* (New York: Oxford University Press, 1985).

2. Michael Brown, *The International Dimensions of Internal Conflict* (Boston: MIT Press, 1996); Barbara Walter, "The Critical Barrier to Civil War Settlement," *International Organization* 51 (1997): 335–364; Zartman, *Ripe for Resolution;* Thomas Ohlson and Stephen John Stedman, with Robert Davies, *The New Is Not Yet Born: Conflict Resolution in Southern Africa* (Washington, D.C.: Brookings Institution, 1994); Caroline Hartzell, "Explaining the Stability of Negotiated Settlements to Intrastate Wars," *Journal of Conflict Resolution* 43, no. 1 (February 1999): 3–22; Donald Rothchild, *Managing Ethnic Conflict in Africa* (Washington, D.C.: Brookings Institution, 1997); and Michael Doyle and Nicholas Sambinis, "International Peacebuilding: A Theoretical and Quantitative Analysis," *American Political Science Review* 94, no. 4 (December 2000).

3. Phillip Roeder and Donald Rothchild, *Sustainable Peace: Power and Democracy after Civil War* (Ithaca, N.Y.: Cornell University Press, 2005); Hartzell, "Explaining the Stability of Negotiated Settlements"; and Benjamin Reilly, *Democracy in Divided Societies: Electoral Engineering for Conflict Management* (Cambridge: Cambridge University Press, 2001).

4. Obviously, this is only a subset of interim regimes as defined in this volume, which would include those cases in which interim arrangements relied heavily upon existing state structures and wartime incumbents remained in power. In these cases, interim arrangements will quite clearly offer the advantage to existing power holders. I have excluded those cases in order to make the point that, even where wholly new arrangements are created, interim governments rarely succeed in shifting the balance of political power that obtains at the end of the war.

After a discussion of the lasting effects of interim choices, I will dissect a selected set of postwar interim government arrangements, identifying three dimensions that are most relevant for the purpose of understanding the process of elite construction that these governments set in motion. This discussion of interim choices—and the implications of different choices along selected dimensions—will provide the needed backdrop for an exploration of the potential impact of interim government structures on elite construction, which is tackled at the end of the chapter.

Interim Mechanisms and Lasting Effects

It is worth going into more detail about how interim governments are likely to influence the nature of the political system in lasting ways. First, those involved in interim government may have a greater influence and a greater role either in drafting the permanent constitution itself or in making the rules about how the permanent rules of the game will be determined. Either way, those in the interim government have the opportunity to tilt the process in a way that plays to their own strengths.

Second, political actors will absorb a wealth of information from the way in which authority is actually exercised under interim government. The practice of interim government will inform the beliefs of elites about the degree of flexibility in the formal rules of the game, about the nature of informal power and authority within the system, about the strengths and weaknesses of external actors there to enforce the arrangements, and about the points on which these actors are immovable or united and those on which they are flexible or divided. They will gain similar kinds of information about their rivals. Participation in interim government provides political actors with information that is likely to give them a competitive advantage under the permanent regime.

Third, the selection of elites for interim government may occur along lines that are different from those that would be viewed as acceptable for elite selection under a permanent regime. During the transitional stage, external actors exercise unusually high influence and may attempt to use the opportunities this creates to exclude or include certain types of political actors while they can. Thus, interim governments may end up empowering elites who would not make it into government under normal circumstances, and once there, they can leverage that experience to lasting benefit. Similarly, external actors may seek to exclude political actors who would not be excluded under a more popularly based selection process. They might do this, for example, if they believe that certain individuals or groups are responsible for the war, have been playing or are likely to play a spoiler role, or are likely to be opposed to the key interests of external actors.

Even if there is no effort to take advantage of the interim period to include or exclude certain actors, the shift from elite-mediated politics to competitive popular elections—which now constitute the basis of most permanent governance arrangements in post-conflict cases—will imply a major shift in the mentality and strategies of those seeking political power. Yet here again, it is likely that those who have already participated in government structures will find it easier to build parties that can serve as electoral vehicles. They enjoy some degree of incumbent advantage including greater name recognition. Greater access to resources means incumbents can more credibly promise future access to resources/patronage, and this helps with recruitment of activists and potential candidates for office. Voters may see those who have served in interim government as having the blessing of the international community, that is, the ability to work with and thus secure resources from the international community. In some contexts this will help their electoral chances, while in others it may hurt them.

There is little reason to suppose that elite beliefs and strategies or the distribution of political power established by interim governing arrangements can be easily changed. Although institutional frameworks shape the incentives and thus the behavior of political actors, the resource allocations that the major players bring to the table also determine outcomes. This initial distribution of power is likely to influence the ability of institutions to change in the underlying nature of politics. The experience that political actors gain from participation in interim government can be viewed as part of the initial resource allocation at the onset of permanent government institutions, just as the balance of power at the end of a civil war will be one of the factors shaping interim government arrangements. Going into the next stage of governance, domestic rather than external political actors are expected to predominate. As such, the types of elites empowered and the allocation of political authority in interim government merit close attention.

If interim governments do indeed influence the nature of more permanent governing arrangements, we need to take a systematic look at the types of elites that tend to be empowered under interim governments and at the ways in which political authority is allocated within these governments. While an in-depth examination of each case reveals innumerable subtleties in each of these respects, I argue that we can make some tentative, broad-based generalizations that hold across most of the cases considered here.

The Allocation of Political Authority

How do interim governments vary? Here we distinguish among interim governments along three dimensions, under the assumption that differences within these dimensions will be significant for our under-standing of how interim government affects the construction of a more permanent group of political elites. These three dimensions are selection process (how political actors are selected or recruited to take part in interim government); power sharing (the distribution of power among political actors within interim government); and sovereign authority (the interim government's power in relation to external authorities).

As table 3.1 demonstrates, the scope of local, popular participation nar-rows along all three dimensions. However, there is no systematic corre-spondence among the three dimensions. In other words, countries with participatory selection processes may have no power-sharing arrange-ments and limited sovereignty. Any selection process may, in theory, go along with any configuration of power sharing and any degree of sover-eign authority. In practice, most interim governments fall in the middle, indicating that selection processes are mediated by elites (domestic and international) rather than by voters; that power-sharing arrangements are reached on the basis of inter-elite negotiations rather than being a reflec-tion of expressed popular support; and that interim governments tend to have limited sovereignty.

It is not surprising, of course, that selection processes and power-sharing arrangements are frequently not based on popular input, since the point of having an interim government is to have some kind of authority in place while decisions are being made about the character of more permanent, more participatory government. Still, the fact remains, as argued below, that these stopgap governments nevertheless may have lasting consequences for the types of elites that can successfully enter the political arena and for the beliefs and strategies elites hold about politics. In turn, such governments influence the nature of participation, representation, and accountability in the political system.

Selection Processes

Two main issues are at stake with respect to selection processes: who should be selected, and how? The processes available for selecting partici-pants in interim governments can be usefully arranged along a spectrum, with direct popular elections for individual candidates at one end and direct appointment by external authorities at the other (see table 3.2). Few real-world cases lie at either end of the spectrum. Between the two extremes we find, among other possible scenarios, direct elections for can-didate lists, election by some sort of caucus system (including national conferences), pacts among elites, and appointment by external authorities, with advice from a local advisory panel (formal or informal).

As we move from left to right on this spectrum, we also see that control from above over who participates in government increases. Frequently, elites

Table 3.1   Variation in Interim Governments on Selected Dimensions

Selection Process	Participatory (national conference or election)	Elite controlled (caucus, pact/negotiation, authoritarian incumbent retains at least nominal authority)	Externally controlled (appointed by external authority)
Power Sharing	Power sharing based on electoral performance	Power sharing determined by elite-negotiated quotas	No power sharing among local factions
Sovereign Authority	Sovereign (full governing authority)	Limited sovereignty (may have extensive powers, but government can be overruled)	Advisory powers only

Source: Author's analysis.

are selected for participation in interim government in ways that are quite different from the selection procedures that are expected to govern political competition in the future (no matter where on the spectrum we begin). We should also note that, in some cases, selection procedures employed by interim government structures at the national level differed from those employed by local-level interim government structures.[5]

Choices about selection procedures themselves, of course, are also indirectly choices about who should participate in government. Those who erect interim governments also frequently resort to more direct ways of determining who should and should not participate. Those who pose the greatest threat to the system (various armed factions, for example) may stipulate their own inclusion in interim government as a condition of peace. Or external actors, on their own, may assume this is a condition of peace. External authorities may seek to exclude or include certain actors in this interim phase in hopes of making free competition "safe for democracy" later on (such as by excluding from politics those believed to be detrimental to stability and democracy). In Bosnia, for example, despite the fact that popular elections have been routinely held to determine who would hold the highest public offices, international authorities have had the power to modify the results of popular selection processes. Additionally, international authorities were given the right to vet candidates, remove public officials from office, and ban politicians from holding office in their political party if they are judged by the Office of the High Representative (OHR) to be blocking the implementation of the Dayton Peace Accords.

---

5. In Iraq under the Coalition Provisional Authority, for example.

Table 3.2   Variation in Selection Processes

Selection Process	Participatory (national conference or election)	Elite-controlled (caucus, pact/negotiation, authoritarian incumbent retains at least nominal authority)	Externally controlled (appointed by external authority)
	Bosnia (all) Kosovo 2 Iraq 3	Afghanistan 1 Afghanistan 2 Cambodia Liberia 1 Liberia 2 DRC Iraq 2	Kosovo 1 Iraq 1

Degree of popular participation in selection process ➡

Notes:

Afghanistan 1 = Bonn Agreement up to the beginning of the interim government (December 2001–September 2002)

Afghanistan 2 = Transitional administration until parliamentary elections in fall 2004

Bosnia = Bosnia case is broken down into Federation of Bosnia and Herzegovina, Republika Srpska, and Republic of Bosnia and Herzegovina.

Cambodia = Paris accord to first postwar general elections (October 1991–1993)

Democratic Republic of the Congo = Formation of interim government in June 2003 to general elections in July 2006.

Iraq 1 = Period of the Coalition Provisional Authority and Iraqi Governing Council

Iraq 2 = Interim government which took office June 28, 2004 (Iraq's first post-Saddam "sovereign national government")

Iraq 3 = Election of transitional assembly (January 30, 2005) to first parliamentary elections (December 15, 2005)

Kosovo 1 = From the end of military action to establishment of provisional institutions (February 2000–February 2002)

Kosovo 2 = Election of provisional institutions (2002) to present

Liberia 1 = Cotonou/Abuja agreements (1995–96)

Liberia 2 = August 2003 agreement among the government of Liberia, the Movement for Democracy in Liberia (MODEL), and Liberians United for Reconciliation and Democracy (LURD) to general elections in October 2005

Source: Author's analysis.

Another important choice must be made between centripetal and consociational formulas. Should interim governments seek to represent existing social and political cleavages, or should they seek to crosscut those cleavages? Whichever model is chosen, those in charge of formulating interim governments must be sure they have correctly identified relevant political cleavages and that the individual political actors who best represent the different sectors have been identified. If there is no past history of competitive politics in the country, this is a difficult task, particularly for external actors. Institutions have predictable consequences only if they have good information about the actors' full range of options.

In practice, what kinds of actors tend to be empowered under different types of interim governments? As shown in table 3.2, selection processes have tended to be negotiated by existing power holders, often in conjunction with the external actors involved in mediating peace agreements or in overseeing implementation of a peace process. There is considerable variation across our cases in terms of when and how elite negotiations take place, as well as in the role of international actors in those negotiations. Nevertheless, we find that interim governments have tended to entrench in power actors who possess (or are believed to possess) "veto power" over the peace process due to their ability to derail it through a return to armed conflict. As Marina Ottaway and Bethany Lacina have cautioned, even in interim administrations with strong international control, "despite the ample military and financial resources available to these international administrations, and the small size of the territories they administer, they have not been able to substantially alter the pre-existing distribution of power and develop democratic regimes."[6] Bosnia, Afghanistan, and Liberia provide ample evidence of this. Even where armed factions are formally excluded, they may still predominate by playing a spoiler role or by retaining de facto authority over territory or militias.[7] This is true notwithstanding the efforts of external actors to include groups that they perceive to have a normative claim to a seat at the table. The latter might include groups perceived as the victims rather than the aggressors in the conflict, members of the "unarmed" civil opposition, women and minority groups, or groups international actors believe will advance their own agendas—stability, good governance, democracy, and foreign policies favorable to outsiders' interests.

This tendency raises a critique that could be made of many efforts to establish interim government—that they are burdened with multiple, unrealistic, and often conflicting expectations. They are expected, for example, to end the conflict—to induce former armed belligerents to remain in the political arena—and at the same time to promote social justice, which quite often would mean removing former armed parties from politics altogether. Thus, we find frequent collisions between realpolitik (peace cannot be sustained in Liberia if Charles Taylor is not the president) and concern for justice (those who are responsible for the war should not be rewarded with political power).

In both Iraq and Bosnia, for instance, an explicit goal of outside interveners was not only to establish the basis for a democratic political system but also to encourage some and to discourage (if not explicitly exclude) other types of political elites from gaining positions of power in the system. In

---

6. Marina Ottaway and Bethany Lacina, "International Interventions and Imperialism: Lessons from the 1990s," *SAIS Review* XXIII, no. 2 (Summer–Fall 2003): 71–92, 85.
7. Ibid.

Bosnia, international authorities were influenced by both normative and pragmatic concerns about nationalist Croat and Serb parties dominating postwar politics. The policies of OHR, the Organization for Security and Cooperation in Europe (OSCE), and the governments involved in funding the peace process reflected the belief that those parties bore the lion's share of the responsibility for the war, and thus their dominance in government after the war would stymie efforts to build a sustainable peace. In Iraq, after toppling Saddam Hussein, the United States initially hoped to install power leaders from exile groups that had long supported intervention to remove Hussein. This plan quickly unraveled in the face of opposition from rival political leaders and other key opinion leaders, such as Grand Ayatollah Ali al-Sistani, who criticized the efforts as undemocratic.[8] Thus, there are few (if any) examples of interim governments bringing about a significant or lasting change in that balance of power among political actors, if only because most interim governments are the product of negotiation between those who already hold power.

What about those cases in which the selection of interim government, and/or the distribution of power within government, is determined by popular election? Is there greater potential there to change the balance of power or even the nature of politics? Here our most important cases are Bosnia, Kosovo 2, and Iraq 3, and there is little evidence from any of these cases to challenge the argument set out above. The efforts of international authorities to build a sustainable peace in Bosnia have been based on the assumption that genuinely competitive electoral politics, and the changes in the civic realm expected to accompany them, would help transform the underlying configuration of political cleavages and lead to the emergence of political parties that would not attempt to mobilize people along eth-nonational lines. But neither elections nor more direct intervention in the political process by international authorities have brought about the eclipse of the wartime nationalist parties in favor of more moderate alternatives. In Kosovo, the Democratic Party of Kosovo (PDK) has had a close rivalry with the Democratic League of Kosovo (LDK) in successive elections, with the LDK consistently edging out the PDK. A third key party was headed by one of the Kosovo Liberation Army's (KLA's) commanders, Ramush Haradinaj. Though the LDK was not an armed faction, there is no doubt that it has been the face of clandestine opposition to Belgrade's rule for decades, long before the emergence of the KLA. Once again, interim government has entrenched forces that were dominant at the onset of interim government.

---

8. Larry Diamond, "Lessons from Iraq," *Journal of Democracy* 16, no. 1 (January 2005): 9–23; "US Sidelines Exiles Who Were to Govern Iraq," *Washington Post*, June 8, 2003.

Bringing substantive change through elections is a long-term process. The key challenge in many cases is how to hold early elections, which may be necessary in order to establish a government but which are bound to entrench existing power holders, while holding open the possibility for longer-term change.

Overall, then, we see little variation among interim governments in terms of the types of people who are recruited or in the types of people who hold effective power in these governments. This is true regardless of the degree of local, popular participation in selecting who will lead in the interim. This also seems to hold true even in those cases where external authorities explicitly seek to prevent the entrenchment of former armed groups in political power, as in Bosnia and Kosovo.

Power Sharing

With respect to the distribution of power within interim governments, table 3.3 makes clear that elite-negotiated power-sharing arrangements are the rule in postwar interim governments. Even where, as in Bosnia at federation and republic levels, elections are held for legislative and executive posts, the specific distribution of power within the executive is constrained by prior agreement among elites and enshrined in the Dayton Peace Agreement. In the cases in which the distribution of power within the executive is determined by elections, as in the Bosnian entity of Republika Srpska, Iraq 3, and Kosovo 2, care has been taken to provide for proportional representation of political parties and, explicitly in all three cases, of social (ethnic or sectarian) groups deemed politically relevant. In Iraq, special efforts—although largely unsuccessful—were made to boost Sunni representation in the transitional assembly after weak Sunni participation in the elections left Sunnis underrepresented there. In Bosnia, there is a complex history of international actors intervening to bolster multiethnic, "moderate" political parties and to balance the interests of all three "constituent nations."[9] In Kosovo, the international community has long sought to boost participation and representation of Serbs, along with Roma and other minorities, in the provisional government institutions.[10]

---

9. David Chandler, *Bosnia: Faking Democracy after Dayton* (London: Pluto Press, 1999); Gerald Knaus and Felix Martin, "Travails of the European Raj," *Journal of Democracy* 14, no. 3 (July 2003): 60–74; Carrie L. Manning and Miljenko Antic, "The Limits of Electoral Engineering in Bosnia and Herzegovina," *Journal of Democracy* 14, no. 3 (2003): 45–60; and Roberto Belloni, "Peacebuilding and Consociational Electoral Engineering in Bosnia-Herzegovina," *International Peacekeeping* 11, no. 2 (2004): 334–353.

10. Details of OSCE's efforts to monitor and promote minority rights in Kosovo, which crosscut all of the organization's initiatives there, are available at www.osce.org/kosovo.

Table 3.3   Variations in Power Sharing

	Power sharing based on electoral performance	Power sharing determined by elite-negotiated quotas	No power sharing
Power-sharing determinants	Bosnia (all) Iraq 3 Kosovo 2	Bosnia (FBiH) Bosnia Republic Cambodia Kosovo 1 Iraq 1 Iraq 2 Afghanistan 1 Afghanistan 2 Liberia 1 Liberia 2 DRC	

Degree of power sharing ➡

Source: Author's analysis.

This noted, there is considerable variation among elite-negotiated power arrangements. In Bosnia, for example, the distribution of power among political parties was determined in the first instance by election, but the results were also mediated by previous agreement among the former armed factions (as enshrined in the Dayton Peace Agreement). In Bosnia's complex constitutional landscape, there are different provisions for power sharing in executive and legislative institutions at municipal, cantonal (in the federation), entity, and republic levels.

In Afghanistan, meanwhile, the second transitional regime was chosen according to a more inclusive process than the first, although it still did not use nationwide elections. In Afghanistan 1, the participants in the Bonn Agreement appointed Hamid Karzai as head of the first interim government. This lasted from December 2001 through the seating of the transitional administration selected by the emergency *loya jirga* in June 2002. The Bonn Agreement provided for the creation of a special independent commission to set the rules for the selection and running of the emergency *loya jirga*. This commission of eminent persons included lawyers, professors, journalists, former civil servants, women's activists, and religious figures, and it was tasked with defining a selection process for delegates to the *loya jirga* and to ensure "adequate representation of women, minorities, scholars, and representatives of civil society groups."[11] Delegates were chosen at several levels: at the most local levels, *shuras*—elders' councils comprised of individuals linked to respected and prominent local families—chose electors, who then chose delegates. The June 2002 *loya jirga* selected the transi-

---

11. Human Rights Watch, "Q&A on Afghanistan's Loya Jirga Process," 2002, www.hrw.org/press/2002/04/qna-loyagirga.htm.

tional administration, again with Hamid Karzai at its helm. In January 2004, a second *loya jirga* adopted a new constitution. A directly elected government replaced the transitional administration in December 2004 in accordance with this permanent constitution.

In Iraq 1 and 2, the distribution of power at the national level, on the Iraqi Governing Council and then in the interim government appointed in June 2004, was the product of negotiations between Iraqi elites, occupation authorities, and, in the latter case, the UN special envoy and his staff. At the local level, both the recruitment of individuals to the governing bodies and the distribution of power within those bodies varied, depending in part upon the discretion of the civilian Coalition Provisional Authority (CPA) and the conditions those authorities found on the ground. In some cases there were direct elections, in others, caucuses. In still other cases councils were appointed by coalition authorities in accordance with their best estimate of how to quickly bring order and effective governance.[12]

In Cambodia, the Democratic Republic of the Congo, and Liberia (1 and 2), interim executive authority was established by agreement among the warring parties and international actors involved in the peace process. In Cambodia and the DRC, it included all of the armed factions, and in Liberia it included armed factions as well as civil society groups that had served in previous, short-lived transitional governments throughout the war. While the formalities of power sharing differed, in each of these cases the actual distribution of power in practice was the subject of ongoing negotiation and squabbling. Relations between power holders from competing factions were characterized by a good deal of tension, uncertainty, and mistrust.[13]

Sovereign Authority

Here we are concerned with the parameters of the interim government's authority vis-à-vis external actors. What is the division of authority, formal and informal, between the interim government and external actors?

Decisions about the scope of interim government authority are determined by a range of factors, including local capacity, the willingness of external actors to devote resources to peacebuilding, the perception of external

---

12. Diamond, "Lessons from Iraq"; Larry Diamond, "What Went Wrong in Iraq?" *Foreign Affairs* (September/October 2004); Celeste J. Ward, *The Coalition Provisional Authority's Experience with Governance in Iraq,* Special Report 139 (Washington, D.C.: United States Institute of Peace, May 2005); and Christophe Wilcke, "Castles Built of Sand: US Governance and Exit Strategies in Iraq," *Middle East Report* 232 (Fall 2004).

13. UN Security Council, "Special Report"; UN Security Council, "Seventeenth Report of the Secretary-General on the United Nations Organization Mission in the Democratic Republic of the Congo" (March 15, 2005); and Jin Song, "The Political Dynamics of the Peacemaking Process in Cambodia," in *Keeping the Peace: Multidimensional UN Operations in Cambodia and El Salvador,* ed. Michael W. Doyle, Ian Johnstone, and Robert C. Orr, 53–81 (Cambridge: Cambridge University Press, 1997).

actors who must make decisions about peacebuilding efforts regarding the causes of the conflict, the likely risk of a return to hostilities, and the parties likely to act as spoilers or good-faith agents. What kinds of political institutions, and what kinds of political actors, do external actors regard as important to building a sustainable peace? What degree of control are external actors *able* to exercise? In Iraq, which presumably represents the upper limit of external intervention in state building, U.S. and coalition forces exercised extensive control over the process of constructing new government structures and selecting and deselecting elites who would participate in the various incarnations of interim government. Nevertheless, they did not have it all their way, even when they had the power to simply appoint ruling elites.

Table 3.4 shows greater variation on this dimension than on the previous two. In Iraq 3, Afghanistan, Liberia, and the DRC, the interim government enjoyed full governing authority, although not necessarily a monopoly on force or capacity to deliver services. While the United Nations has extensive peace operations in Liberia and the DRC, the roles of those missions are linked primarily to enforcing and monitoring cease-fires, to supporting the reestablishment of government structures throughout the national territory, to monitoring and improving the humanitarian situation and human rights, and to overseeing and/or implementing security-sector reform. Yet even in these cases, external actors exercise a significant amount of de facto authority. The sovereign governments of Afghanistan, Iraq, Liberia, and the DRC depend for their continued existence on security provided by international armed forces, and they rely heavily on external aid in order to provide the most basic services to their citizens. Economic dependency is unlikely to change in Liberia, the DRC, and Afghanistan, even after the transition to permanent governing arrangements.

In the cases of Iraq 2, Bosnia, Cambodia, and Kosovo 2, international authorities had or have extensive powers of their own, as well as the power to overrule the interim government on issues related to peace-process implementation, even though some governments (Cambodia and Bosnia) were designated as sovereign.[14] In the cases in which interim government structures have advisory powers only, membership in the interim government structures was based on appointment by an international authority.

---

14. Simon Chesterman, *You, the People: The United Nations, Transitional Administration, and State-building* (Oxford: Oxford University Press, 2004); Carrie L. Manning, "Elections and Political Change in Bosnia and Herzegovina," *Democratization* (Spring 2004); Elizabeth M. Cousens and Charles K. Cater, *Toward Peace in Bosnia: Implementing the Dayton Accords* (Boulder, Colo.: Lynne Rienner, 2001); Chandler, *Bosnia*; and Song, "The Political Dynamics of the Peacemaking Process in Cambodia."

Table 3.4   Variations in Sovereign Authority

	Sovereign (full governing authority)	Limited sovereignty (may have extensive powers, but government can be overruled)	Advisory powers only
Sovereign Authority	Iraq 3 Afghanistan 1 Afghanistan 2 Liberia 1 Liberia 2 DRC	Iraq 2 Bosnia Cambodia Kosovo 2	Iraq 1 Kosovo 1

Scope of interim government authority ➡

Source: Author's analysis.

Elite Expectations and Strategies

What, if any, generalizations can we make about how interim regimes affect the expectations and strategies of elites empowered by them? What advantages and disadvantages do the various factions expect to derive from participating in interim arrangements? And how might participating in those arrangements, or watching from the outside, cause political actors to adjust their expectations? Dankwart Rustow argues that elite expectations about how well they can do under the system are an important determinant of the elites' willingness to invest in the system. The organizational challenges posed by adapting to the political rules of the game, the actor's resource endowment (financial and human resources), the perceived stability or predictability of the rules, and early experience with the new institutions, among other factors, shape actor expectations about their prospects.[15] How are the kinds of interim government structures that have been set up in the cases considered here likely to affect these expectations?

As discussed earlier in this chapter, interim governments privilege power sharing to a greater degree than permanent governments. Our cases in which interim power-sharing arrangements were determined by a process other than (or in addition to) direct popular elections alone include Afghanistan, Bosnia, Cambodia, Kosovo 1, Iraq 1 and 2, Liberia 1 and 2, and the DRC. In all of these cases except Iraq, power-sharing arrangements were either negotiated as part of the peace agreement that concluded hostilities (in Afghanistan, the Bonn Agreement) or, as in the case of Kosovo, informally in side

---

15. Dankwart Rustow, "Transitions to Democracy: Toward a Dynamic Model," *Comparative Politics* 2/3 (April 1970): 337–363.

talks among some of the participating factions at the peace talks.[16] In Afghanistan, the specifics were further worked out through commissions meant to be more broadly representative of society. In all cases, international actors exercised some influence in determining both who should participate and in what capacity.

This type of elite negotiated power sharing in the near term may make for a difficult adjustment to more limited or no power-sharing arrangements later. Parties will likely have significant adjustments to make when electoral competition becomes the basis for achieving or maintaining power. They will have to shift from a system in which their place is secured by virtue of having been armed combatants, to one in which they will have to compete with their rivals on an entirely different footing. Competing in electoral politics will require parties to develop a set of skills, human resources, and material and financial resources that will likely pose serious challenges to the party as an organization and to the authority of its existing leadership. Party leaders may well resist making the shift, or at the very least they may resist making the investments in party development that would likely make them effective electoral competitors, since these investments tend to lead to a liberalization or broadening of authority within the party.[17]

It is thus understandable that those who are empowered during the interim period devote considerable effort to figuring out how to secure a place for themselves in permanent government. Once again, who participates in interim government structures and what they learn there will help determine the character of the rules for the longer-term system. There is no Rawlsian veil of ignorance here. Those who fear they will not be able to compete effectively in elections (because of a small constituency or low organizational capacity) can be expected to try to hold onto interim mechanisms that have benefited them, such as quota systems for representation of each faction. Those who expect to win elections either fairly or by controlling them can be expected, by contrast, to seek to dissolve consensual or power-sharing structures. Thus, it is important to understand the particular incentive structures that party leaders face as they look forward to the transition from interim to more permanent arrangements.

International actors helping to design and implement interim government may have a greater ability to influence the construction of elites and the longer-term character of government by affecting political actors' expectations, both about how well they can do under the system and whether they can successfully circumvent or reform the system. In addi-

---

16. Carrie L. Manning, "Armed Opposition Groups into Political Parties: Comparing Bosnia, Kosovo, and Mozambique," *Studies in Comparative International Development* 39, no. 1 (Spring 2004): 54–76.

17. Angelo Panebianco, *Political Parties: Organization and Power* (Cambridge: Cambridge University Press, 1998).

tion to potential challenges from internal rivals, parties facing the decision whether to invest in competitive politics confront a tremendous amount of uncertainty about the political system itself. Institutions are weak, and there is uncertainty about their final forms and durability. Similarly, there may be doubts regarding the intentions of other political actors (competitors) and uncertainty about the way rules will be applied. External actors, as Barbara Walter and others have pointed out, can make a significant difference here by demonstrating a commitment to maintaining a stable and predictable environment.[18] They can do this by punishing those who transgress, or seek to transgress, the rules and by reinforcing previously agreed-upon norms. For example, external actors sought to proscribe majority domination in Iraq, and so they pressured Shi'a and Kurdish factions to bring Sunnis into the constitution-making process, despite their low representation in the transitional assembly following a boycott of the election in January 2005. What participants in interim governments and their would-be rivals learn about how, when, and why the basic rules of the system can be changed, broken, or ignored, and at what cost, will strongly influence their expectations about and commitment to the political system down the road.

Assessment of Structural Effects

This chapter has merely sketched out some of the possibilities of interim government effects upon elite construction. Each of the questions raised here bears further investigation based on detailed case studies structured for effective comparison. Initially, I set out to describe relevant variations in interim government structures in a selected set of cases and then to trace some of the likely implications of that variation for the construction of political elites.

The variations in these structures, after closer examination, seem less important than the similarities. Interim government structures tend to privilege elite negotiation in determining both who will participate in interim government and how they will divide power among themselves. And those negotiations tend to be dominated by former armed groups and by considerations of how to secure their short-term participation. In the longer term, as Donald Rothchild has pointed out, the principles upon which government is based in the transitional period are unlikely to be sustainable. Even in the short term, such arrangements tend to sacrifice effective governance and the construction of a viable state itself, as has been evident in the DRC, Liberia, and Afghanistan. At the same time, interim government structures create

---

18. Walter, "The Critical Barrier to Civil War Settlement."

vested interests and send unintended signals to those participating in and observing them.

Our cases offer examples of formal power distribution within interim government on the basis of both military and political strength and on the basis of such normative concerns as ethnic proportionality (which, to be sure, can also be a practical concern), gender equality, and representation of social forces that did not participate in armed conflict. The shift from such arrangements to a balance of power based on competition at the polls may hold little appeal for many interim government participants. This is due to the daunting practical challenges associated with retooling their organizations—or creating wholly new organizations—in order to make them capable of competing effectively in the political arena. The issue of how or whether the political actors who tend to predominate in interim governments will seek to build viable parties is crucial to successful peacebuilding.

In situations in which the transition from war to peace is also part of a democratization process—as it is in all of the cases considered here and in virtually all post–Cold War civil war terminations—perhaps the most important way in which interim governments affect the construction of a political elite is by shaping political actors' expectations and strategies regarding democratic politics. In many cases, participation in interim government provides a first opportunity for local political actors to see democracy at work. What lessons will they learn regarding rule of law, representation, accountability, and participation?

Postwar interim governments, like all transitional governments, reflect the power balance that existed at their inception. Unlike other transitional governments, however, in the cases considered here, more than one—sometimes all—of the major participants in government have access to the use of force. Again, the key question is how to create interim governments that will respond to short-term imperatives without damaging the prospects for a more salutary political realignment down the road. As we have noted, external actors have sought in some cases to include or exclude certain actors in the interim period by tinkering with the institutional framework. This seems a reasonable strategy in theory, but in practice it has had little success because political actors have found ways to work around these efforts.

Interim governments also tend to offer their creators (especially external actors) the seductive sense that anything is possible, leading to a voluntaristic approach to politics in which "political will," or the lack thereof, is held to be the key to either success or failure. Of course, the reality is far more complicated. Institutional design can determine political outcomes only when it accounts for the full range of circumstances that shape actors' preferences and drive their choices; otherwise, we cannot accurately predict how actors will behave in a given institutional framework.

What are the implications of interim structure effects upon legitimacy, governance, and political stability? We can think of legitimacy as having both substantive and procedural sources. Governments that are efficacious and that can provide for the welfare of their citizens are more likely to be considered legitimate. Government legitimacy is also evaluated by citizens according to whether the government came to power through procedures considered to be appropriate. From this perspective, there is no generic recipe for legitimacy, and we cannot point a priori to gains or losses in legitimacy for an interim government based on selection procedures, distribution of political power in government, and scope of government power. Legitimacy is a function of the relationship between state and citizen and of the expectations of citizens, which vary according to a large number of factors.

Nevertheless, given the kinds of actors who tend to get entrenched in the kinds of postwar interim governments examined here, legitimacy could be endangered both on the grounds of "appropriate procedure" and on the grounds of government performance. Rewarding warlords with political power may be a practical necessity, but how, for example, does it play in Liberia's Nimba County? And it seems clear that external efforts to influence who gets into interim government run the risk of endangering the legitimacy of interim structures and the more permanent arrangements that succeed them. Indeed, the question of legitimacy is an extremely vexing one for post-conflict interim governments, for it raises very difficult questions, including how much legitimacy matters in the short run and whether anyone finds it possible to look beyond the short run.

There are also implications for governance and stability, which may well be substitutes rather than complements in interim governments. Unity governments have never been among the most efficacious of regime types. Nor is it clear whether broadly inclusive governments are good for stability: there is insufficient evidence to support the claim that mere inclusion in government is enough to reform and co-opt spoilers.

Moreover, if participants view interim government as truly temporary, then interim government is unlikely to serve any of the goals people set out for them: they will likely do little. Everyone will simply bide their time until it is time to write the more permanent rules and will then try to exercise maximum influence over *that* process. If interim governments are responsible for drafting the rules of more permanent governance, they will take the opportunity to entrench themselves in power. Under the latter scenario, the selection and socialization of elites during the period of interim government becomes crucial.

The policy implications for external actors involved in helping to establish and reinforce interim governments are fourfold. First, attempts to alter the balance of power are unlikely to succeed in the absence of direct intervention to remove certain actors before the onset of competitive politics. Electoral politics will not likely change the balance of power between parties even over the long term, unless the sources of party strength are themselves addressed. For example, in many cases where identity-based politics prevails, it is because the allocation of not only political but also economic power has historically been parceled out along those lines. Institutional design can help, but it cannot change this legacy by itself. Bosnia and Iraq provide very different supporting examples on this point. Of course, external actors must be cautious in presuming to know what is best in terms of the balance of political power.

Second, economic development must serve to loosen the link between military power, political power, and economic power. The strengthening of economic governance is an essential, difficult, and long-term process that has received less systematic attention from those engaged in peacebuilding. But it is a key part of building up possibilities for longer-term political transformation. Interim governments tend to mirror power balances at the end of the war. The establishment of strong economic institutions that can promote investment and employment can, in the long term, help diffuse power and promote the gradual weakening of the links among military, political, and economic power which is essential for the creation of a durable democracy.

Third, political institutions themselves do matter. I have argued elsewhere that postwar multiparty politics is not always as competitive as it appears on the surface, owing to the ability of parties to adapt to the game in ways that allow them to lock in a constituency.[19] Those involved in peacebuilding must ensure that competitive politics is truly competitive if they want to see parties and voters respond to the incentives that are presumed to be on offer. There is no simple recipe for achieving this. Instead, it depends on the factors of each particular case: the degree of segmentation in the market for votes, the nature of political cleavage lines, and the particular constitutional and electoral arrangements that are in place.

Finally, for institutional incentive structures to work, uncertainty around the longevity of these institutions must be reduced as much as possible. Only when actors are reasonably certain that the rules are there to stay will they make an investment in those rules. Helping to reduce this uncertainty will require a longer-term commitment by external actors than has customarily been made.

---

19. Manning, "Armed Opposition Groups."

4

Executive Power-sharing Systems

Conflict Management or Conflict Escalation?

Donald Rothchild

Editors' Note

When establishing transitional regimes after civil wars, statesmen and their advisers often experiment with power-sharing institutions. They seek to reassure weaker parties, who are often former insurgents, by including them on a roughly proportional basis in the decision-making process. As Donald Rothchild argues in this chapter, although provisions for such institutions seem logical, they are likely to prove brittle in the later phases of the transitional regimes and in the period that follows those regimes. This fragility is explained by the information and credible commitment dilemmas and by the failure of external actors to protect the peace agreements for an extended period of time. In addition, the weakness of such institutions results from the political elite's fears about a loss of power resulting from inclusion in a power-sharing coalition, incomplete party inclusion in the institutions of state, a lack of shared norms and aspirations, and the constraining economic environment. Paradoxically, then, the power-sharing institutions designed to reassure weaker parties about their security become a cause of conflict and insecurity over time, requiring a search for alternative institutions that will cope simultaneously with the need for security, governance, and development.

"Power sharing" is a broad term connoting a wide variety of institutional and political arrangements that are used to bring various parties into government, with the goal of ensuring their participation in the political process. Often, power-sharing arrangements are implemented in the wake of civil war and are used to incorporate significant power holders into the peace and reconstruction process. Among the various forms of power sharing are at least three main forms: inclusive decision making (for example, shared decision making in the branches of government by the representatives of the major segments of society); partitioned decision making (for example, a limited autonomy exercised by authorities at the regional level); and predetermined decision making (for example, preset formulas for sharing, such as constitutional amendment and electoral formulas).[1] Certainly, some overlap between these categories is evident; for instance, where a powerful leader from an ethno-region gains control of a ministry at the political center, elements of inclusiveness and partition may both be present. Even so, the thrust of these different forms is apparent.

In this chapter I focus on inclusive decision making exclusively, partly for reasons of space and partly because agreement in Africa on meaningful partitioned decision making is so uncommon after civil wars.[2] By establishing formal rules on the inclusion of all major groups in key governmental positions according to the principle of proportionality, executive power-sharing institutions ensure the main actors access to decision making at the highest levels. The intended effect of this is to promote confidence among the bargaining parties about their future roles, for the parties view inclusion in the inner circles of state power as representing a guarantee of participation in the matters that affect them most critically. Furthermore, external mediators and observers—eager to facilitate an end to the fighting and destruction—are inclined to favor institutions that hold out the promise of minimally satisfying the expectations of all negotiators.[3]

I begin by discussing power-sharing institutions in terms of their short- and long-term implications, examining the potential that power sharing, used as an incentive to reach agreements during the negotiation phase, provides as a source of conflict during the longer-term consolidation phase. In the next section I analyze the patterns of Africa's experiences with power sharing, looking in detail at the process in Côte d'Ivoire in the 1990s after the breakdown of stable governance. I then discuss the question of reassuring weaker parties, linking the search for increased political, economic, and strategic security during the negotiation phase with the changed circumstances

---

Earlier versions of this chapter are found in a volume growing out of a conference at McGill University on April 1–2, 2005, titled "Hastening the Day," and the journal *Ethnopolitics* 4, no. 3 (September 2005), 247–267. I wish to thank Nikolas Emmanuel, Camille Sumner, and Eileen Ortiga for their help on research and Stefan Wolff, Daniel Posner, Steven Saidman, and two anonymous readers for their useful suggestions on revising and developing the manuscript.

1. Philip G. Roeder and Donald Rothchild, eds., *Sustainable Peace: Power and Democracy After Civil Wars* (Ithaca, N.Y.: Cornell University Press, 2005).

2. David Lake and Donald Rothchild, "Territorial Decentralization and Civil War Settlements," in Roeder and Rothchild, *Sustainable Peace*, 109–132.

3. Samantha Power, *"A Problem from Hell": America and the Age of Genocide* (New York: Basic Books, 2002), 382.

that prevailed during the consolidation phase. Finally, in the conclusion, I probe the anticipated and unanticipated consequences that may follow from the adoption of power-sharing systems in Africa.

This discussion raises a number of questions. First, does this widespread support for power sharing among practitioners and academics in the transitional regimes take full account of the dilemmas of implementing such arrangements in the later, political consolidation phases? Second, is the outcome of such systems likely to be a transition to the joint exercise of political power over time or a step on the way to the dominant party's consolidation of power, as in South Africa? Third, can power-sharing institutions be constructed to provide for patterns of governance that will prove durable?

The Short- and Long-term Implications

Reassuring weaker parties (and sometimes stronger ones as well) about their future participation in governance is a problem during negotiations and implementation because the short-term motives for adopting power-sharing arrangements may conflict with the long-term incentives to consolidate political power.[4] Power-sharing institutions are attractive to weaker parties during negotiations on a peace agreement, for they hold out the prospect of inclusion in decision-making activities. In their view, this gives them the ability to protect their interests and those of their communal membership. "In times of crisis," writes Ahmedou Ould-Abdallah, the UN secretary-general's special envoy to Burundi in the mid-1990s, "the presence of a community's representatives within a government acts as some reassurance to that community that its vital interests will not be ignored."[5] In most African countries, with the state a critical actor in terms of allocating resources and providing security and the private sector small in size and offering limited opportunities, weaker groups feel that it is crucial for them to be a part of governmental deliberations at the highest level. Group leaders reason that to be shut out of the cabinet, the legislature, or other decision-making bodies is to be unable to protect their group against exploitation, even victimization. This urge for inclusion has led numerous political oppositions to negotiate for a proportional role at the country's political center after civil war.

Thus, power-sharing arrangements respond to a weaker party's perceived need for participation in affairs of state. In situations where weaker parties have not been defeated on the battlefield and a continuance of the war holds out no prospect of military victory, their leaders are likely to consider some

---

4. Roeder and Rothchild, *Sustainable Peace*.

5. Ahmedou Ould-Abdallah, *Burundi on the Brink 1993–95* (Washington, D.C.: United States Institute of Peace Press, 2000), 74.

form of power sharing to be less costly than prolonged fighting. When dominant parties or ruling coalitions are prepared to act in an accommodative way on this issue, it becomes an incentive to weaker parties to reach agreement. Barbara Walter's data show that if a peace treaty includes power-sharing guarantees, 38 percent of the combatants are more likely to sign the agreement.[6] Walter adds, "Rival factions appear concerned with the postwar distribution of power and do seem to demand guaranteed representation as the price for peace."[7]

Being unable to achieve a military victory and at the same time unprepared to accept partition or separate independence, the negotiating teams may compromise on a transitional arrangement to share power in the major institutions of state. They seek to allay the uncertainties that weaker parties have about coexistence in a common state by designing institutions for joint decision making on the basis of some predetermined formula of group representation.

Power sharing under post–civil war circumstances essentially represents a concession by a more powerful actor to a less powerful one in an effort to gain the latter's assent to the peace accord. As Ben Reilly and Andrew Reynolds assert, in a context of prevailing distrust and uncertainty, weaker parties "typically have a greater need for inclusiveness and a lower threshold for the robust rhetoric of adversarial politics than their established counterpart."[8] Concessions therefore become essential, even though the effects are often to create a weak state with limited reach and capacity for effective governance.

When parties sign on to a power-sharing agreement, what does this compromise entail? In contrast to the Westminster model, which is based on "competitive," even adversarial, relations, a power-sharing regime is "coalescent" and involves rules to ensure the inclusion of the main parties in a government of national reconciliation.[9] Third parties can encourage local actors to agree to a grand coalition of elites, but the survival of this fragile institution over the long term depends upon the negotiators' acceptance of the rules of the game and their preparedness to deliver on their bargains. "Power-sharing practices are likely to have conflict-mitigating effects," warns Timothy Sisk, "only if the disputants arrive at them through a process of negotiation and reciprocity that all significant parties perceive as fair and just, given their own changing interests and needs."[10]

---

6. Barbara F. Walter, *Committing to Peace: The Successful Settlement of Civil Wars* (Princeton: Princeton University Press, 2002), 80.

7. Ibid.

8. Ben Reilly and Andrew Reynolds, "Electoral Systems and Conflict in Divided Societies," in *Papers on International Conflict Resolution* (Washington, D.C.: National Academy Press, 1999).

9. Arend Lijphart, *Democracy in Plural Societies: A Comparative Exploration* (New Haven, Conn.: Yale University Press, 1977), 25.

10. Timothy D. Sisk, *Power Sharing and International Mediation in Ethnic Conflicts* (Washington, D.C.: United States Institute of Peace Press, 1996), 9.

Current data suggest that the presence of a mediator facilitates both the negotiation and the implementation process. Walter finds that once peace agreements have been signed, the parties are 20 percent more likely to implement the arrangement if a third party acts as a protector.[11] Yet, in the later phases of implementation, when the external actors disengage, it is the local parties who must take up the slack and make the arrangement a credible one. Hence, the likely durability of the formal and informal rules on interchange and distribution and their ability to meet the essential needs of the stronger and weaker parties for security, participation, and effective governance are critical to continued cooperation.

In sum, power-sharing measures are a logical response to the configurations of power in contexts where the forces are deadlocked politically and militarily and view the costs of compromise on peace as lower than the continuance of war. Power sharing is a face-saving mechanism that enables the adversaries to avoid a worse outcome. Power sharing is an implicit recognition of the finding, formally put forward by World Bank economist Paul Collier, that ethnic dominance doubles the likelihood of conflict occurring after civil wars.[12] However, the short-term benefits in terms of bringing organized violence to a halt may come at a long-term cost in terms of effective governance and political uncertainty about future relations. This results in a dilemma. Power-sharing arrangements may enhance the prospects of peace in the short term, providing incentives to weaker parties to sign on to agreements, but they are a potential source of instability, ineffective governance, and intergroup conflict in the long term. The problematic remains unresolved: how can an energetic dominant coalition and insecure weaker parties coexist simultaneously within a state during the consolidation phase after civil war?

Patterns of Experience with Power Sharing in Africa

Not surprisingly, power-sharing institutions have attracted considerable support in contemporary Africa. African governments have found that signaling a willingness to collaborate with insurgents in national reconciliation governments after civil wars is costly but acceptable in order to maintain their country as a single entity. In signaling a preparedness to concede the sharing of power, the dominant coalition is indicating an understanding of the security fears that weaker parties have about their future and a

---

11. Caroline Hartzell, Matthew Hoddie, and Donald Rothchild, "Stabilizing the Peace After Civil War: An Investigation of Some Key Variables," *International Organization* 55, no. 1 (Winter 2001): 199; and Walter, *Committing to Peace*, 83.

12. Paul Collier, "Policy for Post-conflict Societies: Reducing the Risks of Renewed Conflict" (presented at the Economics of Political Violence Conference, Princeton University, March 18–19, 2000), 3.

willingness to establish institutions to protect them against the possibility of a reemergence of majority tyranny. Provided the fears and antagonisms of civil war are superseded by the emergence of shared norms and practices on constitutionalism and moderation, power-sharing agreements can set the foundation for democracy and for governmental respect for human rights. Where the best-case scenario prevails, as occurred in South Africa, problems of credible commitment may ease, and civility and respect for difference may become expected practice.

However, moderation and civility are normally in short supply after the brutality of civil war. Suspicion and mistrust wither slowly and only after members of the dominant groups are perceived as displaying a genuine concern for the well-being of weaker peoples. Moreover, the economic scarcities and the lack of opportunity that mark relations in a post–civil war context heighten conflictive relations. As Victor Azarya observes, "Civility in social conduct may be hard to expect in countries with acute shortages and extreme gaps between levels of aspirations and accomplishments."[13]

Not surprisingly, therefore, contemporary African experiments with power-sharing institutions display mixed outcomes. Following the signing of peace accords in my sample of recent cases—Burundi, Côte d'Ivoire, the DRC, Liberia, Rwanda, and Sudan—several patterns are in evidence. First, a shaky coexistence is present in Burundi, the DRC, and Liberia, where, following mediation efforts by external parties, local patrons have agreed to power-sharing institutions (in principle, at least), but the implementation process has proven difficult and incomplete. The partial nature of these consolidations is indicated by the continuance of lawlessness and violence and the slow emergence of trust that has developed among the cartel of elites making up the ruling coalition. Burundi's National Forces for Liberation (FNL), which continues to engage government forces in the field, still has not agreed to talks to bring the decades-long war to an end.14 On the other side, the Tutsi-dominated National Union for Progress (UPRONA) resisted implementing the Pretoria Agreement provisions on power sharing in July 2004, urging that the percentage of seats reserved in the National Assembly for the Tutsi be designated for the Tutsi parties only and not include Tutsi who are members of Hutu-led parties.

In Liberia, serious divisions surfaced in 2004 not only among the factional patrons who make up the cabinet but also within the main rebel group, Liberians United for Reconciliation and Democracy (LURD).[15] Order was restored, but only after the UN secretary-general's special adviser, Jacques

---

13. Victor Azarya, "Civil Society and Disengagement in Africa," in *Civil Society and the State in Africa,* ed. John Harbeson, Donald Rothchild, and Naomi Chazan, 91 (Boulder, Colo.: Lynne Rienner, 1994).

14. "Burundi: Broken Ceasefire," *Africa Research Bulletin* 41, no. 4 (April 2004): 15720.

15. "Liberia: LURD Rift," *Africa Research Bulletin* 41, no. 1 (January 2004): 15608.

Paul Klein, and the U.S. ambassador, John Blaney, helped shore interim president Gyude Bryant against opposition leaders from within his own cabinet and only after Bryant himself took measures to halt the crisis at that time within the LURD leadership.[16]

The second pattern of power sharing is that negotiations progress to the point of an agreement in principle, but they remain to be implemented fully in practice. This pattern is exemplified by Sudan, where the bargaining parties achieved a milestone with the signing of the Nairobi Declaration on the Final Phase of Peace in the Sudan on June 5, 2004, reaffirming, among other things, the "Protocol between the Government of Sudan and the Sudan People's Liberation Movement (SPLM) on Power Sharing." The December 31, 2004, Comprehensive Peace Agreement negotiated by the Sudanese government and the SPLM in Naivasha, Kenya, reconfirmed the protocol on power sharing.

However, Sudan's peace seems incomplete, with intense fighting still taking place in the northern enclave of Darfur.[17] How can the incompleteness of Sudan's peace process be explained? Certainly, the Darfur conflict is separate in key respects from Sudan's north-south conflict. The Darfur conflict is more recent in origin, appears in part to be racially inspired, and lacks the religious overtones associated with the conflict in the south. But an interconnected aspect may also be involved—namely, the diffusion of conflict across subregional boundaries.[18] It is possible that northern leaders, fearing that successful negotiations with the SPLM will provoke a contagion of autonomy demands in northern enclaves, have come to fear a process that could culminate in the country's fragmentation. As one journalist commented, northern political leaders are less concerned about the potential economic costs of the north-south agreement than with "the precedent of a region winning terms which allow it to secede. With this comes the threat that other marginalized and disaffected groups will be encouraged to follow suit."[19] Consequently, despite years of careful and effective deliberations, the Sudanese peace process has reached an apparent impasse.

The third pattern of power sharing includes cases of partial or full breakdown in power-sharing institutions. In the Rwanda experiment, the institutions were designed to promote a sharing of power among President Juvénal Habyarimana's largely Hutu Mouvement Révolutionnaire National pour le Développement (MRND) and the Tutsi-led Rwandan Patriotic Front (RPF), as well as various moderate opposition parties. In the externally mediated

16. "Maintaining Group Power: Liberia: Silencing the Guns," *Africa Confidential* 45, no. 3 (February 6, 2004): 2; and "Liberia: LURD Rift."

17. Integrated Regional Information Networks, "Sudan: Think-tank Links Lack of Progress in Peace Process to Darfur Conflict," January 26, 2005, www.irinnews.org/report.asp?ReportID=40275&SelectRegion=East_Africa&SelectCountry=SUDAN.

18. David Lake and Donald Rothchild, eds., *The International Spread of Ethnic Conflict: Fear Diffusion, and Escalation* (Princeton: Princeton University Press, 1998).

19. "Sudan: Last Minute Hitches," *Africa Research Bulletin* 41, no. 5 (May 2004): 15770.

Arusha Peace Agreement, power was distributed equally in the cabinet between Habyarimana's MRND and the insurgent RPF, although a significant bloc of positions was allocated to the opposition as well. The effect of this compromise was to shift the perceived balance of forces in the cabinet to the advantage of the RPF and the moderate Hutu opposition parties. This proved highly destabilizing, for the hard-line Hutu leadership "perceived [this] negotiated outcome to be inimical to their power,"[20] causing Habyarimana to lash out in late 1992 against the protocols and to call upon the militia for continued backing.

Habyarimana pursued what Alan Kuperman describes as a two-track strategy, attempting to co-opt the Hutu moderates while simultaneously working with the extremists to develop "a forceful option." Perception of a changing balance of forces resulted in a sense of imminent potential Hutu exclusion (especially on the part of the hard-line Coalition pour la Défense de la République [CDR]). Indeed, the power-sharing coalition created under the 1993 Arusha protocol (negotiated from October 1992 through January 1993) prohibited the CDR from attaining ministerial portfolios and seats within the transitional National Assembly.[21] The effect of this provision was heightened tensions among the Hutu extremists, contributing to their fateful decision to launch a concerted program of genocide. The power-sharing formulas in the broad-based transitional government featured significantly in this terrible outcome because, writes Bruce D. Jones, "it pushed well beyond what was acceptable in key sectors in Kigali."[22]

In Côte d'Ivoire, a peace agreement negotiated by the government of Laurent Gbagbo and the northern rebel groups in Marcoussis, France, was shaky in both political and military terms from its outset. This compromise arrangement split power at the top between Gbagbo, who remained president, and Seydou Diarra, a northern Muslim who became prime minister charged with heading the government of national reconciliation. Political balance was evident in the selection of government ministers, for two members of the cabinet were appointed from Laurent Gbagbo's Ivorian Popular Front (FPI), two from the rebel forces, two from former president Henri Konan Bedie's Democratic Party (PDCI), and two from former prime minister Alassane Ouattara's Rally of the Republicans (RDR). Instead of bringing a sense of relief to the country, the peace agreement was born amid rioting against French interests by Gbagbo's supporters, who viewed the French diplomats as biased in favor of the northern Muslims. This sense of southern

---

20. Gilbert M. Khadiagala, "Implementing the Arusha Peace Agreement on Rwanda," in *Ending Civil Wars*, ed. Stephen John Stedman, Donald Rothchild, and Elizabeth Cousens, 469 (Boulder, Colo.: Lynne Rienner, 2002).

21. Rwanda Arusha Accords 1993, 27–31, www.incore.ulst.ac.uk/services/cds/agreements/pdf/rwan1.pdf.

22. Bruce D. Jones, *Peacemaking in Rwanda: The Dynamics of Failure* (Boulder, Colo.: Lynne Rienner, 2001), 95.

uncertainty was heightened, particularly in the army, by rebel demands that northern leaders be appointed to the important ministries of defense and the interior.[23]

Given the prevailing hostility and the ambitions of the Ivorian elite, it is not surprising that implementation of the Marcoussis power-sharing agreement has proven difficult. Southern political leaders frequently criticize the Marcoussis Agreement, describing it as a French-mediated sellout to terrorism, while northern leaders claim that Gbagbo reneged on private and public promises he made regarding the powers to be exercised by the prime minister and appointments to the cabinet. In a conciliatory gesture, Guillaume Soro, the secretary-general of the northern-based Côte d'Ivoire Patriotic Movement (MPCI), announced in February 2003 that the rebels no longer insisted that the ministries of defense and interior be placed in northern hands, but he did demand that the president transfer effective powers to Prime Minister Diarra.[24]

Northern resentment threatened the continuing operation of the power-sharing system in March of that year, as rebel representatives failed to appear for meetings, and in July rebel military commanders ordered their ministers to suspend further participation in the government. Matters reached a new level of intensity on September 23, 2003, when the rebel group, now renamed New Forces, again suspended their participation in the government and in the disarmament program to protest Gbagbo's failure to give effective powers to the prime minister. "If the conditions [on implementing the Marcoussis Agreement] are not met," Soro declared, "we will not go to Abidjan."[25] However, it was only the key New Forces ministers who temporarily terminated their participation in the power-sharing cabinet, for the ministers of such lower-ranked ministries as Handicrafts and Organization of the Informal Sector, Technical Education and Professional Training, Territorial Administration, and Youth and Civil Service stayed on in Abidjan to meet with their colleagues. Nevertheless, tensions rose to a new level at this time when Gbagbo insulted the northern representatives, describing them as "kids with pistols," and thereby further complicated cabinet relations.[26] The rebels did return to the cabinet in late December, a decision that not only reflected intense international pressure but also a determination to overcome rifts developing within the New Forces, only to leave once again in March 2004.

---

23. BBC News, "Trouble Mounts for Ivory Coast Leader," January 29, 2003, news.bbc.co.uk/2/ hi/africa/2706431.stm; and BBC News, "Rebels Boycott Ivory Coast Peace Talks," February 10, 2003, news.bbc.co.uk/2/hi/africa/2743323.stm.

24. "Côte d'Ivoire: Can Marcoussis Be Implemented?" *Africa Research Bulletin* 40, no. 2 (February 2003): 15180.

25. Radio France International, "Côte d'Ivoire: Rebel Leader Explains Withdrawal, Condition for Return to Cabinet," Foreign Broadcast Information System, September 24, 2003.

26. BBC News, "Ivorian Leader Ridicules Rebels," September 24, 2003 newswww.bbc.net.uk/2/ hi/africa/3135728.stm.

The deeper meaning of these departures lay not in differences over policies on appointments but in the polarization of perceptions and the evident lack of trust among the parties. In such a context, the competition that is likely to accompany forthcoming elections may prove to create further tension.[27] In that event, attempts to manage conflict by means of power sharing will have already proven counterproductive.

This lack of trust also translates into when concessions are accepted and when they are not. As suggested in table 4.1, dominant party concessions on power sharing were acceptable to the various weaker elements in at least half of these cases. The concession on inclusion of group leaders in the governing institutions at the political center goes far toward satisfying the elite's desire for political power and the members' need for security and access to scarce resources.

African experiences with executive power-sharing institutions also vary in terms of the preparedness of both stronger and weaker parties to commit to agreements, and these commitments are more likely when power-sharing institutions are included than when they are not. Power sharing is certainly not everyone's preferred solution, but it is a readily available one that may be mutually acceptable to all the main negotiating parties. Matthew Hoddie and Caroline Hartzell appear to be right that "at the end of civil wars no alternative set of rules can provide the reassurances demanded by groups in polarized societies to initiate the transition to peace and democratic practices."[28] Moreover, in terms of durability, it is apparent that another factor is at work: when the terms of power sharing were carefully negotiated by the local parties over time, as in the pattern one case of Burundi 2003 and in the pattern two case of Sudan 2004, the possibility of a stable transition seems more likely. Both of the settlements were marred from the outset by uncompromising factions acting as spoilers, but in each case the process of cooperation at the national level was hammered out carefully by the negotiators. By contrast, where power-sharing institutions seem incomplete or have gained only partial legitimacy in the eyes of local parties, as in Côte d'Ivoire and Rwanda, the prospects for instability and a return to civil war seem greater.

Power-sharing institutions are up and running in contemporary Africa. Few scholars or practitioners would contend that these are ideal institutions; rather, they represent pragmatic adjustments to difficult circumstances in

---

27. International Crisis Group (ICG), "Côte d'Ivoire: 'The War Is Not Yet Over,'" *ICG Africa Report*, no. 72 (Freetown/Brussels: ICG, 2003): 37.

28. Matthew Hoddie and Caroline Hartzel, "The Role of Power Sharing in Post-Civil War Settlements: Initiating the Transition From Civil War," in Roeder and Rothchild, *Sustainable Peace*, chapter 4.

Table 4.1   Stronger–Weaker Party Interaction in Recent African Power-sharing Agreements[a]

		Weaker Party Accepts Stronger Party Reassurances?	
		Yes	No
Stronger Actor Offering Reassurances	Yes	Liberia 2003[b] Burundi 2003[c] Sudan 2004[d]	DRC 2002[e] Burundi 2000[f]
	No	Rwanda 1993[g]	Burundi 1994[h] Côte d'Ivoire 2003[i]

a. This table represents the interactions between the majority (that is, the group in power) and the minorities (that is, the groups out of power) in a given peace agreement. It asks two questions. First, does the majority make an offer of credible reassurances to the minority? Specifically, is the majority group (that is, the group in power) willing to offer significant concessions on political representation and security to minority group(s) (that is, groups not in power)? If yes, the majority proposes to share power with the minority. If no, the majority fails to propose a credible deal. Second, does the minority find this offer reassuring and acceptable? Specifically, does the minority group (that is, the group out of power) find the offer on political representation and security put forward by the majority (that is, the group in power) adequate? If yes, the minority accepts the agreement. If no, the minority declines the agreement.

b. Liberia, Accra Comprehensive Peace Agreement, August 18, 2003: In August 2003, the international community (ECOWAS and the United States) brokered a deal in which President Charles Taylor leaves office and goes into exile in Nigeria. An interim power-sharing arrangement is reached after negotiations in Accra among the Government of Liberia, opposition political parties, civil-society movements, and the two main rebel factions, LURD and MODEL. Divisions emerge within the leadership of the LURD movement (between the leader Sekou Damateh Conneh and his wife, Aicha Keita Conneh, over the naming of the finance minister), and some clashes break out over the poorly organized disarmament process, but the power-sharing institutions remain on track. Nigerian troops under the guise of the Economic Community of West African States Monitoring Group (ECOMOG) move into Liberia. By the end of 2003 they are slowly replaced by a UN peacekeeping force of fifteen thousand.

c. Burundi, Pretoria Protocol, October 8, 2003: The Pretoria Protocol agreed to on October 8, 2003, was a continuation of the Arusha peace process agreed to in 2000 but was not successful due to the lack of a cease-fire among all the main armed factions (notably the CNDD-FDD and the Palipehutu-FNL). After months of continuing violence after the Arusha process began, President Ndayizeze met with Hutu rebels from the CNDD-FDD and concluded a cease-fire and peace agreement under which their leader, Pierre Nkurunziza, was brought into a power-sharing government. However, the other primary armed Hutu rebel movement, Palipehutu-FNL, continued to carry out military offensives. The CNDD-FDD is brought into the power-sharing government, which stipulates that they are to have four seats in the transitional cabinet and fifteen seats in the National Assembly. In addition, the CNDD-FDD is granted 40 percent of the officer corps in the armed forces and 35 percent of the positions in the national police force. The Palipehutu-FNL announced early in 2004 that they would observe a unilateral cease-fire and would be willing to enter into negotiations with the transitional government.

Burundi Global Peace Accords, November 16, 2003: After one year of negotiations from the first cease-fire agreement signed in Arusha in 2002, a global cease-fire agreement was signed among CNDD-FDD and the transitional government in Dar es Salaam on November 16, 2003. These accords modified the last power-sharing agreement within the transitional government to include, by presidential decree, a new government with four members of the CNDD-FDD and with Jean Pierre Nkurunziza as their legal representative. According to the accord, the CNDD-FDD will obtain three ministry positions as well as the minister of state. At the legislative level, the accord allots CNDD-FDD the representation of fifteen deputies, two of whom are the second vice president and the deputy secretary of the National Assembly. However, the CNDD-FDD has refused participation in the senate (50 percent Hutu and 50 percent Tutsi representation) due to its bipolar ethnic composition. Nonetheless, this Hutu party will hold more than three provincial governor posts, five councilor posts, two ambassador posts, and thirty community administrator posts, and will acquire 20 percent of the direction of public enterprises. Finally, because security is such an important issue, the Global Accords take into consideration security forces and officers. At the end of January 2004, the implementation of an integrated "Headquarter" took place, composed of 60 percent Burundi Armed Forces (FAB) officers and 40 percent CNDD-FDD officers. The institutional framework set out by Arusha is upheld.

d. Sudan, Machakos Protocol, July 20, 2002; Naivasha Protocol on Power Sharing, May 26, 2004: After more than two years of negotiations, the Machakos Protocol, which was originally signed by the government of the Sudan and the Sudan People's Liberation Movement/Army (SPLM/A) on July 20, 2002, has been complemented by several additional protocols on security (September 2003), wealth sharing (January 2004), and integrating the areas of Nuba Mountains and Southern Blue Nile and Abyei into the agreement. Sudan will be managed by a national government, which will act as the sovereign body of all Sudan. A bicameral parliament will operate alongside a national unity government in which the south would be proportionately represented. This guarantees southerners a share of senior and middle-ranking positions within the civil service, and the government is also committed to the principle of "collegial" decision making by the executive and to the fair division of revenue between the north and south. The principle is that the unity of Sudan will remain the ultimate aim of any peace agreement and it is to be considered the priority for both sides. However, it also stipulates that the south has a right to control and govern affairs in its own region and has the right to self-determination through a referendum, to be held six years after the signing of an accord. However, the current conflict in the Darfur risks undermining the recent gains. According to an interview with the BBC, Abdel Aziz Adim, a senior SPLA commander, said that his organization would reconsider cooperating with a planned coalition government if atrocities in Darfur continue.

e. Democratic Republic of the Congo, Pretoria Agreement, December 17, 2002: The Inter-Congolese Dialogue, an ongoing process brokered by South Africa, is a complex power-sharing arrangement aimed at ending the civil war in the DRC, which since 1997 has killed, directly or indirectly, some 3 million people. The current efforts originated from the Lusaka cease-fire agreement reached in 1999 and has led to a transitional power-sharing government that includes representatives of the government of the DRC, three different rebel movements, the progovernment Mai-Mai militia, several political parties from what is known as the "unarmed opposition," and representatives from civil society. It is headed by the president, Joseph Kabila, and includes four vice presidents, a thirty-five-member cabinet, a 500-seat legislature, and a 120-member senate. These institutions are divided along the lines reached in negotiations under the Inter-Congolese Dialogue. However, the unity government has been unable to assert its authority throughout the country, leaving populations, especially in the east of the country, at the mercy of armed gangs and ethnic militias supported by the DRC's neighbors, such as Rwanda and Uganda. As of July 20, 2004, there have been many delays in the implementation of the Global and All-Inclusive Peace Accord. The major problems seem to be the nomination of provincial governors and regional military officials as well as the reintegration of the army. Additionally, each component is hanging on to its command and control structures, helping to further divide the country. The existing distrust among the parties, coupled with an unwillingness to compromise on appointments, continues to undermine the peace in the country as a whole.

f. Burundi, Arusha Process, August 28, 2000: Nelson Mandela brokered the Arusha Peace Agreement, signed August 28, 2000, following the death of Julius Nyerere. Unfortunately, although the Tutsi-dominated government of Pierre Buyoya, the Burundian armed forces, and most of the Tutsi armed factions agreed to the accord (after heavy pressure from Mandela), the agreement was reached without a cease-fire among the principal rebel groups, namely, the predominately Hutu CNDD-FDD and Palipehutu-FNL, which denounced it and stepped up their military campaigns. Under the agreement, the government of the president, Pierre Buyoya, was allotted eighteen months in office. The agreement stipulates that once this period has elapsed, Buyoya is to be replaced by a Hutu president who will rule for a further eighteen months, when a general election will take place. In addition, a transitional power-sharing cabinet is designed and comprised of 60 percent from the G7 (Hutu parties) and 40 percent from the G10 (Tutsi parties). The transitional constitution leaves the president with considerable powers, but it also envisages an active role for the transitional national assembly and the transitional senate. The assembly is composed of representatives of all the parties that signed the Arusha Peace Agreement, as well as civil society representatives appointed by the president. As stipulated by the agreement, the assembly is 60 percent Hutu and 40 percent Tutsi. The senate is a new body, which includes former presidents, other dignitaries, several Twa, and equal numbers of Hutus and Tutsis. However, violence by Hutu and Tutsi armed factions continues to destabilize the peace process and terrorize civilians. In the instability, Tutsi soldiers in the Burundian armed forces staged two coup attempts against President Buyoya and the peace process in 2001.

g. Rwanda, Arusha Accords, July 25, 1993: After repeated military success by the mostly Tutsi RPF in early 1993 and increasing international pressure, the Habyarimana government is forced to enter into peace negotiations in Arusha, Tanzania. A power-sharing agreement is signed there on July 25, 1993, by representatives of the majority Hutu government (ruling-MRND), the Rwandan opposition parties, and the minority Tutsi RPF. The agreement is met with hostility by extremist factions of the MRND, who fear exclusion from the new power-sharing government and form a new party, the CDR. The CDR, along with some Hutu army officers and politicians who had remained in the MRND but were hostile to the accords, began arming and training civilian militias, recruiting particularly among those displaced by the RPF in the north of the country. They also established a radio station called Radio Television Libre Des Mille Collines (RTLM) to help organize the militias and to spread Hutu-supremacist propaganda. This was part of a larger plan to eliminate Hutu moderate politicians and all Tutsi in Rwanda. The assassination of Burundian Hutu president Melchior Ndadaye in October 1993 by Tutsi elements in the Burundian army served only to accelerate the activities of these Rwandan Hutu extremists and their desires to exaggerate the fears of average Rwandan Hutus. The accords officially ended on April 6, 1994, after the shooting down of the plane bringing President Habyarimana back from Arusha. The extermination of Hutu moderates and Tutsis, along with the RPF, began within hours.

h. Burundi 1994: Violence broke out in Burundi after the October 1993 assassination of recently elected Hutu president Melchoir Ndadaye and the death of his successor, Hutu Cyprien Ntarayamira (killed in a plane crash in April 1994 with Rwandan president Habyarimana). This came along with the growing fear of the diffusion of violence from the Rwandan genocide. In October 1994, all of the major political factions agreed to the Convention of Government, which would replace the existing constitution and install an interim power-sharing government. The convention establishes a new executive body, the Conseil national de securité (CNS), comprising twenty-five members (55 percent from the presidential majority [Front pour la démocratie au Burundi or FRODEBU] and 45 percent from the opposition minority) and is given broad powers. The new coalition government represents seven of the thirteen main political parties in Burundi. However, the CNS power-sharing government was unable to curb the escalating ethnic violence between Hutu and Tutsi militias after it was put into place. This was most probably due to the lack of credible commitment of the members of the coalition government to the convention and their covert support for the various armed ethnic militias. The convention ended with a coup d'état carried out by former president Pierre Buyoya in July 1996. According to the conclusion of a 1995 report by the United Nations Security Council Mission to Burundi, "Extremist elements, both Tutsi and Hutu, both within the coalition Government and outside it, have for their own reasons not accepted the power-sharing arrangements contained in the Convention. Those extremists have usurped the political initiative, at the expense of the moderate elements that constitute the majority of the population and have been silenced through threat and intimidation. This is the root cause of continuing political instability in the country. . . . Activities of all these extremist forces have also contributed to crippling the coalition Government and putting its future in doubt, thus undermining peace and stability in Burundi."

i. Côte d'Ivoire, Linas-Marcoussis Agreement, January 24, 2003: The Linas-Marcoussis Agreement, brokered under close French supervision, is signed January 24, 2003, by all major political parties (ruling-FPI, PDCI, RDR) and rebels movements (New Forces), and a transitional consensus government is set up among the major factions, which begins meeting in April 2003. However, shortly after, antinortherner violence and inflammatory rhetoric in Abidjan by pro-Gbagbo and youth militias lead to the withdrawal of rebel leader Guillaume Soro and his New Forces ministers from the power-sharing institutions. In addition, the New Forces claim that central questions such as the issue of Ivoirité (Ivorian citizenship and electoral eligibility—chapter 35 of the constitution) were not properly addressed in the Marcoussis talks. After a brief attempt to reconvene the consensus government, starting in January 2004, Soro's New Forces and several opposition parties withdraw their representatives. The decision of the New Forces to end participation in the power-sharing executive cabinet solidifies in April 2004 when pro-Gbagbo militias in Abidjan attack northerners and foreigners, killing at least 120 people.

deeply divided societies.[29] Certainly in the best of circumstances, power-sharing institutions offer at least two potential benefits. First, they can assist the parties to end the fighting or, as in Burundi and the DRC, to significantly reduce the violence. By bringing the leaders of the various warring factions into the ruling cartel, power-sharing agreements help to make them stakeholders in the political process. This enables leaders of weaker parties to gain an advantage by working through the system, instead of rebelling against it, to achieve their objectives.

Second, the proximity to other patrons opens up new possibilities for interaction between political parties as well as between former adversaries. As the government of national reconciliation meets to engage in common problem-solving activities, it fosters reciprocities and the development of bargaining norms that can have a stabilizing effect. By promoting an iterated exchange process, power-sharing institutions can lay the basis for an ongoing relationship. Over time, these iterated exchanges can create networks of trust among separate political actors that are the basis for crosscutting perspectives on specific issues. The effect of this can be to encourage self-sustaining encounters. Power sharing, like democracy, does not end uncertainty, but it can create institutions and facilitate relationships. These institutions may hold up during the transition in part because the alternatives are so frightening.[30]

The Limits of Reassurance

Despite these possible benefits, however, power-sharing institutions awaken skepticism regarding their ability to survive in the face of intense conflict or to protect the interests of weaker groups. All the cases show that it is important not to obscure the messiness of the situation on the ground or the continuance of feelings of suspicion and political insecurity. Hence, the strategy of returning to peace by means of power-sharing arrangements often comes into conflict with the uncertainty of implementation, especially during the longer-term phases of the consolidation process. The implementation of peace accords after civil wars encounters multiple and complex challenges. If settlements are to prove durable, they must cope simultaneously with the challenges of political—even physical—insecurity,

---

29. Arend Lijphart, *Power-sharing in South Africa.* (Berkeley: Institute of International Studies, University of California, 1985), 133. A leading advocate of the consociational democracy approach, Lijphart states, for example, "It is nobody's preferred ideal." See also Brendan O'Leary, "Comparative Political Science and the British-Irish Agreement," in *Northern Ireland and the Divided World*, ed. John McGarry, 81–82 (Oxford: Oxford University Press, 2001).

30. Adam Przeworski, *Democracy and the Market* (Cambridge: Cambridge University Press, 1991), 26, 32.

self-determination, representativeness, effective governance, and economic development. Power-sharing institutions appear to be logical responses to the need for ethnic self-determination and representativeness, yet these institutions can involve a possible cost in terms of political stability, effective governance, and economic development.

In the uncertain conditions after a civil war, groups have negative political memories, whether real or unreal, of their opponents, and they project these images into the future. Such memories and projections lead to fears of imminent exploitation or to uncertainty over the possibility of physical harm at the hands of tenacious foes who will search for the first opportunity to take advantage of their vulnerability. Hence, the task of transforming the interactions among groups toward closer, more predictable relations is a sensitive and difficult process.

In many instances, the uncertainty of a post–civil war context seems likely to persist into the peace that follows. Power sharing, which rests on the maintenance of a balance of forces, may do little to facilitate political consolidation. In attempting to explain the limited ability of power-sharing arrangements to reassure weaker parties, I will begin by analyzing three general factors that complicate implementation. After that, I will turn to some of the more specific aspects drawn from the African experience.

Unreliable Information

Following a civil war, communal polarization remains extreme and intergroup connections are circumscribed and specific. Although political elites meet formally for prescribed purposes, groups live for the most part within recognized and separate boundaries. With contact essentially confined to the group, reliable public information is scant, contributing to widespread uncertainty over the intentions of former combatants. Suspicion over the goodwill of rivals who otherwise live a separate existence often emerges and complicates negotiations within power-sharing institutions, as leaders fear that their opponent is not bargaining sincerely and will renege on an agreement when it becomes advantageous to do so. This problem is further complicated when parties deliberately misrepresent the facts in an effort to minimize these weaknesses or to maximize their strengths. Either way, lack of reliable information or the presence of misinformation contributes significantly to bargaining failure.[31] Such failure undermines political stability and undercuts the assurances that emerged from the peace agreement, possibly contributing to new spirals of violence.

---

31. Lake and Rothchild, *The International Spread of Ethnic Conflict*, 12.

The Lack of Credible Commitment

If peace agreements are to be viewed as the equivalent of binding contracts between former belligerents, they require trust on all sides that their terms will be respected. This means that each party must believe that the other party will honor the bargain it made. Rival leaders will be expected to persuade their ethnic or religious supporters to uphold their commitments, even in the face of militant outbidding by ambitious politicians or of reluctance by some people in the field to abide by the agreements made by their representatives. In theory, all parties will gain by maintaining the peace and abiding by the agreement; in practice, however, majority party leaders cannot credibly commit that they will give support to the bargain in the future. Despite expressions of goodwill, for example, current Sudanese government leaders cannot guarantee that future leaders will actually hold the promised referendum on southern self-determination, scheduled for six years after the agreement was reached in 2005.

Over time, commitment to fulfilling the provisions of peace accords also falls behind more pressing concerns. After the confidence-building period has elapsed and the agreement has begun to structure stable relations, the urgency of maintaining the compromises accepted during the negotiation phase may well fade and majority elites may no longer feel the need to reassure weaker parties about the future. They therefore come to place a higher priority on achieving their programs and fulfilling the interests of their constituents and, in the process, pay less heed to fulfilling the peace bargain. With little in the way of accepted norms and values or an established high court system to prevent them from reneging on the agreement, in whole or in part, the ruling coalition may decide to alter the accommodations originally put in place to reassure the weaker parties.

This inability to commit in a credible way underlines the fragility of compromises on power-sharing institutions. Power-sharing arrangements, which carefully balance competing group claims in order to reassure the weaker parties regarding their inclusion in the decision-making process, are seriously impaired by the decision of the dominant majority to alter the rules of the game in favor of a more integrated approach. Because the power imbalance facilitates majority party leaders in their determination to move their country in a more centralized direction, there is little the opposition can do on its own to defend the agreement. This can contribute to the opposition's dismay and even its sense of betrayal. Paradoxically, then, the very provisions in the agreement intended to promote the security of the weaker parties may become a cause of insecurity and lead to intense intrastate conflict.

Inappropriate External Protection

Because it is difficult for the ex-belligerents to overcome the information and credible commitment dilemmas on their own, they often rely on external actors to play an important role in sustaining their formally agreed-upon relationship. For example, external actors can help to keep open the lines of communication between the parties and to mediate issues left unresolved in the peace agreement. They can also reassure the parties that the other side is delivering on its bargains, monitoring the implementation process, and verifying to other actors that their opposite number has been carrying out the terms of the agreement in good faith. That the third-party interveners are critically important in building support for the implementation process is suggested by recently compiled aggregate data indicating that the presence of a third-party state increases the chances of maintaining the peace during the consolidation phase by an estimated 98 percent.[32]

When the external actor intervenes and is effective in protecting the peace agreement, the parties are reassured by its involvement. However, as the third party fails to assume its role fully and as it seeks to disengage from the risks and responsibilities of protecting the agreement, the weaker parties are likely to lose confidence in the dominant majority's willingness to remain committed to accommodations, such as a power-sharing compromise that had been reached earlier. The United Nations, which had been asked by both sides to assist in implementing Rwanda's 1993 peace agreement and to support the transitional government, failed to deploy sufficient forces to the area, and as a consequence, the transitional government was never inaugurated.[33] This failure contributed to a loss of faith in outside protectors that still lingers.

Thus far, I have been assuming that the third party plays the role of a reasonably impartial protector of the agreement. But what happens if the third party is a biased actor that favors one participant in the power-sharing arrangement as against the others? This was indeed the case in Lebanon, where in different periods, French authority was partial toward the Maronites during the mandate period and the Syrian administration favored the Muslims after the Ta'if Agreement was negotiated. In these cases, moreover, the outsider propped up the power-sharing institutions for an extended period of time, but external influence merely masked the fact that deep intergroup resentments divided these interests from within. Clearly, where the survival of power-sharing institutions is dependent on a foreign power as protector, the arrangement is likely to be lacking in legitimacy and will

---

32. Hartzell et al., "Stabilizing the Peace after Civil War," 199.
33. "Rwanda – UNAMIR Background," *United Nations Assistance Mission for Rwanda–Background Summary* (New York: Information Technology Section: Department of Public Information, 2001), www.un.org/Depts/dpko/co_mission/unamir.htm.

possibly create conflict. As political scientist Marie-Joëlle Zahar explains, the presence of a third-party protector creates winners and losers.[34] Once the third party begins to disengage, it weakens its hold, opening the way to a restructuring of relations. As internal relations shift, the dominant majority may seek to centralize power or the weaker parties may attempt to decentralize it. Either way, as Yeats observes, the political center does not hold.

Insights from the African Experience

In addition to these general difficulties with implementing power-sharing institutions after civil war, several significant aspects drawn from Africa's experience are worth noting. First, groups may fear a weakening of power as a consequence of participation in a national grand coalition. It is assumed that participation in a grand coalition represents a form of pressure that pushes them in the direction of cooperation. However, the political moderation that follows from this may weaken their autonomous power base. In Liberia, for example, the leaders of two former rebel movements—LURD and the Movement for Democracy and Elections in Liberia (MODEL)—who were members of the transitional cabinet reportedly tried for a time to undermine it. "This is partly because LURD leader Sekou Damateh Conneh and MODEL leader Thomas Ninely Yaya want[ed] to keep their militias intact should their services be required again by their respective sponsors in Guinea and Côte d'Ivoire."[35] They feared that if the militias were dismantled, their bases of power would be gravely weakened. The effect was to place a strain on the institutions of power sharing during the initial confidence-building period, because cooperation raised the prospect of uncertainty, possibly to unacceptable levels.[36]

Second, because power sharing results from a bargain among the main parties, it can make no claim to being a fully inclusive arrangement. The incompleteness of the deal creates potential problems in its wake. Those parties that are left out of the arrangement may feel disadvantaged and possibly vulnerable. They feel excluded from the decision-making process. As Devon Curtis explains in her chapter, when the government of Joseph Kabila and Jean-Pierre Bemba's Mouvement de Libération du Congo (MLC) negoti-

34. Marie-Joëlle Zahar, "Power Sharing in Lebanon: Foreign Protectors, Domestic Peace, and Democratic Failure," in Roeder and Rothchild, *Sustainable Peace*, chapter 9, especially p. 238.

35. "Maintaining Group Power: Liberia: Silencing the Guns," *Africa Confidential* 45, no. 3 (February 6, 2004): 2.

36. In November 2004, it was announced that both LURD and MODEL had been disbanded. See Jonathan Paye-Layleh, "Liberia's Three Ex-Warring Factions Officially Disband after Disarmament," *Boston Globe*, November 4, 2004, www.boston.com/dailynews/309/world. Liberia.

ated an agreement at the Inter-Congolese Dialogue in Sun City, South Africa, in 2002, they left out Etienne Tshisekedi's Union pour la démocratie et le progress social and the important rebel group, the Rassemblement Congolais pour la Démocratie—Goma (RCD-G), led by Azarias Ruberwa.[37] Similarly, as E. Philip Morgan and others have noted, in Liberia exclusion from the power-sharing coalition gave "incentives for warlords to 'spoil' the [peace] process . . . and for current groups to further factionalize."[38]

Third, African experiments with power sharing have been handicapped by a lack of shared norms and aspirations. The polarized and hostile perceptions that contributed to civil war are not transformed by power-sharing arrangements after the peace. These arrangements preserve the separate identities of the former belligerents and include them in the grand coalition at the political center, which virtually assures limited compromises but not decisive moves to solve common problems. Without common norms and aspirations, it becomes difficult to maintain a balance of forces, especially where uncompromising leaders enter the cabinet. If the Sudanese negotiators had common aspirations, concludes an Integrated Regional Information Network report, the negotiating parties "would have [achieved] a done deal months ago. It is their lack of common aspirations and conflicting political agendas that have meant they have to fight tooth and nail for every gain they make or loss they concede."[39] Not surprisingly, these political leaders carry conflicting political agendas over into the grand coalitions that are cobbled together to implement the peace.

The power-sharing institutions put in place after civil wars may represent an effective short-term response to the needs that Africa's weaker parties have for reassurance about their security, but they are not likely to be stable long-term solutions unless common rules of interaction and common aspirations develop. As UN secretary-general Kofi Annan wrote in a report on the situation in the DRC, "The peace process faces daunting challenges. The most crucial issue concerns the ability of the transitional leaders to act as a truly unified government and overcome the persistent atmosphere of distrust."[40] More pointedly, a local observer comments on the lack of confidence prevailing in the Congo, stating that "leaders themselves do not have trust in each other; as the power-sharing is conceived in zero-sum game perspective: one

37. International Crisis Group, *Storm Clouds over Sun City: The Urgent Need to Recast the Congolese Peace Process,* ICG Africa Report no. 44 (2002).

38. Timothy Sisk, *Future US Engagement in Africa: Opportunities and Obstacles for Conflict Management,* Special Report 17 (Washington, D.C.: United States Institute of Peace, July 1996), sect. IV, www.usip.org/pubs/specialreports/early/USAfrica3.html.

39. Integrated Regional Information Networks, "Sudan: Peace Unsustainable without Democratization–Think Tank," June 11, 2004, www.irinnews.org/report.asp?ReportID=41617.

40. Carter Dougherty, "Peace Precarious in Eastern Congo; Tensions Simmer a Year after Pact Ended Civil War," *Washington Times,* May 5, 2004, www.publicinternationallaw.org/docs/PNW4/PNW.10May_04.html.

wins, not with the others, but at the expense of the others. The necessary atmosphere of trust is lacking."[41] From these examples it becomes apparent that, unfortunately, power sharing may not prove a sufficient basis for political consolidation after Africa's civil wars.

Fourth, experiments with African power sharing are constrained by the painfully difficult economic situation that follows in the wake of civil war. The immediate costs of financing the disarmament, the demobilization, the return of former combatants to their villages and to socially useful occupations, the reintegration of armies, and the reform of the police are all very expensive undertakings. Moreover, the tasks of getting the economy moving again, opening up secondary schools, and creating new economic opportunities for the citizenry are urgent matters that require substantial investment. As Collier warns, "The more severe is poverty, the greater are the risks of conflict."[42]

Third-party promises of economic assistance if the belligerents will sign a peace accord hold out an attractive prospect of a peace dividend. However, recent work indicates that in a majority of African cases there was little evidence that U.S. relief aid was followed by significant rises in development assistance. The impact of this disappointing performance is to place limits on the possibilities for economic expansion and, with it, the ability of members of the ruling coalition to allocate resources to their clients. As a consequence, the constrained economic circumstances that follow a civil war give the members of the power-sharing coalition little incentive to act with civility toward members of other groups. The pie remains small, resulting all too often in intense competition among the members of the elite cartel for control of the meager resources available to them all.

Conclusion

Can one reasonably expect power-sharing arrangements to reassure weaker parties in Africa about their future after civil wars? In theory, such institutions are logical responses to the need for ethnic self-determination and fair representation. They can, as the experiences of Burundi, Côte d'Ivoire, Rwanda, Liberia, Sudan, and the DRC indicate, help to provide a basis for ending the fighting—at least in the short term. This occurs because they propose a mixed package of incentives to the combatants, offering the stronger parties a means to bring an end to the war while holding out the possibility of inclusion in the inner sanctums of government to

41. Mandisi Majavu, "The Failure of an African Political Leadership," interview with Professor Wamba dia Wamba, July 18, 2003, www.globalpolicy.org/security/issues/congo.2003/0718failure.html.
42. Collier, "Policy for Post-conflict Societies," 3.

the weaker actor or actors. Moreover, agreement during the negotiations on power sharing creates the possibility that the parties may be able to use this arrangement as an initiating point for an iterative bargaining process that can lead to new institutions during the subsequent political consolidation period.

Unfortunately, the political center cannot be expected to hold. If power-sharing arrangements were reassuring to weaker parties during the confidence-building phase of implementation, they all too often become the source of suspicion and intense rivalry as the dominant majority seeks to maximize its interests and feels less and less inhibited by the need to allay the fears and uncertainties of the weaker actors. In the political consolidation phase, new elements come to power and do not necessarily feel bound by the promises made by their predecessors at the bargaining table. In addition, the presence of a third-party protector during the initial phase becomes less and less of a restraint after the general elections and the passage of time. At this point the general constraints of credible commitment, unreliable information, and inappropriate external protection come into play. Also, as seen with the African experiences, such factors as weakening group power as a consequence of participation in the grand coalition, lack of full party inclusion, an insufficiency of shared norms and aspirations, and the difficult post-conflict economic environment all threaten the precarious balance that marks a power-sharing approach to conflict management.

Although power sharing does not appear to be a durable solution to many structural arrangements after intense civil conflicts, it is important nonetheless to recognize the significant contribution that inclusion makes to reassuring minorities about their security and well-being as peace is consolidated. In particular, informal rules on inclusion enlarge the representational depth of the dominant coalition without imposing formal, rigid constraints on the choice of coalition partners. Clearly, it is critical to examine how powerful majorities can design political institutions that will join formal or informal practices of balanced representation with regimes that are capable of coping simultaneously with the challenges of security, effective governance, and economic development.

5

Must They Go through Hobbes?

The Revolutionary Provisional Government Model and Political Challenge in Externally Imposed Regimes

Andrew J. Enterline and J. Michael Greig

Editors' Note

In this final chapter of the theoretical section, Andrew J. Enterline and J. Michael Greig offer a completely different type and level of analysis. Their methodology is quantitative and their argument is at the macro level; they examine how externally imposed governments affect democracy and stability. The coauthors start from the fundamental point that a country must have a state before it can have a democratic state: it must go through Thomas Hobbes before it can get to Thomas Jefferson and James Madison. They examine a particular model of interim government contained in Yossi Shain and Juan Linz's Between States*—the revolutionary provisional government—and, after reassessing that model, they argue that the original model does in fact incorporate a class of cases that the contributors to Shain and Linz's volume did not investigate. The overlooked aspects of the model are revolutionary changes imposed from external actors, a class that Enterline and Greig label externally imposed polities. There are aspects to the revolutionary provisional model that are relevant in regime changes resulting from interstate war and foreign conquest. While Shain and Linz analyzed only half of this model—domestic sources of change—in fact, the model leaves room for international sources of change as well. Enterline and Greig therefore attempt to extend the model to assess the implications of externally induced revolutionary change.*

After arguing that external imposition is a form of revolutionary change, the coauthors then investigate the causes of political instability in externally imposed polities. Their analysis comes up with several interesting findings: imposed democracies initially create increased political instability when compared with imposed nondemocracies; economic development in externally imposed democracies often creates increased discontent and incidences of instability, rather than less; and in ethnically diverse countries, imposed nondemocracies are more stable than imposed democracies. Enterline and Greig also find strong evidence that the commitment of the foreign power that is imposing a polity is a key factor in stability: the longer the occupier remains in the country and the more resources it commits (especially to strengthening the security apparatus), the better the chances for a lasting peace. This finding in particular has enormous consequences for the United States' current project of state building in Iraq. The coauthors also find an interesting neighborhood effect: imposed democracies are not likely to create waves of democratization in their areas, contrary to the tenets of U.S. foreign policy. But if a democratic political system is imposed in an area of democracies, its chances for a stable peace increase. If a democratic system is imposed in a neighborhood of nondemocracies, political instability is more likely.

Enterline and Greig apply their model to Afghanistan and Iraq and find controversial and pessimistic results. The bottom line of their analysis is that unless the United States is willing to stay within these countries for the long haul, they are highly likely to experience conflict. Even if the United States remains as an occupying force for many years, however, peace is not guaranteed, because increasing the length of occupation also increases the likelihood that the citizens of those states will begin to resist the occupation. We are already seeing this in Iraq, as the chapter by Christina Caan, Beth Cole, Paul Hughes, and Daniel P. Serwer shows.

■ ■ ■

The first lesson is that we cannot get to Jefferson and Madison without going through Hobbes. You can't build a democratic state unless you first have a state, and the essential condition for a state is that it must have an effective monopoly over the means of violence.
    —**Larry Diamond,** *Squandered Victory*

Introduction

Larry Diamond's assessment of the transitional process in contemporary, postinvasion Iraq raises several questions pertaining to the sources of political stability in imposed regimes.[1] How politically stable are regimes imposed from abroad? Which domestic and international factors condition the capacity of imposed regimes to establish this power, thereby increasing their durability? In the introduction to this volume, editors Karen Guttieri and Jessica Piombo argue that it is necessary to reassess the theoretical

---

1. See Larry Diamond, *Squandered Victory: The American Occupation and the Bungled Effort to Bring Democracy to Iraq* (New York: Times Books, 2005).

insights contained in Yossi Shain and Juan Linz's pathbreaking work on the subject of interim governments, *Between States*, a theoretical and qualitative inquiry into the relationship between interim governments and democratic transitions.[2] Guttieri and Piombo urge that it is necessary to construct models of interim government that draw on insights from the international and comparative politics subfields in order to understand causal processes underlying interim governments and regime transitions. Indeed, the editors reason that this approach is necessary if questions central to contemporary policymaking puzzles, such as the stability and longevity of democratic transitions in Africa and the Middle East, are to be understood and policy-relevant observations distilled.

In this chapter, we investigate the models of interim government and regime transition introduced in *Between States*. Our inquiry is motivated by two observations. First, developments in contemporary politics—namely, the invasions of Afghanistan and Iraq in 2002 and 2003, respectively, and the subsequent imposition of democratic regimes in each state by the occupying coalitions—suggest that the international stimulus for regime transition associated with post–World War II regimes is not an arcane phenomenon; rather, this policy choice represents the state of the art in some contemporary policymaking circles. Second, a survey of the set of models of interim government explored by Shain and Linz indicates that the "revolutionary provisional model" identified by those authors is only partially vetted. Indeed, *Between States* primarily emphasizes the domestically stimulated sources of revolutionary provisional governments, and de-emphasizes regime changes resulting from interstate war and foreign conquest.[3] Certainly, given the comparatively low frequency of cases of regime change resulting from war and conquest following World War II, Shain and Linz had good reason to explore what they considered to be viable causal sources of regime transitions and attendant interim governments. Yet this research strategy does not fully exploit the relevance of the remaining aspects of the revolutionary provisional model for contemporary policy questions, and we seek to do so in the remainder of this chapter.

Specifically, we develop the concept of *imposed regimes* to reflect instances in which a third party imposes a set of political institutions—that is, a regime—on a target state. The concept of imposed regimes encompasses the concept that is central to this volume, interim governments. Clearly, there is variation in the formality by which third parties formally codify the interim government stage in a target state, thereby differentiating this stage from that of the permanent government that follows. Here, we reason that the early phases of the imposition of a regime constitute an interim period

---

2. Yossi Shain and Juan Linz, *Between States: Interim Governments and Democratic Transitions* (Cambridge: Cambridge University Press, 1995).

3. Ibid., 5.

broadly defined. While we are interested in exploring the revolutionary provisional model identified by Shain and Linz, we draw from the comparative politics and international relations subfields, as well as contemporary policy analysis, to study political stability in the imposed regimes, and in turn, we derive conclusions germane to contemporary policymaking.

The remainder of the chapter is organized as follows. The next section outlines the parameters of Shain and Linz's revolutionary provisional model of interim government and regime change. In the chapter's third section, we discuss the concept of imposed regimes before turning to the issue of developing a causal explanation for political stability in these regimes. In turn, we outline the research design that we employ to investigate our expectations regarding the causal explanations for political stability in these regimes and discuss the results of our empirical analysis. We rely on the parameters estimated with our empirically based statistical analysis to simulate political stability in two cases of imposed democratic regimes, contemporary Afghanistan and Iraq. We conclude our chapter by considering the relevance of the Shain and Linz revolutionary provisional model for the study of imposed regimes.

The Revolutionary Provisional Government Model

The international component of the revolutionary provisional model of interim government and democratic transition is elaborated and tested in limited fashion by Shain and Linz and the additional contributors to *Between States*. In this section, we outline the basic components of their model before applying this model to imposed regimes. The revolutionary provisional government model locates two sources of domestic political regime change, the first domestic and the second international, and we discuss each briefly in turn.

Central to the domestic sources of regime change is internal revolution, the phenomenon from which the model's name is partially derived. In the revolutionary component of the model, "a regime is superseded in a revolutionary struggle (frequently violent) or a coup d'etat, [and] the new ruling elite claims to break completely with the old order."[4] In turn, these revolutionary forces often declare themselves to be a provisional government, or the government that serves while a permanent government is formulated and implemented. Shain and Linz observe that these revolutions, and the provisional governments that emerge from such domestic upheaval, often occur in response to political, economic, and social abuses carried out by "sultanistic systems," that is, systems in which personal ties to a leader or a

---

4. Ibid., 28.

family are at the core of political power.[5] Interestingly, while the revolutionary component of the provisional model clearly emphasizes the centrality of the domestic sources of regime change, Shain and Linz suggest that the international qualities of these sultanistic regimes—namely, their subsidiary role in the superpower rivalry between the United States and the Soviet Union during the Cold War—provided crucial contextual conditions conducive to internal revolution.

Vital to the revolutionary regime changes that are central to Shain and Linz's model is the role of ideology. Revolutionary movements occurring after World War II emphasized variants of Marxist ideology.[6] Furthermore, in several instances revolutionary movements professing as a goal the replacement of sultanistic regimes with democratic institutions failed to carry through with democratization, and the regimes devolved into various forms of Marxist dictatorship.[7] Despite the blanket application of labels, such as "Marxist revolution," revolutionary groups in a given country were often riven by internal divisions; they were united solely by opposition to the incumbent regime but fractured in terms of plans for the postrevolutionary period.

Although it is not explicitly emphasized in *Between States*, Shain and Linz's revolutionary provisional model does provide for international actors to shape political outcomes in conjunction with the aforementioned domestic political forces. Similar to their role as secondary or tertiary conditions influencing the likelihood of revolutionary change, international factors, one might argue—particularly external threats by antagonistic superpowers, as well as policy demands from supportive superpowers—constrained policy decisions made by revolutionary regimes. In this manner, international influences reduced the likelihood of successful transitions to democracy, even in cases in which revolutionary movements professed a desire to replace a deposed authoritarian regime with democratic institutions. These international influences aside, however, Shain and Linz's revolutionary provisional government model is anchored primarily to domestic causal processes.

The second source of interim government and regime transition reflected in the revolutionary provisional model is firmly international, with regime changes occurring as the product of interstate war or conquest by an imperial power. This process is most clearly present in the regime changes occurring as a by-product of World War II and the subsequent emergence of the Cold War between the United States and the Soviet Union. Shain and Linz conclude that the post–World War II wave of democratization was a by-product of "the international conjuncture which represented the victory of the Western forces of democracy over the Axis powers," a process often char-

---

5. Ibid.
6. Ibid., 31–34.
7. Ibid.

acterized by the reinstallation of democratic governments in exile and the resurrection of democratic institutions.[8] Revolutionary and war-induced regime changes exert similar pressures on new provisional governments, as new provisional governments must achieve the following to survive: contend with the legacies of the occupation and its proxies, deal with the issue of collaboration and trials, resettle refugees, work toward generating national solidarity and establishing the foundation for a cohesive military force, enforce law and order and eliminate multiple power bases, determine future international alliances, and reconstruct the political and economic systems.[9] Similar to provisional regimes that emerge via internal revolution, provisional regimes that are imposed following war confront the inefficiencies associated with imposed norms for democratic institutions, institutions that might very well inhibit, or even prevent, settling scores with the representatives of the previous regime. Stated differently, the internal conditions associated with revolutionary provisional change often militate against the successful democratization of the new regime.

The case study research contained in *Between States* is exclusively devoted to investigating domestic sources of regime change. Case studies by H. E. Chehabi and Thomas C. Bruneau on the Islamic revolution in Iran in 1979 and the democratic revolution in Portugal in 1974, respectively, give primacy to domestic, rather than international, factors.[10] As we noted earlier, Shain and Linz's emphasis on the internal, revolutionary causes of provisional regimes squared with prevailing trends in international politics, in which internally driven revolutions in the 1970s, 1980s, and 1990s were the modal type of regime change, and international intervention was carried out either under more subtle forms of "neo-conquest" in the forms of foreign aid and covert manipulation of domestic politics or by multilateral institutions, such as the United Nations.

Despite this trend, the development of what Shain and Lynn Berat refer to as the "fourth model," or the international interim government model, suggests that the authors were well aware that international factors are central to transitional governments in contemporary politics.[11] Specifically, Shain and Berat's chapter focuses on the conditions in which civil war pits two or more domestic parties vying for control of a state against each other and the extent of the animus between the parties prevents the establishment of either an interim government based on power sharing or long-term stability. In addition,

---

8. Ibid., 27.
9. Ibid., 38.
10. H. E. Chehabi, "The Provisional Government and the Transition from Monarchy to Islamic Republic in Iran," in Shain and Linz, *Between States,* 127–143; and Thomas C. Bruneau, "From Revolution to Democracy in Portugal: The Roles and Stages of Provisional Governments," in Shain and Linz, *Between States,* 144–159.
11. Yossi Shain and Lynn Berat, "The International Interim Government Model Revisited," in Shain and Linz, *Between States,* 64.

the authors argue that "these conflicts are further exacerbated by the strong influence and sometimes actual physical presence of foreign powers, which may view certain peaceful solutions as inimical to their interests."[12] If such conditions prevail, the prospects for a lasting democratic transition are remote, although intervention under the right conditions by the United Nations might offer hope for escape from seemingly irresolvable conflicts.[13]

The paradox of analyzing contemporary international politics rigorously so as to provide policy-relevant recommendations is that scholars have a tendency to assume that contemporary modes of behavior are reflective of the range of behavior in international politics, when in fact, observable behavior represents a mere sample of potential behaviors. In part, this is what occurs with the treatment of the revolutionary provisional model of interim governments in *Between States*. Indeed, we argue that the foreign war and conquest dimensions of the model are left relatively underexplored in the volume as a result of the relative infrequency of these events when the volume was assembled. Yet, events in contemporary Afghanistan and Iraq suggest that the international aspects of the revolutionary provisional model remain pertinent to the study of contemporary international relations and bear on the issue of interim governments that is central to the present volume.

In the remainder of this chapter, we draw on the international component of the revolutionary provisional model to explore political stability in political regimes that are imposed by third-party states. In doing so, we are able to investigate several policy-relevant research questions put forth by this volume's coeditors. Namely, we intend to develop a predictive model of political stability (what we refer to as "political challenge") in imposed regimes during the modern state system. Prior to doing so, it is necessary to elaborate on the concept of imposed regimes, and we do so in the following section.

Imposed Regimes

We argue that war and conquest by foreign powers are manifestations of a broader phenomenon that we refer to as *imposed regimes*. Imposed regimes are neither new nor confined solely to the conspicuous cases of post–World War II West Germany and Japan, the archetypal examples of this phenomenon. During the roughly two centuries of the modern state system, states frequently sought to impose political institutions on other states, ranging from near ideal-type democratic regimes to near ideal-type autocracies. For example, the victors of the Napoleonic Wars imposed a moderately autocratic regime on defeated France in 1815, and the United States installed a

---

12. Ibid., 63.
13. Ibid., 64.

new democratic regime in Panama in 1989 after the invasion and removal of the strongman regime of Manuel Noriega. Similarly, while the United States and its allies were cultivating democratic institutions in post–World War II Western Europe and Japan, the Soviet Union was cultivating, if not overtly installing, authoritarian regimes in Eastern Europe.

States attempt to impose political systems on other countries for a number of reasons. First, perpetual occupation of countries defeated in war is costly to potential occupying states. Imposing a political system provides a vehicle for indirect rule over the occupied state and thereby a more cost-effective method of controlling a political system. Second, by imposing a polity, the imposer seeks to fashion a reliable ally, a state with similar foreign policy preferences on issues of strategic importance. Third, states imposing a polity may wish to install a government that will facilitate access to economic markets, natural resources, labor, etc., all of which are reflective of the conquest aspect of the imposition dynamic. Fourth, the imposing state may have ideological or normative reasons for imposing different regimes (for instance, Marxist states might impose Marxist-oriented political regimes as a way to strengthen the ideological community). Finally, imposing states might seek economic conquest of the state into which a political regime is imposed.[14] Regardless of the varied motives underlying states' imposition of a political system on other states, we assume that imposing states prefer to impose political systems that are *stable* enough to preclude high maintenance costs in the form of foreign aid or even a reintervention by the imposing state.

Despite preferences for stable political regimes, imposing parties exert only partial control over the political, social, and economic trajectories of the regimes they impose abroad. This is because additional domestic and international factors influence political stability in imposed regimes. These factors range from the level of economic development in the imposed political regime to the degree of foreign threat confronted by the imposed regime. In the following section, we formulate a set of expectations about political stability in imposed regimes, expectations grounded in the degree of commitment by the imposing parties, as well as examine additional sources of political instability in imposed regimes. In doing so, we are able to provide greater insight into the explanatory power of the revolutionary provisional model of interim governments developed by Shain and Linz in *Between States* and, in turn, develop prospective policy forecasts of the contemporary cases of imposed regimes in Afghanistan and Iraq.

---

14. Peter Liberman, *Does Conquest Pay? The Exploitation of Occupied Industrial Societies* (Princeton: Princeton University Press, 1996).

Theoretical Expectations

Our analysis of political stability in imposed regimes draws on the broader study of political stability and instability that is central to a wide array of research studies in the social sciences, including studies in which political stability and instability are the cause as well as the consequence of several political, economic, and social phenomena.[15] Simply put, political stability represents "regular modes" of political expression within a polity, such that members of a polity rely on institutionalized channels for expressing policy preferences and evaluation of government policy, while political instability reflects "irregular modes" of political expression within a polity.[16] In the remainder of this chapter, we are primarily interested in a specific manifestation of political instability that is referred to in the literature as *political challenge*.

The distinction between the general category of political instability and the subset of actions referred to as political challenge lies in the intent and expression of actions taken within a political system. First, as discussed by Douglas Hibbs, political challenges are distinctly "anti-system" with respect to their intended effect on the polity by the individuals and groups engaging in this form of political behavior.[17] Second, political challenges "pose a threat of at least severe political inconvenience to the normal operation of the political elite."[18] Finally, the political challenges are collective in nature and politically oriented, thereby excluding criminal activity.[19] Robert W. Jackman argues that political challenges are distinct from other forms of

---

15. For example, see Richard C. Fording, "The Political Response to Black Insurgency: A Critical Test of Competing Theories of the State," *American Political Science Review* 95, no. 1 (March 2001): 115–130; Will H. Moore, "Repression and Dissent: Substitution, Context, and Timing," *American Journal of Political Science* 42, no. 3 (July 1998): 851–873; Samuel P. Huntington, *Political Order in Changing Societies* (New Haven, Conn.: Yale University Press, 1968); Steve Poe and Neal C. Tate, "Repression of Human Rights to Personal Integrity in the 1980s: A Global Analysis," *American Political Science Review* 88, no. 4 (December 1994): 853–900; Robert Barrow, *Determinants of Economic Growth: A Cross-Country Empirical Study* (Cambridge, Mass.: MIT Press, 1997); Adam Przeworksi, Michael E. Alvarez, Jose Antonio Cheibub, and Fernando Limongi, *Democracy and Development: Political Institutions and Well-Being in the World, 1950–1990* (Cambridge: Cambridge University Press, 2000); Jack S. Levy, "The Diversionary Theory of War: A Critique," in *The Handbook of War Studies*, ed. Manus I. Midlarsky, 259–288 (Boston, Mass.: Unwin Hyman, 1989); Stephen Walt, "Revolutions and War," *World Politics* 44, no. 3 (1992): 321–328; Edward D. Mansfield and Jack Snyder, *Electing to Fight: Why Emerging Democracies Choose to Fight* (Cambridge, Mass.: MIT Press, 2005); Theda Skocpol, *States and Revolutions: A Comparative Analysis of France, Russia, and China* (Cambridge: Cambridge University Press, 1979); and Cynthia McClintock, *Revolutionary Movements in Latin America: El Salvador's FMLN and Peru's Shining Path* (Washington, D.C.: United States Institute of Peace Press, 1998).
16. Claude Ake, "A Definition of Political Stability," *Comparative Politics* 7, no. 2 (January 1975): 271–283.
17. Douglas Hibbs, *Mass Political Violence* (New York: Wiley, 1973), 7.
18. Ibid.
19. Ibid.

instability in that challenges are "distinguished by at least the threat of force on the party of the challengers. Due to their potential gravity for the political elites and the polity, political challengers confront the potential for high costs in the form of government repression."[20] Ultimately, the emergence of political challenges is an indicator of the erosion of a political regime's legitimacy as well as its capacity to preempt political challenges with side payments or repression; that is, the occurrence of overt political challenge signals government weakness. Finally, Christina Schatzman argues that, while political protests and rebellion vary in terms of the role of violence and the degree of challenge to state sovereignty, these two forms of political challenge have in common the goal to effect change in the political system; that is, they represent overt challenges to the political status quo, broadly defined.[21]

In the contemporary cases of Afghanistan and Iraq, political challenge manifests itself most visibly in the form of insurgency, or militant antigovernment attacks intended to destabilize and possibly even to destroy the respective democratic political institutions in these two states. As a result, political challenges and, more importantly, a political regime's capacity to control their occurrence and impact on the political system are central to an imposed regime's survival. As we noted above, however, the occurrence and impact of political challenges can be moderated to some degree by policy choices made by the imposing states, as well as by conditions exogenous to the imposed regime. The remainder of this section is devoted to developing expectations about several causes of political challenge in imposed regimes.

Democratic Polity Type

Two causal logics link the presence of democratic institutions with the likelihood of political challenges during an imposed regime's persistence. The first argument builds on the idea that democratic institutions provide formal, institutionalized mechanisms for relatively large electorates to engage the political process with their policy preferences. By design, democratic institutions should encourage expressions of political preferences that might manifest themselves in the form of political challenges intended to influence the polity's existence into nonviolent political participation,

---

20. Robert W. Jackman, *Power Without Force: The Political Capacity of Nation States* (Ann Arbor: University of Michigan Press, 1993).
21. Christina Schatzman, "Political Challenge in Latin America: Rebellion and Collective Protest in an Era of Democratization," *Journal of Peace Research* 42, no. 3 (May 2005): 291–310.

such as voting.[22] The logic of this argument squares nicely with policy claims advanced for the contemporary cases of Afghanistan and Iraq, wherein imposed democratic regimes are replacing authoritarian regimes and political systems that severely restricted citizen input into the policy process. Additionally, in response to direct political challenges to the fledgling democratic regime in Iraq, one recent policy argument developed by U.S. foreign policymakers is that democracy will succeed because all individuals embrace democratic ideals.

The second argument is that the nature of democratic institutions will increase political instability in an imposed regime, a relationship that is only exacerbated by the fact that imposed democracies are likely to replace authoritarian regimes. First, while democratic institutions provide formal, nonviolent procedures for making policy decisions, it may take several years, perhaps even generations, for these democratic institutions to engender popular confidence and legitimacy, to establish intra-institutional prerogative and precedent, and to develop efficient policymaking processes. During the interim period, when the delicate chemistry of democracy is established, democratic institutions may actually increase the frustration of the population in the state into which a regime is imposed, as those institutions fail to produce efficient policies, which in turn erodes citizen confidence in democratic institutions.[23] Under these conditions, imposed democratic regimes are likely to experience domestic political challenges.

Political Culture

As states persist they can experience more than one regime or set of political institutions. Some of these political institutions might be imposed, but most are likely to be the product of indigenous characteristics and governing traditions or are institutions borrowed from other political regimes in the interstate system. Regardless of their origins, the institutional designs of prior regimes can leave an imprint on a state's collective political "memory," such that these memories influence the stability and fate of subsequent regimes. For example, a citizenry that experienced democratic institutions during a prior period may be more amendable to similarly designed political institutions in subsequent periods. The converse impact might obtain for dissimilar regimes introduced during subsequent periods, such that the imposition of an authoritarian regime on the heels of democratic political experience might stimulate resistance on the part of formerly democratic citizens. This

---

22. McClintock, *Revolutionary Movements in Latin America*; Timothy P. Wickham-Crowley, *Guerrillas and Revolution in Latin America: A Comparative Study of Insurgents and Regimes Since 1956* (Princeton: Princeton University Press, 1992); and S. N. Eisenstadt, *Revolution and the Transformation of Societies: A Comparative Study of Civilizations* (New York: Free Press, 1978).

23. Schatzman, "Political Challenge in Latin America"; and John Foran, *Theorizing Revolutions: New Approaches from Across the Disciplines* (London: Routledge, 1997).

notion of regime memory is similar to that of "civil culture" in terms of its centrality to the establishment and endurance of political institutions in an imposed regime.[24]

Social Fabric

The contemporary policy literature suggests that the social fabric in a state strongly conditions the likelihood of political challenge, and we anticipate that a similar dynamic will bear out under conditions of an imposed regime. A core element of a society's social fabric concerns the differences between, as well as the relationships among, various political or politicized groups. Ethnic identities (that is, the physical, cultural, linguistic, customary, and historical attributes associated with groups of individuals) represent highly visible symbols of a society's social fabric, as well as the potential for a society's social fabric to break down or fray. In turn, this fraying of intergroup relationships is likely to increase the occurrence of overt political challenges to the regime, particularly if political leaders rely on ethnic cleavages as vehicles for nationalism.[25] We anticipate that the proclivity for such challenges is particularly high in imposed regimes, because these regimes likely bear the responsibility for redistributing a state's sources of political and economic power. This process of power and resource distribution probably results in "winners" and "losers." In turn, the potential losers in this process rely on ethnicity and similar signals of identity differences as vehicles for mobilizing individuals politically.

While the previous argument suggests a general relationship between the number of ethnic groups in a country and the occurrence of political challenge, this positive relationship may be a function of the type of imposed regime. Specifically, some scholars suggest that democratic regimes experience greater difficulty in environments characterized as multiethnic because democracies require power sharing, and they function on policy via majority-rule requirements and decision-making rules that are difficult to implement when political parties are anchored in ethnic differences.[26] Here, we explore whether the link between social fabric and political challenge is moderated by the presence of democratic institutions in an imposed regime.

---

24. Gabriel A. Almond, "The Intellectual History of the Civic Culture Concept" in, *The Civic Culture Revisited*, ed. Gabriel A. Almond and Sidney Verba, 1–36 (New York: Little Brown, 1980).

25. Jack Snyder, *From Voting to Violence: Democratization and Nationalist Conflict* (New York: Norton, 2000); Tanya Ellingsen, "Colorful Community or Ethnic Witches' Brew? Multiethnicity and Domestic Conflict During and After the Cold War," *Journal of Conflict Resolution* 44, no. 2 (April 1999): 228–249; Ted Robert Gurr, "Peoples Against States: Ethnopolitical Conflict and the Changing World System," *International Studies Quarterly* 38, no. 3 (September 1994): 347–377.

26. In particular, see Snyder, *From Voting to Violence*.

Prosperity

Two general causal arguments link economic prosperity with political challenge in imposed regimes. The first argument suggests that economic prosperity and development will generally satisfy the material needs of the population in an imposed regime. In this scenario, an imposed regime is essentially successful in delivering a relatively more prosperous economic environment for its citizens, and satisfied citizens are less likely to engage in political challenges to the imposed regime. The second argument suggests that as the fruits of economic development accrue to the citizens in an imposed regime, this prosperity may be accompanied by increasing disparities in wealth between economic classes. Such economic disparities result in political mobilization, and this mobilization process increases the likelihood of political challenges against the imposed regime that is the focal point of a state's political and economic processes. Thus, despite the seemingly plausible assumption that each individual prefers more versus less prosperity, the development process may result in inequitable economic outcomes, outcomes that stimulate the resort to political challenges directed toward an imposed regime.[27]

Militarization

As evidenced by the experiences of contemporary Afghanistan and Iraq, newly imposed regimes must contend with significant challenges to establishing domestic security in an environment in which domestic political institutions have little initial political legitimacy or political capacity. These new regimes often respond to this insecurity by increasing the capability of the domestic security apparatus, such as the police, security, and military agencies, the first step in establishing political rule, regardless of type, and stabilizing the regime. Militarization is often the first step that imposed regimes take in order to acquire capacity to deliver a central necessity: domestic and international security. We generally anticipate that militarization of an imposed regime will raise the cost to individuals for mounting political challenges and therefore reduce the likelihood of their occurrence.[28]

Commitment of Imposing Parties

The policy choices of the state, or states, imposing a regime are central to the process of regime imposition and the occurrence of political chal-

---

27. Seymore Martin Lipset, "Some Social Requisites of Democracy: Economic Development and Political Legitimacy," *American Political Science Review* 53, no. 1 (March 1959): 69–105; Erich Weede, "Income Inequality, Average Income, and Domestic Violence," *Journal of Conflict Resolution* 25, no. 1 (December 1981): 639–653; and Rudolph J. Rummel, "Is Collective Violence Correlated with Social Pluralism?" *Journal of Peace Research* 34, no. 2 (May 1997): 163–175.

28. Jackman, *Power Without Force*; and Moore, "Repression and Dissent."

lenge. In addition to the task of establishing the political institutions associated with a regime type, the imposing parties also serve to deter threats by enemies of the imposed regime. Specifically, the presence of the imposer—namely, in the form of military personnel—serves to insulate the imposed regime from violent efforts by domestic political groups to destroy the political institutions associated with this regime and to disrupt a state's political, economic, and social infrastructure. In addition to deterrence, imposing parties can serve as the interim provider of domestic and interstate security for the imposing regime. In general, imposing regimes can play a critical role, one that is difficult for them to furnish themselves during the regime's initial existence. In addition to providing the resources necessary for, first and foremost, internal defense, imposing parties also provide the financial and diplomatic resources necessary for an imposed regime to carry out the tasks essential to a political system, such as voter registration, elections, and taxation. Thus, the presence of the imposing party should reduce the need for a populace to resort to irregular channels of political participation, thereby reducing the likelihood of political challenge.

Conversely, the physical presence of imposing parties should deter political challenges, but it is also plausible that the presence of an imposing party can engender a negative reaction to an imposer's presence in the imposed state.[29] Under these conditions, the presence of an imposer may actually incite political challenges against a regime that some political groups consider illegitimate. Although the imposing parties may still be able to insulate the imposed regime from the costs of political challenges, the subsequent departure of the imposing parties might accelerate additional, devastating political challenges directed toward an imposed regime.

Interstate Security

External threats have long been identified in the scholarly literature as exerting strong influences on state and regime well-being.[30] One argument is that threats and the possibility of interstate war increase state power, because war fighting requires the centralization of power and resources. Thus, political leaders prefer the presence of foreign threats because these threats afford the state a rationale for mobilizing domestic resources, as well as for stimulating the convergence of domestic preferences over policy choice. Conversely, the mobilization of domestic constituents

---

29. Daniel M. Edelstein, "Occupational Hazards: Why Military Occupations Succeed or Fail," *International Security* 29, no. 1 (Summer 2004): 49–91.

30. Bruce D. Porter, *War and the Rise of the State: The Military Foundations of Modern Politics* (New York: Free Press, 1994); and Charles Tilly, *From Mobilization to Revolution* (Reading, Mass.: Addison-Wesley, 1978).

to fight enemies abroad can sometimes facilitate the organization of domestic opposition groups, which in turn can mount challenges to the leadership and institutions in an imposed regime. Therefore, we anticipate two alternative expectations: one that anticipates foreign enemies fortifying the legitimacy and capacity of an imposed regime, and an alternative that anticipates foreign threats eroding an imposed regime's legitimacy and capacity, which in turn stimulate political challenges directed toward imposed regimes.

Analysis

Research Design

To test the empirical veracity of our expectations, we rely on a data sample of sixty imposed regimes (both democratic and nondemocratic) drawn from a period that encompasses nearly all of the modern state system (see table 5.1).[31] The sample of imposed regimes is primarily derived from the *Polity IIId* data set, with additional vetting with *The Encyclopedia of World History*.[32] The unit of analysis that we employ is the *imposed-regime-year*, of which there are 1,993 in our sample. In terms of our dependent variable, we rely on *The Encyclopedia of World History* to operationalize political challenge broadly, such that it includes an array of political events that we consider challenging to a polity, including insurgency, rebellion, riots, strikes, bombings, protests, and assassinations (both successes and attempts). In our data sample of 1,993 observations, 309 (15 percent) are coded as experiencing political challenge in a given observation.

We create several independent variables corresponding to our theoretical expectations. Specifically, to measure the regime type of the imposed regime, we create a dichotomous variable scored a value of one if an imposed regime is democratic (that is, where the *Polity IIId* variable is *DEMAUT > 0*), and zero otherwise. To measure the commitment of the imposing states, we rely on *The Encyclopedia of World History* to identify intervals corresponding to the presence of military forces from the imposing state in the imposed regime, differentiating between presence during the initial imposition and subsequent

---

31. The details regarding our empirical operationalization of imposed regimes are reported in Andrew J. Enterline and J. Michael Greig, "Beacons of Hope? The Impact of Imposed Democracy on Regional Peace, Democracy, and Prosperity," *Journal of Politics* 67, no. 4 (November 2005): 1075–1098.

32. For a description of the *Polity IIId* data, see Sara McLaughlin, Scott Gates, Havard Hegre, Ranveig Gissinger, and Nils Petter Gleditsch, "Timing the Changes in Political Structures: A New Polity Database," *Journal of Conflict Resolution* 42, no. 2 (1998): 231–242; and Peter N. Stearns, ed., *The Encyclopedia of World History* (New York: Houghton Mifflin, 2001).

Table 5.1   Externally Imposed Polities, 1816–1994

State	First Year	Last Year	Democracy/Autocracy
Albania	1914	1925	Autocratic
Austria	1946	1994	Democratic
Austria	1920	1934	Democratic
Bhutan	1971	1994	Autocratic
Botswana	1966	1994	Democratic
Bulgaria	1946	1990	Autocratic
Bulgaria	1908	1918	Autocratic
Canada	1920	1994	Democratic
Chile	1974	1989	Autocratic
Cuba	1902	1955	Democratic
Cyprus	1960	1994	Democratic
Dem. Peoples Rep. of Korea	1948	1994	Autocratic
France	1940	1946	Autocratic
France	1816	1848	Autocratic
German Dem. Rep.	1954	1990	Autocratic
German Fed. Rep.	1955	1994	Democratic
Greece	1833	1864	Autocratic
Guatemala	1954	1966	Autocratic
Guyana	1966	1978	Democratic
Haiti	1918	1935	Democratic
Honduras	1908	1936	Democratic
Hungary	1919	1945	Autocratic
Hungary	1948	1989	Autocratic
Iran (Persia)	1941	1979	Autocratic
Iraq	1932	1994	Autocratic
Ireland	1922	1994	Democratic
Italy/Sardinia	1816	1947	Autocratic
Jamaica	1962	1994	Democratic
Japan	1952	1994	Democratic
Kampuchea	1953	1993	Autocratic

Table 5.1 *(cont.)*

State	First Year	Last Year	Democracy/Autocracy
Kenya	1963	1969	Democratic
Lebanon	1946	1990	Democratic
Lesotho	1966	1970	Democratic
Malaysia	1957	1994	Democratic
Mauritius	1968	1994	Democratic
Modena	1842	1860	Autocratic
New Zealand	1920	1994	Democratic
Nicaragua	1909	1990	Autocratic
Nigeria	1960	1966	Democratic
Panama	1989	1994	Democratic
Papal States	1850	1860	Autocratic
Papal States	1816	1850	Autocratic
Paraguay	1870	1937	Autocratic
Parma	1851	1860	Autocratic
Philippines	1946	1972	Democratic
Poland	1947	1989	Autocratic
Rep. of Korea	1949	1988	Autocratic
Rumania	1947	1990	Autocratic
Rumania	1878	1947	Autocratic
Singapore	1965	1965	Democratic
Sri Lanka	1948	1994	Democratic
Sudan	1956	1958	Democratic
Syria	1946	1950	Democratic
Tuscany	1816	1849	Autocratic
Tuscany	1849	1860	Autocratic
Two Sicilies	1821	1860	Autocratic
Two Sicilies	1816	1821	Autocratic
Uganda	1962	1967	Democratic
Zaire	1965	1994	Autocratic
Zimbabwe	1965	1987	Democratic

reinterventions. To measure militarization, we rely on the data generation software *EUGene* to calculate the per capita military personnel in each observation.[33] To measure economic development, we rely on *EUGene* to calculate the natural log of the sum of two components of the Composite Indicator of National Capabilities data (energy consumption and iron and steel production) in each observation. To assess the social characteristics prevailing in the state hosting an imposed polity, we identify the frequency of ethnic groups in the state hosting an imposed regime and log this value. Our two major sources on ethnic groups are *Countries and Their Cultures* and *The Encyclopedia of the World's Nations*.[34] Finally, to assess the impact of international forces on political challenge in imposed regimes, we rely on two empirical indicators. First, we rely on *EUGene* to identify whether an imposed polity participates in an interstate war in any capacity in each observation. Second, we create a variable reflecting regional regime similarity by identifying the frequency of states within five hundred miles that share the same regime type (democratic or autocratic) as each imposed regime in our sample. Having established our sample and operationalized our dependent and independent variables, in the remainder of this section we turn to the results of our hypothesis tests.

Findings

Recall that our theoretical discussion of regime type developed two alternative hypotheses for the impact of imposed democracy on the probability of political challenge. Our empirical analysis of political challenge in imposed regimes suggests that, in many cases, imposing democratic political institutions significantly reduces the likelihood of political challenge in a given year. Furthermore, in ethnically homogenous imposed states, democratic political institutions reduce the probability of political challenge in an imposed regime relative to an imposed nondemocracy by slightly more than 40 percent. This finding is consistent with the historical experience of the imposed regime in post–World War II Japan, a largely ethnically homogenous society.

However, our analysis also suggests that the effect of imposing a democratic regime on the occurrence of political challenge depends significantly upon the ethnic makeup of the states that are the targets of imposed regimes. Specifically, as the frequency of ethnic groups in an imposed regime increases, not only does the stabilizing benefit of imposing

---

33. Scott D. Bennett, D. Scott, and Allan Stam, "EUGene: A Conceptual Manual," *International Interactions* 26 (2000): 179–204.

34. Melvin Ember and Carl R. Ember, *Countries and Their Cultures* (New York: Macmillan, 2001); and George Thomas Kurian, *The Encyclopedia of the World's Nations* (New York: Facts on File, 2002).

democracy wane but also the occurrence of political challenge actually increases. While an imposed democracy in a state with four major ethnic groups is 35 percent less likely to experience political challenge than an imposed autocracy in the same state, our model shows a tipping point of about seven ethnic groups after which imposed democracy makes political challenge more probable. For example, an imposed democracy in a state with fifteen ethnic groups is 61 percent more likely to experience political challenge than an imposed autocracy in a similar country. Indeed, this relationship manifested itself in the imposed democratic regime in Sudan during the 1950s, which not only experienced an insurgent challenge to the imposed regime but also an insurgency that led to the collapse of this regime after only three years.

This relationship between political challenge, democracy, and ethnic cleavages suggests a trade-off that imposing powers make between legitimacy and political efficacy in efforts to impose a stable regime upon another state. On the one hand, imposed democracies, by integrating large segments of the populace into the governance process, appear to facilitate a "buy-in" into the political system that reduces the necessity for challenges to the government and attendant political challenge. On the other hand, the emphasis upon consensus and coalition building also makes governance more difficult, as noted by Shain and Linz. This characteristic of democracies may be particularly problematic in extremely ethnically heterogeneous states, wherein competing groups in societies may quickly conclude that an imposed democracy is unlikely to provide effective governance.

Furthermore, these ethnic groups might perceive that the new democratic regime lacks the capacity to restrain competing ethnic groups from using violence. As a result, these groups might resort to violence over political institutions as the means to achieve their goals, both because they perceive the development of a security dilemma between competing ethnic groups within the society and because they expect to achieve a better outcome by resorting to violence rather than working within existing political institutions.

Beyond the type of regime installed, other policy choices made by imposing states influence the prospects for stability in imposed regimes. One clear finding from our analysis is that the longer an imposing power remains in the imposed state, the less likely political challenge is to occur at any time in the lifespan of the regime, even after the imposing power has left the country. An imposed regime in which the imposing power remains ten years after the imposition is 18 percent less likely to experience political challenge than one in which the imposing power never commits forces to the regime. Similarly, an imposed regime in which the imposing power remains in the state for twenty years is 85 percent less likely to experience political challenge than an imposed regime in which the imposing state is present for a single year.

Interestingly, it is the cumulative effect of the presence of an imposing power that significantly reduces the occurrence of political challenges, not the presence of an imposing power in any particular regime year. The presence of a foreign power is likely to generate opposition both to the imposing power and to the regime the imposing state is seeking to install. At the same time, the presence of an imposing power can serve as a bulwark for the newly imposed regime, both by deterring and by fighting groups challenging the regime. When combined, these two effects tend to neutralize each other. Reinterventions, by contrast, are positively related to the occurrence of political challenges. This effect, however, could reflect the tendency of imposing powers to reintervene in imposed regimes when these regimes experience severe political challenge, rather than vice versa.

The capacity of the new government to resist political challenges also emerges as a key factor in the prevention of political challenge in imposed regimes. Key to the current American effort in Iraq is the development of an Iraqi security force capable of stabilizing the country and ending the current insurgency. Our results underscore the importance of the development of this capability in imposed regimes. Increasing the percentage of the population serving in the military of a state with an imposed regime from just .3 percent to 1 percent reduces the likelihood of political challenge by nearly 16 percent. In this sense, as the capacity of an imposed regime to both resist and deter political challenge increases, the likelihood of political challenge decreases.

In accordance with our argument that the initial increases in economic inequality associated with the outside-in process of regime imposition can cause instability, we find that economic development appears to increase the probability of instability in imposed regimes. We take this finding to corroborate the argument that imposed regimes, because they may bring a rapid influx of development projects and prosperity, in turn might create rising expectations for an imposed regime's governing capacity. It may be that as economic development deepens, the willingness of the populace to continue to accept political institutions imposed upon them by outsiders diminishes, making them more willing to challenge the imposed regime overtly.

Turning to the impact of the simple persistence of imposed regimes on the probability of political challenge, we identify a curvilinear relationship between regime duration and political challenges in imposed states. As imposed regimes persist, they tend to become more likely to experience political challenge. This effect begins to attenuate only in imposed regimes that persist for an extraordinarily long duration. For example, an imposed regime that has persisted for thirty-five years is 157 percent more likely to experience political challenge during that particular imposed regime year relative to a regime that persisted for nine years. An imposed regime that persists for sixty-eight years, however, is nearly 13 percent less likely to experience political challenge during that particular imposed regime year than one that has persisted for thirty-five years.

Although the capacity of imposed regimes to prevent political challenge is tied to the decisions imposing powers make during the imposition process, we also found strong evidence of positive neighborhood effects. The regional environment in which an imposed regime is imposed influences its ability to avoid political challenge. Specifically, as the frequency of neighboring states with the same regime type as an imposed regime increases, the probability of political challenge declines. An imposed regime with four states with a similar regime type within five hundred miles is 37 percent less likely to experience political challenge than a state with no similar neighbors. This finding holds for imposed autocracies and democracies, suggesting that this relationship is tied to both the support neighboring states provide to an imposed regime and the example that neighboring states set for imposed regimes, influencing expectations of governance among the citizens in an imposed regime.

Finally, while a nurturing environment can act as a force for stability in an imposed regime, external threats provide a destabilizing effect. An imposed regime at war is 81 percent more likely to experience political challenge than one at peace. This result parallels our findings with respect to the impact of military capacity upon political challenges. Rather than rallying the people and generating support for the government, wars function to increase political challenges by reducing the capacity of imposed regimes to deter and fight them.

Forecasts for Afghanistan and Iraq

Having developed a model of political challenge in the previous section, we now apply these estimates to assess their implications for the imposed democratic regimes in postwar Afghanistan and Iraq. We use our statistical model to predict the probability of political challenge in these imposed democracies five years after their imposition. Initially, we simulate the predicted probability of political challenge in an average imposed regime that has endured for five years. In an average, five-year-old nondemocratic imposed regime, the probability of political challenge in that year is .039. As our model illustrates, imposed democracies, ceteris paribus, tend to be more stable than nondemocracies, as a five-year-old imposed democracy has only a .028 probability of experiencing political challenge.

To assess the validity of our model as a predictive tool, we use the estimates from our statistical model to "post-dict" the probability of political challenge in the imposed democracy of post–World War II Japan. Japan represents an imposed democratic regime that did not experience any political challenges during the first five years of its existence. We generate the model predictions for Japan using the conditions that prevailed in the country at the time of imposition and find that in the first year of the imposed Japanese democracy (1952), the predicted probability of political challenge is .436. Yet, as the imposed democratic regime in Japan persists and avoids political challenge, the regime becomes increasingly more stable. As a result, by 1957 the predicted probability of political challenge in Japan decreases to .036. As the Japanese case illustrates, the best way to reduce the probability of future political challenge is to prevent its outbreak in the first place or to end it quickly when it does occur. In this respect, stability begets stability in imposed regimes.

Employing our model to make predictions with respect to Afghanistan and Iraq, we simulate both an optimistic and a pessimistic scenario for each five years after the imposition of the regime (that is, the year 2008 for Afghanistan and the year 2009 for Iraq). In the optimistic scenarios, we make a number of assumptions. First, we assume that each state will develop an army of the size prescribed by U.S. political and military leaders (70,000 troops for Afghanistan and 150,000 for Iraq). Second, we assume that the democratization of these two countries will promote political liberalization among their closest neighbors, placing Afghanistan in a region of six democracies and Iraq in a neighborhood with a total of seven democracies within five hundred miles of its borders. We also assume that the current insurgent movements in both Afghanistan and Iraq will have terminated at some point in 2006. Finally, we assume that neither state is involved in an interstate war during the year for which the model is being simulated.

Under the optimistic scenario, the probability of political challenge in Afghanistan in 2008 is .038 and the probability of political challenge in Iraq in 2009 is .027, both of which are below the mean probability of a typical imposed regime and approximately that of an average five-year-old imposed democracy. In this scenario, three primary factors drive Iraq's lower predicted probability of political challenge relative to Afghanistan: (1) the duration since the last experience with political challenge; (2) the level of militarization of the regime; and (3) the number of democratic neighbors. As noted, the longer a regime endures without the occurrence of political challenge, the more the regime tends to avoid political challenge. In this respect, if political challenge ceased in both Afghanistan and Iraq in 2006, Iraq would enjoy one year more of political stability before the fifth anniversary of the imposed regime than Afghanistan.

Further contributing to stability is the level of militarization in the state hosting the imposed regime. We argued earlier in this chapter that the larger the size of the military of an imposed regime, the better equipped it will probably be to both deter and defeat political challenges. In this respect, because the prescribed size of the Iraqi army is more than double that of the Afghan force despite Afghanistan's larger population, the model predicts a lower probability of political challenge in Iraq than in Afghanistan in the best-case scenario. Finally, as we previously discussed, as the number of neighboring states with a similar regime type increases, the probability of political challenges in an imposed regime decreases. We argued that this finding reflects the level of stabilizing support regional neighbors tend to provide to imposed regimes with regimes similar to their own. In this respect, assuming that the imposed democracies in Afghanistan and Iraq in turn stimulate democratization in their neighbors (admittedly an arguable assumption), our model predicts that the larger number of regional neighbors for Iraq will function to dampen its prospects for political challenge relative to that of Afghanistan. In short, under the optimistic scenarios, Iraq enjoys a larger regional support network.

As hopeful as the projections of the optimistic models are, there is certainly reason to question their assumptions. First, although policymakers have touted the tendency of imposed democracies to stimulate regional democratization, the scholarly literature suggests the opposite: regional imposed democracies may not stimulate more regional democracy, and they may actually undermine the likelihood of regional democratization.[35] As a result, it is possible that neither Afghanistan nor Iraq will stimulate democracy among their neighbors, leaving them to deal with a region consisting mostly of autocratic regimes. Second, thus far, efforts to develop and equip a capable indigenous military force in both Afghanistan and Iraq have proven difficult, suggesting that these forces may ultimately fall short of these goals both in terms of force numbers and of effectiveness. Finally, although the recent elections and adoptions of constitutions in Afghanistan and Iraq provided reason for hope, the insurgency movements in both states have proven difficult to quell. In Iraq, the insurgencies even accelerated in late 2005 as attacks against American forces and Iraqi civilians continued to mount. As a result, there is certainly reason to doubt the assumption that both political challenges will be defeated in 2006. Based upon these conditions, we conducted a second set of simulations using a more pessimistic set of assumptions for both Afghanistan and Iraq.

In the pessimistic simulations, we make several key assumptions for both Afghanistan and Iraq. First, we assume that the current insurgency movements in both countries continue: through 2007 in the case of Afghanistan and 2008 in the case of Iraq. In this respect, in the years being simulated for Afghanistan and Iraq, the duration since the end of the last political challenge event is zero. Second, we assume that both countries fall short of their

---

35. Enterline and Greig, "Beacons."

prescribed levels of army size, reaching only 35,000 troops in the case of Afghanistan and 75,000 in the case of Iraq. Finally, we assume that neither Afghanistan nor Iraq encourages democratization among any of its neighbors. As a result, in the case of Afghanistan, we assume that none of its neighbors within five hundred miles is a democracy. Similarly, rather than existing in a region with seven other democracies as the optimistic scenario envisions, the Iraqi democracy in this scenario exists in a region in which only Israel is a neighboring fellow democracy. Finally, given the more threatening environment this scenario constructs, we also assume that both states are involved in war during this period. All other parameters are held constant with respect to the optimistic model.

The pessimistic scenarios for both Afghanistan and Iraq, not surprisingly, forecast a significantly higher predicted probability of political challenge in each state. What is surprising, however, is the amount of the increase based upon these parameters. Afghanistan, under the pessimistic scenario, has a predicted probability of political challenge in the year 2008 of .619. The projections are even worse for Iraq, which has a predicted probability of political challenge in the year 2009 of .684. Iraq's higher predicted probability of political challenge results, in large part, from its higher level of ethnic heterogeneity relative to Afghanistan. In the optimistic scenario, the effect of these societal cleavages on political challenge in Iraq was dampened by the assumption of more democratic neighbors and a longer period without insurgency for the country. In the pessimistic simulation, neither of these assumptions holds, and as a result, we find a higher probability of political challenge in Iraq than in Afghanistan.

Recall that we found the performance of imposed democracies to depend significantly upon the ethnic makeup of the states in which they are imposed. More heterogeneous states have less stable imposed democracies. In this respect, Japan, because of its relatively high level of ethnic homogeneity, is particularly well suited for the imposition of democracy. Given these findings, we conducted a third set of simulations evaluating the performance of a hypothetical imposed *nondemocratic* regime in both Afghanistan and Iraq. Each run of the simulations reveals that, ceteris paribus, both states are more stable with an imposed *nondemocratic* regime than an imposed *democratic* regime. Under the optimistic scenario, the probability of political challenge drops to .037 percent in Afghanistan and .023 in Iraq. The effects, however, are particularly striking in the pessimistic scenario. For imposed nondemocracies in Afghanistan and Iraq, the probability of political challenge reduces by approximately 30 percent from the forecast probability for imposed democratic regimes. The predicted probability of political challenge under the pessimistic scenario is .439 in a nondemocratic Afghanistan and .477 in a nondemocratic Iraq (a drop from .619 and .684, respectively).

Although these results seem counterintuitive and certainly run opposite to the arguments of policymakers, they reflect the degree to which imposed governments have the capacity to withstand and terminate political challenges. In multiethnic states such as Afghanistan and Iraq, it may be difficult for an imposed democratic regime, at least in the nascent years of its development, to develop the institutional capacity to deal with these competing interests and to prevent the outbreak of political challenges. Instead, imposed nondemocratic regimes may, at least initially, be better equipped to assert control over a state with a large number of ethnic cleavages. Furthermore, nondemocratic regimes in Afghanistan and Iraq would, under the scenario outlined by the pessimistic model, be more similar to their regional neighbors, making them more likely to avoid efforts at destabilization by dissimilar regimes, if not attracting outright support from these neighboring states.

Choosing to impose a nondemocracy in either Afghanistan or Iraq, however, is likely to be unpalatable both politically and ideologically to U.S. policymakers even if such a regime is more inclined toward stability. Thus, the key question then becomes, how can other conditions associated with imposed regimes in the contemporary cases be adjusted in order to provide the stability that nondemocracies offer and the political and ideological appeal of democracy? By focusing upon the capacity of imposed regimes to resist political challenges, our model provides some ways to think about how to achieve these competing goals. In Iraq, for example, expanding the size of the new Iraqi army from the proposed 150,000-troop level to 300,000 troops significantly increases the capacity of the regime to deal with and resist political challenges. This capacity is further strengthened if Iraq avoids conflict with its neighbors and can focus its attention inward. Finally, this capacity to resist political challenge can be further heightened if U.S. forces remain in Iraq through 2009 rather than withdraw in 2006. If each of these conditions prevails, the predicted probability of political challenge in a democratic Iraq in 2009 under the pessimistic scenario is .483, nearly identical to that of a nondemocratic Iraq under the same scenario. In this respect, the stability of the imposed regimes in Afghanistan and Iraq, while related to the form of government imposed, is not fully determined by the choice of regime type.

Implications for the Revolutionary Provisional Government Model

What are the implications of our investigation for the revolutionary provisional model proposed by Shain and Linz in *Between States*? Although the international dimension of the revolutionary provisional model of interim government and democratic transitions is the one least developed in *Between States*, our analysis of political challenge in imposed regimes suggests that Shain and Linz's volume provides important insights into the political processes associated with regime imposition resulting from war and conquest. For example, Shain and Linz assert that the democratic regimes that are the by-products of foreign intervention can experience difficulty reconciling the diverse policy preferences of many groups. Our analysis of the impact of democratic institutions under conditions of multiple ethnic groups corroborates Shain and Linz's expectation, such that when multiple ethnic groups are present, foreign powers will be more successful in reducing political challenge by cultivating nondemocratic institutions.

Additionally, our analysis demonstrates that international conditions do significantly influence the political stability of imposed regimes. The degree to which a regime is located in a geographic region with similar regime types significantly affects the probability of political challenge in imposed regimes: greater similarity leads to less instability. Furthermore, the degree of conflict between the imposed state and the international community influences the degree to which the imposed regime experiences political challenge. In short, greater conflict with other states corresponds to greater political challenge in imposed regimes.

Finally, the role of the imposing power is central to stability in imposed regimes. Specifically, the presence of a foreign power can serve as a bulwark for the newly imposed regime. The presence of the imposer can deter and fight groups challenging the regime, yet our analysis suggests that imposing states must remain in the imposed state for a very long period of time in order to reduce instability. However, long tenure by an imposer is a double-edged sword: while the presence of an imposer increases stability, it also increases the chance that over time citizens will start to resist the occupation, a development that is also emphasized in *Between States*.

Overall, Shain and Linz's model of provisional interim regimes provides a fruitful point of departure for considering political stability in imposed regimes. Many of the policy choices confronted by interim governments that are the product of internal revolutions also present themselves to states seeking to impose political institutions on other states. In particular, imposed regimes, like internally generated revolutionary regimes, must create centralized, legitimate authority with a monopoly over the use of force, while limiting aggressive interventions by neighboring states. Our analysis suggests that whether and how imposed regimes address these issues will significantly influence whether "going through Hobbes" is a transition marked by political stability or instability and whether the specter of political challenge will loom over these fledgling political systems and, in turn, hasten their demise.

Part Two

Case Studies

6

Multiple Transitions and Interim Governance in El Salvador and Guatemala

William D. Stanley

Editors' Note

William D. Stanley's chapter on Guatemala and El Salvador, the first in the case studies section, provides an example of the classic interim government model in which a military regime came to power via coup d'etat and then found itself with a legitimacy crisis. In both of these countries, splits within the ruling junta caused repression and then the eventual decision to cede power to a civilian regime. In El Salvador the military junta began to remove itself from power to prevent internal strife from imploding the military, while in Guatemala the military ceded some power with the understanding that this was the best way to maintain influence. The transitions in both El Salvador and Guatemala were therefore spurred by domestic processes and a crisis of legitimacy for military regimes that induced them to create temporary civilian governments to manage a transition back to democratic rule. Multiple stages of interim governance followed, as even constitutional, semi-democratic regimes proved unable to quell insurgencies, finding it necessary to carry out formal peace talks and to commit to deeper democratization as a condition for rebel disarmament.

Even in these cases of primarily domestically initiated and managed transitional regimes, however, the involvement of the international community was important. In both cases, the international community provided guidance and management at crucial junctures in the transitional process. In El Salvador, for example, during a critical period of voter registration, the interim regime balked at registering voters who were critical of the military. The UN mission, ONUSAL, moved beyond its observer functions and forced the electoral commission in El Salvador to register the citizens who had been prevented from registering to vote under previous administrations, thus preserving the integrity of the electoral process. Aside from such moments of effective international assertiveness, however, outcomes depended heavily on domestic factors, including the strength and coherence of national political parties, institutional arrangements such as procedures for constitutional reforms, and the specificity of political accords. The transitional government, biased by the continuity in the interim government populated by domestic power elites, would not have otherwise done this.

From these cases we can see that the international community can play an important, though limited, role even in interim regimes that are domestic affairs, but it has limited short-term capacity to overcome some domestic obstacles. Decades-long international efforts to shape domestic political conditions proved at least as important in affecting outcomes as did short-term missions to assist transitions.

■ ■ ■

Introduction

This chapter will review two cases, El Salvador and Guatemala, in which a series of domestic interim governments oversaw a complex, multiphase transition from failed military regimes to competitive democracies. In both cases, de facto interim governments with no credible claims to constitutionality followed the collapse of institutional military regimes. These interim regimes were unsustainable in both countries. The de facto governments were followed by the election of constituent assemblies, the drafting of new constitutions, and the election of new executives and legislatures under partially democratic conditions, with the Left excluded.

While these governments enjoyed greater public and international legitimacy than their predecessors, both partial democracies faced ongoing insurgencies that they were unable to eliminate militarily. Unable to establish a single governmental authority throughout the national territory by force, both governments ultimately negotiated peace accords under which insurgents put down their arms in exchange for comprehensive democratization and state reforms. The partially democratic governments then oversaw the implementation of these measures, bringing the transitional period to an end.

These cases offer three dimensions of comparison that make them analytically useful. First, within each case the partially democratic interim governments performed far better than the initial, de facto juntas. Second, El Salvador's interim government proved significantly more effective and capable than Guatemala's in implementing the democratizing reforms agreed to in the respective peace accords. This chapter seeks to explain these differences in outcome.

Third, while mostly domestic affairs, these two interim regimes shed light on many of the issues under consideration in this volume and have interesting parallels to their internationally organized and managed cousins. At certain junctures, the international community exerted influence to keep these domestic processes on track; at others, it found itself powerless to aid a faltering regime because domestic regulations, laws, and political alignments prevented outsiders from wielding greater influence. Long-term international efforts—such as those to build more moderate, more coherent political parties—had significant effects. These dynamics, discussed in this case study, reveal the delicate relationship between domestic and international politics, and they demonstrate that even the most "domestic" interim regimes are, in fact, intimately connected to and influenced by international politics.

I date the interim period as 1979 through 1994 in El Salvador and 1982 through 2000 in Guatemala. These dates mark the collapse of the institutional military government and the installation of the first post–civil war governments elected under the new, more fully democratic political rules established under the peace accords. While the initial, de facto governments in both countries necessarily considered themselves "interim," given their lack of constitutional foundations, the partially democratic governments of the 1980s and early 1990s considered themselves the constitutional governments of their countries, period. Neither would have recognized itself as interim. Yet if, in accordance with the guidelines provided by this volume's editors, a transitional period ends when a new regime establishes the rule of law throughout the national territory, then by definition the governments of El Salvador and Guatemala were "interim" until their insurgencies ended, founding elections were held under the new rules, and the new governments were in place.

This chapter begins by examining the origins of the transitions and the performance of the early de facto interim governments. It then turns to the initial period of partially democratic interim governance, during which norms of civilian authority were gradually established, parties were formed or broken down, state reforms were attempted, and peace negotiations began. The chapter then examines the contrasting performance of the partially democratic governments in implementing peace accords and explains these differences on the basis of the political capacity of government parties, the strength and agendas of insurgents, the specificity of the framework for reform provided by the peace accords, the ability of existing state agencies to resist change, the design of constitutional reform mechanisms, and the effectiveness of international missions.

Collapse of Institutional Military Governments

In 1979 in El Salvador, reformist military officers formed a Revolutionary Governing Junta (JRG) in partnership with a coalition of social democratic parties and reformist elements of the Catholic Church. Two months later, when the social democrats withdrew from government in protest over human rights violations, the army formed a new alliance with the Christian Democrats (PDC). This new junta ruled, with occasional internal reshuffling, until an interim government and constituent assembly were elected in 1982. A civilian president was elected in 1984 under the new constitution, with legislative elections following shortly after.

In Guatemala, there was less effort to incorporate civilian supporters: two consecutive de facto military governments ruled without significant civilian party support. The second of these allowed constituent assembly elections in 1984, and an elected civilian government took office in 1986. Transitions to limited, elected civilian rule based on legitimate constitutions were complete by the mid-1980s in both countries.

Neither of the initial, nondemocratic interim governments was very effective, a factor driving these governments to hold elections fairly quickly and to step aside. The reasons for their failures differed somewhat, however. In El Salvador, the JRGs were deeply divided internally between factions that favored deep reforms and democratization and factions that favored a violently repressive strategy. I have argued elsewhere that the depth of internal divisions actually increased the severity of violence used by hard-line factions against the general public, as hard-liners sought to veto political compromise with the Left. This intensified state violence further radicalized the Left, pushing thousands of members of nonviolent popular organizations to join the nascent guerrilla forces. Killings were directed particularly against moderate members of the Left who were actively seeking compromise solutions to the political crisis; by the end of 1980, most of the surviving moderates had fled the country, along with military officers whose reformist project had unraveled.[1]

Although the military/Christian Democratic junta succeeded in implementing a limited land reform, this did not diminish the slide toward civil war, which began in earnest in January 1981. The newly inaugurated Reagan administration in Washington simultaneously strengthened U.S. military assistance in El Salvador and began pressing for democratization. The administration viewed greater political legitimacy as a sine qua non for effective counterinsurgency; it also considered it essential for retaining the political

---

1. William D. Stanley, *The Protection Racket State: Elite Politics, Military Extortion, and Civil War in El Salvador* (Philadelphia: Temple University Press, 1996).

support of the U.S. Congress for increased military assistance.[2] A second source of pressure for democratization was internal: conservative activists associated with the business community were alarmed by land expropriations carried out by the military/Christian Democratic junta and sought opportunities to compete directly in elections in hopes of establishing a government more protective of private property.[3] The military ultimately agreed to this, and elections for an interim government and constituent assembly were held in 1982.

In Guatemala, the 1982 coup brought to power General Efraín Ríos Montt. Junior officers called Ríos out of retirement and invited him to take power in an effort to counteract what they saw as the extensive corruption and incompetence of much of the high command. This reflected the primary line of internal division in the military between the established, "institutionalist" leadership and various wildcat groups—particularly junior officers who were actively involved in combat operations against the rebels. However corrupt the mainline officers were, General Ríos brought his own complications, including weekly broadcast sermons from the presidential house that blended Protestant evangelism and counterterror in a way that did not enhance the government's legitimacy in majority-Catholic Guatemala. He also earned very little international acceptance. Despite the comparative success of Ríos's aggressive counterinsurgency strategies, establishment officers overthrew him after less than two years and then orchestrated a highly controlled transition to elected civilian rule. A significant push for a transition to civilian rule came from within the military: a growing current of senior officers viewed indefinite military government as damaging to the military institution and likely to result in ongoing civil conflict. These same officers also expected to be able to control the transition and any civilian government that resulted.[4]

Thus, the de facto governments that followed the collapse of established regimes in both El Salvador and Guatemala failed to achieve sustained legitimacy, capacity to govern, or stability. In line with the predictions of Shain and Linz, internal conflicts within these regimes contributed to instability, and their lack of constitutional standing undercut their claims for popular support. The Salvadoran junta's policies actually accelerated the growth of insurgency, while Guatemalan de facto governments turned the tide against the insurgents through mass murder in the countryside. Neither government had any prospects for achieving lasting order and legitimacy, and so both

---

2. Mark Peceny, *Democracy at the Point of Bayonets* (University Park: Pennsylvania State University Press, 1999), 115–147.

3. Author interview with Juan Vicente Maldonado (executive director of the National Association of Private Enterprise of El Salvador, 1978–87), August 24, 1989, San Salvador.

4. Jennifer Schirmer, *The Guatemalan Military Project: A Violence Called Democracy* (Philadelphia: University of Pennsylvania Press, 1998); and George Black, *Garrison Guatemala* (New York: Monthly Review Press, 1984).

created civilian governments to take over governance by the mid-1980s. It thus fell to successor civilian governments, elected from among parties from the political center and right, to continue the counterinsurgency efforts and eventually negotiate peace agreements that ended the civil conflicts through further democratization.

Partially Democratic Interim Governments

El Salvador

Ironically, El Salvador's initial transition to democracy produced an outcome that was unacceptable to the United States, ultimately leading to an undemocratic political intervention by the U.S. government. The 1982 constituent assembly elections pitted the Christian Democrats against two conservative parties, the former official National Conciliation Party (PCN) and the newly formed National Republican Alliance (ARENA). The Left did not (and could not) participate openly. While the PDC won a plurality, together ARENA and PCN had won more seats than the PDC and sought to install ARENA party founder Roberto D'Aubuisson as provisional president. D'Aubuisson, a retired army major, had been deeply involved in domestic intelligence and death squad operations during the previous military government. After the 1979 coup, he had led various efforts to overthrow the JRG by force. The United States viewed him as an unacceptable choice and pressured the Salvadoran military to prevent his ascent. In his stead, Alvaro Magaña, a banker with no strong party affiliation but close personal ties to the military, was sworn in as interim president.[5]

Magaña governed competently and oversaw a marked increase in the size and capabilities of the Salvadoran military. Yet he presided over continued extreme human rights violations, which began to decline only after the United States sent both Vice President George Bush and CIA director William Casey to hand deliver lists of officers who should be removed from troop commands. Magaña's own political legitimacy was limited by the mode of his selection, and he was never able to exert clear civilian authority vis-à-vis the military. In 1984 José Napoleón Duarte (PDC), who outpolled ARENA's D'Aubuisson, succeeded Magaña as president. Assembly elections in 1985 established a regular legislature with a PDC majority.

The PDC's term in power presents a mixture of accomplishments and failings. In collaboration with the United States, Duarte oversaw some modera-

---

5. Stanley, *Protection Racket State*, 231–233; and author interview with Alvaro Magaña (former Salvadoran president), September 7, 1989, San Salvador.

tion of the human rights abuses of the armed forces, though he never achieved civilian supremacy and no officers were held accountable for abuses. Duarte began a process of negotiation with the Farabundo Martí National Liberation Front (FMLN) but was unable to proceed beyond an initial dramatic meeting. With the improvements in human rights conditions, some leaders associated with the nonguerrilla Left returned to the country to begin exploring their political prospects. Duarte was unable to move ahead with additional land reforms or other measures to address socioeconomic grievances. Police reforms met with little success, as did efforts to improve the judiciary. The war remained in a stalemate; the economy remained relatively weak despite massive U.S. assistance and remittances from Salvadorans living abroad. Corruption and economic mismanagement took a toll on the PDC's political standing; the business community in particular continued to feel excluded from economic policymaking.

While nominally supporting the PDC, the United States began building a new, more democratic Right through investments in a think tank known as the Salvadoran Foundation for Economic and Social Development (FUSADES). Prominently located adjacent to the new U.S. embassy, FUSADES served as an ideological incubator for a more moderate, constructively neoliberal ARENA party. Promoted and funded by the United States Agency for International Development ($67 million between 1985 and 1987), FUSADES's staff of professional economists produced extensive analyses of regulatory bottlenecks in the Salvadoran economy while also offering seminars and technical assistance designed to promote nontraditional exports. For the first time, the modernizing sectors of the Salvadoran business community had an institutional base, and FUSADES helped them to develop a coherent critique of the statist policies of the Christian Democrats. The foundation's analysis, although economically conservative, also emphasized the view that if a market economy were to be successful, a country must first develop a social consensus around the value of market mechanisms.[6] This new capacity to formulate pro-business economic proposals in turn reinforced the more moderate sectors of ARENA.

During the Duarte years, ARENA underwent a process of internal transformation. Faced with U.S. obstruction, the party leaders debated among themselves. Hard-liners wanted to stick to ARENA's radical Right platforms, while moderates, such as coffee and pharmaceuticals magnate Alfredo Cristiani, favored a milder, more business-oriented style that placed less emphasis on

---

6. Kenneth Lance Johnson, *Between Revolution and Democracy: Business Elites and the State in El Salvador during the 1980s*, PhD diss., Tulane University (Ann Arbor: University Microfilms Incorporated, 1993), 213–274; and Herman Rosa, "El papel de la asistencia de AID en el fortalecimiento de nuevas instituciones del sector privado y en la transformación global de la economía salvadoreña: El caso FUSADES" (paper presented at the 17th Congress of the Latin American Studies Association, Los Angeles, September 27, 1992).

organized violence and that could appeal to a broader constituency.[7] In a surprise move in 1988, D'Aubuisson threw his support behind Cristiani, who became party president and then ARENA candidate for the national presidency in 1989.

The shift in ARENA reflected the culmination of various factors. Hardliners within the party had been weakened by the involvement of ARENA members in a kidnapping ring that was preying on wealthy businesspeople. Many of the old-guard oligarchs who had supported the party in the early days had left El Salvador. Business associations were increasingly dominated by younger, more internationally sophisticated business leaders who were less convinced by the reactionary project. In various ways, the war changed the material interests of the capitalist class: coffee growers with plantations in the eastern part of the country could not operate their farms. Many turned their attentions to other economic opportunities presented by the massive flow of remittances from Salvadorans abroad. As commercial agriculture waned and other sectors expanded, important sectors of the elite became less dependent on the labor-repressive services of the military.[8] This shift in the business community was reflected within the party. Moreover, by 1988, the party had seven years of experience with legislative negotiation, bargaining, and playing by (and exploiting) electoral rules.[9] ARENA leaders came to recognize the advantages of building as broad a political base as possible and of having at least the grudging acceptance of the United States.

In the 1988 assembly and municipal elections, ARENA proved its vote-getting ability, winning an absolute majority of seats in the legislature and an overwhelming 70 percent of mayoralties. It used its newfound strength to hamstring PDC president Napoleón Duarte during his final year in office and to build up strong local political machines based on patronage. For the 1989 presidential campaign, ARENA mobilized large numbers of young people and used its financial advantage to convey an image of youthful energy, style, and success. In the presidential race, ARENA received only slightly more votes than in previous elections, but in a context of declining turnout, it was enough to win.

The emergence of ARENA paved the way for the peace process that eventually brought the transitional period to an end. Thus, however imperfect, the partial democracy established between 1982 and 1985 had important effects in establishing norms of electoral competition, contributing to party formation and moderation, and creating a gradually less violent environ-

---

7. Daniel Wolf, "ARENA in the Arena: Factors in the Accommodation of the Salvadoran Right to Pluralism and the Broadening of the Political System," *LASA Forum* 23, no. 1 (Summer 1992): 10–18.

8. Elisabeth Jean Wood, *Forging Democracy from Below: Insurgent Transitions in South Africa and El Salvador* (Cambridge: Cambridge University Press, 2000), 52–77.

9. Ibid., 13.

ment in which a broader range of political opinions could be expressed. At the same time, it also brought leaders of the business community more directly into the political and policymaking process, breaking their previous decades-long habit of deputizing the military to look after their interests.

Once in office, President Cristiani moved quickly to open negotiations with the FMLN rebels. Initially, these talks went nowhere, as the military very publicly vetoed any concessions to the insurgents. In November 1989, the FMLN rebels occupied and held parts of the capital city for more than a week. This offensive was militarily costly for the FMLN, which suffered heavy losses to government airpower. However, the episode also embarrassed the military, which was almost completely unprepared. Moreover, the military reacted by murdering six Jesuit priests and two witnesses at the University of Central America. This placed U.S. military assistance in jeopardy.

These events moved both Cristiani and the FMLN leadership to seek UN mediation. Negotiations began anew in 1990 and culminated in January 1992 with the signing of final accords that opened the political system to the Left, disarmed the rebels, and greatly reduced the powers of the armed forces. ARENA proved to have substantial political capacity to negotiate independently of the armed forces and further proved able to implement difficult aspects of the accords. In the midst of the peace negotiations, legislative assembly elections took place in which a newly formed party of the Left, the Democratic Convergence, won a respectable 17 percent of the vote. The Left's ability to do so well despite little time to prepare encouraged the FMLN to go forward with substantive talks. (I will return to the subject of implementation in detail later on in the chapter.)

Guatemala

Less than a year after overthrowing General Ríos, General Mejía Victores held partially competitive elections for a constituent assembly. The constitution-writing process took nine months and was followed by the election of a new civilian executive. Christian Democrat Vinicio Cerezo Arévalo won a strong majority and assumed the presidency at the beginning of 1986. Cerezo is widely quoted as stating that he held only 30 percent of the power, and indeed he was threatened with coups d'état throughout his presidency and was thus sharply constrained in his ability to address Guatemala's numerous political and economic challenges.[10] The military, under the rubric of counterinsurgency, had put in place a comprehensive system of social and political control at the local level. Military authorities exercised de facto control over local and regional development policies through euphemistically named Inter-Institutional Coordinating

---

10. James Painter, *Guatemala: False Hope, False Freedom* (London: Catholic Institute for International Relations and the Latin American Bureau, 1989), 85.

Councils.[11] Nearly one million peasants were forced to participate in Civilian Self Defense Patrols, which served mainly to give local military commanders control over the whereabouts and activities of residents.[12] Extensive corruption and criminal activity continued within the military.[13] Cerezo was occasionally able to exert authority over the military on specific issues, but he proved unable to crack military control over day-to-day governance. Coup attempts in 1988 and 1989 reduced Cerezo's ambitions to simply surviving his term in office and handing the presidency to a civilian successor.

As was the case in El Salvador, the Christian Democrats (DCG) suffered considerable erosion of political support during their term in power. The 1990 elections brought in a new president, Jorge Serrano, who lacked strong backing from any permanent political party. Serrano undertook some important initiatives, including initial peace talks with the Guatemalan Revolutionary National Union (URNG) rebels. Frustrated by governing without a reliable congressional majority, however, Serrano attempted to follow the model of Alberto Fujimori of Peru by closing the legislature and the Supreme Court.

This looked like a massive setback for the nascent Guatemalan democracy, but reactions to the event actually demonstrated that democratic norms were already taking root. A multiclass movement demanded Serrano's ouster, and key elements of the military leadership shifted against the coup. Ultimately, the Constitutional Court ordered his removal, and the military stood ready to enforce that order. Congress elected former human rights counsel Ramiro De León Carpio to serve out the balance of Serrano's term. De León faced similar challenges in governing without party support; however, his survival in office reinforced democratic rules, and he was able to make further progress in talks with the URNG rebels, reaching four substantive agreements and advancing negotiations on a fifth.

In January 1996 Alvaro Arzú, representing the National Advancement Party (PAN), succeeded De León. Arzú narrowly defeated a more conservative candidate from the Guatemalan Republican Front (FRG), a party headed by former dictator Efraín Ríos Montt. Arzú quickly completed negotiations with the URNG rebels, signing final accords in December 1996.

The period of interim governance leading up to the peace accords in Guatemala presents a mix of accomplishments and limitations. In contrast to El Salvador, there was comparatively little conservative party building. The political Right remained deeply divided over economic policies, how

---

11. Suzanne Jonas, *The Battle for Guatemala* (Boulder, Colo.: Westview, 1991), 150, 165.

12. Margaret Popkin, *Civil Patrols and Their Legacy* (Washington, D.C.: Robert F. Kennedy Center for Human Rights, June 1996).

13. Susan Peacock and Adriana Beltrán, *Hidden Powers in Post-Conflict Guatemala: Illegal Armed Groups and the Forces Behind Them* (Washington, D.C.: Washington Office on Latin America, 2003).

open the economy should be, the role of the state, and the role of the armed forces. The PAN and the FRG both competed for votes from traditional conservative constituencies, including portions of the business and commercial agriculture sectors, Hispanic (nonindigenous) smallholders, urban middle classes, and indigenous communities in some rural areas. The most reactionary, pro-military elements supported the FRG. As later became clear when Alfonso Portillo of the FRG was elected president in 1999, the party was deeply entwined with elements of organized crime (the so-called "hidden powers"), weakening its potential appeal for much of the business community.[14] Relative to the FRG, the PAN positioned itself as representative of the modernized, pro-neoliberal sectors of the business community. In contrast to ARENA, the PAN was newer and lacked both political experience and a clear, unified agenda. Guatemala thus had a highly fragmented and unstable party system going into the crucial period of peace implementation.

Peace Processes and Final Stages of Transition

In both countries, the period of partially democratic governance built increased support for liberal norms, even within the factions of the business communities that initially supported authoritarian solutions. During this period, actors in both countries built habits of negotiation and compromise, and parties of the Right, as well as nascent parties of the Left, gained a degree of confidence in their own political viability in a competitive system. Once the UN-mediated negotiations got under way in each country, the governments and rebels quickly converged upon liberal norms as the basis for any peace settlement. This should by no means be taken for granted, given the nonliberal, power-sharing approaches to civil war settlements sometimes attempted elsewhere in the world.

El Salvador and Guatemala entered the final, peace implementation stage of transition under similar conditions. The peace agreements themselves looked superficially similar. Both required (1) the rebels to disarm; (2) legal acceptance of former rebel organizations as political parties; (3) the armed forces to relinquish internal security roles and confine themselves to defense against external enemies; (4) the government to create new civilian police forces; (5) intelligence reforms; (6) strengthening and professionalization of the judiciary; (7) material assistance to demobilizing combatants; and (8) truth commissions with international representation that would investigate and report on past human rights crimes. Both agreements were achieved through UN mediation, and both mandated UN verification missions.

---

14. Ibid.

Elections were to go forward in accordance with constitutionally mandated schedules but with a broader spectrum of political parties able to participate. The international community was not given any specific mandate with respect to elections in either country, though in both cases international monitoring took place.

There were differences in how the agreements addressed socioeconomic reforms. The Salvadoran accords delegated socioeconomic questions to a forum consisting of labor, business, and government representatives. The accords also provided for land transfers and other economic support to civilian supporters of the FMLN who lived in high-conflict areas. The Guatemalan peace agreement provided little for the noncombatant URNG supporters, but it laid out broad requirements for the state to increase its tax revenues and associated social spending. It also included language that could be interpreted as requiring the government to address historical usurpation of indigenous lands (potentially a very expansive and explosive undertaking in Guatemala!), as well as reforms to increase the accessibility of government services, justice, and education in indigenous languages. The Salvadoran accords included provision for an Ad Hoc Commission charged with evaluating the records of military officers and determining which of them were appropriate for military service in a democracy.

The Salvadoran government eventually delivered on almost everything promised, although with delays and resistance on some issues. The government was initially reluctant to create the new civilian police and tried to maintain existing security forces that should have been demobilized. The FMLN set very ambitious goals regarding how much land would be transferred to its former combatants and civilian supporters, and the government refused to comply with the FMLN's demands. These disputes ultimately required arbitration. The Ad Hoc Commission surprised most observers by calling for the removal of 102 officers from the armed forces, including the minister and vice minister of defense and the entire high command. Several of the top officers resisted and finally retired only after the United States made $11 million in aid conditional on their departure.[15] In the end, however, all elements of the accords were implemented, and in ways that satisfied the high standards set by the UN mission. A series of elections took place, beginning with simultaneous presidential, legislative, and municipal races in 1994. As of 2005, ARENA continued to dominate the political scene after winning the presidency in three consecutive races. But ARENA faced strong competition from the FMLN, particularly in the legislature and in municipalities.

In Guatemala, in contrast, little of what was agreed to was actually implemented. The military's role was never formally changed; the government

---

15. Charles Call, "Assessing El Salvador's Transitions from Civil War to Peace," in *Ending Civil Wars: The Implementation of Peace Agreements,* ed. Stephen John Stedman, Donald Rothchild, and Elizabeth Cousens, 383–420 (Boulder, Colo.: Lynne Reinner, 2002).

failed to raise taxes and social spending; the civilian police consisted initially of the old police in new uniforms; and many aspects of the indigenous and socioeconomic accords remained unfulfilled. As the civilian police force was expanded, it was done in a way that guaranteed its ineffectiveness and its subordination to an officer corps drawn entirely from the old, military-controlled police.[16] The military itself remained largely independent of civilian authority. It carried out its own limited purge of corrupt officers and independently demobilized its paramilitary organizations, leaving substantial intelligence-gathering and social control mechanisms in place at the local level. Intelligence reforms languished. Judicial and prosecutorial reforms have moved very slowly, and the performance of the judiciary has been far from adequate. Accomplishments included the demobilization of the rebels, the legalization of the URNG as a political party, and a series of elections that were generally considered free and fair. There were a few successful prosecutions of human rights violators, largely through the very intensive and courageous actions of Guatemalan non-governmental organizations (NGOs), with international support.[17]

What accounts for these contrasts in the capacity of the Salvadoran and Guatemalan interim governments to implement change and usher in a new regime? The following section will review several factors that appear to contribute to these divergent outcomes: (1) party strength; (2) the strength and negotiating capacity of insurgents; (3) the specificity of the framework for reform provided by the accords; (4) the capacity of old institutions to resist change; (5) the inherited mechanisms for constitutional reform; and (6) the political capacity of the international verification missions.

Party Strength

By the time peace talks began, El Salvador's ARENA had eight years of political experience and had forged a comparatively strong and unified agenda. It had strong electoral legitimacy and a diverse support base that included strong middle-class and lower-class constituencies, as well as the oligarchic families who had helped found the party in the first place. It had unassailable anti-Communist credentials. It had established and sustained a high degree of party discipline in the legislature, even on controversial issues. These resources positioned the party well to negotiate, and later to enforce, a deal that required substantial sacrifices by the armed forces.

---

16. William D. Stanley, "Business as Usual? Justice and Policing Reform in Postwar Guatemala," in *Constructing Justice and Security After Wars*, ed. Charles T. Call, 113–155 (Washington, D.C.: United States Institute of Peace Press, 2007).

17. Ibid.

In contrast, the PAN in Guatemala was a comparatively recent party that had not worked out its internal differences. It also faced a strong challenge from the Right from the FRG. After narrowly beating the FRG in the 1995 elections, the PAN had sufficient coherence and clout to negotiate the final accords with the weakened URNG, but then it proved unable to deliver majority congressional votes for crucial tax increases and early congressional approval of constitutional reforms. The PAN executive failed to maintain clear civilian authority over the armed forces, and it showed poor party discipline.

The PAN's weakness is evident in its electoral defeat by Alfonso Portillo (FRG) in 1999, just two years after peace implementation began. Portillo's administration degenerated into extensive criminality and corruption and made little further progress on the many unfulfilled elements of the peace accords. The FRG administration was so damaging to the country that individuals with deep pockets in the business community engaged in a new round of efforts at party building in the run-up to elections in late 2003. Most of the money went into a new coalition known as the Great National Alliance (GANA); other funds went to the National Unity for Hope (UNE). GANA won the 2003 presidential elections, but it failed to achieve a legislative majority.[18] Whether GANA will develop a sustained capacity to govern remains to be seen.

Thus, in contrast to El Salvador, neither of the Guatemalan parties that negotiated the peace accords have prospered nor maintained their prominent political role. The PAN has withered to a minority role in the legislature, and the URNG has polled only a minor share of the national vote since it was legalized.

Rebel Strength and the Specificity of the Accords

Differences in the political strength of the rebels and the specificity of the reforms they were able to demand during negotiations account for part of the contrast in outcomes during the final stages of interim governance. In El Salvador, the FMLN was in a fairly strong negotiating position. It had withstood repeated military offensives in various parts of the country, had been able to attack targets in the capital city, had the ability to substantially interfere with the economy, and had, in the final stages of the conflict, obtained and used antiaircraft weapons that partially neutralized the government's advantage in airpower. ARENA leaders perceived economic opportunities slipping away as the war continued and thus felt some urgency to reach a settlement. Astutely, the FMLN set aside most

---

18. Mike Leffert, "Guatemala Elects Berger without Legislative Majority," *NotiCen* (January 8, 2004); and Mike Leffert, "Guatemalan Businessmen Pursue Lost Power on the Campaign Trail," *NotiCen* (July 24, 2003), both available at ladb.unm.edu.

socioeconomic demands and focused their political leverage on demilitarizing the state.

The resulting peace accords incorporated specific reforms to the constitution, with the language already drafted; they included as an annex the secondary legislation needed to create the new police and provided extensive details regarding personnel selection, educational requirements, organization, doctrine, use of force, and mechanisms of control and internal discipline. The annex also provided detailed requirements regarding military demobilization, change in doctrine, and civilian oversight. Overall, the accords were concrete in their requirements, making it politically more difficult for the government to fudge during implementation. Moreover, the FMLN maintained its political coherence following demobilization, reflecting their former military strength, the extent of their popular support, and their extensive connections abroad. When there were delays or problems with the government's implementation, the FMLN generally pushed hard for government compliance.

In contrast, the URNG in Guatemala was largely spent as a military force. The civilian government had incentives to end the conflict and reap whatever political and economic benefits might be available by doing so; there was little sense of urgency, however, and the rebels were not in a position to insist upon strong, specific measures in the accords. On close inspection, it becomes clear that much of the language of the Guatemalan accords is equivocal. Firm, quantifiable commitments to deliver outcomes were few. Moreover, the specifics of constitutional reforms were not preagreed, and the provisions for police and military reform were very general. The drafting of specific measures was delegated to a series of postdisarmament citizen committees that varied substantially in their effectiveness and authority. The URNG was caught up in a humiliating scandal in the final stages of the negotiations resulting from their kidnapping for ransom an elderly woman from a prominent family. From the outset of implementation, the URNG had little remaining leverage.[19]

The Capacity of Old Institutions to Resist Change

Massive state reforms inherently generate resistance from those individuals and institutions that have vested interests in the previous order. Among those opposed to the democratizing transitions required by the peace accords were elements of the armed forces, the intelligence services, the existing police, the reactionary factions within the judiciary, the members

---

19. William Stanley and David Holiday, "Broad Participation, Diffuse Responsibility: Peace Implementation in Guatemala," in Stedman et al., *Ending Civil Wars*, 421–462.

of political parties whose interests were threatened by the reforms, and some social elites (particularly in Guatemala).

The Guatemalan military was in a stronger position to resist change than its Salvadoran counterpart for two reasons: first, whereas the Guatemalan military had dominated the rebels and prevented them from significantly disrupting the economy, the Salvadoran military (FAES) had been fought to a politico-military draw; and second, whereas the Guatemalan military relied mainly on domestic resources, the FAES had become highly dependent on U.S. aid flows that became uncertain after the 1989 Jesuit murders and declined sharply after the final peace was signed. Once U.S. policy shifted firmly in favor of a negotiated settlement, the FAES had few options but to comply.

FAES leaders sought to resist the Ad Hoc Commission process, but ultimately they had to comply. The FAES initially engaged in petty resistance, such as stripping all the hardware out of buildings before handing them over to the National Civilian Police (PNC). Ultimately, however, the FAES could not resist substantial cuts in its budget and force levels, with the result that it is now smaller and less politically consequential than the civilian-controlled PNC. In Guatemala, such a civilian-controlled purge of the military was completely out of the question. Moreover, the Guatemalan military was able to obtain substantial supplemental appropriations after the end of the war, achieved through direct transfers of funds originally allocated to such new institutions as the civilian police. Key domestic intelligence organizations of the Guatemalan military resisted being dismantled until several years after the peace accords were implemented.

With respect to the judiciary, the contrast between the cases is less clear. In El Salvador, the UN Truth Commission recommended the removal of the head of the Supreme Court, Mauricio Gutiérrez Castro, whom the commission found to have been complicit in upholding a system of impunity for gross violations of human rights. Gutiérrez responded that "only God" could remove him; he and his colleagues served out the balance of their terms. Efforts at judicial reform and improvements in human rights compliance remained stalled until the post-1994 Legislative Assembly selected new members for the Supreme Court under new procedures designed to depoliticize the courts. In Guatemala, there was some support for reform within senior levels of the judiciary, and senior jurists contributed to designing significant reforms to the system. Resistance was found more at the lower levels of the courts, where judges and administrators adapted reluctantly to the new Criminal Procedure Code.[20]

With respect to police, the start-from-scratch design for the new PNC in El Salvador minimized resistance by the old guard. A limited number of members of the old national police were incorporated into the PNC, along with a

---

20. Stanley, "Justice and Public Security Reform."

limited number of former FMLN combatants. They, along with new civilian recruits (who would make up the majority of the PNC), underwent a comprehensive training program that created a substantially new corporate and professional identity. Problems arose when certain specialized units, including detective and antinarcotics units trained by the United States, were incorporated wholesale into the PNC without significant retraining and resocialization. These units attempted to resist the new force's doctrine, engaged in human rights violations and corruption, and were ultimately disbanded at the insistence of the UN mission.[21] Guatemala's old-order police had more opportunities to resist change, since most of them were "recycled" into the new force with minimal additional training. Initially, there was no means by which new civilians could be brought into the middle and upper command ranks of the police, so the organizational norms were set and reinforced entirely by leaders drawn from the old police. The results, not surprisingly, were poor performance, high levels of abuses, and a high degree of politicization.[22]

Established political parties in El Salvador resisted change mainly through reluctance to register new voters who might disproportionately support the FMLN. By law, the Supreme Electoral Tribunal (TSE) consisted of personnel drawn from the parties already represented in the Legislative Assembly. This was problematic during the final transition since the Left, which constituted nearly half the eligible electorate, had been excluded from the political system. The United Nations estimated that as of August 1993, some 768,000 voters (27 percent of eligible voters) lacked the required electoral documentation and were not on the voter roles.[23] Incumbent parties in the legislature had little incentive to address this problem, and the TSE dragged its feet. Ultimately, the UN peace mission took a very active role in voter registration, picking up TSE employees at their homes, delivering them to their offices, providing generators and photocopy machines, and closely supervising their work. Some two hundred UN civilian police were temporarily assigned to this effort. This rather intrusive approach resulted in much of the work getting done and a more than 50 percent reduction in the number of unregistered eligible voters.

In contrast, the Guatemalan parties were not so much resistant as ineffectual. Voter registration was comparatively uncontroversial, probably because the URNG had less potential for attracting new voters. Existing parties thus had less reason to exclude voters. The major political parties coincided in supporting the broad constitutional reform package, yet that package was

21. See Charles T. Call, "El Salvador: The Mugging of a Success Story," in Call, *Constructing Security and Justice*.

22. Stanley, "Justice and Public Security Reform."

23. Ian Johnstone, *Rights and Reconciliation in El Salvador* (Boulder, Colo.: Lynne Rienner, 1995), 52, cited in Charles T. Call, "Assessing El Salvador's Transition from Civil War to Peace," 383–420 in Stedman et al., *Ending Civil Wars*.

defeated in the 1999 public referendum (see below), signaling the weakness of the parties relative to powerful, antireform social groups.

The Inherited Mechanisms for Constitutional Reform

The constitutional reform procedures in El Salvador actually facilitated the finalization of the peace accords and simplified their implementation, while those in Guatemala ultimately and definitively prevented implementation of key aspects of the democratizing reforms. Both accords called for reforms to establish civilian authority over the armed forces, to exclude the military from domestic security roles, and to limit the military's powers to interfere in politics. Reforms were also needed to change judicial appointment procedures. In Guatemala, the indigenous accord required several constitutional changes related to the collective cultural and linguistic rights of indigenous peoples.

In El Salvador, the 1983 constitution required amendments to be approved by a majority of one legislative assembly, followed by a two-thirds majority of the next legislative assembly.[24] This requirement, in combination with the electoral calendar, created a deadline for the government to accept proposed constitutional reforms early in the negotiations in 1991. Both negotiating parties knew that if the sitting assembly in April 1991 did not approve a package of constitutional reforms, implementation of the peace process would be delayed an additional three years. Faced with this constitutionally imposed deadline, the government of Alfredo Cristiani requested and obtained legislative approval of major constitutional reforms. This accomplishment greatly increased the confidence of the FMLN rebels regarding Cristiani's intensions. It also demonstrated ARENA's political capacity to deliver on concessions made at the bargaining table. Subsequent ratification by the new assembly elected in 1991 was relatively uncontroversial.

In Guatemala, constitutional reform procedures were less auspicious. The constitution of 1985 required a popular referendum in addition to legislative approval. Rather than allowing an up or down vote on the whole package of fifty constitutional reforms, a court ruling required the government to group the reforms into four ballot questions. To the chagrin of Guatemalans who supported the reforms (including all the major political parties), all four ballot questions were defeated by the voters by margins of roughly two to one, reflecting a particularly strong no vote in the capital city.[25] Turnout was only about 18 percent (21 percent in the capital) despite months of publicity

---

24. *Constitución de la República 1983, Reformas de 1991/1992*, Title IX, Art. 248, 95–96.

25. If one discounts the capital city vote, two of the four ballot questions (those related to social and cultural rights and to reform of the judiciary) would have passed.

and get-out-the-vote work, much of it funded by international donors. The defeat was attributable to at least two main factors: a powerful, expensive antireform publicity campaign during the final few weeks before the vote, which portrayed the reforms in a negative, almost apocalyptic light; and public ignorance regarding the content of the reforms, which were complex and easily misunderstood. The defeat of the reforms in May 1999 definitively blocked implementation of much of the institutional transformation agreed to by the government and the rebels.

The International Role

Neither case involved the kind and extent of international intervention that would pose a risk of undermining the legitimacy of national governments. UN verification missions were the international keystones in both peace processes. These missions—the United Nations Observer Mission (ONUSAL) in El Salvador and the United Nations Verification Mission (MINUGUA) in Guatemala—were of course subject to occasional criticism. Right-wing commentators in El Salvador characterized the UN observer mission as the "white plague" (in reference to the white UN vehicles), and indiscretions by UN staff received a great deal of publicity. But much of the political Right and the business community accepted the UN role and found it generally constructive. Attitudes toward the United Nations in Guatemala were sometimes more menacing and resentfully nationalistic, leading the United Nations to maintain a low profile.

ONUSAL played an assertive verification role and assumed direct duties with respect to voter registration and public security. Overall, ONUSAL was highly effective in its mix of ongoing mediation, authoritative interpretation of the accords, verification and forceful criticism of the parties for noncompliance, and coaching and field training of personnel in new governmental institutions. ONUSAL was deployed as a human rights observer mission for eighteen months before the final accords were signed. With the beginning of the cease-fire, ONUSAL quickly and conspicuously expanded its role to include military, police, and, later, electoral divisions. While not interventionist in comparison with missions in more troubled cases such as Cambodia, ONUSAL was active, politically high profile, and sufficiently strong to defend the integrity of the transition. At crucial moments ONUSAL was backed by senior, New York–based UN officials who visited El Salvador and brought to bear the political influence of the Security Council. In cases where the FMLN had agreed to tolerate government violations of the accords in exchange for concessions in which it was interested, the United Nations took principled positions, insisting on compliance with the letter of the accords.

ONUSAL usually won these fights, although sometimes after significant delay. ONUSAL's main weakness was a tendency to displace local capacity, particularly in human rights monitoring. ONUSAL eventually shifted to an institution-building strategy, but it did so too late to have a fully beneficial influence on local human rights capacity. UN peace building in El Salvador was undercut throughout by the zeal of international financial institutions in promoting structural adjustment at a time when tensions over socioeconomic inequities were high.[26]

MINUGUA played a much weaker verification role. First, MINUGUA was constrained by the length of the peace process: it was deployed for more than two years as a human rights mission prior to the signing of the final accords and was slow to transition to a comprehensive mission, in part because of resource constraints. As a result, many Guatemalans (including otherwise well-informed business elites) never realized that MINUGUA's mandate required it to verify the accords in their entirety. Second, because MINUGUA was a UN General Assembly mission, it lacked Security Council involvement. In turn, this reduced the extent of perceived big-power commitment, affecting MINUGUA's ability to compel compliance. Third, the very vague, unverifiable requirements of the peace accords gave MINUGUA little to work with in pressuring the government to move forward with agreed-to reforms, as it was difficult to point to any specific points of the accords against which to measure progress. Finally, MINUGUA may also have been hampered by the fact that the chief of the mission, Jean Arnault, had earlier been the lead mediator/negotiator on behalf of the United Nations. It proved difficult to shift from the confidence-building role of mediator to the more confrontational role of verifier. In the wake of difficult cases such as Somalia and Bosnia, the United Nations was under considerable political pressure to have a success in Guatemala, which provided disincentives for political confrontations with the government. In interviews, MINUGUA staff expressed frustration with the mission's very diplomatic positions on obvious and grave violations of the accords by the government.

Nevertheless, MINUGUA introduced some effective innovations: it operated on a shoestring and drew heavily on UN volunteers for lower-level staffing, an experiment that was generally successful. Early on, the mission began to focus on institution building, in contrast to ONUSAL's late start on capacity building. Unfortunately, MINUGUA's institution-building strategy met with

---

26. Roland Paris, *At War's End: Building Peace After Civil Conflict* (Cambridge: Cambridge University Press, 2005), 12–128; and Alvaro de Soto and Graciana del Castillo, "Obstacles to Peacebuilding," *Foreign Policy* 94 (Spring 1994): 69–83.

limited success because of the government's weakness and lack of commitment in such key areas as police, judicial, military, and intelligence reform.[27]

MINUGUA benefited from a high degree of consensus between the mission and international financial institutions (IFIs) regarding the need to increase taxation and government expenditures. Whereas in El Salvador the peace mission and the IFIs had clashed over the priorities of peacemaking and structural adjustment, the usually austere World Bank, the International Monetary Fund (IMF), and the International Development Bank agreed that Guatemala's state was clearly too small to meet public social needs. They endorsed MINUGUA's view that the government should tax and spend. Unfortunately, the Arzú administration lacked the will or capacity to follow through on raising taxes. Faced with relatively minor opposition and a few demonstrations, Arzú withdrew a measure that would have begun the process of increasing state revenues. Thus, one of the few objective, quantifiable, and verifiable government commitments in the peace accords went unimplemented.

Conclusion

The early phases of the Salvadoran and Guatemalan transitions illustrate the challenges facing de facto interim governments overseeing transitions from one regime type to another. The juntas in El Salvador and the military governments in Guatemala had no basis in constitutional procedures and were patently illegitimate in the eyes of much of the public. While the Salvadoran juntas initially put forward a vision of socioeconomic reform and moderation, this quickly wore thin and lost credibility as the military and intelligence services systematically murdered many of the ostensible beneficiaries of these reforms. Moreover, the tactical alliance between the military and the Christian Democrats was strained from the start. The Guatemalan governments of Ríos Montt and Mejía Victores lacked liberalizing visions, faced increasing international isolation, and had no capacity to move toward sustainable governance without first permitting a transition to civilian rule.

---

27. This discussion of the two missions is, of course, extremely compressed. Coauthors and I have treated these questions at length in the following papers: William Stanley and Mark Peceny, "Liberal Social Reconstruction and the Resolution of Civil Wars in Central America," *International Organization* 55, no. 1 (Winter 2001): 149–182; William Stanley and David Holiday, "Peace Mission Strategy and Domestic Actors: United Nations Mediation, Verification and Institution Building in El Salvador," *International Peacekeeping* 4, no. 2 (Summer 1997): 22–49; and David Holiday and William Stanley, "Under the Best of Circumstances: ONUSAL and the Challenges of Verification and Institution-building in El Salvador," in *Peacemaking and Democratization in the Western Hemisphere,* ed. Tommie Sue Montgomery, 37–65 (Coral Gables, Fla.: North-South Center Press at the University of Miami, 2000).

Even after partial transitions to democracy, neither of the successor civilian governments achieved full legitimacy, capacity to govern the national territory, or stability. The obvious role of the military as a parallel power at the national level—and in some cases as the only de facto authority at the local level—undercut legitimacy. The internal instability of the military, particularly in Guatemala, and its very tenuous deference to civilian authority, created a constant risk of coups. While the Guatemalan military's counterinsurgency campaign was so effective as to prevent the URNG from seriously threatening the state in the latter stages of the conflict, the military was nonetheless unable to eradicate the URNG from many areas of the country. Only a political settlement ultimately made that possible.

Partial democracies have obvious advantages as interim governments. Where the incumbent regime has a degree of domestic political legitimacy, the scope for international involvement can be more limited. Issues of sovereignty and international legal authority are less likely to arise; there is also less risk that international missions will create dependency or undercut the legitimacy of successor governments and institutions. There is a downside to such domestic legitimacy, however. Whereas internationalized interim governments (neo-trustee types) can scale their capacity up or down in accordance with need (and the degree of commitment of member states), in cases where a partially democratic government is in place, the international community depends almost entirely on the capacity of the local state and regime. International missions may substitute for inadequate state capacity in limited ways or to force interim administrations to more fully comply with peace accords (as ONUSAL did in El Salvador), but the overall outcome depends on local regime capacity.

The El Salvador–Guatemala comparison illustrates this clearly: the failure to implement much of the peace accords in Guatemala was largely attributable to shortcomings of the incumbent administration. Even though international missions in Guatemala emphasized institution building, they could not overcome the obstacles presented by the domestic political system.

Moreover, some democratic institutions are more conducive to effective interim governance than others. The Guatemalan case suggests that procedures requiring direct referenda to accomplish constitutional reform are vulnerable to manipulation, particularly in countries with high levels of illiteracy and political ignorance. The preexisting balance of power between civilian and military authorities appears to be crucial as well.

The El Salvador–Guatemala comparison suggests that interim governance is likely to be more effective where the parties making up the governing coalition have accumulated some years of political experience or have at least achieved a measure of party discipline and coherence. The United States' prolonged effort to shape and moderate ARENA paid off in an interim government with impressive political capacity, while the lack of such party building in Guatemala crippled that peace process.

International actors assisting a partially democratic interim government face real dilemmas if the local government proves to be incoherent. There will be little legal and political latitude for taking over deficient government functions. As a practical matter, international missions may be able to do little more than sit back and watch the interim government stumble.

7

Inchoate Opposition, Divided Incumbents

Muddling toward Democracy in Indonesia, 1998–99

Michael S. Malley

Editors' Note

Michael S. Malley offers up Indonesia as a case study of an incumbent caretaker model of transition from authoritarian rule that was spurred by a combination of internal and external factors. Malley's description of the transitional regime in Indonesia demonstrates that even in this world of increasingly internationalized transitions, internally directed change, first described by waves of Latin Americanists, and shades of which can be seen in William D. Stanley's chapter, can still occur. In Indonesia, a performance-based authoritarian regime was brought down by the East Asian financial crisis of 1997, which had sparked a global currency crisis that undermined the Soeharto regime's hold on power. Soeharto first tried to repress dissent, but ultimately he was forced to make some concessions to liberalization. Limited liberalization then snowballed into a full-blown transition, forcing Soeharto to step down in favor of a domestically appointed and managed caretaker government. During this process, dissent over the right course of action strengthened divisions within the ruling regime, and rivalries within the armed forces critically shaped the resultant transitional processes.

Although the conditions for an incumbent caretaker government were hardly auspicious—Indonesia was deeply divided by communal cleavages—it succeeded in creating the world's largest Muslim democracy. Because Soeharto left office quickly after opposition first surfaced, the opposition was too weak and divided to form a united front and therefore to create a provisional revolutionary regime. The weakness of the opposition and the division within the military allowed the incumbent caretaker, B. J. Habibie, to control the transition, although he left the country and politics after it was achieved. The resultant weak democracy was unable to attack corruption or to fully control the military.

■ ■ ■

Introduction

The economic crisis that began in Asia in mid-1997 touched off a process of political change that made Indonesia the largest democracy in the Muslim world. However, the process was far from smooth. In addition to a national movement pressing for democratization, the country experienced separatist movements and communal conflicts on such a scale that observers inside and outside the country feared it would become another failed state. Despite these challenges, the interim government that ruled Indonesia between May 1998 and October 1999 managed to lay the foundation for a more democratic and decentralized political system, and the country emerged from the interim period to join the ranks of the world's democracies, not its failed states.

Indonesia's interim government came to power when President Soeharto unexpectedly resigned from office and transferred the presidency to his vice president, B. J. Habibie. Massive, widespread protests had been strong enough to crack Soeharto's three-decade-old regime, but they were too weak either to replace it with a revolutionary provisional government or to impose a power-sharing arrangement. With the military riven by internal divisions and unsure of their role in a rapidly changing political environment, the way was open for Habibie to form a government that, in retrospect, closely resembled the "incumbent caretaker model" sketched by Yossi Shain and Juan Linz: members of the outgoing regime controlled the transition, the interim government's term in office was limited by Habibie's commitment to hold elections quickly, and the interim government limited its work mainly to the process of amending and replacing laws that protected the regime from effective political competition.[1] Indeed, the interim government was so successful in the latter regard that its end is easily identified as the day in late October 1999 when Habibie peacefully surrendered power to the country's first competitively elected president.

---

1. See Yossi Shain and Juan Linz, eds., *Between States: Interim Governments and Democratic Transitions*, chapter 3, "The Caretaker Government Model," 52–62 (New York: Cambridge University Press, 1995).

In comparative terms, Indonesia's experience presents several analytical and practical challenges. First, Habibie's government democratized under conditions that were clearly inauspicious for the advent of democracy. In particular, Indonesia had been deeply divided by communal cleavages that had worsened under authoritarian rule. "An incumbent-led transition," according to Shain and Linz, "is less desirable when there are deep-seated historical divisions within society of a national, ethnic, religious, or cultural character."[2] Nonetheless, the Habibie government was able to lay a foundation for electoral democracy and avert state failure. Second, some of the same decisions that made Indonesia's transition to democracy possible also contributed to political instability during the following period. This is especially clear in the choice of electoral institutions, in decisions about the military's role in politics, and in the newly formed relationship between national and subnational governments. Third, the end of the Habibie presidency was not accompanied by the achievement of "effective internal sovereignty."[3] Quite the contrary, under the next president separatist challenges intensified, and law and order was impossible to establish in regions where communal conflicts raged. To explore these challenges, this chapter considers how Indonesia's interim government came into being, the decisions that it made, the challenges that it faced, and the legacies that it has left.

Origins of Indonesia's Interim Government

In contrast to several other cases discussed in this volume, Indonesia's interim government was formed by incumbent politicians in response to the breakdown of an authoritarian regime, not by formerly warring factions following civil war or by foreign agencies seeking to rebuild a collapsed state. In some sense, this meant Indonesia faced a more manageable set of challenges than many other countries. Nevertheless, the conditions that led to the formation of Indonesia's interim regime government included the most severe political and economic crises since Soeharto had established the military-dominated New Order regime in the late 1960s.

On its own, the economic crisis that struck several countries in East Asia and Southeast Asia in 1997–98 did not cause the collapse of Soeharto's government and initiate the process of regime change. Instead, it brought about a political crisis by exacerbating tensions rooted in the regime's repression of political opponents during the mid-1990s. In turn, the political crisis led to a fracturing of the regime and, finally, to Soeharto's resignation and the formation of an interim government.

---

2. Ibid., 53.

3. This criterion of effective internal sovereignty was elaborated by Jessica Piombo and Karen Guttieri in a communication to the volume's authors on August 19, 2005.

The economic crisis that struck several Asian countries in 1997–98 affected Indonesia more severely than any other. In 1998, Indonesia's economy contracted by about 14 percent, while inflation rose to 80 percent. During the previous decade, growth had averaged about 7 percent annually, and government policy had kept inflation below 10 percent. In addition, the country's currency suffered a massive devaluation. From a precrisis level of 2,400 per U.S. dollar, the rupiah swung wildly between 8,000 and 17,000 before settling into a wide band between 7,000 and 9,000 during the tenure of Habibie's interim government in late 1998 and 1999. This result, too, must be measured against prior conditions. For more than a decade before the crisis, Indonesia's financial authorities had managed the currency's value to achieve a consistent annual depreciation of about 3 to 4 percent.[4]

This crisis directly threatened the regime's legitimacy. Ever since Soeharto took power in 1966, he had promised to bring development, not democracy. Relying heavily on the advice of professionally trained economists, his regime achieved "performance legitimacy" by delivering the longest sustained period of economic growth since the pre-Depression era under Dutch colonial rule.[5] From the outset, Soeharto justified political repression as an essential condition for economic growth. In fact, he and his fellow army officers spoke proudly of their success in 1965–67 in "annihilating" what had been the world's third-largest communist movement; more than half a million suspected leftists were killed, and many more were interned for a decade or longer.[6] Those killings laid the foundation for an explicit policy of depoliticizing society and asserting military (mainly army) dominance over the political system.

Soeharto's political system rested on three pillars. One was the appointment of military officers to bureaucratic and political leadership positions at all levels of government. In addition to holding top leadership posts in the cabinet, officers headed provincial and local government and held 20 percent of the seats in national, provincial, and district legislatures. Their presence was so pervasive that by the time the regime collapsed in the late 1990s, about four thousand officers held political and bureaucratic

4. These figures are compiled from the "Survey of Recent Developments" that appears in each issue of the *Bulletin of Indonesian Economic Studies*.

5. On technocratic management of the economy, see John Bresnan, *Managing Indonesia: The Modern Political Economy* (New York: Columbia University Press, 1993); on "performance legitimation," see R. William Liddle, "Soeharto's Indonesia: Personal Rule and Political Institutions," *Pacific Affairs* 58 (1985): 68–90.

6. See, for example, Robert B. Cribb, "Problems in the Historiography of the Killings in Indonesia," in *The Indonesian Killings of 1965–1966: Studies from Java and Bali*, ed. Robert B. Cribb, 1–44 (Clayton, Victoria: Centre of Southeast Asian Studies, Monash University, 1990); and Robert B. Cribb, "How Many Deaths? Problems in the Statistics of Massacre in Indonesia (1965–1966) and East Timor (1975–1980)," in *Violence in Indonesia*, ed. Ingrid Wessel and Georgia Wimhöfer, 82–98 (Hamburg: Abera, 2001).

positions.[7] The second pillar was the regime's political party, Golkar, to which all bureaucrats were required to pledge "monoloyalty" and which enjoyed the strong support of the military. Golkar's command structure paralleled the civilian political structure all the way down to the village level. Third, the government actively disrupted, reorganized, and monitored opposition political parties as well as all manner of social organizations.[8] For instance, in the 1970s it compelled all political parties to merge into two: the larger, Islamically oriented Development Unity Party and the smaller Indonesian Democracy Party, a fusion of Christian and nationalist parties. Candidates from both parties were subject to government screening, and new parties were forbidden. Unsurprisingly, the regime's party secured victory in the general elections held every five years, winning 62.8 to 74.5 percent of the votes.

Despite the severity of the crisis that began in 1997, nine months passed before Indonesians began to mobilize and demand political change. The regime had established a tradition of taking strong measures against its opponents and had intensified repressive policies during the mid-1990s. These policies deterred Indonesians from taking to the streets and deprived them of leaders. In the early 1990s, confident of his grip on power, Soeharto had tolerated a period of "political openness." A loose but broadly based coalition of labor unions, Islamic organizations, and liberal NGOs united behind the smallest opposition party. That party was led, coincidentally, by Megawati Soekarnoputri, the daughter of the man whom Soeharto had deposed a quarter-century earlier. Her chief ally was Abdurrahman Wahid, the leader of the country's largest religious organization, an association of mainly rural Islamic schools. In the 1992 general election, Megawati's party nearly doubled its share of the vote to 14.9 percent and appeared to be gaining momentum across the political spectrum.

To stem the growth of this opposition, the government increasingly resorted to the sort of harsh military tactics it had employed during its early years. In addition to closing down major print media, it jailed labor activists, harassed Wahid's organization, and organized a violent takeover of Megawati's party headquarters in 1996 in order to allow government-selected leaders to run her party. At the next election in 1997, Wahid sought political cover by campaigning for the government's political party alongside Soeharto's daughter. Megawati silently watched as the rump of her former

---

7. International Crisis Group (ICG), *Indonesia: Keeping the Military under Control*, ICG Asia Report no. 9 (September 5, 2000): 4; and Geoffrey Robinson, "Indonesia: On a New Course?" in *Coercion and Governance: The Declining Political Role of the Military in Asia*, ed. Muthiah Alagappa, 234–235 (Stanford, Calif.: Stanford University Press, 2001).

8. See Edward Aspinall, *Opposing Suharto: Compromise, Resistance, and Regime Change in Indonesia* (Stanford, Calif.: Stanford University Press, 2005); and Richard Robison and Vedi Hadiz, *Reorganising Power in Indonesia: The Politics of Oligarchy in an Age of Markets* (London: RoutledgeCurzon, 2004), 120–144.

party garnered only 3.1 percent of the votes and Soeharto's Golkar secured its largest victory ever (74.5 percent).

With major social and political organizations and their leaders sidelined, university students took the lead in mobilizing opposition. The focal point for their efforts was Soeharto's uncontested "reelection" by a largely hand-picked People's Consultative Assembly in March 1998 to a seventh five-year term, and his appointment of a "friends and family" cabinet that seemed more likely to protect its own business interests than to help the country recover from the economic crisis.[9] For several weeks their protests were con-fined to campuses, where they demanded Soeharto's resignation and an end to "corruption, collusion, and nepotism," a signal that the regime's "military-dominated" character had acquired "sultanistic" qualities.[10] Then, in late April, security forces could no longer confine protests to university cam-puses, and hundreds of thousands of people joined in. Some protests turned violent, and in mid-May, while Soeharto was abroad, security forces killed several student protesters at an elite university in Jakarta, touching off three days of rioting in which hundreds of people died.

The turn to violence shocked Soeharto's supporters, fractured the regime, and quickly led to his resignation and the formation of Habibie's interim government. In the days before Soeharto resigned, civilian leaders scrambled to find a way to withdraw their support from him without destroying the regime. Showing little embarrassment, the chairman and four vice chairmen of the assembly that had unanimously "reelected" Soeharto two months ear-lier demanded his resignation. The assembly chairman was one of the most prominent Soeharto loyalists; he had led Golkar to its enormous, if tainted, electoral victory in 1997. The vice chairmen represented each political party as well as the armed forces delegation in the assembly. Privately, about a dozen cabinet ministers withdrew their support for Soeharto and pledged to support Habibie if Soeharto resigned.

The military was deeply split between two Soeharto loyalists, and this proved a crucial factor in the success of Habibie's interim government. On the one side was a former presidential adjutant, General Wiranto, who served as armed forces commander and defense minister; on the other was Soehar-to's son-in-law, General Prabowo Subianto, who headed the army's Strategic Reserve Command, an elite force.[11] During the anti-Soeharto protests, generals aligned with Wiranto often met with the students and appeared

---

9. Michael S. Malley, "The 7th Development Cabinet: Loyal to a Fault?" *Indonesia* 65 (April 1998): 155–178.

10. See Houchang E. Chehabi and Juan Linz, *Sultanistic Regimes* (Baltimore: Johns Hopkins Uni-versity Press, 1998).

11. Their rivalry is well described in Jun Honna, *Military Politics and Democratization in Indonesia* (London: RoutledgeCurzon, 2003), 159–164.

sympathetic to their demands.[12] Prabowo's troops, by contrast, turned out to be responsible for the abduction and probably the shooting of student protesters. They had instigated three days of rioting, burning, looting, raping, and other violence in Jakarta in mid-May, apparently in an effort to demonstrate Wiranto's inability to maintain civil order and thereby undermine his relationship to Soeharto.

This rivalry within the armed forces played a critical role in shaping the transition. Most immediately, it led to Soeharto's resignation when Wiranto persuaded the president that Prabowo was responsible for the violence and assured him of military protection once he left office. The rivalry and its resolution had longer-lasting effects, however. Although Wiranto declared his loyalty to Habibie's government and transferred Prabowo and his associates to less important positions, the officer corps remained divided and lacked a common position on reform. Moreover, the activities of Prabowo's groups further discredited the army in the eyes of a public that had become increasingly critical of the army's involvement in political life. Consequently, at the time Indonesia embarked on its political transition, the military was less than firmly under the control of a Soeharto loyalist (Wiranto) and was too internally fragmented and publicly unpopular to influence decisions about the course of political reform.

In sum, the mid-1990s' legacy of repression mediated the political impact of the economic crisis. This legacy created conditions that favored the emergence of a civilian-dominated, incumbent-led caretaker form of interim government rather than the provisional or power-sharing alternatives that Shain and Linz described. The official opposition, represented by two parties that the regime itself had created and continued to control, was in no position to call for the dictator's ouster, and other social organizations with strong networks and prominent leaders likewise had been intimidated. Although university students were able to muster large numbers of passionate protesters, the suddenness of Soeharto's resignation deprived them of the opportunity to forge a strong organization that could form a provisional government in place of Soeharto and his associates, or even compel Soeharto to enter into a power-sharing arrangement. Indeed, the opposition remained too weak and inchoate even to bargain over the terms of the transition. This situation left Habibie, who had been vice president for only two months, and a legislature whose members Soeharto had screened prior to their election in 1997 substantially in control of the country's political transition.

---

12. One of the leaders of this group was Susilo Bambang Yudhoyono, currently president of Indonesia.

Incumbent-led Transition

Shain and Linz argue that "a caretaker government of incumbents . . . might provide a better chance for a successful transition than power-sharing administrations or revolutionary provisional governments," and the reasons they offer to support this contention largely match the conditions under which Habibie inherited the presidency.[13] In their view, an incumbent caretaker committed to democratization allows members of the authoritarian regime to believe that they may be able to retain power, while creating an incentive for moderate opponents to "start organizing for elections instead of concentrating on mass mobilizations and protest actions."[14] In other words, such a regime encourages moderates on both sides of the regime-opposition divide to push forward with reform while isolating regime hard-liners and radical opponents.

In Indonesia, this is more or less the course that Habibie's interim government charted, but it was hardly obvious at the outset that it would succeed. The size and scale of the protests ensured that military and civilian leaders alike understood that their own survival depended on quick and substantial reforms. The rapid pace at which protests led to Soeharto's resignation, and the absence of any formal agreement between the regime and its opponents, also meant that the agenda for reform remained vague and that the political actors lacked a firm sense of each other's strength and commitment to reform. Moderate opposition leaders focused, as Shain and Linz would have predicted, on organizing new political parties and preparing to contest elections, while radical student groups continued to denounce Habibie's government as illegitimate and to demand that he resign and allow them to create a provisional government. Within the regime, too, there was deep division and great suspicion between its civilian and military factions. The armed forces had never been subordinate to civilian control, and during the Soeharto years they frequently had been at odds with Habibie, who exercised control over key defense industries. Under these conditions, reform proceeded along two essentially separate tracks. For the most part, the civilian government focused on political reform, and the military was left to consider its own reforms. In neither case did moderate or radical regime opponents participate directly in the reform process.

Political Reform

In an effort to reassure opponents who questioned his right to rule and his commitment to democratic reform, Habibie freed the press and many

---

13. Shain and Linz, *Between States*, 55.
14. Ibid.

political prisoners, and he announced a detailed agenda and timetable for reforms that would lead to free and fair legislative elections within a year and a presidential election in eighteen months. Toward these ends, his government pursued a very specific agenda that involved rewriting laws on political parties, elections, and legislatures to prepare for elections.[15]

The revision of those laws proceeded in two stages, as his government sought legitimacy by adhering closely to processes required by the 1945 constitution. The first stage required preparing and conducting a special session of the People's Consultative Assembly in November 1998. Under Soeharto, the assembly met only once every five years in a general session to reelect him, approve policy guidelines for the next five years, and set a date for the next election. Although Soeharto had kept the assembly politically weak, it was the highest constitutional body; only it could rescind its March 1998 decision that elections would next be held in 2002. Despite its dry legal role, the meeting presented an enormously sensitive political challenge. Only two special sessions had ever been held: one in 1967, to remove the country's first president, Sukarno, and another in 1968, to appoint Soeharto as his successor. Holding another raised the possibility that, in an uncertain and contentious political environment, delegates might be convinced or coerced to vote Habibie out of office.

Habibie's approach succeeded in marginalizing his radical opponents and winning over the more moderate opposition leaders. Radical reformers, mostly university students, still sought Habibie's removal and the formation of a governing presidium. They denounced the assembly as unconstitutional. They charged that the laws under which delegates had been selected were themselves unconstitutional and that any decisions the body reached would be equally invalid. Yet moderate reformers and government leaders alike preferred to follow constitutional requirements rather than question their legitimacy. They differed primarily over the extent to which existing rules should be changed. All agreed that political and electoral laws should be changed prior to holding elections. Indeed, Habibie had appointed a team of seven experts, including at least three U.S.-trained political scientists, to draw up new laws to be submitted to the House of Representatives after the assembly session.

The assembly session quickly developed as a focal point for political mobilization and demonstrated the serious challenges that the interim government faced. Just before the assembly's special session opened, radical student activists organized a meeting of the four most prominent senior opposition leaders, including Megawati Soekarnoputri and Abdurrahman Wahid, to seek their support for the creation of a provisional government

---

15. On these reforms, see Dwight Y. King, *Half-Hearted Reform: Electoral Institutions and the Struggle for Democracy in Indonesia* (Westport, Conn.: Praeger, 2003), especially chapter 3, "The 1999 Electoral Reforms: Debate and Design," 47–74.

that would replace Habibie with a presidium of opposition figures. When they failed to win that support, they mounted massive protests outside the assembly building, and on the third day, security forces shot and killed about a dozen people.

Despite the turmoil in the streets, the assembly session proceeded rather smoothly. The Development Unity Party, the only potential opposition voice in the assembly, made clear its desire for sharp reduction in the number of military officers appointed to legislative seats and called for an investigation into Soeharto's alleged corruption. After three days of debate, the assembly had made progress. In addition to allowing elections to take place sooner than 2002, it issued a number of decisions to advance the reform process. One decision directed the government to investigate corruption and, by including a specific reference to Soeharto, indicated the degree to which even Golkar members were willing to turn against their former patron. Another decision permitted the military to continue to hold legislative seats by appointment rather than election, but it directed that the number should be reduced by an unspecified amount. It also issued decisions limiting presidents and vice presidents to two terms, revoking extreme powers granted to presidents, upholding human rights, and calling for political decentralization.

Though radical reformists were dissatisfied with the outcome of the assembly meeting, the moderates within the regime and opposition quickly accepted its decisions. Within a week, members of the House of Representatives were at work on bills to revamp laws on parties, elections, and legislatures. These bills were passed in late January 1999 following extensive public debate. Even though none of the new political parties were able to participate directly in the legislative debates, the main positions on each issue were well known.

Debate focused on two central issues: whether to ban civil servants from participation in political parties and how greatly military representation in the legislature should be reduced. Since the regime had built its power on the backs of the bureaucracy and army, these debates focused attention on the core institutions that needed to be changed in order to effect a change in regime. These issues pitted military and civilian members of the regime against each other as much as they did moderate against radical reformers.

In the end, military representation was cut back by about 50 percent, and soft restrictions were placed on civil servants' political involvement. The House of Representatives rejected proposals by the opposition and many government advisers to adopt a district-based electoral system in place of the proportional representation system employed under Soeharto. The rules that emerged from this process laid a foundation for the freest and fairest legislative elections since 1955 and the first competitive presidential election ever, but they also produced an outcome that virtually ensured weak and unstable political leadership. To demonstrate its support for democratic reform and to avoid further antagonizing the opposition, which was excluded from the process of drafting the legal framework for democracy, the Habibie government adopted electoral rules that nearly guaranteed a House of Representatives in which no party controlled a majority.

In this regard, two decisions were crucial. First, despite the recommendations of the expert team that drafted the new laws, the interim government decided to retain the Soeharto-era electoral system, which featured closed-list proportional representation and extraordinarily high district magnitude—some electoral districts had as many as one hundred representatives. In other words, voters would select parties, not candidates, and parties needed to obtain only 1 percent of the vote in certain districts in order to secure a seat in the national legislature. Second, the interim government set an extraordinarily low legal threshold for political parties to participate in the election and left responsibility for determining which parties met the threshold to an independent panel of mainly academic experts. A national presence was one of the main conditions of being certified, since one of the chief goals of the legislation's drafters was to eliminate regional parties. In the short run, this enabled the government to demonstrate its commitment to political liberalization, but in the longer run it ensured that a large number of parties would compete in the election: of 141 legally registered parties, 48 qualified to contest the election, and the rules were not strictly implemented.[16] In combination with Indonesia's enormous regional and cultural diversity, these two features virtually ensured that the resulting legislature would include a vast array of small parties, rather than the small number of large ones that the law-drafting team had wanted.

As in the case of legislative elections, the interim government decided to retain the basic features of the Soeharto-era indirect presidential election procedure but made two changes intended to enhance the democratic accountability of the president. Both changes added parliamentary qualities to Indonesia's presidential system, tipping the balance heavily in favor of the legislature. First, in addition to cutting the number of appointed assembly members from five hundred to two hundred, it took the authority for choosing those members away from the national government and assigned it to provincial governments (five members per province) and the electoral commission (which selected sixty-five delegates to represent various social groups—for instance, farmers, religious minorities, and women). To this it added a well-intentioned requirement that the president deliver an annual

---

16. For the mechanics see King, *Half-Hearted Reform.*

"accountability report" to the assembly, which added another parliamentary element to an ostensibly presidential form of government.

Together, these legislative and presidential electoral rules yielded a unique combination of multipartism and presidentialism even more vulnerable to deadlock and instability than the sort against which Juan Linz and other Latin Americanists have warned so strongly.[17] Although the legislature chose the executive in quasi-parliamentary fashion, its fate was not tied to that of the executive; thus, it faced little pressure to form and maintain a stable majority coalition, and its factions could quarrel freely with the president, without worry that the legislature would be dissolved and fresh elections called. Moreover, the rules for electing legislators meant that the legislative power would almost inevitably be fragmented among many political parties, further diminishing the prospects for stable legislative coalitions.

Military Reform

Resisting radical demands and establishing a new legal framework for democratic elections left the government little time and fewer resources to devote to military reform, but changes to the country's political system put pressure on the military to adapt. For instance, soon after Habibie took power he reversed Soeharto's policy of using the information ministry's fifty thousand employees to monitor and control the flow of information and allowed the ministry to freely issue publication licenses.[18] Long accustomed to respectful treatment in the press and other public forums, military leaders now faced "an onslaught of criticism in the media which soon turned into unrestrained condemnation."[19]

In the face of such pressure, the military took several steps to repair their image and retain a prominent role in politics. Soon after Soeharto resigned, Wiranto convened a military tribunal that examined Prabowo's role in the May riots, and in August Wiranto dismissed Prabowo and two associates from the army. The next month, the armed forces held a seminar at which they presented their own agenda for military reform, called the New Paradigm. So-called "intellectual" generals had convened a seminar on reform in 1996, and after Soeharto fell they took a prominent role in apologizing for military abuses and articulating plans for reform. Still, the pledges made at the September seminar illustrated how reluctant even "reformist" military leaders were to withdraw entirely from politics: they agreed that the military did not need to be at the "forefront of politics" or to exercise "control" over

---

17. See, for example, Juan Linz and Arturo Valenzuela, eds., *The Failure of Presidential Democracy* (Baltimore: Johns Hopkins University Press, 1994).
18. Kevin O'Rourke, *Reformasi: The Struggle for Power in Post-Suharto Indonesia* (Crow's Nest, NSW, Australia: Allen and Unwin, 2002), 146.
19. ICG, *Indonesia*, 2.

politics, but they insisted on continuing to share power with civilians and affirmed their commitment to "influence" political decisions.[20]

These concessions marked a sharp break with previous military policy and doctrine, but they did not stanch civilian pressure for further reform. Just after the New Paradigm was announced, the national human rights commission visited Aceh, a province in which mass graves left from the military's counterinsurgency campaign in 1989–92 were being unearthed. This kept the armed forces in a politically weak position precisely at the time the new legal framework for democratic elections was being debated. As a result, the incumbent regime—largely under civilian control—was able to satisfy public pressure for reform by curbing the military's formal role in politics, and the military was forced to accept significant changes. In particular, the military committed itself to political neutrality, broke its formal ties to the governing party, accepted the halving of its appointive seats in the House of Representatives to thirty-eight after the next election, and agreed that its members no longer would fill civilian political and bureaucratic positions (though currently serving officers could complete their terms in office).

As Shain and Linz expected, an interim government dominated by incumbent civilians and committed to democratic reform was able to forge compromises that won the support of moderates in the regime and among the opposition. By moving quickly and steadily to establish a legal framework for democracy, the government created powerful incentives among moderates of all stripes to devote their energy to forming political parties and preparing to contest elections in June 1999 and presidential elections in October 1999. Indeed, the assembly's special session in November 1998, just six months after Habibie became president, marked the end of any serious efforts to unite radical and moderate opponents against the interim government. The appeal of elections, combined with the short period of time available to prepare for them, encouraged moderate, senior opposition figures to concentrate on creating parties and mustering public support.

Regional Separatism and Communal Conflicts

As Indonesia moved toward legislative elections in mid-1999, two new sets of challenges confronted the interim government. The first was a resurgence of separatist movements in three provinces, and the second was the outbreak of communal violence, mainly between Christians and Muslims,

---

20. Honna, *Military Politics*, 164–167; and Rizal Sukma and Edy Prasetyono, *Security Sector Reform in Indonesia: The Military and the Police,* Working Paper no. 9 (Netherlands Institute of International Relations, February 2003), 22–23.

in three other provinces.[21] These developments raised the possibility that Indonesia, like Yugoslavia, might be consumed by violence and disintegrate into several new states. Indeed, foreign and domestic media alike frequently asked whether Indonesia was likely to become the "Balkans of the East."[22] Despite these threats, the Habibie government managed to hold elections and transfer power to a new government on schedule in October 1999. It was able to do so mainly because the timing, extent, and location of the violence did not pose a direct threat to preparations for the elections. However, measures that Habibie's government took in response to the rising level of regional violence had mixed effects, which were felt mainly after his government left office.

As president, Soeharto confronted persistent armed separatist movements in the provinces of Aceh, Papua, and East Timor, but none of these movements forged ties with antiregime protesters in 1998 or played a significant role in shaping the terms of the political transition.[23] The main reason is that repressive Indonesian policies during the 1990s had isolated nationalist movements in these regions and rendered them militarily and politically weak. Even after Soeharto resigned, leaders of these movements did not seek to participate in the broader process of political reform. Instead, they aggressively moved to resume their independence struggles, doubting that an incumbent-led transition would bring significant change to their regions. In Jakarta, the intensification of these movements combined with proindependence rumblings in other resource-rich provinces contributed to a sense that secessionists might destroy the state before they could

---

21. On the causes and dynamics of these conflicts, see Jacques Bertrand, *Nationalism and Ethnic Conflict in Indonesia* (Cambridge: Cambridge University Press, 2004).

22. For views that a breakup was likely, see John R. Bolton, "Indonesia: Asia's Yugoslavia?" *Far Eastern Economic Review* (April 1, 1999), 31; "Indonesia: Balkans of the East?" *Time* (June 7, 1999), www.time.com/time/asia/asia/magazine/1999/990607/index.html; Anthony Spaeth, "Is Indonesia Starting to Break Up?" *Time* (August 3, 1998); "An Asian Balkans?" *Economist* (November 13, 1999), www.economist.com/world/asia/displaystory.cfm?story_id=E1_NVRVPD; Michael Richardson, "Southeast Asians Fear a Breakup of Indonesia," *International Herald Tribune* (November 16, 1999), 6; and David Rohde, "Indonesia Unraveling?" *Foreign Affairs* 80 (2001): 110–124. Academic observers tended to discount such apocalyptic views. See, for example, Anne Booth, "Will Indonesia Break Up?" *Inside Indonesia* 59 (1999), insideindonesia.org/edit59/booth.htm; Robert Cribb, "Not the Next Yugoslavia: Prospects for the Disintegration of Indonesia," *Australian Journal of International Affairs* 53 (1999), 169–178; Donald K. Emmerson, "Will Indonesia Survive?" *Foreign Affairs* 79 (2000): 95–106; Michael van Langenberg, "End of the Jakartan Empire?" *Inside Indonesia* 61 (2000), insideindonesia.org/edit61/mvl.htm; and Michael S. Malley, "Indonesia: Violence and Reform beyond Jakarta," in *Southeast Asian Affairs 2001*, ed. Anthony Smith and Daljit Singh, 159–174 (Singapore: Institute of Southeast Asian Studies, 2001).

23. The major efforts to chronicle and explain Indonesia's political transition pay virtually no attention to regional conflicts, and one specifically excludes consideration of secessionist movements on the grounds that they "proceeded on the basis of very different political logics" than the groups that brought about regime change (Aspinall, *Opposing Suharto*, 19). But the generalization applies equally to Robison and Hadiz, *Reorganising Power in Indonesia*; O'Rourke, *Reformasi*; and Kees van Dijk, *A Country in Despair: Indonesia between 1997 and 2000* (Leiden: KITLV Press, 2001).

install a democratic regime. The causes of violence varied from region to region. Separatist movements were driven mainly by anger at the massacres and human rights abuses they had suffered during the Soeharto era. In addition, Aceh and Papua were major exporters of such natural resources as natural gas, gold, and timber, and people there deeply resented the exploitation of their resources for the benefit mainly of national government and foreign investors.

The interim government, focused mainly on retaining power and overseeing preparations for democratic elections, responded in an ad hoc fashion to the increasing level of separatist sentiment and communal violence. In early 1999, Habibie adopted an accommodating stand toward Papua, whose armed separatists were few, and he invited one hundred prominent Papuans to hold a National Dialogue. But rather than discuss their concerns with Habibie, they delivered a blunt demand for independence, which led the military to initiate a crackdown.

In Aceh, where Soeharto's government had defeated a guerrilla movement in the early 1990s, a new, nonviolent movement was formed to demand a referendum on independence. However, as the Acehnese uncovered mass graves and other evidence of Indonesian military atrocities, and national leaders responded mainly by issuing only apologies, support for peaceful along with armed resistance grew.

Of all these challenges, the one arising in East Timor was the most serious. Throughout the 1990s, Indonesia had come under growing foreign pressure to ease its grip on East Timor. The East Timorese resistance was much more organized and internationally networked than its counterparts in Papua and Aceh, and activists seized on Soeharto's fall as an opportunity to mobilize locally, in Jakarta, and internationally to achieve independence.

Habibie's policy on East Timor illustrated some of the key characteristics of his interim government. First, in the fluid environment of the transition, he and a close circle of advisers were able to reverse one of the New Order regime's most strongly held positions—that East Timor was irrevocably an Indonesian province—and to permit a UN-sponsored referendum on the territory's future status. The exact reasons for Habibie's decision, which he announced in January 1999 just after the adoption of the new electoral rules, remain unclear. Mainly, it seems, he was no longer inclined to bear the diplomatic, political, and economic burdens of continued occupation. Second, although he had the autonomy to make this decision, he lacked the power to control the military, which organized and equipped militias in East Timor to intimidate proindependence supporters, disrupt the referendum, and violently resist separation from Indonesia. Indeed, although the referendum was conducted peacefully at the end of August, horrific violence followed in September. After nearly 80 percent of East Timorese voted in favor of independence, pro-Indonesia militias killed several hundred East Timorese and drove about one-third of the tiny territory's 850,000 people out of their homes and across the border into Indonesian West Timor.[24] East Timor's separation from Indonesian control was a by-product of the regime transition in Jakarta.

Unlike armed separatist movements, which were well known and long-standing, widespread intercommunal violence took most Indonesians by surprise. Such violence had occurred during the Soeharto era, but on a much smaller scale than it achieved during the years after he resigned. The Norwegian Refugee Committee, which maintains a database of internally displaced persons (IDPs) throughout the world, estimated that the number of IDPs in Indonesia jumped from fewer than twenty thousand at the end of 1997 to about six hundred thousand by the end of 1999, the year the interim government left office. The main cause of this dramatic increase was not separatist movements but intercommunal conflicts, mainly in parts of Maluku but also in parts of Kalimantan and Sulawesi. The origins of each conflict varied, but each seemed to center on conflicts between indigenous and immigrant groups that typically profess different religious beliefs and compete for access to similar economic resources, such as timber, land, or government patronage. In the uncertainty of the country's political transition, some groups felt threatened enough to resort to violence.

The extent and seriousness of intercommunal violence became apparent only in early 1999, as the interim government proceeded toward elections. The first major violence occurred in January in Ambon, the capital city of Maluku Province, where the population was about evenly divided between Muslims and Christians. Within a few months, that city was a war zone, and violence had spread to adjacent areas.[25] The security forces clearly were unable to contain the violence, and Christians and Muslims alike accused army and police units of taking sides in the violence. Media reports stirred people elsewhere in the country, especially Muslims, to demand effective government action and to begin to organize private militias to defend Muslims in Maluku. Nevertheless, the government response continued to be inadequate, and the last months of the interim government witnessed devas-

---

24. For details, see the report by James Dunn, special rapporteur of the United Nations Transitional Administration in East Timor, "Crimes Against Humanity in East Timor, January to October 1999: Their Nature and Causes," February 14, 2001, www.etan.org/news/2001a/dunn1.htm.

25. Bertrand, *Nationalism and Ethnic Conflict in Indonesia*, 126.

tating violence that destroyed large parts of Ambon and displaced thousands of people from their homes.

Despite the scale of these conflicts, their impact on the principal agenda of Indonesia's interim government—democratic elections—was limited. To understand why, it is useful to consider their timing and location. In the first place, a national reform agenda was well established, and its implementation well under way, before violence became severe and widespread. Since the leaders of regionalist movements had not joined the national reform movement, their demands, whether for independence or the protection of minority rights, were initially marginal to the Jakarta-centered debate about reform. Second, the conflict-ridden regions are located very far from Java, the main island in the political and geographic center that is home to nearly 60 percent of the country's 220 million people. Each of the troubled provinces is located on a separate island, and all but one (Kalimantan) is well over one thousand miles from Java. Moreover, the population of each of these provinces is quite small, ranging from just 2 million to 4 million.

Although individual regions had little capacity to influence political decisions in Jakarta, the accumulation of regional conflicts exerted a powerful impact on the interim government. In late 1998, the same team of academic specialists who had drafted the country's new laws on parties, elections, and legislatures turned its attention to the problem of overcentralization. In January 1999, the Habibie government submitted two bills to the House of Representatives: one to share political power with regional governments and the other to share fiscal resources with them. The laws are remarkable in three respects. First, the bills attracted little debate or controversy, a testament to the extent to which the Jakarta political elite accepted the need to accommodate regional interests. Second, however, the bills were drafted without consulting regional leaders to learn what provisions would appeal to them. Thus, rather than attending to the interests of groups increasingly drawn into communal violence, the bills aimed to forestall further support for independence movements. These provisions were more focused on granting power to groups that might seek independence than attending to groups that were increasingly involved in violence due to other intercommunal grievances. Third, because the laws called for sweeping changes to the structure of the state, their implementation was delayed for two years in order to provide the government time to prepare. Thus, their impact on contemporary regional crises was limited and their actual impact was not felt until the interim government had been replaced.

Legacies of the Interim Government

The interim government's character and decisions shaped the possibilities for domestic peace and political stability, and the quality of governance in subsequent years. Habibie's government was not simply an "incumbent-led caretaker government," but one that came to power under particular conditions, because opposition forces were too weakly organized even to engage the regime in direct talks about the future and the military was too deeply divided to intervene directly in political reform. It was moderate in the sense that it did not advocate the restoration of military-backed authoritarianism, and it supported a transition to electoral democracy. However, opposition forces and the military tolerated rather than supported the interim government, and their tolerance depended on steady, measured progress toward reform that did not threaten their interests too directly. In the case of the opposition, this led to rules that allowed enormous improvements in press freedom and a very accommodative approach to new political parties. It allowed the military to withdraw gradually from the formal political arena and effectively postponed serious reconsideration of civil-military relations until an undefined point in the future. The implications of the interim government's actions, and its inactions, are particularly clear in three areas: elections and political instability; regional conflicts and civil-military relations; and corruption and the quality of governance.

Elections and Political Instability

Although widely heralded as free and fair, the legislative elections held in May 1999 failed to produce a majority party or even an obvious majority coalition. Twenty-one parties won at least one seat, but five parties split about 87 percent of the votes. Megawati's secular nationalist party, the Indonesian Democratic Party-Perjuangan (PDI-P, or PDIP-P) won 34 percent, the old regime's party (Golkar) took 22 percent, Wahid's largely rural Muslim party (PKB) won 13 percent, the Islamic party permitted under the old regime (PPP) won 11 percent, and a new, predominantly urban, Islamic party (PAN) won 7 percent. In the House of Representatives, these shares were diluted further by the armed forces' thirty-eight appointive seats.[26]

The political impact of this ambiguous election outcome became increasingly evident as the October presidential election approached. Although

---

26. The parties' names and abbreviations are PDIP-P—Partai Demokrasi Indonesia-Perjuangan, Indonesia Democracy Party-Struggle; Golkar—Partai Golongan Karya, Functional Groups Party; PKB—Partai Kebangkitan Bangsa, National Awakening Party; PPP—Partai Persatuan Pembangunan, Development Unity Party; and PAN—Partai Amanat Nasional, National Mandate Party.

Megawati's party had secured the largest number of seats, she was unpopular among the other parties—mainly Golkar and an assortment of smaller Islamic parties. These parties forged brief but effective alliances, and in a series of separate elections they chose PAN's leader to head the assembly, a Golkar leader as speaker of the House of Representatives, and Wahid as president. In a final election, following protests by her supporters, Megawati was relegated to the post of vice president. In exchange for their support, the new president, Abdurrahman Wahid, selected a cabinet in which all major parties and the armed forces were represented.[27]

The most obvious result of all these compromises was the weakness of the democratically elected central government. After a brief honeymoon, nearly the entire legislature turned against Wahid, and he was forced to divert scarce political capital from pursing policy objectives to defending his own power. Members of the House of Representatives accused him of failing to respond effectively to the economic crisis and regional conflicts, of engaging in corruption, and, generally, of providing weak leadership. In 2001, after the House had censured him twice, the assembly removed Wahid from office and replaced him with his vice president, Megawati.

Megawati's election brought stability to national politics but little progress toward resolving the country's major problems.[28] Since her party was nearly three times the size of Wahid's it was easier for her to maintain support in the House. Yet her party was too small to govern alone, and deep personal differences among party leaders, and ideological ones among the parties, inhibited the formation of a stable coalition. As a result, she found it difficult to translate greater political stability into more effective policies, and when her term in office (the remainder of Wahid's five-year term) expired in 2004, she lost the next election to a retired army general who had served as chief security minister in her own cabinet, Susilo Bambang Yudhoyono.

Civil-Military Relations and Regional Conflicts

Democratic institutions survived the weak Wahid and Megawati presidencies, but the military remained beyond civilian control. Wahid had appointed the first civilian defense minister since the 1950s and sought to promote change in the military by promoting reformist generals. However, these efforts failed to address structural sources of military autonomy from civilian control. In particular, the armed forces retained autonomy

---

27. A detailed account of the political maneuvering behind these elections can be found in O'Rourke, *Reformasi*, chapter 19, "Guerilla Politics," 297–322.
28. Michael S. Malley, "Indonesia in 2001: Restoring Stability in Jakarta," *Asian Survey* 42 (January/February 2002): 124–132.

from the defense ministry, which in any case was run largely by military officers. Moreover, the military maintained its traditional fiscal autonomy from the government, whose budget meets only about one-third of the military's needs and leaves each military unit reliant on its own network of business interests. As a result, Wahid mainly succeeded in riling the officer corps rather than winning its support for his initiatives.

Weak civilian control over the military contributed to a worsening of regional conflicts. Wahid, in contrast to his generals, adopted a generally accommodating stance toward separatist movements in Aceh and Papua. In addition to visiting both provinces, his government oversaw the drafting of bills that would grant each province "special autonomy," although provincial actors and their allies in the House of Representatives were probably more influential in this process. In addition, his government signed an agreement with Acehnese rebels for a "humanitarian pause" in the conflict, and he contributed a large sum of money toward the cost of the largest-ever gathering of Papuan nationalists.

Wahid's moves failed to dissuade separatists in either province from pressing their cases, in part because the military undermined the president's policies by continuing to target peaceful and armed supporters of secession alike. Toward the end of his presidency, as rebel attacks in Aceh escalated, Wahid was forced to authorize harsher military action against the rebels and was unable to achieve the "comprehensive solution" he desired. Communal conflicts, especially in Maluku, worsened dramatically during his presidency. His government, mainly because it lacked authority over the military, failed to prevent a private Muslim militia from sending thousands of members to the violence-plagued region, even after he met with the leaders and expressed his opposition to their plans.

Megawati also chose cabinet members from all main political parties and retired military officers. But unlike Wahid, she had cultivated a closer relationship to segments of the military since her rise in the early 1990s, and after replacing him she moved to strengthen this relationship further. She, too, appointed a civilian defense minister but chose someone with little knowledge of military affairs, and after he suffered a debilitating stroke, she did not replace him. In this as in so many other ways, she allowed officers to run military affairs.

Megawati also shared the nationalist outlook common among the officer corps and many members of her political party and was more inclined to support a hard line against separatist movements than compromise with them. Indeed, even though she signed laws that promised "special autonomy" to both provinces, she adopted other policies that "resulted in the virtual suspension of special autonomy in Aceh and its increasing emasculation in Papua."[29] For instance, soon after she became president, she authorized the creation of a new army command for Aceh, and the army and police stepped up their campaign against Aceh's rebels. In 2003, after another truce failed, she declared martial law in the province and sent tens of thousands of troops to combat an insurgent force that numbered several thousand. In the fighting that followed, the Indonesian military claimed to have killed more than one thousand rebels and detained more than two thousand.

With respect to communal conflict, Megawati's tenure witnessed significant improvements. In late 2001 and early 2002, an influential Golkar leader in her cabinet brokered peace agreements among warring factions in two regions that had endured the most widespread violence, Maluku and Central Sulawesi. These agreements were made possible not just by his leadership but also by the exhaustion of the combatants, the increasingly sharp segregation of religious communities in war-torn regions, peacemaking efforts by NGOs, and the replacement of locally garrisoned troops with an elite force composed of troops from outside the affected regions.[30]

Corruption and the Quality of Governance

The interim government devoted little attention to fighting corruption and, consequently, failed to bring about any substantial improvement in the quality of governance. The interim government's choice of political institutions thus contributed to political instability, and its lack of control over the military exacerbated regional conflicts. The interim government also failed to take action against corruption. Consequently, democratization did not bring substantial improvement in the quality of governance. It is difficult to overstate the extent and seriousness of corruption in Indonesia, which Transparency International regularly ranks among the most corrupt countries in the world (in the bottom 10 percent, with a corruption perception index score of 2.0 or less between 1998 and 2004). Despite intense scrutiny by the media, NGOs, and even official audit agencies working in tandem with international accounting firms, the prosecution of government offi-

---

29. Rodd McGibbon, *Secessionist Challenges in Aceh and Papua: Is Special Autonomy the Solution?* (Washington, D.C.: East-West Center Washington, 2004), 2–3.

30. ICG, *Indonesia: The Search for Peace in Maluku*, Asia Report no. 31 (February 8, 2002): 22–23; and ICG, *Indonesia Backgrounder: Jihad in Central Sulawesi*, Asia Report no. 74 (February 3, 2004), 14–16.

cials was rare, and convictions that were upheld on appeal were even less common. Moreover, major new corruption scandals emerged even during the period of the interim government. In the most glaring of these, the attorney general, supposedly in charge of the anticorruption drive, resigned after taking nearly $2 million from businessmen.[31] In retrospect, it is clear that the incumbent character of the interim government, combined with the intense pressure to compete in elections, militated against an aggressive anticorruption policy.

The cost of failing to attack corruption was visible in many areas. Foreign investors, some of whom lost major court battles for dubious reasons, have shied away from the country, and foreign direct investment has remained flat or negative since 1997.[32] In 2002, a UN special rapporteur on the independence of judges and lawyers said that he "didn't realize that the situation could be as bad" as he had found, and a prominent Indonesian watchdog group described judicial corruption as "systemic."[33] The political cost of continuing corruption was high, too. Wahid, an Islamic cleric, was impeached in part because of financial scandals, including one in which his masseur obtained $3.5 million from the state food distribution agency. The public regarded Megawati's record on corruption as poor—in 2002, 85 percent said they were "very disappointed" with her efforts on this front—and the winner of the 2004 presidential election defeated her in part by stressing his commitment to attacking corruption.

Conclusion

To describe Indonesia's interim government as an "incumbent-controlled caretaker" is to say at least as much about the configuration of social forces that brought it to power as about the character of the government itself. In the face of widespread antiregime protests, political leadership fell into the hands of civilian members of the regime who could not count on military support. Yet the protesters were too weak to replace the government, and the armed forces were hobbled more by a lack of internal unity than by a lack of military capacity. Thus, to say that Indonesia's incumbent-controlled interim government *controlled* the process of regime change would exag-

---

31. For a review of election-related scandals and political groups' efforts to protect their economic interests, see Robison and Hadiz, *Reorganising Power in Indonesia*, chapter 8, "Reorganising Economic Power," 187–222.

32. R. William Liddle and Saiful Mujani, "Indonesia in 2004: The Rise of Susilo Bambang Yudhoyono," *Asian Survey* 45, no. 1 (January/February 2004), 125.

33. "RI Judiciary Worse than First Thought: UN Rapporteur," *Jakarta Post*, July 22, 2002, www.thejakartapost.com/detailheadlines.asp?fileid=20020722.@01&irec=0; "Report Reveals Corruption in Court Is Organized," *Jakarta Post*, July 23, 2002, www.thejakartapost.com/detailheadlines.asp?fileid=20020723.@01&irec=0.

gerate its role. Instead, it struggled mightily to retain power amid uncertainty about its own strength and legitimacy as well as doubts about the intentions, influence, and identity of political actors that ranged from radical activist networks and newly formed political parties to a fragmented military and resurgent separatist movements.

Under these conditions, the interim government articulated a clear but limited agenda for reform and hewed closely to established legal and constitutional procedures. This approach won the support, or at least acquiescence, of influential groups within the regime and among the older, more established opposition groups without alienating the military. In this way, the interim government insulated itself from persistent opposition of radical groups and laid a framework for a smooth transition to electoral democracy.

The impact of the interim government's incumbent character was more apparent in the decisions that it postponed than in the ones it made. It did not attempt to assert civilian control over the military, conduct serious investigations of corruption, prosecute violations of human rights, or even make substantial amendments to the constitution. It left these challenges to subsequent governments, whose capacity to design and implement policies of any type turned out to be very limited. As a result, its legacy includes not just democratic mechanisms for choosing the government and making policy but also widespread corruption and military autonomy, which diminish the quality of the country's democracy.

8

Transitional Governance in Burundi and the Democratic Republic of the Congo

Devon Curtis

Editors' Note

Devon Curtis's chapter presents two cases of externally facilitated peace agreements that led to domestic power-sharing interim governments. Here, the peace processes are by and large domestic, but the international community has taken an active role in the process of transition. In the cases of Burundi and the Democratic Republic of the Congo (DRC), regional actors and organizations pushed forward the peace processes. While domestic actors managed these interim governments, external actors had significant input as to who could participate in the peace talks leading to the creation of the temporary regimes and who could lead those transitional governments once they were created. In this way, external facilitation in creating peace agreements left a strong imprint on the character and functioning of the subsequent domestic regime in each country.

Burundi and the DRC are beset with significant spoiler and legitimacy problems, as well as external actors whose involvements are not always benign. Curtis's chapter revolves around two central themes: the limits of local transitional arrangements when significant local and regional actors do not want peace, and the trade-offs between inclusion and legitimacy created by power-sharing interim governments. First, Curtis takes up the issue of spoilers. Pushing forward with peace processes and creating temporary governments before the combatants agree to a cease-fire and a disarmament, demobilization, and reintegration program create contradictions and tensions that can threaten the entire process. Curtis finds that without a comprehensive, credible cease-fire, groups retain their ability to return to violence, leaving these groups as potential spoilers with incentives to stay out of the process and to continue to bargain for concessions. Yet there is a dilemma in that it may simply not be possible to reach such an agreement in a reasonable time period.

Second, Curtis finds that local transitional arrangements based on power shar-
ing impose significant constraints on the ability to restructure politics and that the
elite focus of power-sharing bargains create a sharp disconnect between the elite-
centered transitional government and the citizens on the ground. Together, these
dynamics create domestic legitimacy problems. In this analysis, Curtis matches the
insights of both Antonio Donini and Carrie L. Manning, fleshing them out with
rich empirical detail. When external actors facilitate the peace agreement, they play
a role in deciding which groups come to the bargaining table. Because inclusion in
the talks and subsequent membership in the transitional government was earned by
being able to threaten violence, many of the members in the transitional govern-
ments lacked strong ties to the community. Furthermore, as a product of elite bar-
gaining, the transitional governments in Burundi and the DRC were concerned
with dividing the spoils of office among those who were able to secure positions.
This focus on dividing the spoils among the elite, rather than structuring a new
government that could deliver services and improve the lives of people on the
ground, exacerbated the legitimacy problems that had already been created when
groups without popular support populated the interim governments.

Ultimately, both peace processes are moving forward, and the transitional govern-
ments succeeded in putting in place the mechanisms to transfer power to permanent
domestic governments. In both countries, however, the processes are problematic, and
in the DRC, violence continues in the eastern part of the country. At best, therefore,
these are limited and tentative successes in delivering post-conflict governments that
are legitimate, stable, and democratic.

■ ■ ■

Introduction

The conflicts and extraordinary violence in Burundi, the Democratic
Republic of the Congo (DRC), and Rwanda have reverberated across the
African continent and have received significant regional and international
attention. With the help of regional facilitators, both Burundi and the DRC
implemented transitional governments as part of their peace processes.
The transitional period of the Burundian peace process formally came to
an end in August 2005 when Pierre Nkurunziza, the former leader of a
rebel group, became president of Burundi following a series of elections. A
new government was established and the UN peacekeeping mission withdrew. Nevertheless, there are still a number of uncertainties in Burundi
and the situation remains volatile. The DRC is also at the end of its transitional period. In the largest electoral process ever conducted with UN support, the DRC held the first round of national elections in July 2006 and the

second round in October that year, bringing an end to the transitional period. Nonetheless, violence continues in some parts of the country, and a number of key issues have not been resolved. While there have been several hopeful signs in both Burundi and the DRC and the transitional governments did lead to elections and permanent institutions as intended, it is still not possible to declare a decisive end to the horrific rounds of violence that have overwhelmed the two countries.

Local transitional power-sharing governments, along with the establishment of new unified national armies, have been the cornerstones of the externally facilitated peace agreements that were intended to resolve the civil wars in Burundi and the DRC. Yet many incoherent and hostile factions populate the political and military environments in each of those countries, and the transitional governments were plagued by difficulties and reversals. While there have been notable improvements, peace and stable governance are not certainties in either country.

In Burundi, the peace process has been more far-reaching than the process in the DRC. Following the signing of the Arusha Peace and Reconciliation Agreement for Burundi (Arusha Peace Agreement) on August 28, 2000, a transitional government was established, but it was severely hampered by the lack of a comprehensive cease-fire. The peace process received a boost in November 2003, when the largest remaining rebel group, the National Council for the Defense of Democracy (CNDD)-Front pour la Défense de la Démocratie (FDD) joined the transitional government. A series of elections were held at the end of the transitional process, starting with a referendum on the permanent Burundian constitution in February 2005, then local, provincial, and national elections culminating in the indirect election of a new president in August 2005. The last rebel group signed a cease-fire agreement in September 2006, but at this writing it has still not been fully implemented. Outbreaks of violence continue and the new government has adopted authoritarian tendencies to consolidate its hold on power.

The transitional process in the DRC has faced even more daunting challenges. The legacy of the predatory, privatized state in the DRC and the weakness of formal state structures have posed enormous obstacles to any transition toward peace and legitimate governance. The Sun City Agreement of April 2003 established a transitional government that brought together many of the Congolese former belligerents. However, divisions within the transitional government made governance difficult in the transitional period, and war continued in the east of the country. Political disputes, strategic maneuvers, and the mere logistical complications of governing such a large country with such poor infrastructure meant that the challenges of transitional governance were formidable.[1] Furthermore, extensive natural resources

---

1. Infrastructure in many parts of the DRC is very poor or nonexistent. The country is eighty-four times larger than Burundi. At 2,345,410 sq. km., it is slightly larger than Greenland. Burundi is 27,830 sq. km., slightly larger than Haiti and slightly smaller than Maryland.

in the DRC and the corresponding battle for control of resource-rich areas have given some actors both inside and outside the country powerful incentives for continued instability in the DRC. With considerable pressure and encouragement from donors, elections marking the official end of the transitional period have been held, but politicians continue to position themselves for political advantage and access to the DRC's economic resources. Violence continues in some parts of the country, and many requirements for peace and stability, such as an independent judiciary and army reform, face serious delays and obstacles.

The conflicts in Burundi and the DRC have involved many outside actors. Neighboring countries have hosted large numbers of refugees fleeing violence. In the case of the war in the Congo, many countries sent troops to assist either the government or rebel groups. Outside actors have also been involved as mediators and facilitators, with South Africa playing a particularly prominent role in the peace processes of the two countries. Both Burundi and the DRC had large Chapter VII–mandated UN peacekeeping missions to help support peaceful transitions. Before the deployment of the UN peacekeeping force, Burundi hosted the first-ever African Union (AU) peacekeeping mission to assist the transition. In the DRC, the European Union (EU) sent a force to the east of the country for three months in 2003 and also sent a force to help provide security during the election period in 2006. These forces operated alongside the UN peacekeeping mission.

This chapter assesses the record of transitional governance in Burundi and the DRC. The transitional "models" promoted by regional facilitators and their international partners in both countries were broadly similar, even though the contexts of the conflicts in the two countries were quite different. Both peace processes focused on inclusive negotiations involving all main belligerent groups, under the auspices of well-known African statesmen-facilitators. In both cases, a number of other African officials and representatives became involved in the facilitation efforts, supported by Western donors and special envoys. The negotiations led to the establishment of local transitional power-sharing structures that aimed to include most potential spoilers and belligerents. In Burundi, transitional power-sharing offices were divided according to ethnicity and political groupings, while in the DRC they were distributed among armed groups, the unarmed opposition, and civil society. Both countries hosted peacekeeping missions to secure and support the transitional institutions.

These cases fall at a mid-range of influence from the international community: more than was the case in Guatemala and El Salvador, but much less than the extreme cases of East Timor, Afghanistan, and Iraq. In neither Burundi nor the DRC have external actors taken over key governance functions, although they have monitored and assisted the governments. International donors and Western countries were willing to pay for expensive

negotiation processes, but they were averse to long-standing expensive commitments, such as more intrusive transitional involvement. Therefore, these
two cases demonstrate a mix of domestic and international pressures in the
transitional process, illustrating a constant interplay between the two levels
of analysis in the process of constructing peace.

For both countries, the chapter will discuss the process leading to the
establishment of these transitional regimes, the role of international and
regional actors, the nature of transitional institutions and obstacles in their
implementation, and the ongoing challenges in achieving domestic legitimacy and stability. The transitional experiences of Burundi and the DRC
point to the severe limits of local transitional arrangements, where a number
of significant local actors, sometimes helped by neighboring groups, do not
want peace. Furthermore, so far, neither country has been able to adequately
share power and resources between the governors and the governed, leading
to potential problems in the future.

Nonetheless, due to the lack of alternative arrangements, the transitional
structures in Burundi and the DRC have opened some space for peace, if they
operate alongside credible efforts to address the regional dimensions to the
conflicts. The outcomes of transitional governance in Burundi and the DRC
depend heavily on the broader politics in the region, particularly on the presence or absence of a regional commitment to peace. Whether the region is
committed to peace is not yet clear.

Conflict in the Great Lakes Region of Africa

Violence and atrocities in the Great Lakes region of Africa have their roots
in historic processes.[2] Burundi, the DRC, and Rwanda have each suffered
repeated cycles of violent conflict, sometimes leading to genocide. Violence
in one country has influenced events in neighboring areas and countries;
therefore, conflict in the Great Lakes must be understood through a
regional perspective.

The most prevalent view of conflict in Burundi is that of a long-term ethnic
conflict between the historically disadvantaged Hutu (85 percent) and the
dominant minority Tutsi (14 percent), with the 1 percent Twa completely marginalized. The Tutsi ethnic group has dominated political, economic,
and military structures since independence in 1962, but viewing the Burundian conflict exclusively through an ethnic lens fails to capture many of the

2. For accounts of the roots of conflict in the Great Lakes region, see, for instance, Jean-Pierre
   Chrétien, *Two Thousand Years of History* (New York: Zone Books, 2003); René Lemarchand,
   Rwanda and Burundi (New York: Praeger Books, 1970); Collette Braeckman, *Dinosaure: le Zaïre
   de Mobutu* (Paris: Fayard, 1992); and Crawford Young and Thomas Turner, *The Rise and
   Decline of the Zairian State* (Madison: University of Wisconsin Press, 1985).

important nuances in Burundian history and social structure.[3] Ethnicity is a critical element of the conflict, and ethnicity has certainly been used as a tool for mobilization, but other factors have also been important, such as regional divisions, urban-rural divisions, a politicized military, political and economic ambitions, and links to politics in neighboring Rwanda and the DRC.

Under heavy international pressure, majoritarian-style democratic elections were held in Burundi in 1993. The winner of the elections was Melchior Ndadaye, a Hutu from the Front for Democracy in Burundi (FRODEBU) party. This was a clear break from years of rule by successive Tutsi presidents from Bururi Province who gained power through military coups. However, Tutsi army officers assassinated President Ndadaye and other high-ranking FRODEBU members less than three months after they took office. These assassinations sparked interethnic massacres across the country and sent thousands of refugees to neighboring countries.

The genocide in neighboring Rwanda in April–July 1994 contributed to an already polarized, tense, and volatile environment in Burundi. In an attempt to stabilize the situation, international officials brokered a power-sharing agreement in Burundi between the predominantly Hutu FRODEBU party that won the 1993 elections and the predominantly Tutsi National Unity and Progress Party (UPRONA) that had been in power since independence.[4] Despite the agreement, the country remained divided and violence continued. The FRODEBU party split into two factions. One faction, led by Léonard Nyangoma, formed a new party, the CNDD, which was committed to winning back power through violent means.[5] Arguing that the stability and governance problems in the country had become untenable, former president Pierre Buyoya (a Tutsi member of UPRONA) launched a military coup in July 1996 and was reinstalled as president of Burundi. There was widespread international and regional condemnation of the coup, and Hutu rebel movements, based in neighboring countries, continued to gain strength and engaged in frequent violent clashes with the government. Comprehensive multiparty peace negotiations known as the Arusha negotiations began in 1998.

The Rwandan genocide was also the spark that triggered the current conflict in the DRC, even though the DRC's colonial legacy and former President Mobutu's thirty-two year reign of predatory politics—assisted by his Cold

---

3. For a discussion of ethnicity and conflict in Burundi, see René Lemarchand, *Burundi: Ethnic Conflict and Genocide* (Cambridge: Cambridge University Press, 1994); and Liisa Malkki, *Purity and Exile: Violence, Memory and National Cosmology among Hutu Refugees in Tanzania* (Chicago: University of Chicago Press, 1995).

4. The Convention of Government was signed by twelve of thirteen political parties in Burundi on September 10, 1994.

5. The CNDD had an armed wing, called the Forces for the Defense of Democracy (FDD). Another active Hutu rebel group was the Palipehutu, which had been founded in the refugee camps in Tanzania in the early 1980s.

War patrons—provide underlying explanations for instability and violence. Following the Rwandan genocide, many Hutu *génocidaires* retreated to the refugee camps in eastern Zaire (as the DRC was then called), creating a security threat for the new post-genocide Rwandan government. In October 1996, the Rwandan army invaded eastern Zaire to break up the camps and find the *ex-génocidaires*. The Rwandan army subsequently helped several anti-Mobutu rebel movements drive the Zairean army out of the eastern part of the country. The leader of these rebels, Laurent Kabila, marched on to Kinshasa with his troops. Mobutu was forced into exile, and Kabila became president in May 1997. Kabila had come to power with Rwanda's strong military support, but the Rwandan influence on his new government was unpopular among Congolese. In July 1998, Laurent Kabila turned against his former allies and ordered the Rwandan army out of the country. In response, the Rwandans once again invaded eastern DRC, this time in an attempt to remove Kabila from power.

To help topple Kabila, Rwanda sponsored a local rebel movement in eastern DRC, the Rassemblement Congolais pour la Démocratie (RCD). Uganda also became involved in the conflict and established a new rebel movement in eastern DRC, the Mouvement de Libération du Congo (MLC), led by Mobutu ally Jean-Pierre Bemba. In the ensuing war, elements of the armed forces of Zimbabwe, Angola, Namibia, Sudan, and Chad came to the assistance of Kabila's government, while Rwanda, Burundi, and Uganda helped various rebel groups against the government.[6] Other armed groups, such as the local Mai-Mai militias, fought the rebels in the east. By the end of 1998, the government of the DRC had lost control of approximately one-third of the country's territory, and peace negotiations were held among most of the belligerents, including outside countries and their proxies.

The Peace Agreements and the Establishment of the Transitional Governments

In both Burundi and the DRC, transitional governments were established as part of broad, comprehensive peace processes. The composition and workings of the transitional institutions were agreed upon during detailed negotiations among belligerents facilitated by outside actors. In Burundi, negotiations began in June 1998 in Arusha, Tanzania, bringing together nineteen Burundian delegations under the facilitation of former Tanzanian

---

6. Neighboring and regional countries became involved in the Congolese war for a number of different political, security, and economic reasons. See John F. Clark, ed., *The African Stakes in the Congo War* (New York: Palgrave MacMillan, 2002); Gérard Prunier, *From Genocide to Continental War: The Congolese Conflict and the Crisis of Contemporary Africa* (London: Hurst and Co., 2004); and Filip Reyntjens, "The Second Congo War: More than a Remake," *African Affairs* 98, no. 393 (October 1999): 241–250.

president Julius Nyerere. The negotiations eventually led to the signing of the Arusha Peace Agreement and the establishment of transitional institutions. In the DRC, negotiations that started in 1998 led to the signing of the Lusaka Cease-fire Agreement in July 1999, including the commitment to further talks on political and military arrangements. These later talks, the "Inter-Congolese Dialogue" and the Sun City and Pretoria negotiations in 2002–2003, led to the establishment of transitional institutions in the DRC.

The Arusha Process

Starting in 1998, therefore, the Arusha process was a comprehensive attempt to bring about peace in Burundi. Five committees were established to look at five themes: the nature of the Burundian conflict, democracy and good governance, peace and security, reconstruction and development, and implementation and regional guarantees.[7] It was the committee on democracy and governance that established the principles underlying transitional governance and the post-transition constitution.

The Arusha negotiations were characterized by constant strategic adjustment, backtracking, and fragmentation of the Burundian political parties. Progress was slow, particularly in the committees dealing with democracy and transitional governance, and peace and security. The armed conflict continued throughout the negotiations. After Nyerere's death in October 1999, Nelson Mandela took over the facilitation of the peace process. Mandela had a strong desire to conclude the process, and even though there were still significant areas of disagreement, the Arusha Peace Agreement was signed in August 2000.

The Arusha Peace Agreement was a very limited agreement. Due to heavy regional and international pressure, several Tutsi parties signed the agreement, but they did so with formal reservations on fundamental points related to transitional governance, such as the future electoral system. Two breakaway major Hutu armed factions that had not participated in the negotiations, the Palipehutu-FNL and the CNDD-FDD, did not sign and continued their armed struggle.

The Arusha agreement provided for a transitional period of thirty-six months. Transitional political positions were divided between the G7 (predominantly Hutu parties) and G10 (predominantly Tutsi parties).[8] The par-

---

7. Each committee had one or two members from each Burundian delegation as well as a chair and vice chair. The chairpersons were international figures chosen by Nyerere. They were Armando Guebuza of Mozambique, Fink Haysom of South Africa, Reverend Matteo Zuppi of Italy, and Georg Lenk of Austria. Mandela was the chair of the Fifth Committee on Implementation and Guarantees, which was established later in the negotiations process.

8. The Arusha agreement specified that the G7 parties would have more than half but less than three-fifths of the ministerial portfolios, and 60 percent of the seats in the National Assembly. The Senate would be divided evenly between G7 and G10 members, but the president of the Senate would come from the G10.

ties could not agree on the leadership of the transitional period. Due to this disagreement and the lack of a cease-fire, it took more than a year for the transitional government to be installed. In July 2001, Mandela broke the deadlock by announcing that Buyoya (from UPRONA) would remain president for the first eighteen months of the transition and that a FRODEBU member would be vice president. In the second eighteen months of the transition, a FRODEBU member would be president and an UPRONA member would be vice president.[9] The transitional government was inaugurated on November 1, 2001, and a transitional constitution was adopted, based on the principles outlined in Protocol II of the Arusha agreement. These transitional institutions were in place until a series of multiparty elections were held, ending in August 2005.

The Inter-Congolese Dialogue and the Pretoria and Sun City Agreements

The 1998 negotiations in the DRC were quite different from the Arusha negotiations for Burundi. Since the armed forces of several African countries were actively involved in the hostilities in the DRC, the governments of these countries participated in the peace negotiations. After lengthy negotiations, a peace agreement was signed in Lusaka in July 1999 by the governments of the DRC, Rwanda, Uganda, Namibia, Zimbabwe, and Angola. The two main Congolese armed groups signed the agreement one month later. The Lusaka Agreement called for an immediate cease-fire, the withdrawal of all foreign forces from the DRC, the disarmament and repatriation of "negative forces" (including the ex-FAR [Forces Armées Rwandaises] and Interahamwe, as well as anti-Ugandan rebels based in the DRC), and the deployment of a UN force. The agreement also called for the establishment of comprehensive inter-Congolese political negotiations involving the armed groups, the Kabila government, the unarmed opposition, and civil society. These negotiations, called the Inter-Congolese Dialogue, would lead to the installation of a transitional power-sharing government, followed by multiparty elections. In November 1999, through the good offices of the Organization of African Unity (OAU), Ketumile Masire, former president of Botswana, was appointed facilitator of the Inter-Congolese Dialogue.

The inter-Congolese negotiations took a long time to begin. President Laurent Kabila refused to work with facilitator Ketumile Masire. Meanwhile, the Lusaka cease-fire was not implemented, and large numbers of individuals profited from continued conflict. As Filip Reyntjens wrote, "Local, national and regional state and non-state actors indeed act

---

9. Domitien Ndayizeye was chosen by FRODEBU to be vice president for the first half of the transition. He became president in April 2003, for the second half of the transition, and Alphonse Kadege from UPRONA became vice president.

rationally, engaged as they are in cost-benefit analyses, whose outcome often shows that war, instability and state decay are more attractive than peace, stability and state reconstruction."[10] In January 2001, Laurent Kabila was assassinated by his bodyguards, and his son, Joseph Kabila, became president. Joseph Kabila recognized Masire as facilitator for the Inter-Congolese Dialogue. Initial meetings for the Inter-Congolese Dialogue were held in Gaborone in August 2001, and the dialogue began in Addis Ababa two months later, in October. However, substantive discussion was blocked due to technical, financial, and political constraints, and the United Nations attempted to push the peace process forward through informal consultations with the Congolese parties between November 2001 and February 2002.

The Inter-Congolese Dialogue finally resumed in Sun City, South Africa, in February 2002. Eight entities were represented: the government, the MLC, the Rassemblement congolais pour la démocratie-Goma (RCD-G), the Rassemblement congolais pour la démocratie-mouvement de liberation (RCD-ML), the Rassemblement congolais pour la démocratie-national (RCD-N), the Mai-Mai, the unarmed political opposition, and civil society representatives (Forces Vives). The dialogue suffered from a number of problems, and initially the parties could not reach a comprehensive agreement. Eventually the DRC government and the MLC delegation concluded a deal between themselves. In July 2002, South Africa brokered an agreement between the DRC and Rwandan governments, in which Rwanda promised to withdraw its forces from the DRC in return for the disarmament of Rwandan Hutu rebels. In September 2002, Angola brokered an agreement between the DRC and Uganda.

Following several more months of consultations, shuttle diplomacy, and negotiations, an all-inclusive peace agreement was signed in Pretoria in December 2002.[11] Using this all-inclusive agreement as a foundation, further negotiations under joint UN–South African auspices led to agreement on the text of a transitional constitution and a memorandum on military and security issues, signed in Sun City, South Africa, in April 2003, with facilitator Masire. The transitional constitution and the all-inclusive agreement were the centerpieces of the peace package and set out the structures of the transitional government.

The transitional government was a power-sharing government consisting of President Joseph Kabila (Parti du peuple pour la reconstruction et la

---

10. Filip Reyntjens, "The Democratic Republic of Congo, From Kabila to Kabila," *African Affairs* 100, no. 401 (October 2001): 312.

11. By the end of 2002, most of the Angolan, Zimbabwean, Ugandan, Rwandan, and Burundian troops had withdrawn from the DRC, although the Congolese government failed to disarm or demobilize the Hutu rebels. This later proved to be a critical factor in the continuation of Rwandan interference in the peace process.

démocratie, or PPRD) and four vice presidents from different groups: Abdoulaye Yerodia Ndombasi (PPRD), Jean-Pierre Bemba (MLC), Azarias Ruberwa (RCD-G), and Z'Ahidi Ngoma (civilian opposition). Thirty-six cabinet ministries were divided among the different armed groups, the unarmed political opposition, and the Forces Vives. There were twenty-five vice ministers, who were also divided up among the groups in order to accommodate prominent people from each of them. The legislature consisted of a 620-seat parliament. There were 500 representatives in the National Assembly and 120 representatives in the Senate, all designated by the parties.

The transitional government was sworn in on June 30, 2003, and was intended to govern for two years, leading to the first national elections held in the DRC since 1965. Elections were delayed, but the first round was eventually held in July 2006 and a second round was held in October 2006, bringing an official end to the transitional period.

The Role of International and Regional Actors

The transitional governments in Burundi and the DRC were local power-sharing governments that reflected the existing power structures in the two countries. Nonetheless, both regional and international involvement were significant in each country, and the transitional institutions bore the imprint of this external involvement.

The Arusha process leading to transitional institutions in Burundi was distinctive due to the high levels of African involvement. There was significant international support for Arusha, including financial support from the European Union and other Western countries, but for the most part African leaders and experts facilitated the Arusha process and provided advice on the nature of transitional institutions and arrangements.

In the early stages of the peace negotiations, large numbers of external actors were involved, and problems of coordination were quite severe. For instance, there were special envoys from a number of countries and organizations, mediators from international NGOs, and regional actors. During the early period of the Arusha negotiations, the different Burundian parties and factions were able to manipulate the large number of regional and international actors. Sometimes, the different external actors worked at cross-purposes. There were disagreements, for instance, between the facilitator, Julius Nyerere, and the Western envoys over the economic sanctions that had been placed on Burundi after Buyoya's coup. There were also disagreements about whether to recognize the different Burundian party wings and factions. Nyerere had his way in both of these disagreements, but he was accused of bias by President Buyoya and the UPRONA party and was seen as sympathetic to certain Hutu parties.

When Nelson Mandela took over as facilitator, some changes were made in the Arusha peace process strategy. Desiring to establish his role as a peace negotiator, Mandela took a tough stance on all parties in Burundi and dealt with them heavy-handedly. Mandela was criticized for pushing the process and forcing Burundian politicians to sign an incomplete agreement. He was also criticized for viewing the conflict through a "South African lens," equating the Tutsi with white South Africans under apartheid.[12] Despite these flaws, Mandela did put great effort into attracting global attention to Burundi and coordinating the regional and international response to it, and his involvement made South Africa emerge as a decisive actor in the peace process. At some points during the process, tensions arose among the South Africans, the Tanzanian facilitation team, and the regional initiative led by Ugandan president Yoweri Museveni, but the South Africans took the lead in negotiating both the transitional arrangements and the cease-fire. Indeed, it is unlikely that the Burundian transitional institutions would have been established without South African pressure and support. For instance, it was Mandela who broke the deadlock over the leadership of the transition by unilaterally declaring that Buyoya would remain president for the first half of the transition. Mandela also persuaded the South African government to provide a 700-member military protection force for the Burundian politicians returning from exile to take up positions in the transitional government. Without this force, it is unlikely that many of the politicians would have returned to Burundi, thus blocking the transitional institutions.[13]

The war continued even once the transitional institutions were established. Different African leaders attempted to mediate between the Burundian rebels and the transitional Burundian government, but the then–deputy president of South Africa, Jacob Zuma, was the main mediator throughout most of the transitional period. In October 2002, following intense pressure from South Africa, agreements were signed with two smaller wings of the rebel groups, but the larger wings of the movements continued to fight. In June 2003, faced with UN reluctance to send a peacekeeping force to a country without a comprehensive cease-fire, the AU established its first peacekeeping mission, the African Mission in Burundi (AMIB). The existing

---

12. For a discussion of this comparison, see Jean-Pierre Chrétien, "Le Burundi après la signature de l'accord d'Arusha," *Politique Africaine*, no. 80 (2000): 136–151, 142.

13. For a discussion of the South African role in Burundi, see Kristina Bentley and Roger Southall, *An African Peace Process: Mandela, South Africa and Burundi* (Cape Town: HSRC Press, 2005). For a discussion of the South African role in Burundi and the DRC, see Devon Curtis, "South Africa: 'Exporting' Peace to the Great Lakes Region?" in *South Africa in Africa: The Post-Apartheid Era*, ed. Adekeye Adebajo, Adebayo Adedeji and Christopher Landsberg (Scottsville, South Africa: University of Kwazulu-Natal Press, 2007); and Devon Curtis, "The Great Lakes Region," in *Constitutionalism and Democratic Transitions: Lessons from South Africa*, ed. Veronica Federico and Carlo Fusaro (Florence: University of Florence Press, 2006).

South African protection force formed the backbone of this larger AU mission. In November 2003, South African mediators finally succeeded in reaching an agreement with the larger rebel faction (CNDD-FDD's Nkurunziza wing) that included a protocol on power sharing in the transitional government and in the army. The transitional government was restructured to take the new agreement into account.[14] In light of this new ceasefire, in June 2004 the United Nations deployed a peacekeeping mission, the United Nations Operation in Burundi (Opération des Nations Unies au Burundi, or ONUB), to take over from the AU forces.[15]

Some Burundians, particularly several hard-line politicians, were critical of the far-reaching South African involvement, especially when key decisions were made by South Africans, such as the question of leadership of the transitional institutions.[16] In some ways, this criticism is unfair because, in the absence of South African involvement (especially the initial security protection provided by South Africa), it is unlikely that the transitional government would have been established or the Arusha Peace Agreement implemented. Even if the institutions were established, it is likely that they would have collapsed without South African commitment and support. Nonetheless, the criticism of South Africa in particular and outside involvement in general uncovers a more serious problem, which only started to be addressed in the later stages of the transition in Burundi. The Arusha process had international legitimacy and regional legitimacy, but it had difficulty garnering domestic legitimacy.

In the DRC, the nature of international and regional involvement in the peace process was quite different because many countries were directly involved in the fighting, and they had strong preferences regarding the outcome of transitional arrangements. The war in the DRC was both an internal and an international conflict. At all stages of the DRC peace process and transition, external actors played a critical role, sometimes helpful and sometimes less so.

Compared to both Julius Nyerere and Nelson Mandela in Burundi, the facilitator of the Inter-Congolese Dialogue, Ketumile Masire, was seen as relatively weak.[17] Masire perceived his role to be minimalist, and the initial

---

14. The Global Cease-fire Agreement was an agreement that finalized earlier political and security power-sharing agreements signed in Pretoria on October 8, 2003, and November 2, 2003. The CNDD-FDD was given four ministerial positions, fifteen seats in the transitional national assembly, and 40 percent of the officer positions in the new Burundi National Defence Force.

15. ONUB was authorized under UN Security Council Resolution 1545 to have a maximum of 5,650 military personnel. ONUB's mandate ended on December 31, 2006. On January 1, 2007, the UN Integrated Office in Burundi (BINUB) was established to coordinate UN activities in the country and to continue to provide support to the new government.

16. Bentley and Southall, *An African Peace Process*.

17. International Crisis Group (ICG), *Storm Clouds over Sun City: The Urgent Need to Recast the Congolese Peace Process*, ICG Africa Report no. 44 (May 14, 2002).

discussions about transitional arrangements and power sharing progressed slowly as he had difficulty mediating and putting pressure on the Congolese belligerents. By 2002, South African president Thabo Mbeki put the negotiations back on track. Nonetheless, many Congolese questioned the neutrality of the South African government, believing it to be overly supportive of Rwanda and the RCD-G. Outside economic interests, particularly the competition over mining contracts, also contributed to delays in the inter-Congolese negotiations.

The governments of the United States, France, and Belgium also put pressure on the belligerents and their allies. The Western countries pressed the Congolese participants on the need to give Kabila special status as president during the transitional period, the need to withdraw all foreign troops, and the need to adopt a timetable toward elections. For the most part, this pressure was effective. As soon as the Sun City Agreement was signed, the DRC government and the World Bank signed a loan agreement of US \$120 million to rebuild the economy, followed by US \$214 million in emergency support a few months later.[18]

Once the transitional power-sharing government was established, it continued to be influenced by external developments and ambiguous and incoherent outside support. The direct involvement of Rwanda and Uganda in sending their troops across the border and in sponsoring different Congolese rebel groups is only the most obvious manifestation of external involvement. Even among external "peacebuilders" (as opposed to external belligerents), the record in the transitional period in the DRC was mixed. Unlike in Burundi, where the South Africans eventually assumed a lead role, the transition in the DRC suffered from an insufficient and often disjointed response.

When the Security Council first authorized its mission to the DRC (the UN Mission in the Democratic Republic of Congo, or MONUC) in 1999, it was little more than a cease-fire observation mission.[19] Through a series of resolutions, MONUC was expanded and strengthened.[20] However, even though MONUC gained Chapter VII authorization, it was hampered by a lack of resources and a lack of political will. For example, in May 2002, when 160 civilians were killed in Kisangani very close to a camp of one thousand MONUC soldiers, MONUC said they did not have sufficient resources to intervene.

---

18. *IRIN News*, July 31, 2004, and September 15, 2004, www.irinnews.org. In addition, the IMF said it would provide aid of US \$472 million in net present value terms, to be delivered through an average annual reduction in debt service of about 50 percent until 2012.

19. UN Security Council Resolution 1279 (1999).

20. UN Security Council Resolution 1291 (2000); UN Security Council Resolution 1376 (2001); UN Security Council Resolution 1399 (2002).

The UN secretary-general appealed for an international force when violence once again erupted in Ituri in 2003. France agreed to lead the force under the auspices of the EU. Operation Artemis was launched in July 2003, deploying 1,500 peacekeepers for three months under a Chapter VII mandate, with the limited aim of stabilizing the city of Bunia. The operation was generally viewed as a success in filling its small mission, and it gave the United Nations time to attain authorization and forces to reestablish its presence in Bunia. Once the United Nations expanded MONUC in Security Council Resolution 1493 (July 2003), the mission had evolved from a cease-fire observation mission to a broader peacekeeping mission supporting the DRC transition. In UN Security Council Resolution 1565 (October 2004), MONUC was further mandated under Chapter VII to deploy 16,700 troops to discourage violence and to protect civilians in imminent danger. It also had a mandate to support the Government of National Unity and Transition, including contributing to the successful completion of the electoral process stipulated in the Global and All Inclusive Agreement. Its mandate also included supporting three joint commissions on essential legislation (including the future constitution), security sector reform, and the electoral process.

As specified in the Sun City Agreement, an International Committee in Support of the Transition (CIAT) was established to assist in the implementation of the agreement and to arbitrate any disagreements that may arise among the parties. The committee was chaired by the United Nations (MONUC) and was made up of diplomatic representatives of the permanent members of the Security Council as well as Mozambique, South Africa, Zambia, Angola, Belgium, Canada, Gabon, the AU, and the EU. It met regularly during the transitional period and was instrumental in supporting the elections, but there was less progress on other issues, including security-sector reform. External actors in general, and MONUC in particular, faced the dilemma of not wanting to alienate the parties they were trying to encourage to collaborate in the peace process, but this led to ambiguous policies toward the armed groups. It was unclear whether certain leaders in the DRC should be considered potential partners or threats to the peace.

International actors were involved in the DRC peace process in other ways as well. Following the renewal of violence in the Kivus in 2004, the United States sponsored talks in November 2004, which eventually led to an agreement among Rwanda, Uganda, and the DRC. The United States also sponsored a Joint Verification Commission, composed of Rwandan and Congolese army officers and MONUC officials, and a tripartite agreement among Rwanda, the DRC, and Uganda to deal with security and diplomatic issues.

Overall, then, the role of external actors in the peace process of the DRC has been ambiguous. Faced with so many different interests, it has been difficult for the international community to present a fully coordinated transitional assistance strategy. The involvement of neighbors, particularly Rwanda and Uganda, constituted an important challenge to the Congolese transitional government and continues to influence post-transition politics.

Stability and Legitimacy

The transitional governments in Burundi and the DRC faced a number of important obstacles and challenges in implementation, even though the processes did lead to elections in the two countries. Indeed, for every step forward, there have been serious challenges, uncertainties, and backsliding. While stability has improved in most parts of the two countries, violence continues elsewhere, and there is no evidence that violence will not be used to resolve future disputes. Achieving domestic legitimacy and popular support has been very difficult in both countries.

Power-sharing Governance, Violence, and Legitimacy in Burundi

The transitional institutions in Burundi were based on the division of power and offices between Hutu and Tutsi political groups. This, of course, responded to the problem of Hutu exclusion from political structures since independence but ignored other roots of the Burundian conflict, such as the lack of economic opportunities, regionalism, and the role of the military. Furthermore, the high degree of factionalism in Burundi shows that ethnic groups are not cohesive and that other considerations (such as personal and regional ties and economic interests) were also extremely salient. New parties and alliances were constantly being formed during the interim period, as Burundian leaders and politicians maneuvered themselves according to strategic, economic, or personal interests.

Indeed, the interim power-sharing arrangements and the continual cease-fire negotiations encouraged factionalism in Burundi. When individuals and parties did not get the office they wanted from the political negotiations, they threatened to break away and pursue their interests through violent means. These groups were able to do this, in part, because of the lack of a comprehensive cease-fire agreement and a disarmament and demobilization process; they continued to constitute genuine potential spoilers. The process inadvertently gave some individuals and parties an incentive to continue fighting, to wait for better offers in subsequent rounds of negotiations. Since external facilitators were so concerned about spoilers, they tended to make increasingly attractive offers to those who remained outside the transitional institutions, providing further incentives for groups to remain outside the process for as long as possible.

Despite the delays and concessions to potential spoilers, in the end the sequencing gamble of establishing transitional institutions *before* a comprehensive cease-fire may have had important positive effects. Burundi was much safer at the end of the transitional period compared to the beginning. This is largely because the CNDD-FDD rebels (Nkurunziza faction) joined the process in 2003, thus enabling the disarmament, demobilization, and reintegration (DDR) programs and army reform to begin. The last active rebel group, the FNL, signed a cease-fire in September 2006, one year after the new government had been in office, but by March 2007 it had not been fully implemented due to disagreements over the FNL's place in state institutions. So while there may not have been a realistic alternative to the sequencing of the Arusha process and it did lead to the establishment of new permanent institutions, it had the unfortunate side effect of sending a message that violence reaps rewards. As long as the Arusha process was not seen as conclusive, violence remained a strategy for gaining office.

The process of implementing peace and creating stability was hindered not just by continuing violence but also by legitimacy and efficiency gaps. The Arusha process achieved international and regional legitimacy, but it lacked domestic legitimacy. This was partly a result of the process itself, which focused on elite negotiations. In a dynamic similar to that outlined in Antonio Donini's chapter in this volume, many of the politicians at Arusha had very little support among the broader population, and they tended to be invited to Arusha due to their capacity for violence rather than their espousal of particular policy proposals. The focus of the Arusha negotiations and the post-Arusha cease-fire talks was on dividing political and military offices among potential spoilers.

Because the negotiations occurred among elites concerned with dividing the spoils, they created an unwieldy government that had little interest in implementing other parts of the economic and social reform package included in the accords. From the point of view of many Burundians, Arusha divided positions among a small, select group of elites, but it had very little impact on their lives. By the middle of the transition period, observers pointed out that conditions had not improved for the bulk of the Burundian population. Poverty had increased, violence continued, and the new transitional institutions benefited only a slightly enlarged group of elites based in Bujumbura.[21] The transitional government was disconnected from the population. There was a referendum on the new

---

21. See, for instance, Jan van Eck, *Absence of Peace Dividends Undermines Legitimacy of Whole Transition: War Continues and Poverty Grows* (Pretoria: University of Pretoria, Unit for Policy Studies, April/May 2002).

post-transition constitution in February 2005 and 92 percent of Burundian voters were in favor of it, but holding a referendum at the end of the transitional process is not sufficient in terms of engaging the broader population in the peace process. In the national elections in 2005, the CNDD-FDD, led by Nkurunziza, won by a large margin. The victory of the former rebels was, in part, due to their late arrival and disassociation from the transitional institutions and to the belief among large sections of the population that the election of the CNDD-FDD would bring an end to violence. Despite its electoral victory, however, the new post-transition government has ruled in much the same way as its predecessors. It has increasingly adopted authoritarian practices. For instance, just under a year after taking office, the CNDD government arrested several prominent opposition politicians on what was largely viewed as trumped up accusations of coup plotting.

Continued Conflict and Weak Transitional Governance in the DRC

The transitional government in the DRC faced even more challenges than its counterpart in Burundi in terms of achieving stability and legitimacy. A highly factionalized and ambiguous transitional power-sharing government in the DRC was unable, and in some cases unwilling, to establish security and stability across the country. Lacking cohesion and control, the various Congolese parties were unable to remove hard-liners from power, which helped facilitate the ongoing military confrontation in the east. The government also had problems in its day-to-day functioning, as well as in its perceived domestic legitimacy. While the transitional process did lead to elections and a new government, enormous problems remain and the outcome is not conclusive.

There were serious problems in implementing the Sun City Accords. It was easier for international and regional pressure to convince Congolese parties to sign an agreement dividing up political offices than to implement that agreement. Two main areas of contention have been power sharing in the army and the continued conflict in the eastern part of the country, particularly in the provinces of North and South Kivu and Ituri.

According to the transitional agreement and constitution, the former belligerents were to hand over control of their armed groups to a unified (power-sharing) new national army, the Forces Armées de la République du Congo (FARDC). However, many of the three hundred thousand combatants in the DRC are controlled by the same military hierarchies as before the transition. Despite the creation of a unified army general staff in Kinshasa in 2003, there are still parallel chains of command in both the capital and the provinces. Kabila's supporters, the various RCD factions, and the other armed groups have very little trust in one another, and MONUC is not strong enough to resolve the security dilemma. New military leaders have been appointed to the DRC's ten military zones, but most of the troops on the ground maintain their allegiances to individual commanders. A further crisis occurred when Kabila wanted to place the intelligence and security services under the presidency, which Ruberwa (RCD-G), vice president in charge of security and defense, refused. Ruberwa was also concerned about the large presidential guard (ten thousand to fifteen thousand strong) that Kabila still controlled, the Groupe spécial de sécurité présidentielle (GSSP). Vice President Bemba also controlled a large protection force.

The signatories of the Sun City Agreement lacked strong command and control over their military and political wings, and there were numerous factions and shifting alliances. There were parallel chains of command in the army, the former rebel groups, and the transitional civilian government. Various factions continued to compete for favors and resources. Kabila was hampered by a lack of cohesion in his party: many of the hardliners around him were opposed to elections and were eager to put an end to transitional power-sharing governance and to pursue a military solution. Some of these people believed that there was no chance for reconciliation with the RCD-G, the "puppets of Kigali." Furthermore, although Kabila declared the Forces Démocratiques de Libération du Rwanda (FDLR) unwelcome in the DRC in 2002, many hard-liners close to Kabila continued to support it. Kabila was hesitant to take on the FDLR militarily, despite his obligations under the Pretoria Agreement to do so.[22] Due to these internal disputes, Kabila shuffled the transitional cabinet and military leadership several times.

The RCD-G also faced serious internal dissent and factional disputes. The RCD-G has no coherent overarching structure. Its base support comes from Kinyarwanda speakers of the province of North Kivu, but there was a split between hard-line RCD-G commanders and representatives in the east, and RCD-G representatives in the transitional government in Kinshasa. Hard-line representatives of the RCD-G in the eastern town of Goma criticized Vice President Ruberwa for failing to represent their concerns, particularly their fears of ethnic persecution. These RCD-G dissidents felt they had nothing to gain from the transition and formed a coalition in the Kivus.[23] This coalition was an unstructured group of dissidents with only a loose hierarchy, but they were supported by Rwanda. For the most part, RCD-G transitional representatives in Kinshasa distanced themselves from the dissidents, but Ruberwa wavered between supporting and criticizing

---

22. Most supplies for the FDLR were believed to come from Mai-Mai militias, which fought against the RCD-G.
23. The hard-line RCD-G governor of North Kivu, Eugene Serufuli, and other RCD-G dissidents sometimes refused to follow Ruberwa's orders.

them.[24] In June 2004, three RCD-G parliamentarians created a new movement called RCD-G *rénovateur*, which regularly criticized Ruberwa and
Rwanda.[25] Therefore, Ruberwa was marginalized by members of his party
in Kinshasa as well as by his base in North Kivu. This lack of coherence
within the RCD and other parties contributed to continued conflict in the
east throughout the transitional period.[26]

Indeed, fighting continued in several parts of the country during the transition. Rwanda repeatedly sent troops to eastern Congo to pursue the Hutu
extremist FDLR and to secure a share in lucrative economic opportunities.
The FDLR had an estimated eight thousand to ten thousand troops in the
DRC, and it could still launch cross-border raids into Rwanda.[27] Fighting in
eastern Congo escalated in 2004, including bloody battles in the city of
Bukavu in May–June 2004.[28] In June 2004, Kabila sent ten thousand ex-FAC
(ex–Congolese Armed Forces) and ex-MLC troops to North and South Kivu.
Yet some members of RCD-G interpreted this as a hostile act by Kabila
against their forces. The deployment led some RCD-G representatives to
withdraw from parliament. Fighting also intensified in the east in the lead-
up to elections in 2006.

Regional actors therefore aggravated tensions in the transitional process:
at times, both Rwanda and Uganda have exacerbated and encouraged the
confrontations. Financial networks established in the first Congo war of 1996
were significant, and some of the fighting between different parties and factions can be understood as violent struggles to preserve these networks.[29]

Regarding domestic legitimacy, the problems are similar to those discussed in the case of Burundi. As in the Arusha Peace Agreement for Burundi,
the Sun City Agreement for the DRC focused on power sharing and the divi-

---

24. ICG, *The Congo's Transition Is Failing: Crisis in the Kivus,* ICG Africa Report no. 91 (March 30, 2005): 6.

25. When Ruberwa suspended his party's participation in the transitional government following the massacre of Banyamulenge refugees in Burundi, sixty-two of the ninety-four RCD-
G deputies refused to follow him.

26. The dynamics within other parties and armed groups also changed continually, driven by
economic and political considerations. For a discussion of the complex politics in the Ituri
region, see ICG, *Maintaining Momentum in the Congo: The Ituri Problem,* ICG Africa Report no.
84 (August 26, 2004).

27. ICG, *The Congo: Solving the FDLR Problem Once and for All,* ICG Africa Briefing no. 25 (May 12,
2005), and "EU May Support Military Action Against Hutu Rebels, Ajello Says," *IRIN News,*
June 24, 2005, www.irinnews.org.

28. A report by the UN expert panel on the Illegal Exploitation of Natural Resources and Other
Forms of Wealth in the DRC documented Rwanda's involvement in the Bukavu fighting.

29. To illustrate the economic stakes, at their peak in December 2000, revenues from the export
of coltan exceeded US $1 million a month. That year, the RCD also exported gold and dia-
monds worth US $30 million. Denis Tull, "A Reconfiguration of Political Order? The State of
the State in North Kivu (DR Congo)," *African Affairs* 102 (July 2003): 429–446, 435. See also
"Final Report of the Panel of Experts on the Illegal Exploitation of Natural Resources and
Other Forms of Wealth of the Democratic Republic of the Congo," United Nations
(S/2002/1146), October 16, 2002.

sion of offices. By giving the main power brokers in the DRC a stake in governance, it was hoped that they would be persuaded to stop fighting and learn to work together. Instead, the nature of the transitional structures allowed power holders to continue to pursue their clientelistic relations and predatory behavior. Although the transition did provoke some shifts in power dynamics, business continued as usual for the most part, including deadly business, as just discussed.

Furthermore, as in Burundi, the emphasis of the Congolese agreement was elite power sharing, which did not strengthen the relationship between leaders and the citizenry. In the DRC, there was no significant pressure to rebuild state capacity or to finance social services. Rather, the transitional structures allowed Congolese political and military leaders to continue to follow old patterns: a reliance on aid, outside assistance, foreign investment, and extraction to compensate for their lack of domestic support. Foreign donors financed 53 percent of the transitional government's budget.[30]

These elite bargains translated into difficulties in day-to-day transitional governance, because they created an oversized government populated by politicians with diverse, often competing, agendas. By design, a "national unity" transitional government brings together individuals with competing political, economic, and security interests. There is an explicit trade-off in this kind of government. Bringing everyone together in the ruling structures is designed to stop violent conflict, but the trade-off is low governance efficiency and effectiveness. Inefficiencies and delays are to be expected in this type of government. More serious impediments, however, relate to the extensive corruption across the administration.[31] The establishment of transitional structures did not bring an end to previous patterns of corruption, clientelism, and informal networks. An audit of state-run companies in September 2004 showed very high levels of corruption. Six ministers were dismissed from the transitional cabinet. However, the mechanisms to deal with corruption in the transitional government were not fully functional, and no criminal charges were laid.

The DRC does not have a strong, differentiated bureaucracy governed by the rule of law. As with the security situation, good governance was hampered by the weakness of political parties and programs and the weakness of the judiciary. In the lead-up to the elections, the absence of well-defined political platforms was an indication that the elections would be fought on

---

30. ICG, *The Congo's Transition Is Failing*, 3.

31. Corruption and the possibilities of personal enrichment have also fueled the conflict in the east. The individuals who control the army's supply contracts and payrolls have benefited enormously. The area of North Kivu controlled by the ex-ANC produced US $1.1 million a month in declared revenue, mostly through taxes on imports and exports. Even more revenue from North Kivu passes outside official administrative channels. The control over lucrative mines in the west of North Kivu has been at the center of the recent conflict. See ICG, *The Congo's Transition Is Failing*, 13–17.

the basis of personalities, ethnic affiliations, and personal ties. There were thirty-three presidential candidates and more than 250 parties competing, but parties are fluid, and individuals move in and out depending on personal ambitions. The electoral law provided for open lists, meaning that voters voted for individuals, not parties, further weakening political parties.

In the Kivus, the RCD-G continued to extract resources through taxes and minerals, but public employees received virtually no salaries, and there was little effort to improve the socioeconomic well-being of the population.[32] These patterns are not dissimilar to patterns established under Mobutu, when systems of political patronage meant it was not necessary to offer extensive public services to the population. Many transitional politicians were aware of their lack of domestic legitimacy and were reluctant to go to the polls. It remains to be seen how they will react to their defeat, particularly under conditions of continued state weakness and easy access to the instruments of violence. The fragility of the DRC transitional process can be highlighted by the military clashes between Bemba's militias and Kabila's Presidential Guard, which occurred in Kinshasa only days after the first round of election results were announced.

Conclusion: Uncertain Transitions

Local, transitional, power-sharing governments ought to provide security by giving former belligerents a piece of the political and economic "pie" and therefore a stake in peace. These aim to bring about domestic legitimacy through elaborating a step-by-step process toward elections and governance reforms. These two objectives, however, have proven difficult to meet in Burundi and the DRC.

First, on security, the competing factions in these two countries are plentiful and incoherent. When leaders have "signed on" to the agreements, their party or group is prone to factional splits. Alliances shift and are inspired by personal or factional interests, rather than national interests or policy platforms. Even though the transitional structures are bloated, it is not possible to accommodate everyone. In both countries, local actors have not eliminated the possibility of using violence to achieve their aims if they do not receive what they want through the transition (despite elections). In the DRC in particular, many powerful politicians and military leaders felt that the transition did not personally benefit them. Elections presented a great

---

32. Tull, "A Reconfiguration of Political Order," 435, 445. As Prunier points out with respect to an earlier period in Congolese politics, ignoring the concerns of the population can lead to further violence, because feelings of political neglect and economic marginalization make it easier for outsiders to activate ethnic solidarity networks. See Gérard Prunier, "Rebel Movements and Proxy Warfare: Uganda, Sudan and the Congo (1986–99)," *African Affairs* 103, no. 412 (2004): 359–383.

potential threat to some of these leaders. While international involvement in the DRC has affected the balance of power among Congolese domestic elites, international efforts thus far have not been able to either marginalize or to co-opt hard-line leaders. The presence of belligerents in the interim institutions was intended to have a pacifying effect, but inclusive structures can also end up rewarding violence. Also, stability in both countries depends on the ability to achieve security-sector reform. The creation of new national armies in Burundi and the DRC has been slow, although the DDR process in Burundi did produce relative success.

Second, interim governments in Burundi and the DRC have not achieved popular domestic legitimacy. Many of the groups represented in the transitional structures had little or no support among the population. Regional and international facilitators focused on reaching agreements to distribute power, political posts, and privileges rather than on trying to root these agreements in a shared vision for the future. Perhaps such a nebulous goal would have been difficult to reach, but the failure to articulate a vision for society and a program for reform will have future consequences. Despite their electoral victories, the new governments in both Burundi and the DRC show signs of continuity with the past and have adopted a number of authoritarian practices. Yet popular expectations in both countries are high and social discontent can rise quickly and easily if these expectations are frustrated.

Finally, the involvement of regional and international actors in the two countries has not always been positive or coordinated. At times, various external actors promoted different, and sometimes opposing, strategies toward the same groups, and their strategies were sometimes motivated by self-interest first. The experiences of Burundi and the DRC show that the establishment of a local power-sharing transitional government does not remove the need for sustained, coordinated international involvement. To the contrary, since the establishment of the transitional governments and even after the elections, both countries need more, not less, coordinated international attention.

This chapter has emphasized the tensions and difficulties in the transitional processes in the DRC and Burundi. Yet this assessment does not mean that the peace processes are doomed to failure in the two countries. There are, indeed, some formidable challenges, but there are also some hopeful signs. Although violence remains a concrete possibility, many leaders are now using political channels to contest issues such as the new constitutions and legislation. In Burundi, competition is primarily centered between two Hutu groups rather than between Hutu and Tutsi, partly as a result of power-sharing arrangements and electoral laws. Although conditions in Burundi are more favorable than before, it is still not possible to determine whether a genuine compact between leaders and the population will be forthcoming.

The DRC faces greater challenges, and several powerful players have much to lose in the postelection period. Yet these shortcomings are as much a commentary on the regional conflict environments and the interests at stake as on the nature of the transitional structures themselves. In other words, inclusive, transitional domestic structures are not enough. Rather, domestic structures must exist alongside mechanisms to address the wider regional conflict and efforts to increase state capacity and accountability.

9

Interim Government in Liberia

Peace Building toward the Status Quo

E. Philip Morgan

Editors' Note

In this chapter on Liberia, E. Philip Morgan provides an analysis of an interim regime located midway between traditional models and the neo-trusteeship models described in the introductory chapter. His chapter stresses the hard choices that creators of interim governments face: should they include combatants and therefore potentially create a government with questionable legitimacy on the ground, or should they exclude combatants and therefore leave potential spoilers out of the peace process? As we saw in Devon Curtis's chapter, there are trade-offs to each approach: including combatants alleviates the spoiler problem, but including them creates a domestic legitimacy crisis. Morgan's case brings out the insight that internationally governed transitional governments (the Liberian Government of National Unity created in 2003) have difficulties gaining legitimacy on the ground, even if the United Nations and other international actors consider the government viable. When military victors are included in governments without consideration for the extent of their local followings, the resulting transitional governments have little support on the ground, and they are concerned more with dividing spoils among the victors than with delivering services and improving the quality of life.

Morgan also introduces the impact of economic relationships on transitional processes. In countries where civil war evolved out of competition to control resource-rich economies, the transitional process will not work without fundamental economic change. In these scenarios, the international community can retain a trump card to push forward the transitional process, even after it turns over an international interim government to a domestic government. This trump card is control over the economy: by creating domestic institutions with significant international oversight and/or control, the international community retains leverage over the transitional process and therefore retains influence even in domestic processes. This influence, however, can be double edged, as the citizens on the ground may, as they did in Liberia, come to see this as an infringement on their sovereignty. It remains to be seen, at least in the Liberian case, to what extent this jeopardizes the legitimacy of the permanent regime.

■ ■ ■

Introduction

This volume is intended to advance an understanding of transitional political processes in countries moving from a condition of conflict to one of peace building and, possibly, democracy under the aegis of an international interim government. While the meaning of *international interim government* is the subject of increasing distinctions and refinements, what all definitions have in common is that an external international party (for example, the United Nations or NATO) is either exercising executive authority or is sharing authority with the government of a vulnerable state experiencing debilitating conflict. The role of interim government is in combination with peacekeeping, peace building, and progress toward political liberalization. That is why this volume contains case studies along with more theoretically grounded essays.

What illumination, whether of theoretical insights or policy implications, might derive from analyzing Liberia's recent experience with several international interim governments? First, Liberia's twentieth-century history is a good case of a resource-rich country beset by factions with a zero-sum outlook on the control of those resources. Second, Liberia is the prototypical failed state, eroded first by privilege and subsequently by ambitious individuals whose armed gangs captured, corrupted, or crushed attenuated political institutions. Third, Liberia and Sierra Leone together provide an optic on contemporary warlord politics, a phenomenon in which political actors opportunistically exploit inchoate public institutions and public resources to serve the personal ambitions of a "big man" and his cronies. Fourth, Liberia's disintegration, its civil war, its interim governments, and its future governance arrangements are intimately tied to an unstable region: the Mano River basin (Guinea, Liberia, Sierra Leone, and Côte d'Ivoire). Finally, Liberia's experience with regional peacekeepers and regional economic arrangements provides both cautionary tales and positive precedents with respect to peace building, legitimacy, and governance.

Origins of the Liberian State
and the Seeds of State Failure

The factors that led to the civil war that devastated Liberia in the 1990s were intimately tied to the creation of the country in 1847. Liberia is an artifact of the emigration of freed American slaves to Africa under the agency of the American Colonization Society. Described as "an alternative to abolition," this movement began in the 1820s, culminating in a settler "republic" in 1847.[1] Over the next hundred years, the coastal settlers evolved into a tightly knit community of privilege. They governed a unitary sovereign state through which they variously fought, exploited, and, to an extent, co-opted the indigenous people in the countryside. From the 1920s a Liberian Frontier Force (LFF), along with a department of "interior," secured peace, order, and revenues from the tutelary population in the countryside.[2] The 1926 agreement with the American Firestone Company to further develop the rubber industry was motivated by the government's need for revenue, jobs for laborers, and, by extension, extra organizational assistance in keeping "order."[3] Power and wealth were highly concentrated, and a few families controlled great quantities of land: the twenty largest Liberian logging concessions covered 8,500 square miles, and 3,000 independent private rubber estates (15 percent of the territory) turned local inhabitants into laborers dependent on those families. By the 1940s, political and economic power reposed in roughly 300 families of Americo-Liberians.

For much of the mid-twentieth century (1944–71), William Tubman served as the president of the sovereign Republic of Liberia. His great power derived from his role as godfather/broker to the elite families, his control of the LFF and public revenues, and a singular political organization, the True Whig Party, which he used to manage national affairs until his death in 1971. Government and businesses were dominated by, as William Reno writes, a "circle of relatives, other Americo-Liberian families, and more recent local assimilated tribal entrants to this 'honorable' class."[4]

By the 1960s, no longer able to contain aspirations for greater participation, especially given the wholesale expansion of political independence of all his neighbors along the West African littoral, Tubman was forced to open up the system. New county jurisdictions were established, binding the countryside

---

1. Amos Sawyer, *Beyond Plunder: Toward Democratic Governance in Liberia* (Boulder, Colo., and London: Lynne Rienner Publishers, 2005), 11.
2. Ibid., 14–15.
3. J. Gus Liebenow, *Liberia: The Quest for Democracy* (Bloomington: Indiana University Press, 1987), 56.
4. William Reno, *Warlord Politics and African States* (Boulder, Colo., and London: Lynne Rienner Publishers, 1998), 82.

to the coast in the same political-administrative framework. The extension of
the franchise to indigenous people, along with greatly expanded educational
opportunities, combined to create a slightly more inclusive society, at least at
the margins.[5]

As in other countries, the reforms served only to evoke more expansive
ambitions among younger people of Tubman's own class. His successor in
1971, William R. Tolbert, was cross-pressured by the conservative elites
who wanted to extend the privileges of their own progeny. They induced
him to privatize more communal land to generate export income. While
this served the intended purpose of extending opportunities for already
powerful elites, it also ejected indigenous farmers from their land. Moreover, the Tolbert government continued to turn a blind eye to the low wages
paid to both rural and urban labor, leaving the majority with a mean, subsistence existence.

These conditions were noted by local intellectuals and professionals and
by returning overseas graduates and local youth. They were well informed
as to how politics and government had changed among the neighboring
states in the 1960s and 1970s and were imbued with the ideas of self-
determination and majority rule implicit in the decolonization process.
Accordingly, two organizations emerged in the 1970s that offered a modest
challenge to the monopoly on authority enjoyed by the True Whig Party and
the Tolbert government: the Movement for Justice in Africa (MOJA), which
advocated for social justice, rule of law, and democratization generally, and
the Progressive Alliance of Liberians (PAL), which focused more specifically
on multiparty electoral competition.[6]

While Tubman had been able to balance competing demands, thus insu-
lating his power base from challenges, Tolbert had developed neither the
temperament nor the political skills to manage ever more contradictory
demands. States Amos Sawyer, "Demands for the introduction of a multiparty democratic political process, including electoral reform, peaked in the
late 1970s at a time of economic decline"—in part due to the cost of petroleum
product imports.[7]

Events came to a head in April 1979, when in response to a 50 percent
increase in the price of a bag of rice, the PAL called for a protest march. The
police overreacted and started shooting into the crowd, killing "somewhere
between 40 and 140" and wounding an "additional 400."[8] The Tolbert government was so rattled that it asked neighboring Guinea to intervene to restore
order. With seven hundred Guinean troops patrolling the streets, MIG planes
flying overhead, the arrest and subsequent charges of treason of PAL leaders

5. Sawyer, *Beyond Plunder,* 16.
6. Ibid., 28.
7. Ibid., 17.
8. Liebenow, *Liberia,* 172.

and other political dissidents, and the closure of the university, the government played a very heavy hand in crushing a protest that it had precipitated by its own policies.

The Doe Interlude: From Lumpen Military to Armed Gangs

These events revealed the government's vulnerability. Tolbert's vacillation between a personal instinct to try to manage reform and his overriding need to appease the old Whig aristocracy (which consistently demanded the use of sticks without carrots) left him appearing weak to all sides. Almost one year later to the day—April 12, 1980—Sergeant Samuel K. Doe and a few other noncommissioned officers from the Liberian military seized power in a coup d'etat and summarily executed William Tolbert and thirteen former government officials. Although these events were stunning in themselves, they also represented a profound break with the past. As J. Gus Liebenow comments, "Although the president could not fully control events or the settler group, he had become the Indispensable Man with respect to the survival of the caste relationship. When the president fell . . . the entire structure of dominance fell with him."[9] As the indigenous Liberians seized power, a century-old oligarchy came to an end and with it the "end of a distinct system of patrimonial rule."[10]

The Tubman and Tolbert governments had maintained power through patronage and indirect control over the economy through a network of business partners. Controlling the economy had always been the key to maintaining power in Liberia, and it continued to be one of the decisive factors shaping events under the new regime.

While Doe initially tried to establish a credible government as head of state and through the initial loyalty of many senior civil servants, the role of the state as the primary broker in allocating and managing commercial power was fading fast. Without any other source of influence and legitimacy, Doe could not maintain control indefinitely. "Commercial operations shifted away from the heavy reliance on access to state power, and thus on presidential patronage, to establishing independent connections to global markets and regional non-state actors," writes Reno.[11] The big foreign investors upon whom Doe could rely for revenue began to leave: the National Iron Ore Company joint venture left in 1985, the German Bong Mining Company in 1988, and the Liberian American Mining Company in 1989.[12] "Fiscal and administrative

---

9. Ibid., 183.
10. Sawyer, *Beyond Plunder*, 17.
11. Reno, *Warlord Politics*, 85.
12. Ibid., 86.

malfeasance tended to favor smaller, better-connected Americo-Liberian and ethnic Lebanese operations, which could use personal connections and capacity to conceal commerce in more portable and marketable resources such as timber, rubber, gold and diamonds."[13] The connections of the locals were often with outlets in neighboring Côte d'Ivoire, Guinea, or Sierra Leone.

Further complicating the scene, Doe lacked an extensive personal network to compensate for the lack of an economic power base. Having come to power as he did, he was isolated from the Americo-Liberian network of influence. Doe's own ethnic group came from a remote area of the country, which left him without an ethnic power base in the capital city to provide a loyal core of ethnic solidarity.

Since Doe had no other networks of support, especially in Monrovia, he began to mobilize what Sawyer calls the "lumpen" military: the urban poor population that sought a living in the army but had no cultivated loyalty either to the mission of the national military or to any indigenous group.[14] Doe, a Krahn, did extend patronage to his homeland group in the southeast (Grand Gedah), but he soon found it necessary to mobilize support among his peers who had few links to indigenous roots. After all, with no broad ties to either the countryside or to the former Monrovia oligarchy, young soldiers were mobilized—and too easily, as it turned out. In 1985, after a coup attempt by his top general, Thomas Qwiwonkpa, Doe purged the other old lineage-based elements of the Liberian military, the Gio and Mano, who in turn retreated to the border areas of Guinea and Côte d'Ivoire (only to subsequently become commandos in Charles Taylor's militia).[15]

Between 1981 and 1984 the U.S. government had supported Liberia financially and militarily, while simultaneously pressing Doe to initiate a new constitutional drafting process. After extensive consultation with the Liberian people all over the country, the document drafted by the Constitution Commission provided checks on executive authority and limited power sharing with other bodies, such as county governments. However, Doe had the text radically revised by a second-stage Advisory Assembly. By the time the constitutional referendum occurred in 1984, the public was confused, having taken seriously the three years of consultations and assurances that their views were important. Thus it came to be that the 1985 election was not only tainted procedurally, but it also restored Doe to a very autocratic presidency.[16]

---

13. Ibid.

14. Sawyer, *Beyond Plunder*, 23–25.

15. Ibid.

16. Ibid., 102–107. Here is a full account of the constitutional consultation and drafting process that began in 1981, right up through the revisions, the referendum, and the reelection of Doe in 1985. Sawyer was the chairman of the original Constitution Commission, but he was arrested and jailed in August 1984 in the wake of the publication of the text, which would have reduced the power of the presidency.

By the late 1980s Doe was weakened on all fronts: economically, politically, and in terms of any legitimacy he had garnered at the outset of his rule. He also lost the confidence of the American foreign patron, for by this time, the Reagan administration had lost interest. Doe's treasury was empty and could no longer buy him support, and those who had their own now-privatized connections to commercial resources did not need him any longer. Doe became isolated and vulnerable to more and more challengers during the second half of the 1980s. Ever in search of resources, he tripled public employment in five years and began to pillage the state enterprises for his own purposes. He took over the Forestry Development Authority himself as well as the Liberian Petroleum Refining Corporation for the subsidized oil imports that he, in turn, sold for personal profit.[17]

Civil War, Regional Intervention, and the First Interim Government (1990–96)

Eventually, rebel forces led by someone Doe himself had set up in government overthrew Doe's government. In the early 1980s Doe appointed or promoted a number of people who had strong ties to the Liberian network in the United States. Among these individuals was Charles Taylor, whom Doe had appointed director of the General Services Agency, the procurement authority for the Liberian government. By 1984, however, while on an official business trip to the United States, Taylor was arrested on Liberian charges of embezzling nearly $1 million. It is generally assumed that because of his intimate ties to the Liberian diaspora through the Union of Liberian Associations in the Americas (ULAA) and the access that provided him to members of the Congressional Black Caucus and a notable attorney, Ramsey Clark, Taylor was never formally extradited. Mysteriously, and for reasons never explained, Taylor escaped from prison while awaiting extradition, and he disappeared.[18]

The scope of his ambition became clear on New Year's Eve in 1989, when Taylor invaded Liberia from the north with a mixed militia of mercenaries, regional and internal supporters called the National Patriotic Front of Liberia (NPFL). Chaos reigned in the next few months, during which somewhere between thirteen thousand and twenty thousand people died.[19] Most sources agree that by mid-1990 Taylor's forces controlled 90 percent of the country. Throughout this period of the war, Taylor stayed in the north, consolidating his connections with various private commercial

17. Reno, *Warlord Politics*, 85–86.
18. Ibid., 92.
19. Stephen Ellis, *The Mask of Anarchy* (New York: New York University Press, 1999), 2.

interests. He had also taken advantage of his years in exile to visit Libyan training camps and to network with an array of dissidents from Liberia's neighbors.

When he launched his assault on Doe's government in 1989, Taylor exploited the relationships he had forged in Libya. It is at this time that the conflict became regionalized. While in Libya, Taylor had developed a relationship with Foday Sankoh of Sierra Leone who, with Taylor's assistance, began a war against his own government by attacking the rural diamond areas with a militia that became the Revolutionary United Front (RUF). There, Sankoh ruthlessly acquired diamonds to sell on the international market. Taylor's investment paid off, as Sankoh provided both himself and Taylor the means to acquire weapons to further advance their ambitions to seize power in their respective countries.

The mix of regional nationalities involved in Taylor's NPFL made neighboring countries nervous, especially the Nigerians and Ghanaians. In what has to be *the* authoritative treatment of the complexities of the next six years, Adekeye Adebajo provides a compelling interpretation of the regionalization of Liberia's civil war through the prism of a *Pax Nigeriana*.[20] In mid-1990 Nigeria took the lead in securing formal support from the Economic Community of West African States (ECOWAS) to sponsor a military "monitoring group" (ECOMOG) made up initially of Nigerian, Ghanaian, and Sierra Leone soldiers. The Nigerian foreign minister presented his case to the UN Security Council in August, although the move was largely a fig leaf for what was going to happen in any case.[21] The international force, along with the remnants of Doe's army, thwarted the NPFL advance on the port and the capital city.

Partisans of different groups were now diffused throughout the Mano River basin. Alhaji Kromah mobilized Liberians on both sides of the northwest Guinea border. A breakaway leader from Taylor's NPFL, Prince Johnson, was determined to benefit from what he regarded as the three-way contest for the post-Doe order: Taylor, ECOMOG, and Johnson's own "Independent" NPFL. Accordingly, Johnson murdered Doe in September, making sure to record the event on videotape. While Taylor was obliged to stay in the north and regroup, Johnson was near Monrovia and welcomed the ECOMOG troops to Liberia.

Unlike many interim regimes, which are based on the principle that a transitional government must share power among all factions capable of spoiling the peace process, ECOMOG insisted that the Interim Government of National Unity (IGNU) exclude the warring parties. Because all the factions were discredited through their participation in the war, the logic was

---

20. Adekeye Adebajo, *Liberia's Civil War: Nigeria, ECOMOG, and Regional Security in West Africa* (Boulder, Colo., and London: Lynne Rienner Publishers, 2002).

21. Ibid., 53. For a full discussion of the run-up to Nigeria's role in Liberia, see pp. 48–65.

that the IGNU should remain untainted by association with these entities and should instead constitute an impartial force to transition the country to a stable government. The international community, whether under the guise of ECOMOG or the United Nations, had no intention of running the Liberian government itself.

Although this left Johnson out (for which he was compensated with a safe exile in Nigeria), it made sense to invite Professor Amos Sawyer, former chairman of the 1981–84 Constitution Commission, to be president under the IGNU.[22] Sawyer used the security of the ECOMOG zone to try to rekindle debate and dialogue on a new plane of constitutional reconstruction. Two attempts resulted in regional, multilateral conferences (Cotonou, 1993; Akosombo, 1994), but Sawyer's efforts to engage Taylor outside the zone of ECOMOG control in reestablishing public trust through a credible democratic process were continuously rebuffed. As months extended to years, ECOMOG failed to deliver anything but minimal security, which further hurt the legitimacy of the IGNU in the eyes of Liberians. The country was awash in armed gangs, such that the situation did not seem different from governance under Doe. In 1994, unable to forge a stable coalition, Sawyer gave up his efforts to establish a new, more democratic order.

Taylor's relentless ambition evolved into creating a warlord state with its own political economy. He mobilized support by forging commercial alliances with local natural resource and merchant interests that had international market outlets. Over time he became the broker with the international connections needed by the smallholders of local resources. Taylor did everything he could with his NPFL to create alliances of opportunity, to capture resources, and to use them to mobilize others. Ultimately, however, what he really needed to consolidate his power was to somehow become the president of sovereign Liberia. In that regard he charmed regional leaders from the Côte d'Ivoire to the Democratic Republic of the Congo into believing he could bring order and peace to Liberia. Through his ULAA network, Taylor impressed a number of American leaders, including former president Jimmy Carter, that he was a democrat who could forge a regional peace if Carter would help him with the Nigerians.

Assessing the Interim Government of National Unity

The first ECOMOG and weak UN engagement (1990–96) took place in an atmosphere of state disintegration. Before assessing its effectiveness, it is

22. Abiodun Alao, John Mackinlay, and Funmi Olonisakin, *Peacekeepers, Politicians, and Warlords* (Tokyo, New York, Paris: United Nations University Press, 1999), 35.

worth pausing to summarize the conditions of state failure in post–Cold War sub-Saharan Africa that allow the warlord alternative to emerge.

- First, the internal features of Cold War–era patron-client politics translate into vulnerabilities for rulers amid increasing external pressures from donors and creditors for reforms, both political and economic (namely, structural adjustment, market liberalization, privatization, civil society, etc.).
- Second, weak patrimonial states are unable to implement policies that would restructure the economy to launch it on a liberal-rational path. Without the Great Power rivalry to justify continued opportunistic support, domestic economies deteriorate amid the demands of creditors and business-as-usual elite corruption.
- Third, weak-state leaders develop new strategies for converting patronage politics into "warlord politics," that is, using private militias, whether domestic or external, to seize and exploit resources in the state. These "commercial partnerships" essentially replace the Cold War bureaucratic state.
- Fourth, other strongman competitors translate entrepreneurship into informal political authority.
- Fifth, all alliances are temporary and know no borders; in fact, among the hallmarks of warlord politics are the cross-border alliances that provide rebel movements safe havens in neighboring territories.
- Finally, weak states reveal a new organization of global capital that exploits commercial opportunities previously out of reach. As these transactions cumulate, the exercise of political authority is "almost indistinguishable from private commercial operations."[23]

Accordingly, any effective international interim government in this situation would require a very strong mandate with a highly specified mission, clear terms of engagement, and an appropriate size of force. As it happened, the motivation of the Nigerians was honorable, if also self-serving, but their numbers and the accompanying UN presence were tentative. The fact is that ECOMOG I arrived too late and was too weak to roll back the Taylor machine, so it had to content itself with protecting Monrovia and the port. Moreover, although Sawyer knew his legitimacy and effectiveness over time depended on reaching out and bringing parties together—and ECOMOG helped in that effort by setting up two international meetings—the international interim government of ECOMOG and Sawyer were too weak to expand their ambit of influence. As events deteriorated in the mid-1990s, the Nigerians simply wanted out.

---

23. Reno, *Warlord Politics*, 13.

Although the Nigerians had never favored capitulation to a Charles Taylor power grab, by 1995 ECOMOG was facing great frustration in the field. Morale dropped, casualties rose (to five hundred in the end), other national contingents grew unreliable, and locals accused them of looting and other behaviors similar to those of the armed gangs. Moreover, Nigerians at home were increasingly unhappy with the open-ended engagement and the drain on resources. After all, Nigeria provided 75 percent of the soldiers and 90 percent of the funding for ECOMOG.[24] The Sani Abacha government was increasingly concerned about the standoff and the loss of prestige if Nigeria were to withdraw with no new institutional outcome. Accordingly, Nigeria mounted a peace conference at Abuja in 1995 to which Taylor was invited as a major participant. This led to a second one a year later, at which ECOWAS heads of state blessed an accord with a transitional government to last until presidential and parliamentary elections in July 1997.

The Taylor Government, 1997–2003: Ongoing Civil War

Remarkably, Charles Taylor got the sovereignty he sought by winning the election decisively. In a thorough, plausible analysis of the election results in which Taylor's National Patriotic Party (NPP)—formed out of the original invasion force—garnered 75 percent of the votes, David Harris concluded that "Taylor's overwhelming victory most likely derived from a heady brew of electoral rules and irregularities, a huge campaign, a backbone of support, a divided and weak opposition, and his apparent dominance over the security question."[25] This election result provided the basis for the ECOMOG forces to withdraw, and it allowed the Nigerians some cover for their failed *Pax Nigeriana*. Liberia had transitioned from an internationally managed interim government to a domestic regime under Charles Taylor.

The next six years revealed the worst aspects of the warlord political economy. Taylor had generated many rivals and bitter enemies by the late 1990s. They raised their own militias against him, using outside resources where possible (for instance, from neighboring Guinea in the case of the Liberians United for Reconciliation and Democracy [LURD]). The mobilization of children as combatants, paying them in the drugs or booty they could seize, brought the world's attention once again to hapless Liberia (and to Sierra Leone, where Sankoh's RUF militia were chopping off people's limbs).

---

24. Adebajo, *Liberia's Civil War*, 48.
25. David Harris, "From 'Warlord' to 'Democratic' President: How Charles Taylor Won the 1997 Liberian Election," *Journal of Modern African Studies* 37, no. 3 (September 1999): 451–452.

It is in this context of political and social disintegration that one also has to appreciate the reemergence of the traditional practice of "medicine," or magic. The spirit world is an important factor in accounting for one's fate in countries of this region. Rural citizens in dire straits retreated into symbolic sacrifices with animal (occasionally human) organs in order to endure the insecurities in their lives. Religious references were also used to pressure, or blackmail, young men into becoming combatants.[26]

By 2003, on the outskirts of Monrovia, the irregular forces of LURD and the Movement for Democracy and Elections in Liberia (MODEL), made up of anti-Taylor dissidents and Liberians returning from refuge in the neighboring states, were challenging Taylor and his increasingly fragmented supporters. There was no longer a Liberian government as that term is normally understood. The civil service had crumbled because unpaid government employees descended into survival mode like everyone else. In the warlord "state," functional ministries no longer existed. Somebody in Taylor's entourage might have been the minister of finance or agriculture, but the minister had no competent staff or, necessarily, any competence in administration of the portfolio. The "cabinet" had no bureaucracy, nor in the end were the combatants themselves being paid. Taylor admitted that his people "paid themselves" with what they could take. As dead bodies were piled up in front of the U.S. embassy in Monrovia as a symbol of total chaos and a plea for the Americans to intervene, a peace accord among the warring factions was forged in Accra, Ghana, in August 2003. To avoid facing a new international military force and appearing in an international criminal court, Taylor accepted exile in Nigeria. A new ECOMOG contingent was mobilized under a UN peacekeeping mandate, and a UN special representative began to restore order.

ECOMOG II/UNMIL: The Second International Interim Government

On August 18, 2003, a peace agreement among the Government of Liberia (GOL), LURD, MODEL, and the political parties was signed in Accra,

---

26. Ellis, *The Mask of Anarchy,* 25–26, 220–223. In this regard it is notable that as recently as June 29, 2005, the interim president, Charles Gyude Bryant, announced in a nationwide broadcast, "It has been brought to our attention that some people are killing their fellow humans and extracting parts to go to the 'juju' man to make them become president or parliamentarian." He further asserted that people convicted of ritual murder aimed at securing political posts through black magic would be given the death penalty. Locally, this statement would be seen as part of the tactical landscape of the coming October election. Nonetheless, it is important to understand the additional challenges to interim governments in this region posed by superstition and by practitioners of magic who prey on people in an already generalized state of distress.

Ghana. The main provisions of the Accra Comprehensive Peace Agreement (ACPA) were as follows:[27]

- a cease-fire and monitoring
- an international stabilization force
- disengagement
- disarmament, demobilization, and reintegration (DDR)
- security sector reforms: disbandment of irregulars, restructuring of the armed forces, and structuring of the national police and other special security services
- the release of prisoners and abductees
- the establishment of an independent national commission on human rights
- the establishment of a Truth and Reconciliation Commission (TRC)
- humanitarian relief
- the creation of a governance reform commission
- the creation of a contract and monopolies commission
- electoral reform and new elections in October 2005
- the founding of a National Transitional Government of Liberia (NTGL), to consist of an executive, a legislative assembly, and a judiciary, the primary responsibility of which was to ensure the implementation of provisions of the peace agreement
- international assistance: a UN special representative, a consolidated UN mission, and specific calls to ECOWAS, the United Nations, the African Union, the European Union, and the International Contact Group on Liberia (ICGL) to mobilize resources for post-conflict rehabilitation and reconstruction
- assistance to refugees, displaced persons, and other vulnerable groups, especially women and children

All these provisions preempted the provisions of the constitution, statutes, and other laws of Liberia until January 2006, when they were to be restored, along with the installation of a newly elected government. The executing partnership of the NTGL is a broad coalition of external players: the United Nations, ECOWAS, the African Union, the European Union, the United States, the International Monetary Fund, and the World Bank (hereafter referred to as the Partners). This interim government was designed to have a much heavier international footprint than the first two.

---

27. For the text of the Accra Comprehensive Peace Agreement, see www.usip.org/library/pa/liberia/liberia_08182003_cpa.html.

Peace First

Restoring public order was the first priority in the summer–fall of 2003. A countrywide state of peace has gradually been achieved over the last twenty-four to thirty-six months. Initially, ECOWAS established an "interposition" force, subsequently integrated into an International Stabilization Force under the auspices of the United Nations Mission in Liberia (UNMIL).[28] The UN force is now fifteen thousand soldiers, the largest such UN peacekeeping force on the ground in the world. This force was to remain until both the UN Security Council and the elected government of Liberia, after January 1, 2006, determine otherwise.

The disarmament and demobilization (DD) of the armed gangs has also made progress after a very rocky start, in which the early weapons recovery effort backfired. This DD work continues as a delicate, piecemeal operation of identifying "leaders" of the youthful groups in the field, convincing them the war is over, and offering opportunities for schooling and a better life. What they want, inevitably, is money. Money continues to be used in direct exchange for weapons. The danger is that most of the former combatants are essentially homeless, many are ill, and the capacity of the rehabilitation and reintegration program to place them in even a subsistence setting is limited.[29]

Complicating this important process is the habit of factional interests to seek influence by passing money out to former combatants. Mrs. Aicha Keita Conneh, a coleader with husband Sekou Damateh Conneh of LURD and a signatory to the peace agreement that draws support principally from the Malinke areas of the northwest, accompanied a UN-sponsored DD mission to disarm groups in that area to use her influence to help persuade the young people to give up their weapons. The UN officer in charge, a Kenyan colonel, had planned to leave this first meeting with the incentive that, upon his return a few weeks later, the young people would turn over their weapons in exchange for selected services and a small amount of cash for each former combatant. After endorsing the Kenyan colonel's admonitions to the group, Mrs. Conneh proceeded to "hold court" on her own in the indigenous language, then took out a wad of cash and threw it out for the boys to scramble over. Mrs. Conneh's unexpected intervention not only created a very dangerous situation among young people with weapons, she also made it unlikely that the United Nations would succeed on that next visit without more plausible incentives for such volatile groups. This episode also illustrates the regional character of the ongoing struggle. Mrs. Conneh is the adopted

---

28. UNMIL is a Chapter VII mission established through UN Security Council Resolution 1509 (2003).

29. Public Broadcasting System, "Liberia: No More War," *Frontline World*, aired May 17, 2005, www.pbs.org/frontlineworld/rss/redir/frontlineworld/stories/liberia/.

daughter of the president of neighboring Guinea, Lansanna Conte, which might explain the source of LURD's resources.

Reforms under NTGL

One of the main problems with the first transitional government had been that none of the armed elements in Liberia had any stake in the government. This time the signatories to the transitional peace accord of August 2003 were largely self-identified political stakeholders with their own militias. The transitional government created in the accord guaranteed representation for these groups. While the various rivals agreed to the processes outlined in the document, implementation of the agreement invariably raised the unresolved distributive claims of those very signatories. This was ensured by the formula by which numbers of seats in the transitional legislature were allocated to specific groups, such as LURD, MODEL, GOL, other political parties, and counties. Similarly, ministerial portfolios were allocated based on negotiations among the stakeholder groups. So, although the transitional chairman, Gyude Bryant, had no partisan past, the other players in the NTGL simply mirrored the factional interests in place at the end of the war.

Peace and security have been more or less restored, but the political institutional "reforms" did not progress in the two years between the cease-fire in 2003 and the election in October 2005. Former president Amos Sawyer (a professor who knows the most about constitutive reconstruction in Liberia, having shepherded a process in the 1980s that died in the Doe-Taylor wars) expressed great reluctance about going ahead with the 2005 election because the contending factions had not really agreed to compromise on much of anything. New parties reflecting civil society organizations, new platforms, and nationwide debates and discussions needed to arise before an election was held that could actually be expected to launch the country on a new trajectory. Sawyer viewed the "reform" path of neighboring Sierra Leone as a model *not* to be emulated. In fact, he proposed a regional reform process because the institutional problems have been shown to be regional at every turn of events.[30]

Similarly, there has been little progress in the reform of the economy. This is especially important for an assessment of the progress and pitfalls of the interim regime, since the *warlordization* of politics that tore the state apart in the first place was based on a desire to manipulate the country's economic resources. The ACPA agreement put a premium on economic and fiscal management reforms that would address the endemic corruption of the warlord state. A Contract and Monopolies Commission was established

---

30. Amos Sawyer, "Violent Conflicts and the Governance Challenges in West Africa: The Case of the Mano River Basin Area," *Journal of Modern African Studies* 42, no. 3 (September 2004): 437–474.

to "oversee activities of a contractual nature undertaken by the NTGL."[31] External audits of the Central Bank of Liberia and the five principal state enterprises, as well as economic investigations, were to be undertaken as the Partners thought necessary if they were to continue to support the reform effort.

At a meeting held in Copenhagen in May 2005, the NTGL and its Partners "concluded that there should be a more robust approach to economic governance in Liberia, with immediate and firm remedial efforts." Audits by Liberia's auditor general, financed by the European Commission, "have shown serious mismanagement of pubic finances in several key revenue earning agencies" and noted "the unprecedented step taken by the ECOWAS for deployment of investigators and economic crime experts to study the situation and report back."[32] Two months earlier, in March 2005, a UN panel discovered that Liberian officials had signed a secret contract giving a European company a virtual monopoly on mining diamonds. The arrangement, apparently, even involved members of the transitional government.[33]

In the meantime, the Partners agreed to a new Economic Governance Action Plan that outlined in some detail a rigorous implementation of sound economic and fiscal management, including the following measures:

- securing the revenue base from the state-owned enterprises and the Central Bank
- improving budgeting and expenditure management
- improving procurement practices
- establishing new judicial measures to control corruption
- requesting international assistance to be targeted at several key institutions, such as the Central Bank, the General Accounting Office, and the Governance Reform Commission, among others
- building the local capacity of these same institutions

The Partners agreed that the plan would be executed within the structure of the Results Focused Transition Framework that coordinates donor resources with national resources and would be replaced by an Interim Poverty Reduction Strategy when the new government took over in January 2006.

The timing of this new agreement on the economic front suggests that much more reform needs to be institutionalized before the "transition" is over. The plan is being challenged by many Liberians at home and abroad as somehow impinging on the country's sovereignty and ignoring the fact that

---

31. Accra Comprehensive Peace Agreement, Art. XVII.
32. *Liberia Observer*, posted July 1, 2005, www.allafrica.com.
33. Stephen Ellis, "How to Rebuild Africa," *Foreign Affairs* 84, no. 5 (2005): 135.

many talented Liberian professionals of integrity can be entrusted with these important economic institutions after the election.

At the same time, little has really changed at the level of connections between the political class and local commercial interests, and corruption still plagues the most central economic management institutions, suggesting that the transition is incomplete. The Partners told the NTGL that they would not continue to support a new government if there is not more palpable progress in reforming the country's economic management. In view of these facts, together with the ongoing, if murky, involvement of Taylor in exercising influence among his loyalists in and around the NTGL from exile in Nigeria, there was much uncertainty surrounding the October 2005 election and transition to a new government in January 2006.

Elections for a Permanent Government

A national election was held on October 11, 2005, for the office of president and the ninety-four seats in the House of Representatives and the Senate. Considering the terrible infrastructure conditions in the country (there is no reliable electric power, for example, even in the capital city), most reports indicate the administration of the election was sound and consistent across the country. After ballot counting, the top two vote getters among the twenty-two presidential candidates were George Weah, a former international football player, and Ellen Johnson-Sirleaf, a former finance minister and Africa region head of the UN Development Programme. A runoff election took place on November 8, 2005, in which Johnson-Sirleaf got 59 percent of the vote. Weah's party filed a complaint with the National Electoral Commission (NEC) alleging fraud, but after several weeks of investigation, the NEC announced that the "evidence adduced was not sufficient to constitute massive fraud."[34] Confirming this outcome, on December 17 George Weah met with President-elect Johnson-Sirleaf to discuss a peaceful transition. She was officially inaugurated on January 16, 2006, the first woman head of state in modern-day Africa.

Reflections on the Second Interim Government

The second interim government had a much more robust peacekeeping force, supported by a determined Security Council that very specifically restrained the export of local resources by anybody, including the transitional government. Despite his meddling from exile, Taylor's physical absence from the country allowed his partisans to recognize that they

---

34. See "Weah Drops Liberia Poll Challenge," December 16, 2006, news.bbc.co.uk/go/pr/fr/-/2/ hi/africa/4549528.stm.

were on their own. The combination of UNMIL and the absence of any warlord to delude Taylor's former fighters allowed the natural exhaustion on all sides to set in.

Although the peace accord left all the partisans in place, the Liberian side of the NTGL interim government forsook more war in favor of trying to manipulate the country's wealth. The Security Council's resolution has kept that under control to this day. A condition of the present postelection settlement is that the United Nations will not lift the embargo until it is satisfied there are responsible institutions and persons in charge of their disposition.

Meanwhile, the international interim government's greatest accomplishment (beyond keeping a cease-fire and demobilizing partisans) was the remarkably effective election in October and runoff in November 2005. Skeptics on all sides were impressed with the quality of organization and logistics where there were no roads, no electric power, petrol stations, etc., in so much of the country. Here was a case where the United Nations, as a coprincipal agent of executive authority and with administrative authority over such important modalities as the election, executed the letter of its mission admirably.

Since the installation of the new Liberian government in January 2006, UNMIL and the government have cooperated in the joint pursuit of security and reconstruction. Some of the unfinished security matters delaying reconstruction include discoveries of armed partisans hiding in rubber plantations. These troublesome legacies must be cleared before the government can begin to show control over its resources. While UNMIL works on such ongoing DDR operations, the UN mission is also funding the recruitment and training of two thousand soldiers and six thousand police.[35] With 75 percent of the population living on less than $1.00 per day and an unemployment rate of 80 percent, credible governance reforms and economic recovery cannot wait.[36] A most encouraging development in this regard was the Nigerian handover of Charles Taylor to the Liberian and, subsequently, UN authorities in March 2006. Taylor is presently awaiting trial on an international war crimes warrant in the Hague.

The Government Reform Commission is now operational under the chairmanship of the previously cited Professor Sawyer. Its tasks include a range of structural and fiscal reforms of the civil service and establishment of vetting conditions for those appointed to cabinet-level posts. However, corruption is so entrenched that suspicion dogs almost anyone associated with any former government or public office. Even the reform commissioners accuse one another of malfeasance. There are so few experienced persons left in the country that the president finds herself appointing people under a cloud as

---

35. Ellen Johnson Sirleaf, "President Calls for Faster aid Flows: Speech at Georgetown University," *News*, posted October 17, 2006, allafrica.com/stories/printable/200610171237.html.
36. Ibid.

ambassadors to important countries like the United Kingdom, however reluctantly. To send a message about anticorruption and to establish role models, the president has appointed women to the top posts in the police department and in the ministries of justice, finance, commerce, and youth and sports.

Because establishing credibility on the financial front is a priority on a par with security, the new government has installed strong anticorruption measures that have already resulted in increased public revenues. Furthermore, it has passed regulatory legislation controlling timber harvesting, which will allow the United Nations to lift sanctions on the forestry sector, and has returned to the good graces of the International Monetary Fund (IMF), particularly with regard to a poverty reduction strategy and cooperation on working toward a debt-relief package.[37]

Another dimension of credibility on matters of governance and institutional reform is the launching of a truth and reconciliation process. Hundreds of interviewers have been trained to take testimony from citizens about violence and crimes perpetrated over the past fourteen years. The TRC staff will operate out of offices all over the country. One of the issues arising immediately in the implementation of this process is the extent to which such testimony should be taken in public. Liberia is such a small country that the fear of reprisals against those who testify is quite widespread.

Broader Reflections on the State, Governance, and Legitimacy

What can we learn from twenty-five years of conflict in Liberia, punctuated by two different national transitional and two international interim governments? We must begin with whether the evident endemic instability since the early 1980s calls into question the very "stateness" of Liberia. Whatever one thinks of the pre-1980 party-boss, patron-client system, the Republic of Liberia was regarded as a sovereign state. At the same time, the claim to sovereignty was based on a historical construction, the legitimacy of which was beginning to be extended to the whole population only in the 1960s, when Tubman extended the franchise and a homogeneous administrative system to the "countryside."

Other analysts, such as Amos Sawyer, would argue that Liberia's problem is not so much one of state sovereignty as one of governance. He has argued for years that the governance problem is essentially one of overcentralization of the presidency, which occurred under Tubman's long tenure. The fact that the president has so much power in Liberia makes it the single

---

37. Ibid.

prize for those with political ambition. Sawyer, a political scientist, activist, and interim president, had conducted three years of consultations with ordinary people all over the country in the early 1980s. He believes that an auspiciously designed decentralized or "polycentric" constitution can garner the legitimacy a national government would require. Apart from the 1980s' constitutional revision, reversed before it could be tested, Sawyer has developed these ideas at length in *Beyond Plunder: Toward Democratic Governance in Liberia.*[38]

At the same time, the instability of the past twenty years could be said to have undermined the state of Liberia, especially as one ponders the regional character of the conflict. Some analysts of the first ECOMOG venture describe the interim government as maintaining "the fiction that Liberia was still a state with Monrovia as the main actor."[39] Visitors to Monrovia during that period easily missed the fact that they were in what today we would call a "green zone." The center of gravity had passed into the hands of substate actors, with contenders setting up their own capitals around the country.[40]

This debate, about whether Liberia's problems are principally those of state legitimacy or governance, comes to a synthesis in the concept of a "failed state." Although the term *weak* is a reference to "state strength" or "a lack of institutional capacity to implement and enforce policies," as Francis Fukuyama states, this weakness is "often driven by an underlying lack of legitimacy of the political system as a whole."[41] Weak governance undermines sovereignty.

Conclusion

What, then, have been the effects of the two respective ECOMOG/UN interventions in Liberia and their parallel interim governments with regard to reestablishing peace, stability, governance, and even legitimacy? Certainly the *Pax Nigeriana* underlying ECOMOG I began as a genuine effort to assert regional leadership, but it was based on an underestimation of the scale and complexity of the task. ECOMOG was not really able to contain conflicts beyond a limited zone, was stretched in having to enter the Sierra Leone theater as well, and faced test after test of rotating and dwindling contingents from its regional ECOWAS partner countries. Sawyer's interim government was unable to extend the dialogue and bring a

---

38. Sawyer, *Beyond Plunder,* 124–130.

39. Alao et al., *Peacekeepers, Politicians, and Warlords,* 116.

40. Ibid.

41. Francis Fukuyama, *State-Building: Governance and World Order in the 21st Century* (Ithaca, N.Y.: Cornell University Press, 2004), 96.

peace settlement home despite heroic efforts mainly because Taylor was ultimately strong enough to resist any compromise. The election of 1997, handing Taylor "legitimate" power, was a shame to all concerned in that he continued to behave as a warlord rather than a statesman. By 2001, for example, he was selling diamonds—even to al-Qaeda.[42]

The second interim government in Liberia did, finally, restore peace; made a good start at DDR functions through ongoing reconciliation programs (schooling, housing, and jobs for the young fighters, for example); guided the execution of a national election; and supported (and continues to support) the new government of President Johnson-Sirleaf in her efforts to implement administrative reforms. It is much too early to say that the interim government has succeeded in establishing national reconciliation and democracy. But this case does suggest that the United Nations can work effectively with local nationals in peace building on the ground.

This case might also suggest that the UN peace-building effort is more effective when it holds onto a trump card, in this case one of economic sovereignty, in the form of controls over the commodity sector. The international partner is more likely to be an arbiter helping to restore sovereignty where endemic instability or a political vacuum attracts exploiters. This is where reconstruction, development, and legitimacy in governance all meet in the new world of stabilization operations.

At present, the new government is assured protection under the ECOMOG/UNMIL mandate for an uncertain period. The apparent determination of the external Partners to restore integrity to the economic management of Liberia is as much a test of the legitimacy of the new government and the effectiveness of the state as the election itself. After just over a year in office, the government of Liberia has persuaded the Security Council to lift the ban on timber exports and diamonds and renegotiated a previous contract with the newly merged Alcelor Mittal Steel for iron ore that better serves the country than the one agreed to by the former Bryant government. Moreover, both the United States and China have cancelled more than $400 million in debt, and the IMF recently forecast that the Liberian economy would grow by 11 percent on average for the next five years.[43]

Would the future have been brighter if the interim government arrangements had provided for a full constitutional review and design to be ratified by the public before the UNMIL mandate expired? Because that configuration of the interim government did not happen, participation by new civil society groups and political parties could not better inform the election or its aftermath. The unrepentant politicians and cronies of the Taylor era, combined with the continuing instability in the region (Côte d'Ivoire, Guinea),

---

42. Ellis, "How to Rebuild Africa," 138.
43. "Liberia Economy 'To Grow by 11%'," April 7, 2007, news.bbc.co.uk/go/pr/fr/-/2/hi/business/6564773.stm.

could still cause the new venture to become unstuck. There is no question that the Truth and Reconciliation Commission is not progressing in ways that reassure the public that perpetrators living in their midst will face a timely formal proceeding. [44]

Interim governance in Liberia remains a top-down process, managed by the former warring parties and the international community. Meanwhile, institutionally speaking, Liberia is back to the status quo of the mid-1980s. The difference lies in the promising leadership of President Johnson-Sirleaf, her domestic allies genuinely committed to reform, and the Partners who are determined that reconstruction will not fail.

---

44. "Liberia Must Do More to Punish War Crimes–Amnesty," www.alertnet.org/thenews/ newsdesk/L14597079.htm.

10

International Interim Governments, Democratization, and Post-conflict Peace Building

Lessons from Cambodia and East Timor

Aurel Croissant

Editors' Note

Aurel Croissant compares the transitional processes in Cambodia and East Timor: one that ended a civil war and another that nursed a newly independent people. In both of these cases, the international community plays a more direct and involved role than in any of the prior chapters. Echoing Antonio Donini, Croissant makes the fundamental point that sustainable peace building and transition from authoritarianism to fully institutionalized liberal democracy require more than ending civil strife. Croissant's chapter extends the theoretical analysis provided in the introductory chapter by providing an excellent synthesis of models of interim governance, focusing on those created by Yossi Shain and Juan Linz and Michael Doyle. Following this, Croissant discusses the inherent contradictions in externally imposed democratization and the problems of democratization, particularly in post-conflict situations: these regimes violate sovereignty and legitimacy in order to return sovereignty and to restore legitimacy.

Croissant also raises the tension, particularly in regard to the UN transitional authority in East Timor, between organizing an international regime to completely run a country and, at the same time, attempting to prepare that country to resume sovereign governance. He argues that there is a delicate balance among creating an effective and impartial international regime, incorporating locals to increase ownership, and preparing citizens to resume control.

Finally, Croissant raises the issue of timing. Cambodia is a cautionary tale about pushing democratization on a war-torn country too quickly, without any change in

underlying power structures. In these insights, Croissant brings together the argu-
ments of Carrie Manning, Andrew J. Enterline, and J. Michael Greig. Reconstruc-
tion takes at least a decade, and democracy can be created prematurely. In East
Timor, the lack of a common understanding of capacity building and the negligence
of these issues in the early stages of the transitional authority retarded the United
Nations Transitional Administration in East Timor's (UNTAET's) efforts at insti-
tution building. Perhaps the most basic lesson to be learned from the UN-led interim
governments in Cambodia and East Timor is that having the support of the local
population is critical, but this alone is not sufficient. Successful UN-led interim
governments also require elite settlement and the support of the regional powers
and international patrons of local clients. Croissant argues, "Obviously it does not
make sense to leave the fate of a young democracy in the hands of antidemocratic
national elites, yet this was exactly what took place in Cambodia. Rather, the inter-
national community must have the will to take responsibility for social and eco-
nomic reconstruction and to intervene even after the transitional process, if any
negative aberrations do occur afterward."

Introduction

Some years ago the British diplomat Robert Cooper created a huge controversy when he argued that "liberal imperialism" is a legitimate response
to the chaos and disorder of civil strife and disrupted states. But yesterday's heresy has become today's conventional wisdom. In his new book,
Empire Lite, Michael Ignatieff declares, "Temporary imperialism—Empire
Lite—has become the necessary condition for democracy in countries torn
apart by civil war."[1] Is he right? Is externally directed and monitored
democratization an appropriate strategy for successful peace building in
post-conflict environments? Are liberal protectorates or international
interim governments stable institutional bridges between regimes that can
carry a society from conflict to sustainable peace?

   This chapter discusses the notion of temporary imperialism with reference
to Cambodia and East Timor. Specifically, to what extent have the international
interim governments contributed to democratization and post-conflict peace
building in Cambodia and East Timor? The study proceeds in five steps. The
first step is to identify general problems of democratization through international interim governments and peace building in territories characterized by

---

1. Robert Cooper, "Why We Still Need Empires," *The Observer,* April 27, 2002; and Michael
   Ignatieff, *Empire Lite: Nation Building in Kosovo, Bosnia, Afghanistan* (Toronto: Penguin Canada,
   2003).

civil strife and disrupted stateness. The second step is to analyze the background conditions, facilitating factors, and obstructive conditions for democratization and peace building through UN-led transitional governments in both countries. Next, the chapter describes the nature of transitional authority, its legitimacy, and the organization and operational methods of the two interim governments. The fourth step is to evaluate the successes and failures of both interim governments and the causes of both governments' achievements and shortcomings. The conclusion draws some lessons from the experiences of the two countries in coping with the challenge of democratization and peace building through international interim governments.

International Interim Governments

In their seminal work on interim governments and democratic transitions, Yossi Shain and Juan Linz developed the model of international interim governments, defined by the authors as those forms of transitional authority "in which the international community, through the aegis of the United Nations, directs and monitors the process of democratic change."[2] Obviously, this is neither the only form of interim government nor the only mode of externally monitored democratization. Additional models of democratizing interim governments developed by Shain and Linz are provisional, power-sharing, and caretaker governments. Another, empirically more frequent mode of externally directed and monitored transition from authoritarianism is democratization through war and imposition, exercised either by a domestic administration under more or less explicit control of external powers (post-Taliban Afghanistan) or directly by the occupation forces (Germany and Japan after World War II).[3]

Michael Doyle recently developed the idea of international interim regimes further by presenting a fourfold typology of transitional authority that allows classifying different subtypes of international interim regimes.[4] The four types of transitional authority (supervisory, executive, administrative authority, and monitor) are differentiated from each other by the degree

2. Yossi Shain and Juan Linz, eds., *Between States: Interim Governments and Democratic Transitions* (Cambridge: Cambridge University Press, 1995), 5.

3. Cf. Alfred Stepan, "Paths toward Redemocratization: Theoretical and Comparative Considerations," in *Transition from Authoritarian Rule: Prospects for Democracy*, vol. 4, ed. Guillermo O'Donnell, Philippe C. Schmitter, and Laurence Whitehead, 64–84 (Baltimore: Johns Hopkins University Press, 1986). See also Andrew J. Enterline and J. Michael Greig's chapter, "Must They Go through Hobbes?" in this volume.

4. Michael Doyle, "War Making and Peace Making: The United Nations' Post–Cold War Record," in *Turbulent Peace: The Challenges of Managing International Conflict*, ed. Chester A. Crocker, Fen O. Hampson, and Pamela Aall, 515–528 (Washington, D.C.: United States Institute of Peace Press, 2003); and Michael Doyle and Nicholas Sambanis, *Making War and Building Peace: United Nations Peace Operations* (Princeton: Princeton University Press, 2006).

of legal authority and effective international capacity the interim regime enjoys. Three of Doyle's types of transitional authority are subtypes of international interim government; the fourth (monitor) is not. While the work of Shain and Linz focuses on the role that interim governments play in enhancing or impeding the democratic outcome in the transition from authoritarianism, Doyle is interested in the role that UN transitional authorities play in post-conflict peace building. As the editors of this volume discussed in their introductory chapter, the latter is a complex, multidimensional challenge that reaches far beyond directing and monitoring the process of democratic change.

International interim governments are common features of peace-building programs. Post-conflict peace building conceivably describes all operations conducted by an interim government organized either through an international organization like the United Nations (as in the case of Cambodia and East Timor) or the government of another sovereign state. Peace building includes fostering economic and social cooperation among the political elites of a specific territory "with the purpose of building confidence among previously warring parties; developing the social, political, and economic infrastructure to prevent future violence; and laying the foundations for a durable peace."[5]

Doyle characterizes second-generation UN peace operations as a much more ambitious process than the traditional first generation of "peacekeeping." This second generation involves "the implementation of complex, multidimensional peace agreements"—including such traditional tasks of peacekeeping as monitoring cantonment and demobilization—as well as resettling refugees, promoting human rights, monitoring elections, supervising transitional civilian authorities, and revitalizing economic development.[6] While legal methods emphasize issues of transitional justice, the focus of political methods is on democratic institution building to promote liberal democracy; economic measures emphasize socioeconomic development. Therefore, democratization through international interim government in post-conflict societies can best be understood as one dimension of the multidimensional project of peace building.[7] Long-term success in relation to democratization critically depends on how much transitional authorities achieve regarding the economic, social, and political components of peace building.

Democratization through international interim government typically occurs in a much more challenging context than other modes of democrati-

---

5. Doyle, "War Making and Peace Making," 530.
6. Ibid., 532–533.
7. See also Denis Austin, "Democracy and Democratization," in *From Civil Strife to Civil Society: Civil and Military Responsibilities in Disrupted States*, ed. William Maley, Charles Sampford, and Ramesh Thakur, 180–204, 180 (Tokyo and New York: United Nations University Press, 2003).

zation. Shain and Linz have formulated five basic propositions for the applicability of the international interim government model.[8] Most fundamentally, this model requires that domestic state institutions remain largely intact; that is, failed states are unsuited to the model. Second, the incumbent regime has not been totally delegitimated and still exerts control over the means of violence; third, foreign patrons of domestic parties support the international interim government; fourth, domestic parties have a genuine interest in conflict accommodation; and fifth, domestic parties communicate and interact among one another. Clearly, in many post–civil war societies, none of these conditions holds.

There are, however, additional reasons why democratization through international interim governments in societies torn apart by civil strife is often more difficult than other transitions to democracy. The sovereignty of the people and the accountability of the government toward its citizens are the core principles of democracy. International interim governments, however, by definition lack democratic legitimacy—the sovereignty de facto (if not de jure) passes from the people on to an external power. Thus, democracy is supposed to be introduced under the imposition of a tremendous deficit of democratic legitimacy.

At the same time, international interim governments, particularly UN transitional authorities, must bear a double, sometimes conflictive, accountability. De jure, they are accountable to the external principal organizing, controlling, and financing their mission. In the case of a UN-led interim government, the UN Secretariat and Security Council are the principals. De facto, however, the interim government is also accountable to the domestic elites and the people of the territory it is ruling and for whom it has to construct a self-sustainable democratic system.[9]

Furthermore, transitions from authoritarianism in post-conflict societies occur under extremely obstructive political, social, and economic conditions. In general, public and social infrastructures are typically underdeveloped in a poor state. There are the challenges of refugees and internally displaced persons. Power resources are concentrated in the hands of military commanders and entrepreneurs of violence, and there is a dramatic need to reconstruct public order and security. Markets do not function properly, and macroeconomics is unstable. Furthermore, comparative studies show that the reconstruction of civil strife–torn economies requires an extensive amount of time. In the past, countries rarely recovered within the first decade following a civil war nor did most develop sustainable growth without

---

8. Shain and Linz, *Between States*, 64–65.
9. Cf. Ian Martin and Alexander Mayer-Rieckh, "The United Nations and East Timor: From Self-Determination to State-Building," *International Peacekeeping* 1, no. 12 (Spring 2005): 125–145.

extensive international assistance.[10] High levels of international assistance, however, often lead to the emergence of an extreme type of rent-seeking economy, in which the accumulation of external rents and its transformation into local rents are the most attractive form of economic activity.[11] This dynamic has strong negative consequences for the transparency and the accountability of the political process. This constellation of factors increases with other, more general problems of successful democratization.

Finally, where civil strife has disrupted the preexisting government, former enemies may have agreed on a cease-fire or peace but not on who should govern the peace. Even where the organization of an international interim government is based on the agreement of the warring parties, this agreement is often based on the factions' inability to change the political status quo in their respective favor. It may be more a tactical agreement than the consequence of a successful elite settlement. As a result, peace elections in post-conflict societies are dramatic events, and the stakes are very high, probably higher than in founding elections in other young democracies.[12]

Therefore, as a rule, those countries that are the most likely targets for liberal protectorates are the most unlikely candidates for successful democratization.

Conditions for Democratization and Peace Building in Cambodia and East Timor

Among the manifold differences between Cambodia and East Timor, the nature of the conflict that preceded the interim regimes is probably the most fundamental. In Cambodia warring parties had been fighting each other since 1970: first, the regime of General Lon Nol versus the communist Khmer Rouge guerrillas (1970–75), followed by a four-year reign of Khmer Rouge terror under the leadership of Pol Pot (1975–79), during which approximately one-fifth of the population was murdered or died as a result of the misrule of the Khmer Rouge. Then, after the Vietnamese invasion of Cambodia in 1979, the so-called Coalition Government of Democratic Kampuchea (CGDK), a three-party coalition of the Khmer Rouge, the royalist National United Front for an Independent, Neutral, Peaceful and Cooperative Cambodia (FUNCINPEC), and the Khmer People's National

---

10. Jonathan Haughton, "Reconstruction of War-torn Economies: Lessons for East Timor," in *East Timor: Development Challenges for the World's Newest Nation*, ed. Hal Hill and Joao M. Saldanha, 288–306, 294 (Singapore and Canberra: ISEAS, 2001).

11. Michael Ehrke, "Von der Raubökonomie zur Rentenökonomie: Mafia, Bürokratie und internationales Mandat in Bosnien [From Predatory Economy to Rent Economy: Mafia, Bureaucracy and International Mandate in Bosnia]," *Internationale Politik und Gesellschaft* no. 2 (2003): 123–154, 142.

12. Austin, "Democracy and Democratization," 190.

Liberation Front (former pro–Lon Nol forces) fought a guerrilla war with the pro-Vietnamese government of the People's Republic of Kampuchea (from 1989 on, the State of Cambodia, or SoC).

By the end of 1986, neither Vietnam and the People's Republic of Kampuchea (with support from the Soviet Union) nor the CGDK forces (with support from Thailand, China, and the United States) were in a position to dictate terms. Faced with military stalemate, a weakened political and diplomatic position, and domestic economic problems, the Vietnamese government withdrew its troops in 1989. The State of Cambodia could now no longer hope for victory, despite its continuing numerical military dominance. Informal negotiations between the CGDK and the SoC led to official peace talks in Paris in 1991. Under the guidance of the UN Security Council's Permanent Five and supported by the governments of Australia, Indonesia, Japan, and other concerned states, the warring parties signed the 1991 Paris Accord, which mandated the establishment of an interim government, the United Nations Transitional Authority in Cambodia (UNTAC).

In contrast, the nearly twenty-five-year conflict in East Timor was between an indigenous liberation movement and occupation forces, not a civil war. As a consequence of the 1974 "Revolution of the Carnations," Portugal's moribund empire, to which East Timor had belonged since the sixteenth century, rapidly crumbled. In the following months, conflicts among the proindependence Frente Revolucionara de Timor Leste Independente, or Fretilin, the pro-Indonesian integrationalist Apodeti, and the anti-Fretilin Timorese Democratic Union (UTD) escalated into intense fighting between both groups.[13] Subsequently, on December 7, 1975, Indonesian troops landed and secured military control of the capital city of Dili. Although Jakarta's full-scale invasion of East Timor aborted decolonization in East Timor, the United Nations maintained a strict policy of nonrecognition of Indonesia's invasion and subsequent annexation of East Timor. As a result, the question of East Timor's independence remained on the international agenda.

The window of opportunity for the decolonization of East Timor, which had been closed by Indonesia, once again opened after Indonesia's transition to democracy in 1998. Partially because of the weakened ability of the Indonesian government to control the situation on the island and partially because of the increasingly diffuse situation in Indonesian politics, the situation in East Timor became progressively more volatile, as Michael S. Malley's chapter in this volume attests. A shift in U.S. policy toward Indonesia and growing support in Australia for the self-determination for the Timorese may have also contributed to Indonesia's interim president, B. J. Habibie, deciding on January 27, 1999, to propose limited autonomy for East Timor. In

---

13. Stephen Hoadley, "East Timor: Civil War—Causes and Consequences," *Southeast Asian Affairs* (1976): 411–419.

subsequent negotiations, Indonesia, Portugal, and the United Nations concluded a set of three agreements on May 5, 1999, in New York. The agreements included a cease-fire between Fretilin and the Indonesian military and the conduct of a consultation vote that would enable the East Timorese to choose between a permanent autonomous status within Indonesia and a transition to independence under the aegis of the United Nations.

On June 11, 1999, the Security Council established the United Nations Mission in East Timor (UNAMET). UNAMET, which had already started to deploy a preparatory contingent in late May 1999, went into Timor without the protection of armed UN peacekeeping troops. The referendum that took place on August 30, 1999, had a voter turnout of 98 percent; 79.5 percent voted in favor of independence. In response, pro-Indonesian militias, either with the support or under the direct command of the Indonesian army, began Operation Clean Sweep, a three-week destruction campaign. About 70 percent of East Timor's building stock was destroyed or damaged, and the public and social infrastructure was almost completely destroyed. Operation Clean Sweep displaced more than two-thirds of the population and murdered approximately 1,500 people.[14]

The orgy of violence created a storm of protest in the international community. Within a matter of days, the deepening humanitarian catastrophe galvanized the United Nations and the major Western governments into action. On September 12, President Habibie announced Indonesia's acceptance of a peacekeeping force. Three days later, the Security Council authorized the establishment of the International Force for East Timor (INTERFET), a Chapter VII multinational force empowered to use all necessary measures to restore peace and security. Led by Australia, and under a unified command, INTERFET began arriving in East Timor on September 20, 1999. The Indonesian parliament eventually recognized the result of the consultation in mid-October. A week later the Security Council, in Resolution 1272, established the United Nations Transitional Administration in East Timor (UNTAET). East Timor's international interim government was born.

In Cambodia, the UN transitional authority faced the task of democratization and peace building after three decades of civil war. In contrast to East Timor, in Cambodia the state was weak, but state institutions remained largely intact. The incumbent regime still exerted some control over the means of violence, and the incumbents initiated the interim regime. In East Timor, there was no state or regime, as both vanished in flames and ashes after Indonesia had drawn back its troops.

---

14. Joseph Nevins, "The Making of 'Ground Zero' in East Timor in September 1999," *Asian Survey* 4, no. 42 (2002): 626–641.

In both countries, changes in international and domestic politics preceded the installation of interim regimes. These changes in the "enabling environment for international intervention" altered the costs and benefits of continuing the conflict for all parties. After the end of the Cold War, external support for all warring parties in Cambodia rapidly declined. Due to the rapprochement among the United States, China, and the ASEAN states on the one hand, and Vietnam and the Soviet Union on the other, the political and economic costs of the conflict increasingly exceeded the potential gains from the stabilization of Cambodia, not only from the perspective of those countries that supported the CGDK but also for Vietnam. Thus, all foreign governments participating in the conflict had an interest to disengage from the civil war through engagement in the peace process. This, in turn, affected the situation in Cambodia because none of the combatants was able to continue the fight without external support. Moreover, the military campaigns in the late 1980s had proven that neither government nor rebels were able to break the military stalemate.

In East Timor, domestic and international factors also reinforced each other. Due to the results of the consultation vote in August, the East Timorese desire for independence had an unambiguous popular mandate, whereas Indonesian claims were discredited. The pro-Indonesian militias in East Timor were dependent on support from Indonesia and could not block any peace solution. It remains an open question why the Tentara Nasional Indonesia (TNI), the Indonesian military, allowed the ballot to proceed at all and why the United Nations and concerned Western governments failed to plan for possible postballot violence before the referendum took place.[15] Once the violence began, however, it strengthened the resolve within the UN Security Council that "East Timor would not be the next Rwanda or Srebrenica." The international community pressured the Indonesian government either to stop the violence or to accept an international intervention force.[16]

Domestic political issues also played a role. As Paulo Gorjão argues, interim president Habibie hoped to improve his government's position vis-à-vis the international community, whose goodwill the government desperately needed in order to manage the financial crisis of the late 1990s.[17] At the same time, President Habibie tried to strengthen his image as a political reformer, which, if successful, would have improved his chances in the upcoming presidential elections. Refusing to cooperate with INTERFET and

15. Cf. Tamrat Samuel, "East Timor: The Path to Self-Determination," in *From Promise to Practice: Strengthening UN Capacities for the Prevention of Violent Conflict*, ed. Chandra Lekha Sriram and Karin Wermester, 197–229 (Boulder and London: Lynne Rienner Publishers, 2003).

16. Nicholas J. Wheeler and Tim Dunne, "East Timor and the New Humanitarian Interventionism," *International Affairs* 4, no. 77 (2001): 805–827, 816.

17. Paulo Gorjão, "Regime Change and Foreign Policy: Portugal, Indonesia and the Self-determination of East Timor," *Democratization* 9 (2002): 142–158.

the United Nations would have undone any possible domestic political gains and would have weakened the government's bargaining power. The Indonesian military also could accept a solution involving East Timorese independence because the destruction of September 1999 had already worked as a warning to separatist movements in other parts of the country, for example, in Aceh and West-Papua.[18]

The United Nations and some Western countries had key roles in the process, which eventually led to the installation of interim governments in both countries. In Cambodia, the United Nations provided the framework for peace negotiations among the warring parties, and external patrons supplied pressure and incentives to induce their domestic clients to cooperate. However, the main actors in Cambodia still were the four hostile factions. In East Timor, by way of contrast, domestic parties played only a minor role. Of course, the indigenous resistance movement's prolonged struggle for independence kept the issue of East Timor's national sovereignty on the international agenda. The East Timorese exile government's diplomacy and the activities of the Timorese diaspora in Europe also played a role. The major actors in the drama of 1999, however, were the UN Security Council and the governments in Jakarta, Canberra, Washington, and Lisbon. Although ASEAN was passive and slow to react to the crisis, some Southeast Asian nations also played a role, which facilitated Indonesia's consent to some form of humanitarian intervention.

Still, the challenges for transitional authority were enormous in both countries. Neither society had democratic experiences, traditions of constitutionalism, or civil society from which the UN administrations could have benefited. Particularly in Cambodia, the deliberate deepening of social conflicts by the autocratic rulers left traditional patterns of internal conflict resolution shattered and the sources of social capital drained. The political, social, and economic infrastructures were destroyed. Most economic and social resources needed for reconstruction were absent. Both societies suffered from the legacies of colonialism, war destruction, genocide trauma, social anomie, and vast poverty.[19] Social reconstruction in both countries required the repatriation of a large number of refugees, the reintegration of former combatants into civil society, and the achievement of national reconciliation.

In addition, state capacity building in Cambodia was retarded by the politicization and underpayment of the bureaucracy and an army that was bloated far beyond national security needs. The warring parties in Cambodia had to be disarmed and their troops demobilized, while antidemocratic ideologies remained prevalent among the domestic actors and some of the

---

18. Kevin O'Rourke, *Reformasi: The Struggle for Power in Post-Soeharto Indonesia* (Crow's Nest, NSW, Australia: Allen and Unwin, 1999), 211–212.
19. Doyle, "War Making and Peace Making," 94–5; and Martin and Mayer-Rieckh, "The United Nations and East Timor."

factions were fundamentally unwilling or unable to abide by their commitment to the peace agreement. As the next section will show, this unwillingness was further aggravated by choices made during implementation.

UN-Led Interim Governments

The United Nations controlled the interim governments in both countries.
However, the depth and effectiveness of the legal authority and de facto
control of the transitional authority varied considerably. This was largely
due to the organizational and juridical status and structure of the interim
government, as well as the domestic situation, particularly the number of
domestic actors involved and their position toward the interim government's policies. Using Doyle's terminology, the interim government in East
Timor belongs to the "supervisory authority" type, that is, the UN transitional authority exercised full legislative, executive, and administrative
powers. In fact, Jarat Chopra compares UNTAET with a "pre-constitutional
monarch in a sovereign kingdom."[20]

Unlike in East Timor, UN transitional authority in Cambodia was restricted
to administrative authority, while the Supreme National Council—the local
power-sharing government of all four warring parties with Prince Norodom
Sihanouk as its head—had full legislative authority. UNTAC and its special
representative, Yasushi Akashi, were given the authority to decide matters
only when the factions within the council were deadlocked and Prince
Sihanouk did not act. UNTAC's primary responsibility was to control the
administration in five areas of sovereign activity—defense, finance, foreign
affairs, information, and public security. UNTAC thus exercised executive
power only indirectly. The previously established bureaucratic structures,
however, remained intact, and the old bureaucracy, which was riddled with
cadres of the ruling Cambodian People's Party (CPP), was responsible for the
execution of UNTAC's directives. In addition, UNTAC had no mandate to
develop a long-term plan for economic reconstruction.

Both post-conflict missions were deployed with the consent of or, as in
Cambodia, by the invitation of all involved domestic parties, expressed in
the 1991 Paris Accord (Cambodia) and the May 5, 1999, agreement (East
Timor). In both countries, the United Nations played a threefold role as peace-
maker, peacekeeper, and peace builder. In Cambodia, the top priorities of the
UN transitional government were enforcing the cease-fire, disarming the
warring parties, holding elections, and preparing the democratic transition.
Furthermore, the interim government was authorized to preserve the integrity and sovereignty of the country and to organize the repatriation of refu-

---

20. Jarat Chopra, "The UN's Kingdom of East Timor," *Survival* 3, no. 42 (September 2000): 29.

gees and war internees. The timely completion of many of the tasks was the essential precondition for undertaking subsequent tasks—a recipe for internal tensions and delays.

Implementation of military and civilian operations started on March 15, 1992. In July, the UN cantonment, disarmament, and demobilization programs began. The interim administration prepared a new election law for the upcoming general elections and began registering voters and implementing various voter education programs in October of that year. UNTAC was able to stabilize the country's security situation so that in May 1993, free and fair elections could be conducted. Based on the framework of the Paris Accord, the newly elected parliament drafted a constitution for the Kingdom of Cambodia. The constitution was officially promulgated in September 1993 after the parliament had approved the new all-party grand coalition government under the equal leadership of FUNCIPEC and CPP. At the end of that month the UN interim administration ceased.[21]

The interim government in East Timor developed in five phases:

1. UNAMET (June–October 1999). UNAMET's mandate was to conduct the consultative referendum on August 30, 1999.
2. INTERFET (September 1999–February 2000). INTERFET was authorized by the UN Security Council to use all necessary measures to restore peace and security in East Timor. A UN peacekeeping force displaced INTERFET in February 2000.
3. UNTAET (October 1999–May 2002).
4. UNMISET (May 2002–June 2005). East Timor became independent on May 20, 2002. On that same day, the Security Council established the United Nations Mission of Support in East Timor (UNMISET) to provide assistance to East Timor over a period of two years until all operational responsibilities were fully devolved to the East Timor authorities. Subsequently, the Security Council extended UNMISET's mandate for another year to permit the new nation of Timor-Leste to attain self-sufficiency.
5. UNOTIL (June 2005–present). The United Nations Office in Timor-Leste (UNOTIL) is a simplified version of the previous mission, with no peacekeeping component.

Strictly speaking, only UNTAET was an interim regime with fully developed supervisory executive authority, while phase 1 and phase 2 each constituted a necessary step toward the interim government, and phase 4 marked

---

21. For details, see Sorpong Peou, "From the Battlefield into the State: Post-UNTAC Political Violence and the Limits of Peacebuilding," in *The Politics of Death: Political Violence in Southeast Asia*, ed. Aurel Croissant, Beate Martin, and Sascha Kneip (Munich: LIT, 2006).

a transition from international interim government to a self-governing democratic polity.

UN Security Council Resolution 1272 endowed UNTAET with a more comprehensive mandate than UNTAC: UNTAET was to exercise full executive and legislative authority during the period of transition from Indonesian rule until full national sovereignty.[22] More specifically, UNTAET was to provide security; establish an effective administration; assist in the development of civil and social services; ensure the coordination and delivery of humanitarian assistance, economic rehabilitation, and development; support capacity building for self-government; and support sustainable development. At the same time, UNTAET's mandate asked the transitional administration to develop the East Timorese state as well: to create a civil administration, a new police force, a judiciary system, a monetary system and banking sector, and a fiscal and taxation system. In other words, as Paulo Gorjão observed, "UNTAET would have to invent a functioning state in East Timor."[23]

From the very beginning, as Dwight Y. King noted, UNTAET suffered from "an underlying tension between the mandate to govern East Timor and the longer-term, strategic objective of preparing East Timor for democratic self-government."[24] The interim government lacked a consistent approach in dealing with the indigenous elites and population. The initial approach was not to integrate Timorese into the transitional structure but rather to recruit locally a separate civil service. Following deepening criticism of this approach, UNTAET reacted with the establishment of a nonelected, strictly advisory National Consultative Council, composed of UNTAET and East Timorese representatives. This ill-received initial approach in "Timorization" of the interim government subsequently was replaced by the National Council, a transitional cabinet with executive authority in which half the portfolios were entrusted to East Timorese representatives from the territory's thirteen districts, political parties, and members of various social organizations.[25] Many Timorese and even some of UNTAET's own representatives criticized the transitional authority for following a mostly cosmetic approach to "Timorization," without having a broader integration strategy of power sharing with the indigenous elites.[26] However, UNTAET still enjoyed broad public support and successfully conducted elections for a constitutional convention in August 2001 and for a president in April 2002.

22. Shalini Chawla, "Shaping East Timor: A Dimension of United Nations Peacekeeping," *Strategic Analysis* 12, no. 24 (2001).

23. Paulo Gorjão, "The Legacy and Lessons of the United Nations Transitional Administration in East Timor," *Contemporary Southeast Asia* 2 (2003): 313–333, 314.

24. Dwight Y. King, "East Timor's Founding Elections and Emerging Party System," *Asian Survey* 5, no. 43 (2003): 747–757, 745–746.

25. Martin and Mayer-Rieckh, "The United Nations and East Timor,"

26. Chopra, "The UN's Kingdom of East Timor," 27–39.

Legacies of UNTAC and UNTAET

Both interim governments achieved their short-term goals; however, there are still questions about long-term achievements in terms of *sustainable* peace building and *durable* democratization. This study argues that in contrast to optimists, who view East Timor as an overwhelming success of peace building and democratization under the aegis of the United Nations, and to pessimists, who describe UNTAC as a flop, the performance of interim governments in both countries is best seen as a limited success.

Cambodia

UNTAC achieved mixed results in a number of its immediate goals: while stabilization was successful, peace building was only a partial success and democratization was mostly a failure. UNTAC was able to repatriate a considerable number of refugees, and its presence forced the warring parties to moderate their tactics.[27] It created an environment in which the threat of a new regional conflict was reduced, and the Cambodian people, for the first time in thirty years, could begin to think about the future of their country.

Regarding democratization, UNTAC did conduct free and fair elections. The election, though boycotted by the Khmer Rouge and held in a context of mutual mistrust, turned out to be UNTAC's biggest success. Voter turnout was 89.5 percent, despite the Khmer Rouge's threats to disrupt the poll (which did not materialize). The elections ended with a surprising victory of the National United Front for an Independent, Neutral, Peaceful, and Cooperative Cambodia (FUNCINPEC), led by Prince Norodom Ranariddh. FUNCINPEC and the Buddhist Liberal Democratic Party together won 68 of 120 total seats in the National Assembly, whereas the CPP, led by Hun Sen, won 51 seats. At the end of the mission, a popularly elected government took over power from UNTAC. For the first time in more than three decades, Cambodia had an unstable but legitimate government. Furthermore, any assessment of the interim government's performance must be placed in historical context. To argue that there are no improvements in human rights, democratic freedoms, or human security in general is misleading.[28]

Yet elections are not all there is to democracy, and for a number of reasons it was unrealistic to expect that the interim government could achieve liberal democracy and political stability in an almost totally unpredictable national

---

27. Trevor Findlay, *Cambodia: The Legacy and Lessons of UNTAC* (Oxford: Oxford University Press, 1995), 155.

28. See Sorpong Peou, "Implementing Cambodia's Peace Agreement," in *Ending Civil Wars: The Implementation of Peace Agreements*, ed. Stephen J. Stedman, Donald Rothchild, and Elizabeth M. Cousens, 499–526 (Boulder, Colo., and London: Lynne Rienner Publishers, 2002); and Sorpong Peou, "Collaborative Human Security? The UN and Other Actors in Cambodia," *International Peacekeeping* 1, no. 12 (2005): 105–124.

environment within an arbitrarily fixed period, after which international support would be dramatically curtailed.[29] First, the UN peacekeeping force could not realize the military component of the peace agreement. The disarmament and demobilization of the various factions were a critical shortcoming of the whole mission. From the summer of 1992, the Khmer Rouge blocked disarmament of its troops and did not allow the peacekeeping force to enter its territory.[30] As a consequence of UNTAC's decision not to force disarmament of the Khmer Rouge, the other parties also refused to demobilize their troops. After the departure of the UN troops, fighting once again erupted, and the ensuing low-intensity civil war did not stop until 1997.

Second, UNTAC also failed to provide a neutral political environment for the assumption of power by the newly elected Cambodian government. Failure to disarm and demobilize aggravated the security dilemma, particularly for the opposition factions. The more time UNTAC lost on the disarmament issue, the more the peace agreement eroded. Political and military tensions, and attacks on UNTAC staff, increased in numbers and intensity especially in the run-up to the elections. This, in turn, led UNTAC to restrict its presence more and more to the capital city.[31] While all political parties violated the rules of the transition game, it seems that CPP and the Khmer Rouge were responsible for most incidences. This development was an unintended consequence of UNTAC's failure to control the Cambodian bureaucracy.

Third, UNTAC's lack of manpower (170 mission staff were expected to oversee more than one hundred thousand Cambodian civil servants under CPP control alone), technical difficulties, and lack of knowledge of Cambodian history, culture, and language allowed the ruling CPP to shield the bureaucracy from UN surveillance. The interim government's operational problems, especially in the beginning phase of UNTAC, increased opportunities for the Khmer Rouge and the CPP not to comply, as well as decreased any embryonic confidence the factions might have had in UNTAC's capabilities to provide neutrality and security.

Fourth, the UN administration had only weak instruments to force the Cambodian parties to accept the outcome of the poll. While UNTAC was based on the consent of the factions as expressed in the Paris agreement, during the implementation period, the transitional authority found itself operating without the continuous or complete cooperation of the two most powerful political parties, the CPP and the Khmer Rouge. Although the success of voter registration and the high voter turnout attested to the interim

---

29. Austin, "Democracy and Democratization," 196.

30. David W. Roberts, *Political Transition in Cambodia 1991–99: Power, Elitism and Democracy* (Richmond, Surrey, UK: Curzon Press, 2001), 93–150.

31. Sorpong Peou, *Foreign Intervention and Regime Change in Cambodia: Towards Democracy?* (Singapore: ISEAS, 2000), 260–261.

government's claim that most Cambodians endorsed the plan to introduce democracy in Cambodia, the CPP successfully reestablished itself as the hegemonic political force. In fact, the CPP, as the main loser in the 1993 poll, refused to accept the outcome, claiming that it was the result of UNTAC's partisanship that gave an advantage to the opposition. The political crisis was temporarily settled by building a grand coalition consisting of all relevant political parties. FUNCINPEC and the CPP formed a coalition government, with Prince Ranariddh and Hun Sen serving as first and second prime ministers, respectively.

This compromise proved fragile. In 1997, conflicts between the two major parties escalated into what is viewed by many as a coup d'etat of Hun Sen (CPP) against Prince Ranariddh. Due to the firm reaction of the international community, Hun Sen was forced to reallow limited standards of competition in the 1998 and 2003 elections. Since the CPP effectively controlled the preparation of the polls, electoral defeat was unthinkable, although the polls, as Jeffrey Gallup states, "were generally well and fairly administered in a technical and organizational sense."[32] The CPP used its overwhelming coercive power and resources to implement a strategy of "intimidation by incumbency," which effectively prevented a level playing field.[33] Although lacking a dramatic shift from electoral democracy to open autocracy, the failure of the UN mission to fulfill critical parts of its mandate has nevertheless paved the way for the emergence of a new hegemonic one-party system that is softer and more stable than any other regime has been for the last thirty years.

Regarding the causes for the shortcomings of democratization, four critical factors can be identified. First, the peace agreement faced a number of birth defects. The agreement constructed the interim regime as a hybrid cogovernment between the deeply divided Cambodian coalition government on the one hand and the UN transitional authority on the other. It forced hostile parties into a political "shotgun wedding"—a marriage that, David W. Roberts states, "brought together political combatants for whom the election was a continuation of the war, rather than the basis for sharing power agreeably."[34] The transitional authority's inappropriate framework, along with the enduring military and political strength of the CCP—especially on local and regional levels—transferred the political struggle from the battlefields into the state itself: it "undermined political transition in the implementation phase as well as in the period between the two elections in 1993 and 1998. . . .

---

32. Jeffrey Gallup, "Cambodia's Electoral System: A Window of Opportunity for Reform," in *Electoral Politics in Southeast & East Asia*, ed. Aurel Croissant, Gabriele Bruns, and Marei John, 25–75, 41 (Singapore: Friedrich-Ebert-Stiftung, 2002).

33. Ibid., 47–48.

34. Roberts, *Political Transition in Cambodia*, 47.

stable democratic political transition was temporal in the short, UNTAC-term, and untenable in the longer term."[35]

Second, bringing all relevant parties into government and giving them their share of posts in cabinet and bureaucracy led to double, sometimes even triple structures. This approach not only sustained a dangerous level of factionalism but also increased the likelihood of corruption. Rather than depoliticizing the CPP-controlled one-party state, power sharing created, as David Ashley writes, "two separate and competing party states operating within every ministry, province, military command and police commissariat. Instead of working with their counterparts from the other party, officials from the prime ministers' level down conducted business with their party clients and colleagues."[36] This retarded the already weak capacity of the public administration, as Ashley continues, "by building and reinforcing parallel structures of personal and party authority, operating both within and outside the state."[37] The size of the armed forces rose disproportionately, resulting in high military expenditures of 30 percent of the total public expenditures. This temporarily avoided the problem of unemployed and dissatisfied soldiers. However, no central command structure under a neutral command developed. Rather, FUNCINPEC and CPP were in fact in control of their troops, promoting the political fractionalization of the army and securing the military predominance of the CPP.

Third, the lack of strategic orientation in the international community also contributed to the negative developments of the 1990s. Even though the interim government's measures led to unintended and negative consequences in the early stages of the interim government, the international community stuck to its goal to democratize a country shattered by thirty years of civil war within only eighteen months. The road map for democratization was essentially restricted to holding free and fair elections without changing the existing structures of political and military power. The constitutional process was rushed and the political institutions were relatively weak at the end of the transition period. Furthermore, the international community took no precautions to bind the warring parties to respect democratic procedures after the election. The international community underestimated the difficulties of the mission, such as the lack of political and social tolerance, civic values, and experience with peaceful and cooperative forms of conflict settlement and elite settlement. At the same time,

---

35. Ibid., 49.

36. David Ashley, "The Failure of Conflict Resolution in Cambodia," in *Cambodia and the International Community: The Quest for Peace, Development and Democracy,* ed. Frederick Z. Brown and David G. Timberman, 55 (Armonk, N.Y.: M. E. Sharpe, 1998), www.asiasociety.org/publications/cambodia/failure.html.

37. Ibid.

governments—especially Western ones—misperceived the strength of the exile parties such as FUNCINPEC.

Finally, the vested entrepreneurs of violence, such as the Khmer Rouge, military commanders, and various party cadres, had no interest in the stabilization of the state's coercive monopoly, civilian control over the military, or the emergence of the rule of law because of their own economic interests in arms sales, timber, gems, and drug trafficking. The UN transitional authority neglected long-term development and capacity-building objectives, which led to weak results in generating economic recovery and impeded democratic development. However, UNTAC was not solely responsible for this, given that international donors provided only a fraction of what they had promised at the beginning of the peace process.[38]

East Timor

UNTAET's achievements are well summarized by Ian Martin and Alexander Mayer-Rieckh: "While the peace operations in East Timor did generally well in the areas of electoral assistance, traditional peacekeeping, humanitarian assistance and emergency rehabilitation, UNTAET consistently faced problems with institution building and governance tasks." The lack of a common understanding of capacity building and the neglect of these issues in the early stages of the transitional authority retarded UNTAET's efforts at institution building.[39]

While planning for UNTAET was cursory, the planning for UNMISET began early, allowing the transitional authority to develop a detailed and comprehensive plan for the follow-up mission.[40] Even though the interim government in East Timor also ended without having established the social and economic prerequisites for a working democracy and sustainable development, most observers considered UNTAET and UNMISET to be successful, and they still can be considered more successful than UNTAC in terms of peace building.[41] Lessons were drawn from UNTAC's numerous mistakes and failures to better prepare UNTAET. Equipped with relatively large financial and personnel resources relative to the country's small size, UNTAET was able to reach an unusually swift economic stabilization.[42] The transition from UNTAET to UNMISET led to only a small decline of international engagement. Indeed, the UN Security Council and international donors realized that international support for East Timor was still vital.

---

38. Peou, *Foreign Intervention and Regime Change.*
39. Martin and Mayer-Rieckh, "The United Nations and East Timor," 142.
40. Ibid., 139.
41. See, for example, Doyle and Sambanis, *Making War and Building Peace,* chapters one and five.
42. Haughton, "Reconstruction of War-torn Economies."

UNTAET provided security, and the transition to independence and democracy was surprisingly smooth. Nevertheless, it is still unclear if and when the young nation's economy and public administration will be able to stand on its own feet: foreign aid made up 45 percent of East Timor's gross domestic product (GDP) in 2001.[43] UN staff still occupy many high-level positions in civil administration, particularly in the judiciary and budget offices. Repatriation of refugees and reconciliation and transitional justice for past crimes against humanity, committed by militias and the Indonesian military, have ceased. Unemployment is estimated at between 60 and 80 percent, and more than 50 percent of the country's eight hundred thousand or so people live on less than US $0.55 a day. Four years after Timor-Leste officially became a sovereign nation in May 2002, the latest UNDP report demonstrated the full extent of misery in the country. In 2006, GDP per capita was about $370; average life expectancy was 55.5 years; more than 50 percent of the population has no access to clean drinking water and is illiterate. After most UN personnel had left the country in 2005, the GDP growth rate even turned negative, and national income declined in 2005.[44]

The slow pace of reconstruction and the high unemployment levels are an additional source of disorder. Antigovernment demonstrations in East Timor's capital city, Dili, in July 2004, involving former guerrilla fighters, indicated a growing frustration among veterans who feel robbed of their independence dividend in a fledging nation with a profoundly weak economy and high unemployment. Clashes between disgruntled veterans and soldiers on the one hand and police and troops loyal to the government on the other turned Dili into a war zone in April and May 2006. President Xanana Gusmao and Speaker of the Parliament Francisco Guterres saw no other option to stabilize the situation than appealing to the international community for assistance. Thus, only weeks before the last UN mission was scheduled to end, Australia, New Zealand, Malaysia, and Portugal once again sent a 2,300-troop international protection force to East Timor.[45] Although most observers attribute the recent instability to the worsening of socioeconomic conditions, the unrest also has a strong political component and even an element of ethnic conflict; the conflict among various factions of the army parallels the cleavage between the new nation's eastern and western districts. Ironically, while regional identity was of minor political relevance under the Indonesian government, it turned into the most salient cleavage in Timorese society after the country became independent because various political

---

43. Ibid.

44. United Nations Development Programme, "The Path out of Poverty: Integrated Rural Development," Timor-Leste Human Development Report 2006, www.tl.undp.org/undp/for_download/NHDR2006/TL-2006-Final.pdf.

45. Manuel Schmitz, "Osttimor in der Krise [The Crisis in East Timor]," *Südostasien aktuell* 4 (2006): 35–46.

actors attempted to capitalize on regionalism as an instrument for political mobilization. Thus, some observers view East Timor as a prime example of how "nation building" in post-conflict (and postcolonial, in the case of East Timor) societies can create new "ethnic conflicts."[46]

Furthermore, frustrated former guerrilla fighters and the remnants of pro-Indonesian militias pose a serious internal security problem for the new country, as do rising crime levels, an inefficient police force, and a weak judiciary. The ability of Timor-Leste's security forces to contain these threats without help from the United Nations must be seriously questioned.

While the former liberation movement Fretilin consolidates its near-hegemonic power and its prime minister openly boasts that the party will be in power for the next fifty years, the politicization of the security apparatus points to various potentially destabilizing effects from East Timor's semi-presidential system.[47] The dual leadership system and institutionalized competition of democratic legitimacies in semipresidentialism in general is a recipe for political trouble, and the fact that "the individuals occupying these two critical leadership positions are political opponents, perhaps even political enemies," as Dennis Shoesmith observes, further hinders democratic consolidation.[48] Indeed, at the time of writing of this chapter, there is ample evidence to suggest that East Timor is at risk to become a failed state, incapable of achieving even the most minimal standards of stateness in a modern nation-state.

Conclusion

Bearing in mind that each country's situation is unique to some degree and that its lessons may in fact be limited, it is nevertheless possible to reach some conclusions.

Differences in the nature of the conflict and the domestic constellation of involved factions had an enormous impact on the challenges the two UN interim regimes had to face. East Timor, to some extent, was "easier" than Cambodia because the United Nations did not have to achieve a just peace through negotiating with warring parties. By the time the interim regime was established in East Timor, conditions of success that are rarely available to peace missions were present. The belligerent power had completely withdrawn, and an effective multinational force could credibly provide security.

46. Manuel Schmitz, *Ethnische Konflikte in Indonesien und die Integrationspolitik Suhartos* [Ethnic Conflicts in Indonesia and Suharto's Policy of Integration] (Hamburg: Institute für Asienkunde, 2003).

47. Anthony L. Smith, "Timor Leste: Strong Government, Weak State," Institute of South East Asian Studies, ed., *Southeast Asian Affairs* 2004, Singapore: 2005, 279–297, 281.

48. Dennis Shoesmith, "Timor-Leste: Divided Leadership in a Semi-Presidential System," *Asian Survey* 2, no. 43 (2003): 231–252, 231.

The local population enthusiastically welcomed the transitional authority. There was a single domestic faction with which to negotiate, rather than a number of hostile factions as in Cambodia.

While it is true that the main challenge in East Timor was to build a state from the ground up, the situation there was different from the conditions of failed states as we think of them. The main obstacles for UN-led interim regimes in failed states are the de facto privatization of violence and the dispersion of political power created by the disintegration of the state. In East Timor, the issue was not power dispersion but the power vacuum that the Indonesians left behind after their retreat. While Fretilin was too weak to take advantage of the situation, INTERFET filled the existing vacuum quickly. In fact, within less than two months, a new "proto-state under United Nations tutelage" emerged.[49] The nonexistence of an incumbent regime prevented the emergence of a dual authority problem between the authority in power and the United Nations Transitional Authority. This institutional and political tabula rasa actually provided opportunities for the effective functioning of the interim government. The question remained as to whether the transitional authority would understand and utilize these opportunities.

Perhaps the most basic lesson to be learned from UN-led interim governments in Cambodia and East Timor is that having the support of the local population is critical, but this alone is not sufficient. Successful UN-led interim governments also require elite settlement and the support of the regional powers and international patrons of local clients. Sustainable peace building and transition from authoritarianism to fully institutionalized liberal democracy require more than ending civil strife. As Dennis Austin writes, "Immediately satisfactory elections do not necessarily mean that a democratic government or any of the essential elements of democracy (the rule of law, and independent judiciary and a professional non-partisan civil service including the police and military, and another 'free and fair' election) will be guaranteed."[50]

Particularly in the case of internationalized interim governments, democratizers face a dilemma: in order to reach an agreement, they must assume all domestic parties will participate in good faith. At the same time, however, they must take reassurances should the parties be unwilling or unable to fulfill the agreement made.[51] So, democratization through international interim governments in countries in the midst of civil war will be successful only if the transitional authority is able to maintain a "hurting balance of power,"[52] in which all parties realize that continuing the struggle will harm them more than benefit them. This was the United Nations' failure

---

49. Maley et al., "Introduction," in *From Civil Strife to Civil Society*, 1–14, 3.
50. Austin, "Democracy and Democratization," 189.
51. Doyle, "War Making and Peace Making," 542.
52. Peou, *Foreign Intervention and Regime Change in Cambodia*.

in Cambodia. UNTAC was neither able to establish a stable hurting balance of power nor could it guarantee the parties' compliance with democratic procedures.

Particularly, the Cambodian experience proves that de facto democratization becomes an exit strategy if the international community focuses on technical problems (holding elections), leaving actual politics to the national elite. The Cambodian elite commenced fighting after UNTAC departed; they had not learned to accept the democratic decision-making process and to behave according to the norms of democracy. The democratization process came to a halt and, finally, led to a new semiauthoritarian regime. Obviously, it does not make sense to leave the fate of a young democracy in the hands of antidemocratic national elites, yet this was exactly what took place in Cambodia. Rather, the international community must have the will to take responsibility for social and economic reconstruction and to intervene even after the transitional process, if any negative aberrations do occur afterward.

Cambodia and East Timor prove that democratization expands beyond the fallacy of electoralism. Instead, it must be embedded in a comprehensive agenda of political, social, and economic methods of peace building. This means that the protectorate will be very expensive for the international community, both in terms of time and in terms of financial and human resources. As a result, interim governments run the risk of becoming never-ending self-replicating political realities. It is a moot point whether the foreign governments and the international community want to accept such enormous responsibilities in countries outside of their own political backyard (Bosnia, Kosovo) and where engagement will not yield significant security or economic benefits. The opposition of the U.S. government and others to UNMISET's extension and their insistence on a limited, one-year mandate for UNOTIL are representative of this problem. However, as the thirteen years' experience of post-UNTAC Cambodia proves, if interim governments end before democracy takes root and democratic institutions are strong enough to stand alone, then the entire endeavor may fail.

11

State Building before Statehood

Kosovo's Evolution from an Interim Polity to "Conditional Independence"

Lenard J. Cohen

Editors' Note

Through an analysis of the origins and evolution of the United Nations Interim Mission for Kosovo (UNMIK), Lenard J. Cohen raises many of the dilemmas facing the international community as it attempts to re-create viable governance in a land torn apart by war. However, the ambiguity of future status—whether Kosovo will achieve status as an independent state, remain part of Serbia, or something in between—adds to the burden of transition. Cohen argues that lingering ambiguity over its sovereign status undermines Kosovo's security and economic and political development. In this situation, there is no credible domestic authority that could oversee the transitional process.

Therefore, a UN transitional administration has governed the formerly autonomous Yugoslav province since a 1999 NATO-led military intervention halted Serbian-supported militia abuses of ethnic Albanians. The numerically dominant Kosovo Albanians, Cohen argues, translated a de facto alliance between the Kosovo Liberation Army and the United States during the intervention itself into prominent positions for Kosovo Albanian activists in governing structures. Serbia's continued influence over the minority Kosovo Serbs, meanwhile, undermined efforts to draw the latter into plural governance within Kosovo. The UN mission faltered without clear goals or organizational cohesion, and local forces, empowered by a greater self-perception of political legitimacy than the UN mission, proved cunning in their efforts to undermine external efforts to force Kosovo's transition. Violent events in 2004 sparked a renewed effort by the international community to move simultaneously toward achieving international standards, such as minority protections, and some form of enhanced sovereignty, if not full statehood.

We are trying to build a transitional country out of a non-country. . . . I've been sent to do an impossible task.

    —Bernard Kouchner, Special Representative of the Secretary-General,
    December 1999

My predecessors . . . were in a difficult situation because they were managing an interim administration where the international community very often seemed very content with having this as an interim mission. . . . I think there's a limit to how long you can keep a place in limbo.

    —Soren Jessen-Petersen, Special Representative of the Secretary-General,
    April 12, 2004

Introduction: From Interim Status to Enhanced Sovereignty

Kosovo—its very sovereign status in continuing question—presents a fascinating and instructive case study of an international model of interim governance. The UN resolution that ended the NATO war with Slobodan Milosevic's Yugoslavia in 1999 gave Kosovo an ambiguous status. Technically, Kosovo remained a part of Serbia, within the imperfectly integrated two-unit federation of Serbia and Montenegro, but in fact it was governed by a protectorate structure, the United Nations Interim Mission in Kosovo (UNMIK). During the prolonged interim interlude, Kosovo held regular elections for central and local assemblies and established governmental institutions.[1] While UNMIK has retained powers in vital areas, it has also slowly transferred powers to local political authorities substantially composed of Kosovo Albanian political party activists. Ministries for justice and security, for example, were established in early 2006.[2] By the onset of 2006, Kosovo was clearly on the cusp of a major change in its status. But the details of that change, only now becoming evident, increasingly appear to alter Kosovo's status in a less fundamental way than many had hoped or expected.

    Widespread anti-Serb riots throughout the province in March 2004, combined with UNMIK's failure to achieve significant advances in democratic consolidation and sustainable economic development,[3] finally galvanized the international community to focus greater attention on Kosovo. This led to

---

1. The electoral system for the assembly is proportional representation with closed party lists. Twenty out of 120 seats are reserved for minority communities: ten each for Serbs and non-Serb minorities.

2. As late as 2005, UNMIK controlled foreign affairs and domestic policing, justice, and fiscal policy.

3. Kosovo is the poorest economy in the Balkan region, with a GDP per capita of US$790 in 2003. Approximately 37 percent of Kosovo's population lives on under US$1.70 a day and another 15 percent are in "extreme poverty," surviving on US$1.17 a day. An estimated 70 percent of the Kosovo Albanian population is under thirty years of age, and 50 percent are under the age of twenty. Alexandre Kolev et al., *Kosovo Poverty Assessment* (Washington, D.C.: World Bank, 2005).

a comprehensive UN appraisal of conditions in the protectorate and, by the fall of 2005, to a UN decision to initiate talks on Kosovo's future status. By the time the imminent talks were announced, the international community had reached a consensus on three points:

1. Kosovo should not return to its pre-1999 de jure linkage with Serbia and Montenegro.
2. There should be no territorial linkage or any new sovereignty association of Kosovo's territory with neighboring states.
3. Kosovo should move to some form of enhanced sovereignty, but its new governance structure should, at least for the immediate future, be something less than "final" status, or full statehood.

The stakeholders in Kosovo's transition hold antithetical positions on the fundamental question of independent statehood. While most Albanians (constituting more than 90 percent of the population) in the protectorate seek full state sovereignty for Kosovo, the Serb minority community desires to retain the status quo, or at least to block outright independence. The agenda of the Serb minority has been advanced—indeed often manufactured—by the Serbian regime in Belgrade. The Belgrade regime has promoted a vague notion for Kosovo's future—"more than autonomy, less than independence"—that envisions very little modification of the status quo.

Two related features—Serbia's influence (including nominal sovereignty over Kosovo) and Kosovo's indeterminate future status—make Kosovo's transitional regime a peculiar case of internationally administered interim governance. By keeping the status of Kosovo ambiguous, the UNMIK administration avoided confrontation in a compromise that left everyone somewhat dissatisfied. At the same time, this ambiguous status and the multiorganizational nature of UNMIK stymied the mission's ability to form an effective and domestically legitimate government, creating many failures in governance and security in Kosovo. UNMIK found itself administering an interim regime that, while not technically a state, desperately needed to develop enough capacity to avoid state failure.

The case of interim governance in Kosovo illustrates the dilemma for the international community when it becomes closely associated with the activities of a secessionist insurgency, however well intentioned its attempt to quell interethnic violence, remove a dictatorial regime, and achieve humanitarian goals. The U.S. alliance with the Kosovo Liberation Army (KLA) in 1999 formed such an association. Enormous difficulties arise if the international community is unable or unwilling to allow the secessionism either to reach its logical outcome, that is, full independence, or, alternatively, to take complete charge and address the complex political and socioeconomic problems that originally motivated the insurgent movement.

Fabricating a Failed State (1999–2004)

The obstacles to successful state building and democratization in post-conflict environments are exceedingly difficult to overcome, even when issues
of state sovereignty and the locus of political power are far clearer than
they have been in Kosovo since mid-1999. The establishment of the UNMIK
mission took place in a highly disrupted and politically volatile interethnic
climate following the ethnic cleansing of Kosovar Albanians by Serb police
and paramilitary forces during the 1999 war and mutual atrocities that
occurred during the ensuing struggle. That context compounded the
already considerable difficulties arising from the antagonistic history of
Serb-Albanian relations in Kosovo; the political repression and violence
carried out in the province by the Milosevic regime in the late 1980s and
1990s; the bloody struggle between Serbian forces and Albanian insurgents
in 1988–99; and the collapsed political negotiations between Kosovar Albanians and Serbian leaders at the early 1999 Rambouillet conference.[4] At the
conclusion of the 1999 war, UN Security Council Resolution 1244 (passed
on June 10, 1999) determined that Kosovo would remain a de jure part of
Yugoslavia (now Serbia and Montenegro) but accorded it "substantial
autonomy and meaningful self-determination."

Initially underprepared and understaffed, the UNMIK mission also
found itself confronted by a potentially threatening power vacuum. The
wartime destruction and apathy of the Albanian community's parallel
institutions that had functioned during the Milosevic period, when combined with the hasty postcapitulation withdrawal of the Serbian governmental and security apparatus, created an authority deficit. The Albanian
parallel structure of the 1990s—led by the internally quite authoritarian
but tactically nonviolent Democratic League of Kosovo, or LDK, of Ibrahim
Rugova—had been politically eclipsed, at least temporarily, by the military
and political representatives of the KLA.

Beginning in the late 1990s, the militant secessionist KLA had waged an
armed struggle against the Belgrade authorities. During the 1999 war against
the Milosevic regime, the KLA became a de facto ally of the United States and
NATO. The KLA was also at loggerheads with Rugova's LDK, which had developed its own armed forces (the National Army of Kosovo, or FARK) during the
war. In the immediate postwar period, KLA activists spearheaded a "reverse
ethnic cleansing." Albanian vengeance against the remnants of the Serb community forced the exodus of thousands of Kosovo Serbs and initiated a violent
settling of accounts with the KLA's Albanian political rivals. A pattern of
revenge, not reconciliation, thus dominated during the early UNMIK administration and troubled Kosovo throughout the years of interim governance.

---

4. See James Pettifer, *Kosova Express: A Journey in Wartime* (London: Colin Hurst, 2005).

Working within the complex environment of an ethnically polarized, factionalized, and violent society and also in the context of a considerable ambiguity regarding Kosovo's future sovereignty, UNMIK officials were often conceptually unsure about whether and how to share power with the local population and political structures. The vast majority of the Albanian Kosovars, including Albanian political parties, viewed the "new" Kosovo as "their" state-in-formation. During and immediately after the war, Albanian officials—particularly KLA operatives—took control of many of Kosovo's municipalities. The newly arrived international officials lacked the capacity or, often, the political will to dislodge them. Meanwhile, vainly believing that somehow with the help of political forces in Belgrade they could recover their lost domination, the Kosovo Serbs—especially in the heavily Serb zone around northern Mitrovica—were closely aligned with, and manipulated by, the Milosevic regime (and after October 2000, by different political forces in multiparty post-Milosevic Serbia).

Very early in its postwar evolution, UNMIK developed a loosely coordinated four-pillar structure: (1) Police and Justice was controlled directly by the United Nations (until 2000 a humanitarian assistance pillar under the UN High Commissioner for Refugees, or UNHCR); (2) Civil Administration was run by the United Nations Department of Peacekeeping Operations; (3) Democratization and Institution Building was led by the Organization for Security and Cooperation in Europe (OSCE); and (4) Reconstruction and Economic Development was led by the European Union. Responsibility for security resided in the hands of NATO through the Kosovo Force (KFOR).

The United Nations quickly improvised a structure during the last months of 1999 that divided and overlapped responsibilities among a multitude of international organizations within UNMIK. This structure, combined with multiple local and factionalized domestic actors and a residual role of the Belgrade authorities, was rife with interorganizational conflicts, turf battles, communication failures, and other coordination and coherence problems related to the UN mission's overall operations. These problems were significantly compounded by the extreme angst regarding the status of Kosovo exhibited by both international officials and domestic actors. The UN mission faltered owing to the absence of a clear set of goals, a lack of organizational cohesion, and serious challenges from a complicated terrain of competing and cunning local forces who believed they appropriately enjoyed far more political legitimacy than the international mission.

Gradually, UNMIK devised various procedures and administrative agencies for managing Kosovo and for engaging the cooperation and reconciliation of the local communities. Early on, UNMIK exercised executive and legislative authority through consultative bodies such as the Joint and Interim Administrative Structure, the Interim Administrative Council, and the Kosovo Transition Council (which all included Albanian and Serb representatives). A "constitutional framework for provisional self-government" was adopted on May 15, 2001. Kosovo's first elected central legislature was inaugurated on December 10, 2001, followed by the formation of the Provisional Institutions of Self-Government (PISG), although UNMIK retained ultimate authority on constitutional and legal matters. By the end of 2003, the PISG had formally been awarded numerous civil administration responsibilities, except for UNMIK's "reserved powers" in major spheres of sovereignty, including security, law and order, foreign relations, minority rights, banking, customs, and other key economic spheres.

Unfortunately, UNMIK never fully recovered from the organizational dilemmas that flowed from the troubled and jurisdictionally confused circumstances of its organizational birth. Most of the deficiencies in the areas of legitimacy and institutional capacity that afflicted Kosovo between 1999 and 2006 can be directly linked to the early stages of the UNMIK mission.[5]

An Outworn Welcome: Stasis and the Struggle for Power

The UN mission's internal organizational rivalries, together with its early difficulties dealing with political forces in Kosovo, undermined UNMIK's consolidation of authority and its ability to develop legitimacy. Over the next six years, it also contributed to UNMIK's highly uneven record in broad areas of interim governance, including democracy building, justice, economic development, and interethnic reconciliation. UNMIK would prove successful at creating a modicum of political stability and economic reconstruction and also at organizing competitive elections at the municipal level (October 2000 and October 2002) and for the central legislature (November 2001 and October 2004). Despite these efforts, Kosovo nonetheless receives the Freedom House's lowest overall governance rating in the Balkans, earning the "not free" overall rating.[6]

The legitimation and effectiveness of the new institutional structure and UNMIK itself were undermined by the persistent polarization of the Albanian and Serb communities, as well as by the uncompromising and often

5. On these issues, see William G. O'Neill, *Kosovo: An Unfinished Peace* (Boulder, Colo.: Lynne Rienner, 2002); Bathsheba N. Crocker, "Kosovo: Learning to Leverage 'Liberator' Status," in *Winning the Peace*, ed. Robert C. Orr (Washington, D.C.: Center for Strategic and International Studies, 2004); Knut Kirste, "Administrative Capacity Building in Kosovo: An Assessment of UNMIK/OSCE's Civil Administration Policy" (paper prepared for the conference Comparing Experiences with State Building in Asia and Europe: The Case of East Timor, Bosnia, and Kosovo, Council for Asia-Europe Cooperation, December 13, 2001); Anne Holohan, *Networks of Democracy—Lessons from Kosovo for Afghanistan, Iraq, and Beyond* (Stanford, Calif.: Stanford University Press, 2004); and Mark Baskin, "Review Article: Post-Conflict Administration and Reconstruction," *International Affairs* 79, no. 1 (January 2003): 161–170.

6. This measure includes the government's transparency and capacity, as well as civil service institutions. Although the score on a seven-point scale (1 is best) improved from 6.0 in 2004 to 5.75 (national) and 5.5 (local) in 2005, it remains well below the 4.0 median for the Balkans. Freedom House, *Nations in Transit: Democratization from Central Europe to Eurasia*, www.freedomhouse.org/template.cfm?page=17&year=2005.

violent pattern of political pluralism within the emergent Kosovo party system. Against the background of Kosovo's unresolved future status, all these problems festered and created a sense of drift.

Debilitated by both its own internal strains and a lack of clarity about what kind of endgame it should promote, UNMIK found it difficult to effectively mobilize support for dynamic economic recovery and intergroup reconciliation. This context made it almost impossible to attract foreign investment and caused efforts at privatization to move at an excruciatingly slow pace. (The latter was also partly due to problems of financing and ownership disputes.) The economic growth that did occur was driven almost entirely by foreign aid and remittances from the diaspora Albanian community. Chronic unemployment ran at above 60 percent (nearly 70 percent by 2005) in a society where nearly half the population was under twenty years of age. A trade imbalance skewed toward imports and revenues was highly dependent on taxing imports. Endemic corruption and organized crime—intensified by the clientelistic-clan character of politics and business—further weakened the economic situation over the course of the international administration. In June 2005, Andre Venegoni, Kosovo's international prosecutor for business crime, suggested that the dominant "economic mentality" in Kosovo supports fraud, misconduct, bribery, and other forms of organized corruption that is like "a cancer, a wound which is crippling economic and all other development in Kosovo."[7]

Despite such economic difficulties, elections did begin to institutionalize competitive pluralism and democratic participation in Kosovo. Unfortunately, due to the tenuous commitment of Kosovo politicians to democratic norms and to the salience of the outstanding status issue, a virulent pattern of nationalist politics also reemerged and intensified in Kosovo. Both Albanian and Serbian parties engaged in ethnic outbidding, with each party's leadership trying to demonstrate that its organization was the most committed to achieving the national goals of its respective ethnic constituency.[8] Each of the three major Kosovo Albanian parties—Rugova's LDK and the two KLA derivative parties (Hashim Thaqi's Democratic Party of Kosovo, or PDK, and the newer offshoot, Ramush Haradinaj's Alliance for the Future of Kosovo, or AAK)—attempted to demonstrate that it alone could best address the overarching goal of the Albanian community, namely, independent statehood. This obsession with quickly terminating Kosovo's interim status drove Albanian party leaders and Kosovo's new PISG into a persistent power struggle with UNMIK.

Increasingly, UNMIK was viewed as maintaining "colonial" rule, hoarding its reserve powers, and limiting the Albanian community's right to move

---

7. *Beta,* June 2005.

8. On this subject, see Bernd J. Fischer, *A Survey of the Development of Albanian Nationalism,* Woodrow Wilson International Center for Scholars, (Washington D.C.: March 23, 2005).

beyond the narrowly defined "substantial autonomy" provided by UN Security Council Resolution 1244. Serbian political activists were equally alienated from UNMIK, which they alleged coddled the Albanian side and encouraged Albanian sovereignty aspirations. As a result, interethnic reconciliation stalled, the UN mission increasingly lost legitimacy, and intraparty relations on the Albanian side overheated and became more violent.[9]

The international community had directly or indirectly encouraged Albanian nationalism in the late 1990s to combat the repression and maintenance of the Milosevic regime. Early on in its interim rule, UNMIK had unwisely acquiesced to the KLA's entrenchment. But after Milosevic's ouster in Serbia, and with the international community busy in other troubled areas, Albanian nationalism began to complicate the continuation of state building in the Balkan surrogate state. The continuing unwillingness of the international community to push the issue of resolving Kosovo's indeterminate status only provided fodder for the increasingly rabid nationalist rhetoric and mobilization. Indeed, Albanian nationalism had spilled out of Kosovo and was seriously destabilizing both southern Serbia and Macedonia.

Explosion and a New "Exit Strategy" (2004–05)

In mid-March 2004 the accumulated problems in Kosovo, particularly the mistakes and delinquency of the interim government structure, came into sharp focus when Kosovo was rocked by a wave of communal violence and chaos. Ethnic Albanians turned against both their Serb neighbors and the international administration. The violence that took place from March 17 to 19 had premeditated features but, as mobs rampaged, also metastasized into spontaneous activities. The riots left nineteen people dead (eleven Albanians and eight Serbs), hundreds injured, and more than four thousand people displaced from their homes. Nearly 750 Serb-owned houses and 36 Serb Orthodox churches and religious sites were destroyed or damaged. According to UN figures, 82 percent of the 4,100 minority group members displaced during the crisis were Serbs, victims of activities that aptly could be termed a "pogrom" or "ethnic cleansing." The UN secretary-general's report of April 30, 2004, characterized the March events as "ethnically motivated violence, a targeted effort to drive out Kosovo Serbs, as well as members of the Roma and Ashkali communities, and to destroy the social fabric of their existence in Kosovo." About 180 members of KFOR,

---

9. Kosovo may have had a multiparty, multiethnic coalition government cobbled together by UNMIK, but its head, Prime Minister Bajram Rexhepi, from the PDK, admitted that cooperation with president Rugova of the LDK was very limited: "We cannot sit together unless someone from the international community joins us" (*Global Newswire*, September 13, 2004).

UN Police personnel, and Kosovo Police Service personnel were among those injured.[10]

The trigger for the March chaos has been traced to specific incidents—such as the drowning of three ethnic Albanian children on March 16 in the divided town of Mitrovica, after they were allegedly chased into the river by Serbs—and to Serb roadblocks in central Kosovo following a violent incident in which a Serb teenager died. But the crisis in March certainly also reflects deeper socioeconomic and ethnopolitical problems, many of which are connected with Kosovo's unresolved status. "The March violence in Kosovo was unexpected," aptly observed James Pettifer, "but causes lie deep in the unresolved future of Kosova and complacency and lack of attention by the International Community."[11] The international authorities did their best to arrest the ringleaders and perpetrators and also to bring those responsible for the riots to trial.

The March upheaval in Kosovo was a profound shock to the interim governance structure. UNMIK and KFOR were badly prepared and proved disoriented in dealing with the crisis, and NATO reinforcements were quickly rushed to Kosovo. A report by the Kosovo Ombudsperson Institution pessimistically concluded, "It has now become increasingly difficult to maintain any form of pretense that there is a reasonable possibility of creating a real multiethnic society in Kosovo in the foreseeable future."[12] Human Rights Watch criticized the international community in Kosovo of being in "absolute denial about its own failures towards minorities in Kosovo."[13]

The crisis of March 2004 prompted the international community to completely reconsider and reorient its strategy for dealing with Kosovo. Veton Surroi summed up the coming change on March 19, even before order had been restored: "A policy died yesterday in Kosovo and it took human lives in the most tragic way. It was a policy that involved a confrontation between UNMIK and the Kosovars over the transfer of powers."[14]

International officials suggested that their policy of implementing standards would continue, and a new (quite comprehensive, but extremely long

---

10. UN Security Council, April 30, 2004, S/2004/348.

11. *Kosovo March 2004: The End Game Begins* (Surrey: Defense Academy of the United Kingdom, Conflict Studies Research Centre, April 2004); see also International Crisis Group, *Europe Report 155: Collapse in Kosovo* (April 22, 2004).

12. *Ombudsperson Institution in Kosovo Fourth Annual Report, 2003–2004,* July 12, 2004, 20.

13. "Failure to Protect: Anti-Minority Violence in Kosovo—March 2004," *Human Rights Watch* 10, no. 6 (July 2004): D.

14. According to a Foreign Broadcast Information Service report of March 18, 2004, Surroi also noted the impressive ability of self-identified "KLA veterans" and "student leaders" to rapidly mobilize Albanian protest during the crisis and their "organizational capacity" as demonstrated by the number of weapons that quickly appeared. But he warned that institutional life, dictated by the leadership of "those anonymous figures cannot be a real kind of institutional life. . . . We are hostages to the incompetence displayed by the Kosova leadership, which paved the way for UNMIK's arrogant behavior" (*IWPR*, March 22, 2004).

and complex) implementation plan was released. There was also broad recognition, however, that a more fundamental policy shift was also necessary. It was Ambassador Kai Eide's August 2004 "Report on the Situation in Kosovo,"[15] prepared for Secretary-General Kofi Annan in order to develop a policy response to the March crisis, that began a new chapter in the evolution of the international administration. Eide noted that UNMIK was in "disarray," lacked "internal cohesion," and had consequently become the target of everyone's blame. Although the UN mission had been "a victim of the lack of clear political perspective," Eide slammed UNMIK for having become "static, inward looking fragmented and routine . . . with a serious lack of a rational, unifying plan." He recommended a gradual overhaul of UNMIK, which would temporarily retain its four-pillar structure. He also urged the United Nations to prepare for a "gradual reduction of its presence to be accompanied by a parallel increase in the EU and a continuation of the OSCE presences."[16]

Eide argued that the notion that Kosovo should meet a series of standards before status talks could be opened was an "untenable" policy that lacked credibility. "In the current situation in Kosovo," Eide remarked, "we can no longer avoid the bigger picture and defer the most difficult issues to an indefinite future." The argument had circulated for some time, particularly among Albanian leaders, that the formula for future progress in Kosovo should be changed to standards *and* (not before) status.

Eide's report accepted that suggestion and made some other interesting policy innovations. He called for a "more dynamic standards policy with achievable priorities reflecting the most urgent needs, including those for the future status process." An accelerated "transfer of competences" to Kosovo provisional institutions was needed, including those in "core residual areas," and also "more ambitious and systematic capacity building." Meanwhile, Eide called for a "robust policy of interventions and sanctions in cases of inappropriate performance." The Albanians, he was confident, understood that they had done "too little, too late to stem the violence" in March, and needed to reach out to the Serbs. For their part, the Serbs realized they could not avoid involvement in the political process.

Although there was actually very little indication that views had changed as much as Eide thought, his report signaled a major policy reversal. In many respects, Eide's subsequent 2005 standards implementation review was a continuation of his August 2004 report to Secretary-General Annan.

Eide's 2004 report and the United Nations' acceptance of its recommendations did not serve to instantly reenergize the UNMIK mission as he suggested or to ensure the achievement of standards, but they did change the overall climate and direction of international and internal discourse regard-

---

15. United Nations Security Council, (November 30, 2004), S/2004/932.
16. Ibid.

ing Kosovo. Harri Holkeri, special representative of the secretary-general, resigned for health reasons in May 2004 and was replaced by Denmark's Soren Jessen-Petersen, who was committed to the Eide recommendations. The March events, the 2004 Eide report, and the anticipated status talks created new momentum within UNMIK to accelerate the transfer of powers to Kosovo institutions and to achieve the implementation of standards.

Toward a Final Interim Model

For several months during the first part of 2005, the issue of Kosovo's future status awaited the completion of yet another situation report under preparation by Eide. This review, again commissioned by Secretary-General Annan, followed the launching of a major policy initiative by the United States that accorded future status talks for Kosovo a very high priority. When submitted at the end of September 2005, the report's conclusions set the stage for the current debate on Kosovo's future.[17]

The report concluded that the economic situation in Kosovo remained "bleak" and that the foundations for a multiethnic society were "grim." Although the institutional vacuum that had existed in 1999 had been filled, the society was still suffering from the effects of a "post-conflict trauma" and the behavior of self-interested politicians who did not view themselves as guardians of the public trust. Kosovo Albanians, Eide observed, had done little to dispel the security fears of the Kosovo Serbs; the rule of law had not been adequately entrenched; organized crime and corruption remained rampant; and political institutions were "fragile." For example, Kovoso's justice system had failed to respond adequately to the March 2004 riots and had fueled perceptions of impunity for ethnic violence.[18]

Launching status talks, Eide argued, would be a stimulus to both economic and political improvement, and in any case, something fresh needed to be tried to achieve forward momentum for the troubled region. Expanding the decentralization process would enable minority communities to control their local affairs and to develop a stake in Kosovo's political system. Determination of future status could not wait until the protracted process necessary to consolidate democratic standards had been completed. Eide conceded, however, that should status changes not be accompanied by real progress on standards, the entire exercise might prove counterproductive.

---

17. United Nations Security Council, "Letter Dated 7 October 2005 from the Secretary-General Addressed to the President of the Security Council (Report on a Comprehensive Review of the Situation in Kosovo, Presented by Mr. Kai Eide, Special Envoy of the Secretary-General)."

18. A report by the OSCE, "Kosovo: The Response of the Justice System to the March 2004 Riots," drew this conclusion in 2005.

Even though determining Kosovo's future status should not wait for this process to take root, Eide sought to strengthen governmental institutions. Kosovo sorely needs to develop a democratic "parliamentary culture" and to establish a public service sector that is not simply composed of various ministries and agencies functioning as the fiefdoms of different political party organizations and party elites. Such institutional capacity building takes a long time and requires the development of a new outlook and mentality (including the need for a depoliticized university).

Given present conditions and recent difficulties, Eide was careful not to inflate expectations: "Kosovo will not in the foreseeable future become a place," he aptly noted, "where Kosovo Albanians and Kosovo Serbs are integrated. They probably never were." International organizations, particularly the European Union, and security forces would need to play a prominent role in the next stage of Kosovo's development.

On November 21, 2005, precisely ten years after the signing of the Dayton Peace Accords to end the war in Bosnia, former Finnish president Martti Ahtisaari arrived in Kosovo as a UN envoy to begin preparing for status talks on Kosovo's future. Ahtisaari's arrival just two months after the submission of the Eide Report demonstrated the international community's determination to move expeditiously. Ahtisaari began a round of shuttle diplomacy, which was to be followed by the start of direct talks between the various actors involved: the Kosovo Albanians, the Kosovo Serbs, the Belgrade regime, and members of the international community. Direct talks were planned to begin in February–March 2006 and expected to last for six months to a year. Although the international community and local and regional actors now shared the view that the Kosovo status issue needed to be addressed, there were still differences among the participants who were about to begin direct negotiations.

Kosovo Albanian Perspectives

Among the citizens of Kosovo, opinions regarding the territory's future status reflect a profound ethnic divide. The Albanians of Kosovo overwhelmingly support the notion that the interim arrangements under which they are now ruled should be quickly replaced by an independent state. For example, one opinion poll conducted in September 2005 revealed that 90 percent of the Albanians surveyed supported full independence, as did 90 percent of the non-Serb minorities.[19] The notion of Kosovo remaining part of Serbia as an autonomous province was supported by 86 percent

---

19. United Nations Development Programme (UNDP), *Fast Facts on Kosovo Early Warning Report* (Pristina: UNDP, 2005).

of the Kosovo Serbs (a view also seen as favorable by 65 percent of Serbs polled in Serbia).[20]

The Albanians of Kosovo, and particularly the various political parties they support, are not monolithic with regard to their respective negotiating positions and willingness to compromise. Not surprisingly, public positions among Albanians in Kosovo regarding the goal of independence range from the uncompromising to the more pragmatic, and the positions espoused reflect the underlying cleavages and competitive features that characterize the current political landscape. Although six major parties endorsed a resolution on independence approved by the Kosovo Assembly in mid-November 2005, such unity masks the considerable tactical differences among various Albanian political forces.

For example, the views of the controversial and popular speaker of the assembly, Nexhat Daci of the LDK, are illustrative of a strong current in Kosovo Albanian society. Daci not only rejects the consideration of Serbian interests regarding Kosovo but also is highly suspicious of the motives and policies of the international community. "Kosovo has a capacity to become a normal Balkan state," he argues. "It would be the wrong investment if we spent money, time and energy seeking new models." He has advocated "urgent" transfer of power from UNMIK to Kosovo institutions in the areas of justice and security and has cautioned against the creation of an "asymmetric decentralization" which would allow predominantly Serb municipalities to become "new enclaves organically related between themselves and administratively connected with Belgrade."[21]

The PDK's Hashim Thaqi takes a slightly more pragmatic, flexible position, which grew out of the wartime UCK (Ushtria Clirimtare E Kosoves). Thaqi has also warned against excessive accommodation of the Serbs and generally stresses the grievances and claims of the Albanian side. Thaqi has admitted, "There is certainly an element of prejudice in [Kosovar] society towards ethnic Serbs." But rather than focusing on the urgency of eliminating such prejudice, Thaqi generally seeks to explain or excuse its origins in recent history, as well as the equivalent hostility of Serbian society toward Albanians and the Belgrade regime's failures to assist aggrieved Albanians.[22] There has been a deep division between Thaqi and Daci, but they and their respective political organizations have recently been cooperating more closely.

Other Kosovo Albanian politicians are very pragmatic about the status talks that lie ahead, and they fully realize that security for the Serb minority is a critical matter for Kosovo's future and that it is also an issue of central

---

20. *Kosovo-Kosova: Coming to Terms with the Problems of Kosovo: The People's Views from Kosovo and Serbia* (Belfast: Institute of Governance, Queen's University–Belfast, 2005).

21. *KosovaLive News Agency*, September 21, 2005.

22. *International Herald Tribune*, November 26, 2005, 4; and *Koha Ditore*, November 28, 2005.

concern for the international community. For example, Veton Surroi of the centrist Citizens List Hour (ORA) Party—who, like Thaqi and Daci, is a member of the Kosovo Albanian team for negotiations on status—recognizes that the protection of Kosovo Serbs, and the future development of their identity and cultural life, must be the subject of negotiation and resolution before the topic of Kosovo's full independence is broached.

Surroi and other Albanian moderates are also more willing to assist in raising awareness of minority rights among the Kosovo Albanian majority and to discuss the various problems of democratization commented on in the Eide report. As Surroi told a Belgrade newspaper in October 2005, "The fact that all [the Albanians] seek independence doesn't mean that we seek an authoritarian society or a society that doesn't respect the rights of minorities and others. . . . Among Kosovo Albanians we must construct a consciousness that Serbs are part of Kosovo . . . and that the Serbian minority is in a position in which it must have mechanisms and instruments for positive discrimination."[23]

As preparations for status talks began in 2005, Kosovo's president, Ibrahim Rugova, and prime minister, Bajram Kosumi, attempted to express the sovereigntist yearnings of their ethnic group: namely, to maintain Kosovo's unity and still leave sufficient room for maneuver in the upcoming negotiations. Rugova enjoyed an extremely high moral and intellectual position in Kosovo Albanian society and politics, and he was regarded by most observers as critical to Kosovo's gradual evolution toward independence. Rugova died of cancer on January 21, 2006, which cast a pall over the debate surrounding the state's future status and led to a temporary postponement of the status talks. Members of the international community counseled the members of Rugova's LDK party to find a quick replacement for him in order to fill the vacant post of president and to renew momentum on the start of status negotiations. In mid-February the LDK chose Fatmir Sejdiu, a moderate leader of the party, to replace Rugova.

Serbian Perspectives

Some Serbian moderates feared that Rugova's death would strengthen the hand of Kosovo Albanian radicals. Other Serbs welcomed the delay in addressing future status or believed that Rugova's absence would compel the international community to delay Kosovo's full independence. On the whole, Serbian elites welcomed the Eide report on Kosovo, mainly because it underlines the serious outstanding problems to be addressed before the protectorate can be transformed into an independent state.

Rugova's moderate presence in the negotiations had been important in part because the majority of Serbs, whether in Kosovo or in neighboring

---

23. *Politika*, October 15, 2005.

Serbia, have been resolutely opposed to the full independence of Kosovo. Recent polls, however, reveal an increasing acceptance over the last few years by Serbs in Serbia that they will not be able to retain even de jure control over Kosovo.[24] Not surprisingly in these circumstances, various views exist in the Serbian community regarding what negotiating position should be adopted in the forthcoming status talks.

In Serbia, opinion makers are divided, but many believe that accepting some kind of an internationally sponsored conditional or limited independence for Kosovo will enable Serbia to extract more concessions in the Kosovo talks and international support for Serbia's entry into the European Union and various Euro-Atlantic institutions, such as NATO. Moreover, an obstructionist Serbian posture on Kosovo will, according to the moderate view, endanger Serbia's own transition to democracy. The Serbian Assembly in November endorsed a resolution that emphasized the "inviolability" of Kosovo's position within Serbia and rejected any "imposed solution," but the document was essentially an initial "patriotic" position statement for the coming status talks.

Prime Minister Vojislav Kostunica's right-of-center (some term it neonationalist) four-party minority government in Serbia has endorsed a "more than autonomy, less than independence" formulation that would technically leave Kosovo within Serbia-Montenegro. Their proposal envisions a highly decentralized Kosovo governance structure and a continuing close linkage between Serbia and the Kosovo Serbs.

Meanwhile, the moderate president of Serbia, Boris Tadic, another member of the Serbian delegation to the Ahtassari talks (but whose Democratic Party is not in the government), has advanced a two-entity plan for Kosovo (an Albanian entity and a Serb entity) that is quite similar to the position of the ruling coalition. Tadic's plan closely resembles aspects of Bosnia's Dayton Peace Accords. It includes the retention of international officials and security forces in Kosovo for some time, as well as strong cultural links of the Kosovo Serb minority community to Serbia. Over time, Tadic's plan has won some support from political rival Kostunica, and now both Tadic and Kostunica stress the urgent need to develop mechanisms for the protection of the Kosovo Serbs and the return of displaced Serbs who have been forced to leave the protectorate.

Despite this seeming consensus, however, the Tadic-Kostunica nexus is complicated by the fact that Tadic hopes to promote early elections in Serbia, both to legitimize his views on Kosovo and to replace the Kostunica-led coalition. While each man agrees that the other one's plan for Kosovo is acceptable, nevertheless each would rather promote his own specific plan, so

---

24. During 2005, the number of Serbian respondents who thought that Kosovo's independence was a realistic possibility increased from roughly one-fourth to one-third of those polled (*Vecernje Novosti,* November 30, 2005).

they compete for influence. In January 2006, in a gesture of reaching out to the Albanians, Tadic tried to attend the funeral of President Rugova, while Kostunica did not even send a telegram of regret. Although the Kosovo Albanian elite who planned Rugova's funeral rebuffed Tadic, the Serbian president did have an informal encounter in early February with Albanian leader Thaqi at an international meeting in Athens.

The Kostunica government's plan for Kosovo's future and the Tadic variant both leave Kosovo within the territorial confines of Serbia and Montenegro. Such a solution is totally unacceptable to the Kosovo Albanians. Supporters of Tadic and Kostunica regard their ideas as substantially more reasonable for Kosovo than more extreme views that favor a formal partition of the protectorate along ethnic lines. The highly nationalist Serbian Radical Party—whose popularity has been growing—and other even more radical nationalist groups are far more intransigent in their rejection of Kosovo independence or any type of enhanced sovereignty for the protectorate.

The Kosovo Serbs, most of whom are concentrated within a few municipalities, are primarily interested in their own security and depend heavily on the advocacy of their interests by the contending political forces in Belgrade. Kosovo Serb leaders have tried to emphasize the need for full realization of democratic standards in Kosovo prior to any kind of enhanced sovereignty or independence for the region, as well as the need for "realistic decentralization" and the meaningful participation of their minority community in Kosovo's governing institutions. The Serbian government and Serbian Orthodox Church led an election boycott campaign in October 2004, and as a result, Kosovo Serb voters stayed home. The fact that major Kosovo Serb parties have chosen to boycott Kosovo political institutions in recent years has contributed to the continuing standoff between the two principal ethnic communities.

International Perspectives

By 2005, the major players in the international community that had assumed responsibility for Kosovo since 1999—centered in the Contact Group (the United States, Russia, the United Kingdom, Germany, France, and Italy)—had reached a general consensus regarding the basic principles for the negotiation of the protectorate's future status. But differences still remained among the international players regarding the details and timetable of moving beyond the current interim arrangements, and in some cases there continued to be disagreement on fundamental issues.

Each of the major international players will have its own special envoys in the status negotiations led by Ahtassari, and different views about what should emerge from the talks. For example, the United States is taking a strong stance in favor of minority protection to ensure the security of the Serbian community and, thus, the need for very substantial decentralization of power to local communities. Russia will be more vigorous than Washington in supporting the retention of close links between the Kosovo Serbs and the Belgrade regime. Serbia's ability to mobilize support from the United States and the European Union will also certainly be limited by Belgrade's lethargic cooperation on the matter of dealing with indicted war criminals who are still at large. In late 2005, both the Albanian and Serbian sides were actively organizing their lobbying efforts in Washington. On balance, the Albanian side appeared better equipped in terms of financial resources and contacts with sympathetic former U.S. officials, think tanks, and international lobbyists. Serbian leaders, for their part, were also beginning to employ high-profile U.S. and foreign lobbyists in order to mobilize support for their views.[25]

The respective roles for NATO and the European Union regarding future security arrangements in Kosovo must also be worked out. The Berlin-Plus arrangements for EU-NATO cooperation that have worked well for a EU takeover of the mission in Bosnia may provide a useful model for Kosovo.[26] The issue of what form EU participation in Kosovo would actually take remained very much an open question in early 2006. Conscious of its failures in the Balkans during Yugoslavia's dissolution, the European Union in recent years has been very active in military security and policing operations in both Bosnia and Macedonia, and through its diplomatic and economic initiatives the European Union has been quite engaged throughout the region. As Javier Solana, the European Union's high representative for common foreign and security policy, commented recently, "The importance of continued EU engagement in the Balkans cannot be overstated. More than any other region in the world this is a European responsibility. Quite simply we cannot afford to fail here."[27]

The Eide report recommended substantially increased EU involvement in Kosovo. EU members' interest and resources, and the receptivity of the Kosovo Albanians and Kosovo Serbs to different forms of international oversight, will influence future EU engagement. In late 2005 there appeared to be substantial disagreement among EU member states about the best resolution of Kosovo's future status. Indeed, diplomats from the Czech Republic, Slovenia, Spain, Greece, and Italy were all promoting different ideas, some of them clearly at odds with the European Union's common policy for Kosovo. For example, in a controversial speech, Czech prime minister Jiri Paroubek suggested that partitioning Kosovo along ethnic lines might be the best solution: "The northern part of the region will belong to Serbia, the majority of the southern part can be given the status of an

---

25. *Financial Times,* September 2, 2005.

26. For more on Berlin-Plus arrangements, see Bastian Giegerich, "Not Such a Soft Power: The External Deployment of European Forces," *Survival* 46, no. 2 (2004): 163.

27. *Radio-Television Kosovo,* September 26, 2005.

independent nation." Kosovo's ethnic groups, he added, "will have a hard time living next to each other, much less together. . . . A soldier or police officer would have to be standing around every corner."[28] The Czech initiative was clearly in breach of earlier EU statements opposed to Kosovo's partition.

Meanwhile, Slovenia's president, Janez Drnovsek, has advanced a plan for Kosovo's full (and unpartitioned) independence, a suggestion that ran considerably ahead of the European Union's policy of first providing protection to the Serbian minority. At the same time, Italy, Spain, and Greece appeared concerned about the prospect of full-fledged independence for Kosovo. Spain's problem of Basque separatism makes the independence scenario for Kosovo a worrisome prospect. Italy and Greece—which had led the "coalition of the willing" that intervened in Albania in 1997—were concerned about potential Albanian refugee outflow should Kosovo fail. The different views within the European Union reflect anxiety about Kosovo and the prospect of forming a new state in the Balkans. At a time when the European states were sorting out the impact of their differences over the failed EU constitution and their various concerns over future enlargement, the potential political implications and financial burden of long-term management over Kosovo's affairs were naturally a subject of considerable debate.

Future Transition: Protracted Protectorate Lite (2006–15)

In early 2006, UN special envoy Ahtassari was continuing his diplomacy and discussions with interested parties in preparation for direct negotiations. He sensibly had warned against "rushing unnecessarily" to any solution in the long-awaited debate on Kosovo's future. But international momentum concerning Kosovo was under way, and debate and controversy were likely to intensify during the spring of 2006. The Kosovo issue was now moving along the international fast track to a new phase of state building and status clarification. The next stage of transitional governance pending statehood will prove critical in terms of improved management and performance by both international and domestic actors if the weaknesses of the earlier interim period after 1999 are to be avoided.[29]

---

28. *B92*, November 23, 2005, and *EUobserver.com*, December 1, 2005.

29. Only minimal reassurance is provided by a recent UNDP report on the capacity of Kosovo institutions to perform their roles: "The foundations for a sound system of public administration are *being established gradually*. . . . In most areas, the level of development of the administrative system is no less advanced than it was in comparable countries at the time of independence, and it even exceeds this level on a significant number of measures." UNDP, "Assessment of Administrative Capacity in Kosovo" (April 2005), 8. On Kosovo's still fragile political, security, and economic conditions, see *Kosovo Early Warning Report*, no. 9 (Pristina: UNDP, January–March 2005).

In early 2006, it remained difficult to predict what shape the international presence in Kosovo would take. It appears that the projected degree of international control exercised over Kosovo's political institutions and local decision making in the near future will probably be far more limited than either the powers currently enjoyed by UNMIK or the power wielded in Bosnia by EU high representative Paddy Ashdown. It is an open question whether this less invasive form of interim governance, or what might be termed *protectorate lite*, can do a better job than UNMIK with respect to status implementation and democracy building.

Although circumstances make it futile to elaborate a single or an ideal template for post-conflict interim governance, many precedents now provide a base of experience. The record of international transitional administration in the Balkans has been spotty thus far. The international protectorates, or interim governmental arrangements, in Kosovo and Bosnia have been fairly criticized for being "phantom states." For example, David Chandler has argued that such states are neither "puppet regimes doing the will of the international community, nor genuine states relating to the will and needs of the population. It is not like imperialism and equally not like the old UN idea of states and sovereignty . . . [but] the worst of both worlds; no responsibility is taken internationally, but it's impossible for local actors to assume responsibility. Kosovo just sums that up."[30]

And yet, despite their admittedly unsatisfactory and uneven performance in state building and democracy promotion, the international administrations and protectorates established in the Balkans during the 1990s arguably filled a critical need in the area of post-conflict stabilization and peace enforcement.[31]

Conclusion

UNMIK endeavored to divert or freeze the course of Kosovo-based Albanian nationalism and to guide the Kosovars toward an internationally devised paradigm of democratic standards within the context of a vaguely defined sovereignty structure. Improvising an interim system of governance in the wake of the turbulent conditions that followed the 1999 war and in a "non-country" protectorate environment proved to be an almost "impossible task," as UNMIK's first chief, Bernard Kouchner, once remarked. UNMIK was to a large extent making it up as it went along.

---

30. David Chandler, testimony before United Kingdom Parliament, Select Committee on Foreign Affairs, Minutes of Evidence (October 4, 2004), questions 4–46.
31. Alexandros Yannis, "The Creation and Politics of International Protectorates in the Balkans: Bridges over Troubled Waters," *Journal of International Relations and Development* 5, no. 3 (September 2002): 258–274.

Today, beset by "transition fatigue," "enlargement fatigue," and "status fatigue," the international community is still engaged, but it is in a quandary regarding the further evolution of governance of the surrogate state. Kosovo is poised for another extended episode of interim rule. Another protectorate or trusteeship phase is unavoidable but, as the March 2004 riots illustrated, fraught with danger.

Epilogue

In 2006, after seven years of the United Nations' interim administration in Kosovo, the protectorate's future status became a subject of internationally sponsored negotiations. From February through mid-September, eight meetings were held between representatives of Kosovo's provisional government on the one side and representatives of Serbia and the Kosovo Serbs on the other side. The direct status talks were presided over by Martti Ahtisaari, the UN secretary-general's special envoy for Kosovo. The bulk of the meetings—held under the auspices of the UN Office of the Special Envoy for Kosovo (UNOSEK)—focused on what were termed "status-neutral issues," such as decentralization of the government structure (including the number, organization, and responsibilities of municipalities), protection of cultural heritage sites, and community rights. One high-level meeting, which included top political executives from Kosovo and Serbia, was also exclusively devoted to the question of future status itself.

In the context of the United Nations' rather checkered performance in Kosovo, and particularly in view of the considerable mistrust and ethnic distance between the majority Albanian Kosovar community and the Serb minority, which was intensified by the anti-Serb violence in 2004, it was an achievement just to launch and sustain the negotiations. But by the end of September, Ahtisaari and his colleagues in UNOSEK had made only very limited headway in reconciling the diametrically opposed views of the Kosovar and Serbian delegations. From the onset of talks, two closely related issues have deeply divided the two sides: first, whether Kosovo would receive statehood at the conclusion of the negotiations; and second, the type of organization and extent of autonomy that should be accorded to predominantly Serb communities. The Kosovar side is unalterably committed to achieving full statehood and ending the protectorate, and it wishes to grant only minimum political control to Serbian majority localities. Serbia's delegation, in contrast, adamantly opposes Kosovo's formal independence and favors the establishment of some type of "maximum autonomy" for the protectorate, including the continuation of formal links to Serbia, substantial rights and security for local Serbs, and the protection of the Serbian cultural legacy in Kosovo. The Kosovar side warns that excessive decentralization will mean the partition of Kosovo, while Belgrade's representatives regard independence as the internationally sanctioned theft of Serbian territory that can destabilize the entire Balkan region. On September 15, 2006, after chairing the eighth round of negotiations, Deputy Special Envoy Albert Rohan suggested that the prospects of progress in the talks had become increasingly slim. He was quoted in a UNOSEK press release that day as saying, "We are approaching the moment whereby talking alone we will not accomplish the goal. We could talk for another ten years and not change anything."

Kosovar and Serbian officials alike have suggested that, should their respective demands be ignored, and if some kind of "imposed solution" or compromise is made by Ahtisaari and the international community, there is a good chance that extremist elements on one side or the other will violently destabilize the region. Meanwhile, the Contact Group, which has overall responsibility for seeing that the negotiations suit the goals of the international community, has indicated it is "desirable" for the talks to conclude by the end of 2006. By the end of September, it appeared increasingly likely that Ahtisaari and UNOSEK would recommend to the Contact Group that it proceed with a unilateral solution for Kosovo if the talks prove inconclusive.

With or without a consensus or a compromise between Pristina and Belgrade, the difficult Kosovo status negotiations will undoubtedly soon be concluded, and at some point in the first half of 2007, Kosovo's interim status as a protectorate will be terminated by the United Nations. Although the details of future status still remain unclear, the course of the status talks and the situation in Kosovo after seven years of UNMIK control underscore several points that may be useful for a general understanding of transitional international administration. First, it is extremely difficult to formulate an exit strategy for an open-ended post-conflict interim administration arrangement, particularly if there is ambiguity at the beginning of an external intervention regarding the prospective political status that the international community is working toward. Second, when the main impact of interim rule has been to only partially dampen violence and maintain a semblance of order, rather than to fundamentally alleviate or eliminate the deeper causes of the original conflict, finding an effective exit strategy becomes far more difficult. Third, and closely related, when an interim administration proves ineffective at achieving fundamental political reforms and intergroup reconciliation, as unfortunately has been the case with UNMIK, and when there is no viable state structure to stand alone after interim status is technically ended, the international community will still be saddled with long-term responsibility for preventing post-interim-status state failure. For example, after the termination of the UNMIK mission, there will be a new and substantial international civil and military presence in Kosovo that is accorded significant "intervening" powers in "state" affairs. UNMIK will probably be replaced by an International Community Office and led by an

International Community Representative, although those labels and acronyms may be altered as negotiations proceed. The European Union has also begun preparations to establish an international civilian mission in Kosovo that will start to operate after the end of UNMIK and will have substantial authority in the police and judicial sectors.

Kosovo's status will likely be "resolved" sometime in 2007. But representatives of the international community will continue to have authority to replace and appoint certain officials and to veto laws. To a large extent, such international powers or a "mandate for implementation of the agreement on status," amount to an extended interim situation. Thus, UNMIK will end in June 2007, but Kosovo will still be functioning under international administration and protection. Finally, those Kosovar and international officials managing Kosovo affairs under the imminent semisovereign status arrangements will still have to face the formidable challenge of democracy building and state building. Kosovo will certainly confront the same, if not a heavier, load of challenges to democratic consolidation when the protectorate is dismantled and future status becomes clarified. Indeed, the UNDP reported that between March 2005 and June 2006, public satisfaction in Kosovo with the provisional institutions of governance decreased by 40 percent![32] The mid-July 2006 report of the Ombudsperson Institution in Kosovo concluded that "the judiciary remains weakened by allegations of widespread corruption and lack of funding . . . Kosovo does not have a strong and independent judiciary to fall back on and . . . most of the judges in Kosovo only started exercising judicial functions after 1999. . . . In Kosovo at the moment the governing structures still resist recognition and support of the rights of minority communities, especially the Serbian and Roma communities, while certain minority groups, including the Serbian community, refuse to recognize the Kosovo institutions."[33] A recent report also found that the situation of minorities in Kosovo was the worst in Europe, with the highest degree of segregation and harassment of people on an ethnic basis.[34] Clearly, in Kosovo, democracy is still not the only game in town, a condition that is sometimes viewed as the threshold for democratic consolidation. However, if the international community maintains a sub-

---

32. UNDP, *Fast Facts on Kosovo Early Warning Report*, no. 13 (Pristina: UNDP, June 2006).

33. *Ombudsperson Institution in Kosovo*, Sixth Annual Report, 2005–2006 (Pristina: Assembly of Kosovo, July 11, 2006).

34. Clive Baldwin, *Report, Minority Rights in Kosovo under International Rule* (London: Minority Rights Group International, July 2006). See also *Kosovo Future Status Process, Knowledge-Attitudes-Practices (KAP) Survey Final Report* (Pristina: KIPRED, July 19, 2006); *Report Submitted by the United Nations Interim Administration Mission in Kosovo to the Human Rights Committee on the Human Rights Situation in Kosovo Since June 1999* (New York: United Nations, March 13, 2006), CCPR/C/UNK/1; *Not on the Agenda: The Continuing Failure to Address Accountability in Kosovo Post-March 2004* 18, no. 4 (New York: Human Rights Watch, May 2006); and *United Nations Security Council, Report of the Secretary-General on the United Nations Interim Administration Mission in Kosovo*, September 1, 2006, S/2006/707.

stantial presence in the new, conditionally independent state and obtains the cooperation of both local and regional actors, there will be a diminishing opportunity for other political games to undermine regime stability and the fundamental legitimacy of pluralist rule.[35]

---

35. Near the end of March 2007, Martii Ahtisaari wrote to UN secretary-general Ban Ki-Moon recommending that because the international administration of Kosovo was no longer sustainable, Kosovo should be awarded a "new status," that is, "independence, supervised initially by the international community." Ahtisaari also presented a "Comprehensive Proposal for the Kosovo Status Settlement," which provides the components for Kosovo's supervised sovereignty. Under the arrangements, the European Union would have the major responsibility for Kosovo's future civilian and economic development. Kosovo's Albanian political forces were, on the whole, delighted with the proposal, while Serbia's major political actors and the Serbs living in Kosovo were appalled and hoped that the Russian Federation would veto the Ahtisaari proposal when it came to the UN Security Council sometime in the spring.

12

Interim Notions of Statehood in Bosnia-Herzegovina

A Permanent Transition?

Mark Baskin

Editors' Note

Writing on Bosnia, Mark Baskin presents a case of a complex international adminis-tration ruling over a country in which war was waged among robustly organized armed forces supported by outside powers. Baskin's analysis brings out the dilemmas created when local transitional administrations share power with international actors: the problems of negotiating cumbersome power-sharing arrangements among the indigenous actors are compounded when power is shared, yet again, with the international actors. Baskin argues that by remaining aloof and continuing to char-acterize themselves as impartial facilitators, international actors miss a critical role to effect more coordination and cooperation. This also means that in Bosnia, the formal responsibility for transformation continues to rest with the affected society. To quote Secretary-General Kofi Annan, "The role of the United Nations is merely to facilitate the process that seeks to dismantle the structures of violence and create the conditions conducive to durable peace and sustainable development."[1]

Bosnia-Herzegovina (hereafter referred to as Bosnia) is emblematic to thinking about interim regimes: it has served as the poster child for the failures of international intervention and the frustrations of reconstruc-tion. The war in Bosnia was a crisis for the international community—for

---

1. United Nations Secretary-General, "No Exit without Strategy; Security Council Decision-Making, and the Closure or Transition of United Nations Peacekeeping Operations," April 20, 2001, S/2001/394, www.un.org/Docs/sc/reports/2001/sgrep01.htm.

European nations in particular, but also for the United States, North Atlantic security institutions, and the United Nations. The international community reacted slowly and inadequately as war raged in the early 1990s, and following the Dayton Peace Accords of 1995, it met many roadblocks as it sought to mend the war-torn society. The war in Bosnia shaped a generation of UN officials, North Atlantic diplomats and soldiers, and NGO staffers and activists. It led to the establishment of influential nonstate actors such as the International Crisis Group, the European Stability Initiative, and the Institute for War and Peace Reporting, and has been a petri dish for the initial international experiments in post–Cold War humanitarian intervention. Any broader effort to understand the deeper dynamics of interim governance and administration sidesteps examination of the Bosnian experiment only at great peril.[2]

This chapter explores the underlying dynamics of Bosnia's "permanent transition" that began in the mid-1980s as the Socialist Federative Republic of Yugoslavia (SFRY) began coming apart at the seams. This unraveling included an unresolved constitutional debate, rampant inflation and declining real income, increasing regional inequality, the rise of a complex civil society, and the political squabbling of regional oligarchs—all in the absence of an authoritative central leadership.[3] This transition continued throughout the 1991–95 war, which was marked by an extensive, international intervention that failed diplomatically to end the fighting until late summer 1995, with NATO's Operation Deliberate Force. With the implementation of the Dayton Peace Accords that were signed in December 1995, there seems no end in sight to Bosnia's political transition. An exploration of the underlying dynamics of this difficult transition can help both to identify a mechanism that would enable Bosnian institutions to win popular support and external recognition (that is, enhance Bosnia's effective sovereignty) and to develop a framework for addressing other, similar cases facing the "international community" today.

A voluminous policy-oriented literature over the past decade has been carefully assessing internationally driven efforts to establish a viable government in Bosnia.[4] It seeks approaches to Dayton implementation that are

---

2. Richard Caplan, *International Governance of War-torn Territories: Rule and Reconstruction* (Oxford and New York: Oxford University Press, 2005).

3. Mark Baskin and Paula Pickering, "Yugoslavia and Its Successors," in *Democracy, the Market and Back to Europe: Post-Communist Europe,* ed. Sharon Wolchik and Jane Curry (Rowman and Littlefield, forthcoming); John Lampe, *Twice There Was a Country: Yugoslavia as History* (Cambridge and New York: Cambridge University Press, 2003); and Sabrina Petra Ramet, *Balkan Babel: The Disintegration of Yugoslavia from the Death of Tito to the Fall of Milosevic,* 4th ed. (Boulder, Colo.: Westview Press, 2002).

4. Among the best examples of work are those by Forian Bieber, Elizabeth Cousens, Susan Woodward, and Richard Caplan, as well as the ongoing accounts provided by the International Crisis Group, the European Stability Initiative, the Institute for War and Peace Reporting, the Bosnian Institute, the United States Institute of Peace, and many other institutes throughout Europe and the United States.

both effective and in accordance with international norms and standards. It explores the implementation of the Dayton Peace Accords as a simple project intended to create an independent, stable, liberal, and democratic government.[5] Additionally, it addresses the capacity and political will of Bosnian institutions, the capacity of international institutions to compel Bosnians to implement the peace in accordance with the Dayton Accords, the desirability of international versus local ownership of developments, the readiness of Bosnia to join regional organizations such as NATO and the European Union, and the unintended effects of internationally led efforts to build Bosnian institutions.

Only occasionally has this conversation among the Balkan or post-conflict policy communities in capitals and in the field included academic area specialists, who tend to view developments in Bosnia from the bottom up.[6] Area specialists are familiar with the broader historical, social, and economic contexts in which the political transition is taking place. The middle and older generation of specialists had been working in Bosnia for decades before the war began. Academic specialists often speak Bosnian-Croatian-Serbian fluently, have worked closely with Bosnian and other former Yugoslav academics through the years, and are conversant with Bosnian and international scholarship and culture. Their work has focused on how the range of parties, organizations, and ordinary people have adapted to the developments in post-Dayton Bosnia. Academic area specialists command a uniquely important perspective in their assessments of developments in Bosnia.[7]

The policy-oriented and area-specialist literatures are each rife with disagreements over the nature of social and economic processes, the optimal locus of activity, the quality of the international action, the character of

---

5. For two clear and intelligent statements criticizing this approach, see Roland Paris, *At War's End: Building Peace After Civil Conflict* (New York and London: Cambridge University Press, 2004); and Michael Barnett, "Building a Republican Peace, Stabilizing States after War," *International Security* 30, no. 4 (Spring 2006): 87–112. The literature is voluminous.

6. For the Balkan cases see, for example, Ramet, *Balkan Babel*; Nenad Demetrijevic and Petra Kovacs, eds., *Managing Hatred and Distrust: The Prognosis for Post-Conflict Settlement in Multi-ethnic Communities in the Former Yugoslavia* (Budapest: Open Society Institute, 2004); and Paula Pickering, "Generating Social Capital for Bridging Ethnic Divisions in the Balkans: Case Studies of Two Bosniak Cities," *Ethnic and Racial Studies* 29, no. 1 (2006), 79–103.

7. Especially useful are Norman M. Naimark and Holly Case, eds., *Yugoslavia and Its Historians: Understanding the Balkan Wars of the 1990s* (Stanford, Calif.: Stanford University Press 2003); Mark Pinson, ed., *Muslims of Bosnia-Herzegovina: Their Historic Development from the Middle Ages to the Dissolution of Yugoslavia* (Cambridge: Harvard University Press, 1993); Robert Donia, *Islam Under The Double Eagle: The Muslims Of Bosnia And Herzegovina, 1878–1914* (Boulder, Colo.: East European Quarterly, distributed by Columbia University Press, 1981); Sarah Kent, "Writing the Yugoslav Wars," *American Historical Review* 102, no. 4 (1997): 1085–1114; and Ivo Banac, "Historiography of the Countries of Eastern Europe: Yugoslavia," *American Historical Review* 97, no. 4 (1992): 1084–1102; Tone Bringa, *Being Muslim in the Bosnian Way: Identity and Community in a Central Bosnian Village* (Princeton: Princeton University Press, 1995); and William G. Lockwood, *European Moslems: Economy And Ethnicity In Western Bosnia* (New York: Academic Press, 1975).

domestic Bosnian factions, and the appropriateness of the outcomes.[8] It would seem important that these two communities engage each other in the assessment of the Bosnian experiment because both have something important to add to the conversation.

This chapter provides a bridge between these two perspectives on Bosnia's interim governments. It further suggests that systematic disagreements in how international and Bosnian officials think about key principles, values, and interests have impeded the transition from interim to a more permanent government and have lowered the effectiveness of well-intended international efforts to contribute to the development of a stable and democratic regime. It will explore these differing perspectives as background to an account of Bosnia's transition as part of the violent dissolution of socialist Yugoslavia and will then turn to the dynamics governing the interim government that has been in place since the Dayton Peace Accords were signed.

The Bosnian Context

Bosnia presents many complexities. It has long been at the center of major European divisions: between the Eastern and Western Roman Empires, between Eastern Orthodoxy and Roman Catholicism, and between the Habsburg monarchy and the Ottoman Empire. In recent history, the SFRY lay geographically and politically between the two Cold War blocs in Europe.[9] Bosnia has also long been an object of dispute between Croatian and Serbian nationalists, and discussion over the "real" national identity of the Bosnian Muslims has gone on since the end of the nineteenth century.

The Socialist Republic of Bosnia-Herzegovina was the only republic in the SFRY that was not nominally associated with a single nationality; it was considered a community of nations (Serbs, Croats, and Bosnian Muslims).[10] It

---

8. David Chandler, *Faking Democracy after Dayton* (London: Pluto Press, 2000) and Gerald Knaus and Felix Martin, "Travails of the European Raj," *Journal of Democracy* 14 (2003): 60–74. See also a debate between Thomas Cushman, Robert Hayden, and Bette Denich that was kicked off by Cushman, "Anthropology and Genocide in the Balkans," *Anthropological Theory* 4 (2004): 5–28.

9. Robert J. Donia and John V. A. Fine Jr., *Bosnia-Hercegovina, A Tradition Betrayed* (New York: Columbia University Press, 1995); Noel Malcolm, *Bosnia, A Short History* (New York: New York University Press, 1996); Ivo Banac, *The Yugoslav National Question* (Ithaca, N.Y.: Cornell University Press, 1984); and Francine Friedman, *The Bosnian Muslims* (Boulder, Colo.: Westview Press, 1996).

10. Substantial numbers of Slavic Muslims are also found in the Sandzak region of Serbia and in Kosovo; they are known as Bosniacs today. The term "Bosniac" is used to describe the Slavic Muslims who live mainly in Bosnia-Herzegovina but also in Serbia, Montenegro, and Kosovo. They had been known as Muslims in a national sense since 1971, but the Congress of Bosniac Intellectuals officially adopted the term "Bosniac" as the name for the people in 1993, and it has been generally accepted among all Slavic Muslims. See Mustafa Imamovic, *Istorija Bosnjaka* (Sarajevo: Preporod, 1998).

was a republic in which three-quarters of the population lived in small cities and rural areas and not in the headline-grabbing cities of Sarajevo, Mostar, or Banja Luka. By the 1960s, the Bosnian Muslims gained formal recognition, first as an ethnic category and then as a nation that was symbolically equal in status to the Yugoslav nations of Serbs, Croats, Slovenes, Montenegrins, and Macedonians.

Bosnia was among Yugoslavia's economically less developed republics and remained a center of orthodox Marxist practice to the end of the socialist era. Under this patina of Leninist unity simmered a series of regionally based and politically complex rivalries that did not provide a basis for a stable political community to emerge. The nasty war in Bosnia-Herzegovina that took place from 1991 to 1995 was one act in the failed drama of the Yugoslav transition from one-party socialism to a liberal, democratic order.

From the late 1940s, the SFRY had pursued a series of political and economic experiments that were intended to place it between Soviet socialism and Western capitalism. A number of policy reforms were initiated, for example, in "market socialism," self-management decision making, non-alignment in foreign policy, "brotherhood and unity" in nationality policy, and political decentralization, or divorcing the League of Communists of Yugoslavia (LCY) from power.[11] Despite all these efforts at reforms, governance in Yugoslavia did not become self-regulating. By the 1980s, government performance began to decline measurably—as seen in increasing unemployment, foreign debt, and regional inequality, as well as extrainstitutional political conflict.

This ineffectiveness, particularly following the death of long-time and founding leader Josef Broz Tito, steadily eroded the legitimacy of the Yugoslav regime. By 1989 pressure for comprehensive change in Yugoslavia was great, but no authoritative central figure was able to manage an increasingly diverse and difficult agenda. The central LCY de facto ceased to exist in January 1990 when the Croat and Slovene delegations walked out of its fourteenth Extraordinary Congress after the Serbian bloc rejected a series of Slovene motions for reform without any meaningful discussion. Most former republican communist organizations soon morphed into Social Democratic parties.[12] For the first time since World War II, nationalist ideas were viewed as wholly legitimate, and by 1991, few political or institutional constraints were commonly accepted throughout Yugoslavia. The significant ambitions of nationalist Serb and Croat leaders in Bosnia did not augur well for a peaceful and democratic transition in Bosnia.

---

11. Dennison Rusinow, *The Yugoslav Experiment, 1948–1974* (Berkeley: University of California Press, 1978); Ramet, *Balkan Babel;* and Baskin and Pickering, "Yugoslavia and Its Successors."

12. Lampe, *Yugoslavia as History,* 354–355; and Ramet, *Balkan Babel,* 54–55.

Bosnia's First Transition

The Yugoslav government barely paused at the precipice of dissolution and war in 1990 and 1991. Elections throughout the federation in 1990 selected republican leaders who were accountable to ethnically based constituencies. These democratically elected leaders did not succeed where the regional communist leaders had earlier failed, namely, in reaching consensus on the architecture of a democratic Yugoslav federation. At this impasse, Slovenian and Croatian leaders held well-orchestrated referenda on independence and began transforming their reserve forces into armies. European mediators failed to prevent a war at this "hour of Europe," and the U.S. government was not sufficiently interested at this early moment to act. Armed conflicts in Slovenia and Croatia in 1991 set the table for the much longer war in Bosnia.

The Slovene government declared independence on June 25, 1991, following careful preparations for defense that effectively stymied an ill-prepared Yugoslav National Army (JNA) offensive. By June 30, Serbian leaders ordered the JNA to prepare to abandon Slovenia. There were eight military and five civilian deaths among the Slovenes, and thirty-nine JNA personnel died. Slovenian independence was formally acknowledged on July 18.[13]

The more difficult conflict in Croatia foreshadowed the war in Bosnia. The Croatian government declared independence on June 26, 1991. Following its initially artful invitation to the leader of the Serb Democratic Party to become a vice president in the Croatian government in the spring of 1990, the Croatian government, led by Franjo Tudjman, awkwardly began firing Serb administrators and police throughout Croatia in the name of achieving ethnic balance in official employment. Armed conflict began in 1990 with a series of skirmishes, and with the aid of JNA officers and arms, the Serbs had consolidated control in the illegally constituted Serb Autonomous Regions by mid-March 1991. Croatian Serbs largely boycotted the Croatian referendum on independence. Former U.S. secretary of state and UN negotiator Cyrus Vance concluded a plan that allowed 13,500 UN troops to deploy to oversee the reintegration into Croatia of the one-third of the republic's territory controlled by Serbs.[14] An estimated twenty thousand people died during the war. Despite European Community (EC) concerns over the Croatian government's treatment of its Serb minority, Germany recognized Croatia's independence in early 1992; the United States and other European governments soon followed.

---

13. Lampe, *Yugoslavia as History*, 370.
14. See www.un.org/Depts/dpko/dpko/co_mission/unprofor.htm for basic information on UNPROFOR.

International negotiators from the United Nations, the EC, the United States, and Russia presided over three years of inconclusive negotiations between the Croatian government and rebel Serbs, who repeatedly refused to begin talks concerning the reintegration of Serb-held territory into Croatia in accordance with the Vance plan. During the Serb occupation of Croatian territory, hard-line elements of the Serb leadership held out for unification with the Republika Srpska (RS) in Bosnia. These Serb officials regularly traveled to Belgrade for meetings in Yugoslav ministries, and ordinary individuals treated the Serb territories from Knin near the Dalmatian coast to Serbia as a single Serbian social, economic, and political unit.[15] The Croatian government launched two offensives to regain control of most Serb-held territory in May and August 1995 after which approximately three hundred thousand Serbs fled Croatia, many for the RS and many for Serbia.[16]

The situation in Bosnia was especially fragile, as its election in November 1990 amounted to an ethnic census. The two reformist offshoots of the LCY lost badly to ethnic parties representing Serbs, Muslims, and Croats. By the autumn of 1991, the delicately balanced coalition government among those three parties broke down, with disputes over Bosnia's relationship to rump Yugoslavia, the departure of the Serbian Democratic Party delegation, led by Radovan Karadzic, and the formation of multiple Serb Autonomous Regions with JNA support. Croatian president Tudjman had already discussed the partition of Bosnia-Herzegovina with Serbian president Slobodan Milosevic by March 1991, in an initiative that would betray Croatia's image as a victim of aggression, strengthen the hand in Bosnia of radically nationalist Croats in Herzegovina, and establish the "territorial integrity of the Croat nation in its historic and natural borders" in a way that would expand the Tudjman government's influence in Bosnia and the hard-line Herzegevonian influence in Croatia.[17]

Following a referendum that was boycotted by most Serbs in Bosnia, the Bosnian government declared independence. Several Western governments recognized Bosnian independence on April 6, 1992. Serb military campaigns then rapidly led to the capture of about 60 percent of Bosnia's territory, gains that remained basically intact until the end of fighting in the autumn of 1995. In an attempt to homogenize Bosnia's ethnically complex social geography, the Serb military engaged in ethnic cleansing and created prisoner camps. The radical Croatian Defense Council subsequently launched offensives in

---

15. This observation is based on the author's own work as a UN Civil Affairs Officer in Croatia's Sector North from 1993 to 1994.

16. An estimated nine hundred Serbs were killed in the Croatian offensive against Serb-held Krajina in 1995 See "Croatia, Impunity for Killings after Storm," Amnesty International EUR 64/004/1998 (August 1, 1998), web.amnesty.org/library/index/ENGEUR640041998.

17. Quoted in Branka Magas, "Franjo Tudjman, an Obituary," *Independent,* December 13, 1999, cited in Bosnia Report New Series 13/14 (December 1999-January 2000), www.bosnia.org. uk/bosrep/decfeb00/tudjman.cfm.

Herzegovina and central Bosnia. Radicalized by foreign Muslim volunteers, a Muslim brigade in central Bosnia also committed crimes. Both Serb and Croat forces destroyed Islamic cultural monuments.[18] The war generated 2.5 million refugees and internally displaced persons (IDPs).

The international community proved to be ineffective at ending the war for more than four years. The United Nations Security Council passed more than one hundred resolutions, presidential statements, and presidential letters. It established an arms embargo that de facto favored the well-armed Bosnian Serb Army against the poorly equipped Army of the Republic of Bosnia-Herzegovina, created six poorly defended "safe areas" for civilians, and addressed daily crises in the provision of humanitarian assistance and protection of civilians. Concurrently, diplomatic negotiators from the European Community, the United Nations, and the Contact Group consisting of the United States, Russia, Great Britain, France, and Germany drafted a series of peace plans based on extensive postwar power sharing. This group, however, took few steps to compel the parties to reach agreement and did not intervene in support of the elected Bosnian government. The UN Security Council deployed twenty-six thousand lightly armed troops in the UN Protection Force (UNPROFOR), who were scattered throughout Bosnia during the fighting in support of humanitarian efforts. But these troops were not in a position to compel compliance with the UN mandate and were, in effect, at the mercy of the strongest and boldest party on the ground—the Bosnian Serb Army.

Legacies of the War

Bosnia's wartime institutional development strengthened informal behavior and a faux traditionalism that has inhibited the postwar political transition. The four years of conflict strengthened informal economies and networks of authority that had earlier emerged at the margins of official Yugoslav socialist institutions.[19] These informal networks wielded real power pragmatically at the expense of very complex formal lines of authority.

The informal networks were rooted in iron triangles among like-minded and regionally based party, government, and enterprise elites that filled in legal and institutional gaps left unfilled by formally endowed Yugoslav organizations. In addition, before the war there already existed an extensive set of alternative networks rooted in the massive emigration of Yugoslavs

---

18. For example, the Croatian Defense Council destroyed the beautiful sixteenth-century bridge that united east and west Mostar, and Serb forces destroyed the Ferhadija Mosque in Banja Luka, the largest in Europe.

19. On the local and informal character of the war, see Mart Bax, "Warlords, Priests and the Politics of Ethnic Cleansing: A Case Study from Rural Bosnia and Herzegovina," *Ethnic and Racial Studies* 23 (2000): 16–36; and more generally, see Stathis N. Kalyvas, "The Ontology of 'Political Violence': Action and Identity in Civil Wars," *Perspectives on Politics* 1 (2003): 475–494.

who had departed for jobs abroad as part of the economic reforms of the mid-1960s.[20] These multiple informal networks became even more resilient during the war, and they were strengthened by the support of humanitarian assistance and reconstruction aid from Western development agencies. They also thrived on transnational trafficking networks—cars, drugs, and human beings. These networks included a mix of Croats, Bosnians, Serbs, and others who often displayed significantly more interethnic cooperation than do any of the internationally driven post-conflict reconstruction and transition efforts. The networks adapted effectively to the extraordinary wartime and postwar conditions by ensuring that they also address the pressing existential, social, cultural, and material needs of the forgotten majority of ordinary people living at the margins. This approach contrasted with the guiding principles of officially mandated international reconstruction's more abstract references to international legal norms.[21]

Important individuals in these informal networks easily mixed with political leaders in nationalist parties, law enforcement agencies, and both domestic and international administrative networks. In fact, the RS and Croatian Herceg-Bosna quasi-state structures established in the course of the war were offshoots of these informal arrangements that had evolved during the dissolution of prewar Bosnia-Herzegovina. Governments in Zagreb and Belgrade then rendered significant direct assistance to these networks. The three dominant nationalist political parties—Croatian Democratic Union (HDZ), Serbian Democratic Party (SDS), and Party of Democratic Action (SDA)—came to be identified closely with administrative and political power within ethnically dominated entities or quasi-entity. These new parties have assumed a position akin to that of the LCY during the period of socialism; many of the new leaders were themselves former members of one of the more hard-line sections (the League of Communists of Bosnia-Herzegovina) of the LCY.

These informal networks shaped the three Bosnian leaderships that emerged from the fighting and were charged with (1) implementing the peace; (2) working directly with the wide array of international military and civilian agencies mandated to implement the agreement; and (3) facilitating a

20. William Zimmerman, *Open Borders, Non-Alignment and the Political Evolution of Yugoslavia* (Princeton: Princeton University Press, 1986); Susan Woodward, *Socialist Unemployment: The Political Economy of Yugoslavia, 1945–1990* (Princeton: Princeton University Press, 1995); and Paul Hockenos, *Homeland Calling: Exile Patriotism and the Balkan Wars* (Ithaca, N.Y.: Cornell University Press, 2003); and Mark Baskin, "The Evolution of Policy Communities in Socialist Yugoslavia: The Case of Worker Migration Abroad," *Governance* 2 (1989), 67–85.

21. Mary Kaldor, *New and Old Wars: Organized Violence in a Global Era* (Palo Alto, Calif.: Stanford University Press, 1999); Michael Pugh, "Transformation in the Political Economy of Bosnia since Dayton," *International Peacekeeping* 12 (2005): 448–462; Peter Andreas, "Criminalized Legacies of War, the Clandestine Political Economies of the Western Balkans," *Problems of Post Communism* 51 (May–June 2004): 1–8; and Amra Festic and Adrian Rausche, "War By Other Means: How Bosnia's Clandestine Political Economies Obstruct Peace and State Building," *Problems of Post Communism* 51 (May–June 2004): 27–34.

transition to stable civilian rule. It should have been no surprise that individuals in these vital and informal systems of authority would resist international efforts to compel them to find consensus on cosmopolitan political principles that appealed far more to lawyers in Geneva than to their true constituents—the ordinary people in Doboj, Livno, or the Srebrenica displaced persons community. It should also have been no surprise that these leaders, powerful in good measure because of their ties to these informal networks, displayed little acceptance of the universal value of modern liberalism that is rooted in market economies, cultural heterogeneity, and Western-style political pluralism marked by the routine transfer of power among relatively similar and mutually loyal parties.

The war also reinforced the Yugoslav "springtime of the nations" that served as a surrogate for more comprehensive economic and political reform. The violence dramatically decreased genuine empathy among groups and increased the ethnic distance among ordinary Croats, Bosniacs, and Serbs.[22] The internationally driven "peace process" actually enshrined the principle of ethnic differences to the point that ethnic identity has become the only remaining legitimate identity on which to act publicly. The delicately balanced and nuanced set of identities—local, regional, republican, professional, ideological, supranational—from which individuals could select in their daily lives has been forever changed. In contrast to the party-imposed "brotherhood and unity" of the socialist era, the militarized enshrinement of contemporary ethnicity and nationality in Bosnia (and in the Balkans more widely) has made interethnic bargaining much more of a zero-sum game than it had been earlier.

As the sense of uncertainty and insecurity has risen, ordinary people have strengthened identification with their ethnic groups as if they were kinship groups. Ethnic identity has provided a sense of symbolic collective security that could mitigate the uncertainty of a very cruel war. These attachments become especially strong among groups of victims, such as refugees, IDPs, organizations of families of missing persons, and others who made great sacrifices during the war. Such groups occupy a sacred political space—as "huddled masses yearning to be free"—as both the constituents of and the shock troops for the political parties acting in the name of the nation. In return, the nationalist parties and governments directly addressed the needs of the victims in ways that often contradicted international legal norms. They provided physical security, employment, housing, and economic assistance. The leaders of the international community could only

---

22. For a useful survey of several cases, see James D. Fearon and David D. Laitin, "Violence and the Social Construction of Ethnic Identity," *International Organization* 54, no. 4 (2000): 845–877. On the Balkans, see Anthony Oberschall, "The Manipulation of Ethnicity: From Cooperation to Violence and War in Yugoslavia," *Ethnic and Racial Studies* 23, no. 6 (2000): 982–1001.

urge the victims to solve their existential problems by engaging in a political process through voting and Western-style advocacy and bargaining in NGOs and other associations.

It would have well served the international leaders who were guiding Bosnia through its transition to pay close attention to the potential social, economic, and political implications of these developments. In their effort to retain the positions and privileges they won during the first transition, these elites appealed to ordinary Bosnians by resting on their familiarity and manipulating the sentiment that "it is better to trust the devil you know than the devil you don't." The internationally driven interim government that emerged from the war would be judged by ordinary Bosnians, above all, on its capacity to resolve their daily security concerns and to provide basic services rather than on its ability to build liberal institutions that resembled those in the developed world.

Internationally Driven Transition at Dayton

The incapacity of the great powers and international organizations to prevent or stop the war during the first half of the 1990s has been well established.[23] U.S. negotiators had succeeded in compelling the Bosnian government and the Croat forces in Herzegovina to cooperate against Serb forces by forming a federation during the war in early 1994, although the Bosnian-Croat Federation (hereafter referred to as the Federation) never realized much of its institutional potential in the period before the Dayton Peace Accords. By mid-1995, Serb forces became increasingly assertive, culminating in their conquest of Srebrenica in the largest single post–World War II European massacre, during which seven thousand to eight thousand people were brutally killed. Soon thereafter, NATO's air intervention and a Bosniac-Croat offensive against the Bosnian Serb Army ended the fighting and resulted in U.S.-led negotiations in Dayton, Ohio, in November 1995. Most estimates hold that between one hundred thousand and three hundred thousand people died in the conflict.

The U.S.-led Dayton negotiations, which resulted in the General Framework Agreement for Peace, involved the principals from the conflict itself only peripherally. The sole Bosnian principal who actively participated in the negotiations was President Alija Izetbegovic, a Bosniac. U.S. negotiators preferred to deal with Serbian president Milosevic and Croatian president Tudjman rather than their Bosnian ethnic subordinates. In any case, RS president Karadzic had already been indicted by the International Criminal Tribunal

---

23. See, especially, James Gow, *Triumph of the Lack of Will: International Diplomacy and the Yugoslav War* (New York: Columbia University Press, 1997); and Laura Silber and Allen Little, *The Death of Yugoslavia* (London: Penguin BBC Books, 1996).

for the former Yugoslavia (ICTY), and Croat leader Kresimir Zubak was not authoritative among dominant Herzegovinian Croats. Therefore, the two Bosnian leaders played no substantive role in negotiations.[24] Although the Serbian and Croatian presidents were not impartial in the overall Balkan conflicts (there were outstanding disagreements over Croatia's Eastern Slavonia and over the Prevlaka Peninsula in the Adriatic, and Serbia sought the lifting of economic sanctions), these two were nevertheless one step removed from the everyday operations of Serb and Croat forces in Bosnia.

In the event, Milosevic and Tudjman assured the U.S. chief negotiator, Richard Holbrooke, that the Bosnian Serbs and Croats would sign an agreement that had been negotiated in their name.[25] It turned out, however, that these assurances did not extend to a guarantee that the accords would be implemented. It may be that the two presidents were insufficiently authoritative to compel their subordinates in Bosnia or that they had no intention of compelling their subordinates in the first place. It is certainly the case that the two presidents were personally associated with expansionist policies at the outset of the war, and that only the threat (or reality) of international punishment or the promise of rewards brought them on board with the U.S. negotiators. It is easy to see why the ethnic Serb and Croat leaderships in Bosnia felt little ownership for elements of the accords that compelled them to share power and build a common state and that Milosevic and Tudjman would do little to end this resistance. This was no secret to political analysts who were closely observing developments at the time.[26]

The Dayton Peace Accords were intended by their framers to be a short-term restoration project that would end the fighting once and for all, facilitate a quick transition to stable rule, and restore Bosnia's multiethnicity.[27] The relatively brief accords contained eleven annexes intended to be a comprehensive guide to a quick transition: military aspects and regional stabilization, the establishment of an interentity boundary line, elections, a constitution, provisions for arbitration, human rights, return of refugees, public monuments, public corporations, civilian implementation (that is, the establishment of the Office of the High Representative, or OHR), and public security. The NATO-led Implementation Force (IFOR) of sixty thousand troops was meant to provide a robust backbone to the implementation of the peace. It might have appeared that the transition period of interim governance would be short indeed.

---

24. Richard Holbrooke, *To End a War* (New York: Random House, 1998).

25. Ibid., 243, 263.

26. The author wrote several internal notes in late 1995 within the UN Peace Forces that analyzed the political incentives to implement the Dayton Peace Accords in just this way.

27. See Elizabeth Cousens and David Harland, "Post-Dayton Bosnia and Herzegovina," in *Twenty-First-Century Peace Operations*, ed. William J. Durch (Washington, D.C.: United Institute of Peace Press, 2006).

Annex 4 of the accords was the constitution. In the name of building a multiethnic political community and government, the Dayton Peace Accords largely recognized the facts created on the ground by the war and created quasi-consociational power-sharing arrangements that actually reinforced the significance of national identity and that resembled the Yugoslav institutions that were created by the 1974 constitution.[28] Post-Dayton Bosnia is an unwieldy configuration of two entities: the RS (49 percent of the territory) and the Federation (51 percent of the territory), each with its own police, army, and powers of taxation. The RS is relatively centralized, while the Federation is composed of ten cantons with substantial autonomy. Of those ten cantons, two are explicitly mixed, five are dominated by Bosniacs, and three are dominated by Croats. Although Croat interests were recognized as equal within the Federation, HDZ leaders in Bosnia never abandoned their goal of a third entity and have acted to build compact Croatian areas with a full complement of Croatian-dominant institutions. The consociational arrangement presumed that the three ethnic leaderships could find consensus on the basic political architecture and rules of the game. In turn, this consensus would then provide a basis for the direct international support and capacity building on which Bosnia-Herzegovina would glide smoothly through a transition to independent statehood. Elections were to be held within nine months of the signing of the accords. All 2.5 million Bosnian refugees and IDPs (over half of Bosnia's prewar population) were supposed to return to their home of origin in security and dignity.[29]

The international community that was deployed to facilitate the implementation of the Dayton Peace Accords was not a coherent force with developed plans for a transitional regime. Rather, it was presumed that the Dayton political architecture provided a viable framework for an independent Bosnia. NATO's robust IFOR was in a chain of command distinct from civilian agencies. Within a year, the force began drawing down and was renamed the Stabilization Force (SFOR), which subsequently became the EU Force (EUFOR) in December 2004. The civilian agencies were distinct and much more decentralized. Some tasks had multiple agencies and some agencies had multiple tasks, and no mechanisms effectively coordinated the activity in the early period.

The OHR coordinated the array of organizations that were overseeing civilian aspects of implementation and a range of distinct agencies. The UN International Police Task Force (UNIPTF) addressed policing, and the

---

28. See Arend Lijphart, *Democracy in Plural Societies* (New Haven, Conn.: Yale University Press, 1980). For an example of the dysfunctions of this strategy in socialist Yugoslavia, see Mark Baskin, "Crisis in Kosovo," *Problems of Communism* 30, no. 2 (March-April 1983): 61–74; and Zimmerman, *Open Borders.*

29. See Robert M. Hayden, "'Democracy' without a Demos? The Bosnian Constitutional Experiment and the Intentional Construction of Nonfunctioning States," *East European Politics and Society* 19 (2005), 226–259.

UN High Commissioner for Refugees (UNHCR) addressed human rights and the return of refugees. The Organization for Security and Cooperation in Europe (OSCE) was responsible for elections and for regional arms control. The World Bank and the European Commission were responsible for reconstruction. In addition, a range of national agencies—such as the United States Agency for International Development (USAID), the United Kingdom's Department for International Development, and Germany's Deutsche Gesellschaft für Technische Zusammenarbeit—played significant roles in giving assistance to Bosnia.

International officials from these organizations played key roles in the domestic affairs of the Bosnian transitional government. Among other elements of influence outlined below, international officials formally assumed key Bosnian posts as governor of the Central Bank and chair of the Provisional Election Commission. In the earliest phases of Dayton implementation, this ad hoc array of agencies had a commanding authority to shape developments with the Bosnian parties but little capacity to use that authority effectively—as would be demonstrated, above all, by the establishment of security in the early stages of implementation.

Security and Power Sharing in the Absence of Consensus

A successful transition to a self-regulating and democratic state would require sufficient security to enable officials and citizens to pursue their livelihoods in physical safety.[30] It would also require freedom of movement and freedom of political expression, assembly, and participation. In theory, security is meant to emerge from the systems of policing and judiciary.[31] Authoritative policing is meant to ensure order, and an effective and fair judiciary is meant to ensure equality before the law.[32] The Bosnian security institutions that emerged after the war were not prepared to provide this sort of security. The police forces that emerged during the war were largely special and paramilitary police forces that served the interests of the various warring parties. Many police lacked the basic training and orientation

---

30. See Charles Call, "Protecting the People: Public Security Choices after Civil Wars," *Global Governance* 7, no. 2 (April–June 2001): 151–172.

31. See Mark Baskin, "Some Lessons for Security Sector Reform from Bosnia-Herzegovina and Kosovo," *Security Sector Reform* (Clementsport, Nova Scotia: Proceedings of the Roundtable on Security Sector Reform, Pearson Peacekeeping Centre, November 29–December 1, 2000), 48–59. More generally, see "Police, Judiciary and Corrections Aspects of Rule of Law," *Handbook on Multidimensional Peacekeeping*, UN Department of Peacekeeping Operations, Best Practices Unit, pbpu.unlb.org/pbpu/handbook/Handbook7.%20Police%20Judiciary%20and%20Corrections.html.

32. Thomas Carothers, "The Rule of Law Revival," in *Critical Mission: Essays in Democracy Promotion*, ed. Thomas Carothers, 121–130 (Washington, D.C.: Carnegie Endowment for International Peace, 2004).

of a civilian police force. Nor were the international police who served in the UN Mission in Bosnia and Herzegovina mandated to meet the initial challenges of providing security, and poor coordination between international military and the civilians diluted the effectiveness of international security for civilians at the outset of Dayton implementation. For well over a year, for example, IFOR explicitly neglected to detain persons indicted for war crimes (PIFWICS) on the excuse that this would amount to mission creep. Similarly, IFOR did little to quell the violence that ensued when parts of Sarajevo were transferred from the RS to the Federation under the terms of the accords, on the excuse that this task fell to civilian agencies. As a result, the first PIFWICS were detained by NATO in July 1997, more than eighteen months after the beginning of Dayton implementation and only after the UN Transitional Authority in Eastern Slavonia supported the ICTY in detaining a PIFWIC in June 1997 and demonstrated that such detentions were not necessarily destabilizing.[33]

Additionally, Bosnian civilian police agencies were not prepared to work in a manner that was in accordance with the precepts of the peace agreement. The UNIPTF was assigned the tasks of restructuring and reforming police, monitoring and advising police, and investigating police abuse of human rights. Only later did the UN mission provide assessments of the judiciary that would enable reform. In practice, this meant selecting police, devising training programs, certifying that police were trained and untainted by the past, overseeing police operations of static checkpoints, working with the police to develop community policing, writing reports on human rights abuses, monitoring some trials, establishing a system for registering automobiles, and establishing a state border service. The genuine progress in providing security and rule of law in Bosnia has not yet fundamentally changed the politicized nature of civilian security institutions. Even after the United Nations departed from this mission in policing in 2002, a European-led police mission continued this work in Bosnia, with little end in sight.

External efforts at police reform provide a useful lens through which to view some broader difficulties of the transition. It proved much easier to compel contending parties to sign agreements than it was to put them into practice. The plans for "democratic policing" drafted at the April 25, 1996, Bonn-Petersberg Conference were supposed to be implemented by September of that year. This agreement was made during the UN mission's honey-

---

33. The UN secretary-general reported that "IFOR declined to undertake any task it considered would draw it beyond the limits of its mandate into policing or law and order functions, and IPTF, an unarmed, monitoring, and advisory force, has no mandate to take action to maintain law and order." See "Report of the Secretary-General Pursuant to Resolution 1035 to the Security Council," March 29, 1996, S/1996/210, 10. This is consistent with the comments of the IFOR spokesman at the time: "IFOR is not going to put itself in a position where it becomes the de facto police force in the area. We have resisted that, we will not do that" (www.nato.int/ifor/trans/t960318a.htm).

moon period, when the relative strength of international officials vis-à-vis local officials was at its peak. But there were no provisions to ensure implementation of the plan or to compel Bosnian police authorities to give their genuine support to policies that were designed by international officials. Although Federation officials resisted implementing the Bonn-Petersberg Declaration over the years, the declaration has continued to provide the benchmark against which all goals in Bosnia are measured.

The declaration's ambitious formula of ethnic representation (the ethnic composition of the police was to reflect the population in the 1991 census) provided the initial basis for far more difficult negotiations, which in turn led to the December 1998 Framework Agreement for the Republika Srpska on Police Restructuring. These latter negotiations passed through two iterations under two different special representatives of the secretary-general. The negotiations took place initially against the background of several elections, the wartime RS leadership's political fragmentation, violent conflict among police loyal to one of the two groups, and increasing international impatience with the RS's recalcitrance.

More recently, the OHR drove the development of a more politically comprehensive police reform that is intended to compel police in the RS and the Federation to cooperate closely together.[34] Following the tortuous process of winning initial RS approval for the plan, its implementation has been overseen by a Directorate for Police Restructuring, under the watchful eye of the EU Police Mission.[35] But the RS authorities have consistently defended their core goals of national sovereignty. They invoke the sanctity of the Dayton Peace Accords in their refusals to implement these internationally driven reforms that promise to diminish the political power of the entity-based officials, especially when they are conflated with constitutional reform initiatives that seek to diminish the entities' authority on many matters of administration. To complicate matters further, the UN IPTF's vetting of police prior to 2003 has been seriously called into question by the OHR and by the Bosnian government.[36]

---

34. See the decision of the High Representative in July 2004, www.ohr.int/ohr-dept/rule-of-law-pillar/prc/prc-key-doc/default.asp?content_id=34149. See also the "Final Report on the Work of the Police Restructuring Commission of Bosnia and Herzegovina" (Sarajevo: Police Restructuring Commission, December 2004), www.ohr.int/ohr-dept/presso/pressr/doc/final-prc-report-7feb05.pdf; and OHR's public relations plan to win support for the plan, www.ohr.int/ohr-dept/presso/pic/police-campaign/.

35. On the "Directorate for Police Restructuring Implementation in BiH," see the Web site of the EU Policing Mission, www.eupm.org/Clanci.asp?ID=653&lang=eng.

36. See Tihomir Loza, "Bosnia: Police Reform Held Hostage," *Transitions Online*, no. 3 (2007), www.ceeol.com/aspx/issuedetails.aspx?issueid=7f399f52-7c51-45e4-924f-ac45ac6cd768&articleId=fc42be58-42e5-4835-a9e0-36433c596609. See also European Stability Initiative, "On Mount Olympus, How the UN Violated Human Rights in Bosnia and Herzegovina, and Why Nothing Has Been Done to Correct It," February 10, 2007, www.esiweb.org/pdf/esi_document_id_84.pdf.

Efforts to enhance security-sector reform point to some common threads in the broader international efforts to support the development of a stable state. The first concerns goals. The local parties look at all internationally proposed changes through the lens of their enduring wartime goals. This means that Bosniac leaders insist that central institutions be strengthened and that they have a prominent position in the emerging institutions. RS leaders act to preserve the sanctity of the entities against the encroachment of central, civic, and non-Serbian institutions, and they continue to focus on a special relationship with the Republic of Serbia. Croat HDZ leaders continue to find the opportunity to support the development of a third entity and to focus on cantons and municipalities where they can play a dominant role.

Analysts in the international community have long described this Bosnian intransigence as a "culture of impunity," one that has been enhanced by the fact that the nationalist Bosnian leaders have been better prepared for the negotiations than the international officials. Many of the Bosnians—hardliners and moderates alike—have studied abroad, speak foreign languages, and are broadly familiar with the cultures and approaches taken by international officials. Conversely, many international officials are poorly informed about Bosnian history, language, or ethnography. In the early years of the deployment, they knew little about the principles or practice of post-conflict operations, and they lacked empathy for the people with whom they were working. It was generally the case that international officials chose not to develop meaningful contact with their national partners in favor of collaborations and friendships with other international officials. This increasing "social and cultural distance" does not work in the interest of developing a stable transitional government.[37]

Power Sharing in the Absence of Consensus

The establishment of security provides the foundation, but the heart of the transition is in the formula for power sharing and, thereby, a multiethnic Bosnia resting on modern principles of administration and state organization. As we have seen, however, the formula for power sharing in the Dayton Peace Accords was rooted in an unwieldy constitution with ineffective state institutions that were dominated by the ethnically based SDA, HDZ, and SDS.[38] None of these parties had changed its political goals apprecia-

---

37. Cf. Jared Chopra and Tanje Hohe, "Participatory Intervention," *Global Governance* 10 (2004): 289–305; and Jared Chopra, "The UN's Kingdom of East Timor," *Survival* 42 (2000): 27–39.

38. European Commission for Democracy Through Law, "Opinion on the Constitutional Situation in Bosnia and Herzegovina and the Powers of the High Representative," (March 2005), www.venice.coe.int/SITE/DYNAMICS/N_RECENT_EF.ASP?L=E&TITLE1=62ND%20PLENARY%20SESSION&TITLE2=62E%20SESSION%20PLÉNIÈRE.

bly with the end of the war, and "Dayton Institutions" provided few incentives to abandon ethnically defined goals. The Dayton framers believed that elections would provide the basis for achieving a genuine political breakthrough.

The first elections that took place just nine months after the initial deployment in September 1996 hardly favored a political breakthrough in accordance with the Dayton Peace Accords. And there the many subsequent elections for state-level, entity-level, and local-level government offices have usually disappointed as well. "Electoralism," the idea that holding elections will jump-start the democratic process, has had the reverse of its intended effect. Indeed, electoralism has heightened interethnic tensions in Bosnia.[39] Since ethnically based parties rarely win votes from other groups, party leaders have strong incentives to make radical appeals to ensure a greater turnout of their own group.[40]

Liberal internationalists had taken some hope that the ethnic party system would change because the nationalists began to win increasingly narrow victories, and by the 2000 elections international officials had convinced diverse social democratic forces to unite behind the Social Democratic Party–led Coalition for Change. However, the coalition's efforts at comprehensive reform failed because of internal bickering and opposition from exclusivist elements that had been forged during the war. In the RS, the Party of Independent Social Democrats remains a regionally based Serbian party that has been willing to enter into meaningful dialogue with Bosniac and international officials as long as the existence of the RS itself is not brought into question. But the party has come a long way from its moderate, anti-SDS positions that won it considerable external support as it emerged in opposition to Karadzic's SDS in the late 1990s. Although Social Democrats have made some inroads into the Serb, Bosniac, and Croat electorates, Bosnia is saddled with an ethnically based party system. Such a system does not provide the basis for effective cooperation among the three groups or the prospect that the transition to a self-regulating state will be a simple matter. To succeed in post-Dayton Bosnia, political parties invariably fall back on nationalist appeals to the lowest common denominator.

This pattern was again demonstrated in the October 2006 elections. International observers noted that the election campaign was "marked by sharp nationalist rhetoric and occasional inflammatory statements." [41] The election

---

39. Sumantra Bose, *Bosnia after Dayton: Nationalist Partition and International Intervention* (Oxford: Oxford University Press, 2002), 117.

40. Donald Horowitz, *Ethnic Groups in Conflict* (Berkeley, Calif.: University of California Press, 1985); and Paul Mitchell, "Party Competition in an Ethnic Dual Party System," *Ethnic and Racial Studies* 18 (October 1995), 773–793.

41. Statement of Preliminary Findings and Conclusions, International Election Observation Mission, Bosnia and Herzegovina—General Elections, October 1, 2006, www.osce.org/documents/odihr/2006/10/20826_en.pdf, 2, 5.

of wartime prime minister and foreign minister Haris Silajdzic as the Bosniac member of the presidency has upset both Serbs and Croats. Silajdzic has called for the further integration of Bosnia as a unitary state without entities, while moderate Serb politicians such as Milorad Dodik have been raising the question of independence and have resisted international efforts at centralizing reforms.[42] The split of the Croat HDZ in Bosnia into two distinct parties in advance of the elections paved the way for the victory of Social Democrat Zeljko Komsic as the Croat member of the presidency. The defeated HDZ incumbent, Ivo Miro Jovic, initially said that he would not relinquish his post because Komsic "did not get a vote from a true Croat."[43]

Intervention of a New Type

Well over ten years of Dayton implementation have not brought Bosnia very close to achieving the status of a self-regulating state in which the three political leaderships concur—either with each other or with the OHR—on the basic understanding of their government. The absence of this common understanding has made much more difficult the international community's attempts to transform politically contentious issues into the cold issues of administration. True, some long and tortuous negotiations have led to modest successes: for example, in the evolution of political and administrative institutions, economic development, Bosnian integration into a range of European institutions, reforms in the military and police forces, the return of refugees, efforts to build a more central government apparatus, and efforts to reform the Dayton constitution. But none of these successes has become self-regulating or institutionalized, and each step forward in Dayton implementation depends heavily on enormous international pressure on Bosnian officials. It is no surprise that this pressure has not yielded much fruit. A recent USAID study on civil society concluded that "the international community continues to drive the development and agenda of civil society," that beyond a narrow critical mass of NGOs in and near the large urban centers, capacities of NGOs remain "limited," and that "domestic funding sources . . . are extremely limited."[44]

It also appears that post-Dayton Bosnia has not been very effective at governing. The last official population census took place in 1991, before the war. As of March 2005, well over three hundred thousand people remained

---

42. RFE/RL Newsline, Southeast Europe Report, May 25, 2007.

43. RFE/RL Newsline, Southeast Europe Report, October 4, 2006, www.rferl.org/newsline/2006/10/4-SEE/see-041006.asp.

44. Catherine Barnes, Milan Mrdja, Selma Sijrcic, and Mirjana Popovic, *Civil Society Assessment in Bosnia and Herzegovina* (Sarajevo: USAID/BiH, 2004).

internally displaced within Bosnia.[45] It also appears that the influence of wartime conditions remains in the countryside, which is wracked with increasing poverty and decreasing employment diversity. One study showed that 40 percent of households are unable to afford necessary health care, that more than half have family members in poor health, and that household spending on education continues to decrease.[46] In other words, all evidence points to an odd type of normalization or equilibrium in Bosnia that neither spells the return to the prewar status quo ante nor signals the development of a viable government that can serve as a reliable international partner within NATO or the European Union. And international organizations that remain in Bosnia are the only guarantors of that equilibrium.

Even with its commanding formal position in post-Dayton Bosnia, the international community in residence appears to be in a relatively weak position to compel nationalist leaders among the Serbs, Croats, and Bosniacs. Senior international officials in the OHR, the OSCE, the United Nations, SFOR, and national agencies actually have relatively low stakes in the outcome of any particular operation in Bosnia as long as developments can be framed in the language of progress in their reports to headquarters, thereby justifying funding for programs in subsequent years. International administrators have personal agendas of advancing their own careers, organizational agendas of ensuring that they get credit for the progress being made, and overall agendas of contributing to a stable and democratic Bosnia. They place Bosnia in the broader context of their own government's foreign policies, which concern the larger European security architecture, the domestic elections in their home countries, the policies toward the United Nations, Europe, and the like. Over the past decade, Bosnia has lost its luster as donors have fled to newly urgent international crises.

The leaderships of all three Bosnian groups treat developments at home as an urgent and definitional matter, not as negotiations to be placed in a broader European context. They all blend the romantic's attachment to their nation and soil with the realist's appreciation of strategy and tactics and to their deep desire to retain their positions and privileges. The Bosnian leaders cooperate with international organizations when such cooperation advances their own goals and/or when their noncooperation could

---

45. Norwegian Refugee Council, Global IDP Project, "Bosnia-Herzegovina: Statebuilding Key to Overcome Ethnic Division and Solve Displacement Issue," www.internal-displacement.org/8025708F004BE3B1/(httpInfoFiles)/5E2544D376C9EE13C12570CA003A1496/$file/Bosnia_overview_mar05.pdf.

46. Elizabeth Stites, Sue Lautze, Dyan Mazurana, and Alma Anic, *Coping with War, Coping with Peace: Livelihood Adaptation in Bosnia-Herzegovina, 1989–2004*, Report of the International Famine Center, Friedman School of Nutrition Science and Policy (Medford, Mass.: Tufts University, April 2005), nutrition.tufts.edu/pdf/research/famine/bosnia_livelihoods_study.pdf.

threaten their removal. However, international officials find it easier to compel Bosnian officials to reach "significant agreements" than to convince those same officials to implement the agreements. The nationalist leaders have learned that failing to conclude an agreement can lead to severe penalties, such as removal by the High Representative, although even this penalty is muted by the tremendous influence that fired officials can continue to exert over policy—and without any formal, international oversight. In addition, the very act of concluding an agreement can actually substitute for the implementation of the agreement in the short to medium term. Recalcitrant leaders "work the output side" of the agreement by devising administrative resistance to that which they did not wish to sign in the first place. It is clear that the well-endowed international community has been forced to pay close attention to its political resources so that it could gain leverage over the three Bosnian parties in almost all instances and at all stages of policymaking.

The international tactics for governance have prioritized immediate success over the longer-term capacity building of the individual institutions in Bosnia.[47] The High Representative compensated for his weakness in two basic ways. First, he won extraordinary powers at a meeting of the Peace Implementation Council in Bonn in December 1997, which enable him to override Bosnian institutions to pass legislation and to remove domestic officials from office. At that meeting in Bonn, the council concluded that the "High Representative can facilitate the resolution of difficulties by making binding decisions on . . . interim measures to take effect when the parties are unable to reach agreement. . . . [and] actions against . . . officials . . . found by the High Representatives to be in violation of legal commitments under the peace agreement."[48] This allowed the OHR to break deadlocks and pass legislation. Between December 1997 and October 2006, this tool of external governance was employed 811 times, at a rate of almost eight decisions per month.[49] A great deal of significant legislation has been passed via the High Representative's Bonn Powers, including that related to adoption of the flag, the currency, a common license plate, and the like. In the period reported above, the High Representative removed from power 168 officials—mainly Serb and Croat nationalists—who were seen as unsupportive of Dayton implementation.

Second, the Bonn powers were linked to an additional tactic—that of conditionality in which international assistance was given to parties that cooper-

---

47. See Richard Caplan, "Partner or Patron? International Civil Administration and Local Capacity-building," *International Peacekeeping* 11 (Summer 2004): 229–247.
48. See the Web site for the Office of the High Representative, www.ohr.int/pic/default.asp? content_id=5182#11.
49. For a listing of each decision, see the Web site for the Office of the High Representative, www.ohr.int/decisions/archive.asp. In this reporting period of 106 months, the High Representative took 811 decisions.

ated with the international community. In practice, this has meant that the RS has not benefited as much from assistance as have the other two parties. On one hand, the Bosniacs in the Federation have been relatively cooperative, in good measure because their goal of strengthened central institutions is in harmony with Dayton's putative goal of a multiethnic Bosnia in which the entities are very much a part of the state institutions. The Croats have been in a better position to win alternative sources of support from abroad—whether from an HDZ-led government in Zagreb or from the well-developed émigré networks that have supported the advancement of exclusivist Croat interests within Bosnia. But the Serbs' patron of Serbia—under consistent pressure from the international community that intensified over Kosovo in 1999—is in a relatively weak position to compensate materially for the absence of international support. Nonetheless, Serb leaders in the RS invariably look to Belgrade for leadership and place the RS squarely in an all-Serbian context by claiming that granting even supervised independence to Kosovo could set a precedent for the RS.

International officials find themselves in a difficult position: although international pressure can force the Bosnian ethnic leaderships to go along with policies they find unpleasant, this pressure has not been artfully employed to help to build effective state institutions. It is common to read that the use of Bonn powers undermines the authority of Bosnian officials elected under Dayton's rules and does little to support the development of a self-regulating and stable state that has passed through its transition.[50] In fact, the Bonn powers may have reinforced the political attraction of regional centers of ethnic authority in Zagreb and Belgrade over state authority in Sarajevo. As a result, they symbolize the fragility of the Dayton institutions.

Conclusion: Replacing Exit with Engagement?

At the time of this writing, there seems to be no end to building the Bosnian state—a goal that seems culturally akin to the Cold War's building of socialism in European Leninist states. The history of Bosnia's brief post-Dayton transition is complex. The official history of the Bosnian transition written by international officials is one of optimism and good prospects, of a peace that has not been broken since late 1995, of tensions that have been dispelled, and of the confidence that has been built. But it is also a history of missed opportunities—to detain PIFWICS, to engage the victims' groups that have been mobilized against the international community, and

---

50. Elizabeth Cousens, "Missed Opportunities to Overcompensation: Implementing the Dayton Agreement on Bosnia," in *Ending Civil Wars: The Implementation of Peace Agreements,* ed. Stephen Stedman, Donald Rothchild, and Elizabeth M. Cousens, 531–566 (Boulder, Colo.: Lynne Rienner Publishers, 2002).

to establish security for the development of normal state institutions. Bosnia is riddled with formal successes whose reality does not equal the tale told in reports to headquarters. This is clear in the very difficult and slow implementation of police reform and constitutional reform, and in efforts to create the conditions for minority refugees and IDPs to return to their homes in safety and dignity. Furthermore, it is seen in optimistic efforts to advance Bosnian membership in a range of international and European organizations meant to mentor Bosnian officials to the norms and values of these organizations.

In a sense, the history of post-Dayton state building is about the evolution of an unusual and modern protectorate in which international organizations have played and continue to play central formal roles in the everyday affairs of government and administration.[51] It is one whose institutions continue to evolve and where governance continues to improve, albeit slowly. And while it is true that the High Representative has limited capacity to compel recalcitrant nationalist leaders to sign on to policies that undercut their influence and way of life, international officials continue to hold the strongest hand in the bargaining over the future of Bosnia as a European country. There are few signs that international organizations active in service delivery and capacity building are about to pack up and leave Bosnia. In fact, if Bosnia is to be a serious candidate for accession to the European Union, there will be increasing numbers of international officials throughout the country.

Here it is important for international officials to accept a long-term engagement in Bosnia. They can learn patience and learn how to listen and consult more fully. They can find ways to make themselves accountable to the Bosnian publics for their performance beyond their accountability to their headquarters in New York, Brussels, and elsewhere. They can develop a policy of engagement that retains the mandate to support the development of stable and democratic institutions and works more effectively with Bosnian officials in formulating and implementing policies.[52]

At the current juncture, this implies specific steps to detain important PIFWICS, such as Radovan Karadzic and Ratko Mladic, as a crucial step in putting the war behind. International officials can take steps to ensure that the police and judiciary function in harmony with international norms and practices. They can assist in the improvement of administration and security, in the efficient management of firms, and in the development of sound investment policies. They can listen more clearly to how to address problems such as unemployment and social welfare, a key skill in building an

51. See Mark Baskin, "Review Article, Post-conflict Administration and Reconstruction," *International Affairs* 79, no. 1 (2003): 161–170.

52. See Mark Baskin, "Between Exit and Engagement: On the Division of Authority Between International and Domestic Institutions in Transitional Administrations," *Global Governance* 10, no. 1 (2004): 119–137.

effective democracy. Finally, they can encourage Bosnian policymakers to think about sovereignty in new ways, in which officials in domestic and international organizations divide their labor so as to benefit their Bosnian constituents. In this sense, the challenge for the international community is to find a way to be both constructive and relevant as Bosnia attempts to move beyond its interim government. There is far less mystery about the type of measures that would help Bosnia to become a self-sustaining, European government than about the specific steps that would be needed to transcend the flaws in Dayton's initial design and to adjust international expectations to the realities in Bosnia.

13

Afghanistan's Post-Taliban Transition

State Building after War

Thomas H. Johnson

Editors' Note

Thomas H. Johnson's chapter on Afghanistan describes an elite-dominated interim government without popular legitimacy, which then drafted a constitution that was more concerned with doling out spoils to the elite participants than in creating a government that could provide for the people. By this point in the volume, this has become one of the more common themes: even in a situation where there is no clear "victor's justice," the groups that are strong at the cessation of conflict write the rules of the game to skew them in their favor for the long term. Johnson describes how the Bonn Agreement, which created Afghanistan's peace process and interim government, ignored the root causes of the Afghan civil war; how it codified existing power relations; and how the Bonn process ignored the domestic legitimacy or illegitimacy of the actors included in the talks. In the resulting transitional government, democracy was just an afterthought. Paralleling Devon Curtis and E. Philip Morgan, who demonstrated how the composition of the participants in peace talks influences the viability of the interim administration, Johnson stresses that the Bonn Agreement was not a peace agreement because the losers were not at the table; only the winners of Operation Enduring Freedom participated in the process. This left the transitional and permanent regimes with spoiler problems that hamper the ability of the Kabul government to extend control outside the limits of the capital city.

Introduction

Is Afghanistan approaching unheralded success or tragic failure?[1] The answer depends upon whom one asks. Several years after an international coalition and U.S.-backed Afghan insurgents removed the ruling Islamic fundamentalist Taliban from power, experts differ as to Afghanistan's future: will it be stability and democracy or a return to its chaotic and turbulent past? On the one hand, after decades of fighting, this volatile state has been the site of watershed elections and significant rebuilding. Much work remains, but significant progress has been achieved in human rights, political and economic reform, and infrastructure development.

On the other hand, a number of extremely disturbing countervailing trends are evident. First, the state is extremely weak. The actual influence and control of the new, democratically elected government of Hamid Karzai extends only minimally beyond the outskirts of Kabul, an increasingly sophisticated insurgency threatens stability, and large areas of Afghanistan are still ruled by warlords and drug lords. Second, there are severe economic constraints: the country has become a narco-state, with opium crops and transport representing 60 percent of the licit GDP.[2] This reliance on a criminal, informal economy strengthens the powers of those resisting the imposition of state authority, thus creating a negative feedback loop. Finally (and perhaps most troubling), ethnic fragmentation is on the rise and old patterns of identity politics continue to exist in the "new" Afghanistan.

This chapter assesses the effectiveness of the "post-conflict" political transitional process that created the Kabul regime upon Afghanistan's stabilization and good governance. I will review and critique the Bonn Agreement and process—the major driver for Afghanistan's post-conflict transition—assess the current situation in Afghanistan, and examine prospects for democratization, development, and stability. I will also identify the opportunities and obstacles generated from Afghanistan's transition for peace, stability, and nation building after three decades of state failure.

The views expressed in this chapter are the author's own and do not reflect the views or opinions of the U.S. government. A version of this chapter was previously published in *Central Asian Survey* 25, nos. 1/2 (2006): 1–26.

1. Gordon Cucullu and Paul Vallely, "Stabilizing Afghanistan: A Promising Template for Iraq," *Washington Times*, January 9, 2006; and John C. Bersia, "Moves Fall Short of What's Needed in Afghanistan," *Orlando Sentinel*, December 13, 2005.
2. United Nations Office on Drugs and Crime and the Government of Afghanistan's Counter Narcotics Directorate, "Afghanistan Opium Survey, 2004," November 2004, www.unodc.org/unodc/en/crop_monitoring.html.

Political Reconstruction: The Bonn Agreement and Process

Since the fall of the Taliban in late 2001, the Agreement on Provisional Arrangements in Afghanistan Pending the Re-Establishment of Permanent Government Institutions, commonly referred to as the Bonn Agreement, has served as the Afghan political road map.[3] Once the imminent defeat of the Taliban became obvious, the United States pushed the United Nations to organize a conference to map out a future plan for Afghanistan. The United Nations complied by convening a conference in Bonn, Germany, on November 26, 2001, and after nine taxing days of meetings and deal making among various Afghan factions,[4] participants signed the Bonn Agreement. Heavily influenced by the desires of the United States, the agreement established the provisional arrangements for Afghanistan to create permanent governmental institutions.[5] The goal was to lay the groundwork for Afghanistan's future political processes and institutions of governance based on the commitment of "the right of the people of Afghanistan to freely determine their own political future in accordance with the principles of Islam, democracy, pluralism and social justice."[6]

Democracy was merely "an afterthought for the White House," according to James Dobbins, a former envoy to Afghanistan and a participant at the Bonn Conference, since the George W. Bush administration believed that democracy "had little application for Afghans." Rather, Bonn was meant to establish international legitimacy for the Kabul government. It was the Iranian delegation, Dobbins says, who introduced the word "democracy." As a result, the agreement was, unfortunately, vague regarding how to achieve a democratic system.[7] The Bonn Agreement created a government but not a state.

The Bonn Agreement was also *not* a peace agreement to end the decade-long Afghan civil war or the conflict between the Taliban and the U.S.-led Northern Alliance, as Bonn brought together only the winners of the U.S.-led Operation Enduring Freedom (OEF), *not* the warring parties. Ironically, many of those "winners" were Afghan factions that were historically opposed to one another; indeed, many were direct opponents during the

---

3. United Nations Security Council, Agreement on the Provincial Arrangements in Afghanistan Pending the Re-Establishment of Permanent Government Institutions, December 5, 2001, S/2001/1154. The text of the Bonn Agreement was endorsed by the United Nations Security Council on December 7, 2001.

4. Key factions at Bonn were the Northern Alliance (primarily Tajik), the Rome Group (representing the former king, Mohammed Zahir Shah), the Cyprus Group (allegedly Iranian backed), and the Peshawar Group (primarily Pashtun).

5. The Bonn Agreement was endorsed by the UN Security Council Resolution 1385, and an international peacekeeping force was authorized by Security Council Resolution 1386.

6. UN Security Council, Agreement on the Provincial Arrangement, 2.

7. Quoted in Sidney Blumenthal, "Democracy Was Only an Afterthought," *Guardian*, July 21, 2005, www.guardian.co.uk/print/0,3858,5243844-103677,00.html.

brutal civil war that began in earnest after the Soviets withdrew from Afghanistan in January 1989. The Bonn Agreement did not try to reconcile differences between the warring parties or attempt to draw members of the defeated group—the Taliban—into the process of government reestablishment or state creation. Bonn did create the agenda and the process for establishing permanent governance institutions, representing a new level of commitment and political will by both Afghans and major powers. However, it ignored many root problems, most notably the ethnic fragmentation and distrust that has plagued the country for decades, narcotics production, and regional "warlords."

The agreement, as critics noted, codified de facto power relations and disregarded certain actors' legitimacy or lack thereof.[8] In particular, Bonn gave control of key ministries to the Tajiks and the Northern Alliance, who at the time of the conference controlled Kabul.

The Bonn Agreement recognized the problem of the multiple armed forces operating in Afghanistan, even if scant resources were applied to address it. The text called for a single national army. Section V(1) states, "Upon the official transfer of power, all mujahedin, Afghan armed forces and armed groups in the country shall come under the command and control of the Interim Authority, and be reorganized according to the requirements of the new Afghan security and armed forces."[9] Bonn and UN Security Council Resolution 1386 (2001) left law and order responsibilities in the hands of the Afghans themselves, but they provided a role for outside help to create a new national force. The external military force provided to address Afghanistan's security challenges initially included the five thousand troops, led by Great Britain, in the International Security Assistance Force (ISAF)—a Chapter VII UN authorized force—and the eight thousand U.S. and coalition troops in OEF.[10] This number of troops was significantly smaller than those provided for Bosnia, Kosovo, or Iraq. The troop-to-population ratio of less than one-half to one thousand in Afghanistan scarcely compares to the more than eighteen per thousand in Bosnia and twenty per thousand in Kosovo.[11] Moreover, of the total U.S. financial assistance to Afghanistan, two-thirds is devoted to sup-

8. See Barnett Rubin, "Afghanistan and Threats to Human Security" (essay adapted from a speech titled "Human Security and Terrorism—Diversifying Threats under Globalization–from Afghanistan to the Future of the World," delivered at the International Symposium on Human Security, Tokyo, December 15, 2001), www.ssrc.org/sept11/essays/rubin.htm.

9. The text of the Bonn Agreement is available from the Afghanistan Independent Human Rights Commission, http://www.aihrc.org.af/bonn_agreement.htm.

10. UN Security Council resolutions 1386, 1413, and 1444 authorized the International Security Assistance Force. The lead passed from the United Kingdom to Turkey and Germany before NATO took on the leadership, beginning in 2003. See www.afnorth.nato.int/ISAF/about/about_history.htm.

11. John G. McGinn, James Dobbins, Keith Crane, Seth G. Jones, Rollie Lal, Andrew Rathmell, Rachel Swanger, and Anga Timilsina, *America's Role in Nation-Building: From Germany to Iraq* (Santa Monica, Calif.: RAND, 2004), 136.

porting the U.S. troop presence there, with $3 billion of the remaining $5 billion per year devoted to supporting the Afghan National Army.[12]

Figure 13.1 provides an overview of the process spurred by the Bonn Agreement. As this figure suggests, an explicit time frame was established for the implementation of interim, transitional, and, finally, fully representative and elective governments. The Bonn Agreement likewise established deadlines and procedures for constitutional development and explicit elections and laid the groundwork for the following:

- the formation of *loya jirgas* (grand councils)—emergency and constitutional
- national elections
- the role of the United Nations in Afghan reconstruction
- the reorganization of Afghan military forces
- the establishment of an ISAF
- the discharge of humanitarian and reconstruction aid

Interim and Transitional Authorities

The Bonn Agreement called for the establishment of an interim governing structure and set a timetable for a transition to a more "broad-based gender-sensitive, multi-ethnic and fully representative" government.[13] The interim authority was to rule for six months until a traditional *loya jirga* convened to elect a transitional authority or government (see figure 13.1 for time line). The delegates at the Bonn Conference chose Pashtun tribal leader Hamid Karzai to serve as head of an interim power-sharing council, which took office in Kabul on December 22, 2001. Most of the remaining administrators or ministers were selected from the representatives at the Bonn meetings.[14]

The United States was unlikely to settle for any Afghan interim leader other than Karzai. After the Taliban's assassination of Abdul Haq on October 25, 2001,[15] Karzai was the one creditable Pashtun leader whom the United States knew well and, more important, trusted. The United States lobbied vigorously to secure Karzai's position as the leader of the Afghan interim government. A Durrani-Polpolzai Pashtun, Karzai was the son of a senator who had served in the government of former king Zahir Shah. After sus-

12. Hugh Riddell, John Ewers, Rebecca Linder and Craig Cohen, *In the Balance: Measuring Progress in Afghanistan* (Washington, D.C.: Center for Strategic and International Studies, July 2005), 16.

13. UN Security Council, Agreement on the Provincial Arrangements, 2.

14. Some of this section is drawn from Thomas H. Johnson, "The Loya Jirga, Ethnic Rivalries and Future Afghan Stability," *Strategic Insights* 1, no. 6 (August 2002): 1–10.

15. "Desperate Call from the Valley of Death: Help Us," *Observer*, October 28, 2001, observer. guardian.co.uk/afghanistan/story/0,1501,582247,00.html.

Figure 13.1 Bonn Process

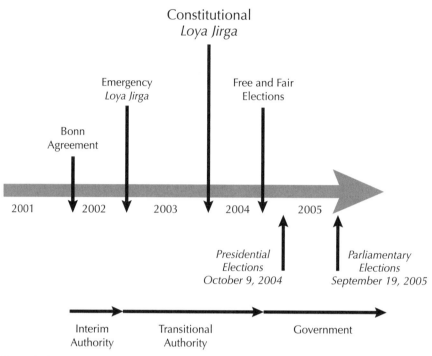

Source: Author.

pected Taliban elements assassinated Karzai's father in Quetta, Pakistan, in 1999, Karzai was named the Pashtun clan chief, positioning him for a high-level leadership role in post-Taliban Afghanistan. The United States' relationship with Karzai was to become a major factor in Afghanistan's post-Taliban transition.

Karzai's interim administration (cabinet of ministers), "entrusted with the day-to-day conduct of state," was significantly composed of victors in the war.[16] The three most powerful ministries of this cabinet went to Panjshiri Tajiks of the Northern Alliance who had controlled the militia in possession of Kabul since the Taliban's defeat. Yunus Qanooni, who led the Northern Alliance's Bonn delegation, was selected interior minister. General Moham-mad Fahim, commander-in-chief of the Northern Alliance, was selected defense minister, and Dr. Abdullah Abdullah was selected as foreign secretary. The thirty-member interim cabinet included eleven Pashtuns, eight Tajiks, five Shi'a Hazara, and three Uzbeks, with the remainder drawn from other minorities. Table 13.1 presents the members of the Afghan interim administration.

---

16. UN Security Council, Agreement on the Provincial Arrangements, 5.

Table 13.1 Interim and Transitional Afghan Authority Administrators/Ministers

Interim Authority Position	Name	Ethnicity	Transitional Authority Position	Name	Ethnicity
Chairman	Hamid Karzai	Pashtun	*President*	Hamid Karzai	Pashtun
Vice Chair	Mohammed Fahim	Tajik	*Deputy President*	Mohammed Fahim	Tajik
Vice Chair and Women's Affairs	Dr. Sima Samar	Hazara	*Deputy President*	Karim Khalili	Hazara
Vice Chair	Haji Mohammed Mohaqqeq	Hazara	*Deputy President*	Abdul Qadir	Pashtun
Vice Chair	Ahmed Shakar Karkar	Uzbek			
Vice Chair	Hedayat Amin Arsala	Pashtun			
			Special Adviser on Security	Yunus Qanooni	Tajik
Defense Minister	Mohammed Fahim	Tajik	*Defense Minister*	Mohammed Fahim	Tajik
Foreign Minister	Abdullah Abdullah	Tajik	*Foreign Minister*	Abdullah Abdullah	Tajik
Finance Minister	Hedayat Amin Arsala	Pashtun	*Finance Minister*	Ashraf Ghani	Pashtun
Interior Minister	Yunus Qanooni	Tajik	*Interior Minister*	Taj Mohammed Wardak	Pashtun
Planning Minister	Haji Mohammed Mohaqqeqk	Hazara	*Planning Minister*	Haji Mohammed Mohaqqeqk	Hazara
Communications Minister	Ing. Abdul Rahim	Tajik	*Communications Minister*	Masoom Stanakzai	Pashtun
Borders Minister	Amanullah Zadran		*Borders Minister*	Arif Nurzai	Pashtun*
Refugees Minister	Intayatullah Nazeri	Tajik	*Refugees Minister*	Intayatullah Nazeri	Tajik
Small Industries Minister	Aref Noozari	Pashtun	*Mines Minister*	Juma M. Mahammadi	Pashtun

Table 13.1 *(cont.)*

Interim Authority Position	Name	Ethnicity	Transitional Authority Position	Name	Ethnicity
Mines and Industry Minister	Mohammed Alim Razm	Uzbek	Light Industries Minister	Mohammed Alim Razm	Uzbek
Public Health Minister	Dr. Sohaila Siddiqi	Pashtun	Public Health Minister	Dr. Sohaila Siddiqi	Pashtun
Commerce Minister	Sayed Mustafa Kasemi	Shiite Muslim	Commerce Minister	Sayed Mustafa Kasemi	Shiite Muslim
Agriculture Minister	Sayed Hussain Anwari	Hazara	Agriculture Minister	Sayed Hussain Anwari	Hazara
Justice Minister	Abbas Karimi	Uzbek	Justice Minister	Abbas Karimi	Uzbek
Information and Culture Minister	Saeed Makhdoom Rahim	Tajik	Information and Culture Minister	Saeed Makhdoom Rahim	Tajik
Reconstruction Minister	Mohammed Fahim Farhang	Pashtun	Reconstruction Minister	Mohammed Fahim Farhang	Pashtun
Haj and Mosques Minister	Mohammad Hanif Balkhi	Tajik	Haj and Mosques Minister	Mohammed Amin Naziryar	Pashtun
Urban Affairs Minister	Abdul Qadir	Pashtun	Urban Affairs Minister	Yusuf Pashtun	Pashtun
Public Works Minister	Abdul Khalig Fazal	Pashtun	Public Works Minister	Abdul Qadir	Pashtun
			Social Affairs Minister	Noor Mohammed Karkin	Turkmen
Water and Power Minister	Ahmed Shakar Karkar	Uzbek	Water and Power Minister	Ahmed Shakar Karkar	Uzbek
Irrigation Minister	Haji Mangal Hussein	Pashtun	Irrigation and Environment Minister	Ahmed Yusuf Nuristani	Pashtun
Martyrs and Disabled Minister	Abdullah Wardak	Pashtun	Martyrs and Disabled Minister	Abdullah Wardak	Pashtun
Higher Education Minister	Sharif Faez	Tajik	Higher Education Minister	Sharif Faez	Tajik

Table 13.1 *(cont.)*

Interim Authority Position	Name	Ethnicity	Transitional Authority Position	Name	Ethnicity
Air Transport & Tourism Minister	Abdul Rahman		*Civil Aviation & Tourism Minister*	Mir Wais Saddiq	Tajik
Labor and Social Affairs	Mir Wais Saddiq	Tajik			
Transportation Minister	Sultan Hamid Hamid	Hazara	*Transportation Minister*	Saeed Mohammed Ali Jawad	Shiite Muslim
Education Minister	Abdul Rassoul Amin		*Education Minister*	Yunus Qanooni	Tajik
Rural Development Minister	Abdul Mailk Anwar	Tajik	*Rural Development Minister*	Hanif Asmar	Pashtun
			Supreme Court Chief Justice	Sheikh Hadi Shinwari	Pashtun

* From a Tajik-dominated party
Source: Author calculations based on data from the Joint Electoral Management Board of Afghanistan.

The composition of this cabinet undermined both the interim and transitional regimes. Critics contended that neither Bonn nor the chosen government was very representative of the traditional power centers in Afghanistan. In particular, relatively few Pashtuns were given administrative or cabinet positions. Pashtuns expected this imbalance to be corrected in the emergency *loya jirga* (or ELJ, which was to select the transitional administration). Karzai was expected to shift the balance of power back to Pashtuns and give the former king a prominent national role. A transitional authority would then "lead Afghanistan until such time as a fully representative government can be elected," no later than two years from the convening of the ELJ.[17] The ELJ would also select a head of state for the transitional administration.

It was no surprise that Hamid Karzai was selected as transitional president at the ELJ of June 2002. The major issues of the ELJ turned out to be the role of the former king—Zahir Shah—and the role of the Panjshiris. Once the former king gave his support for the election of fellow Pashtun Karzai as the Afghan head of state—after considerable pressure was applied by the United States—ethnic issues were temporally defused. (Before Zahir Shah made his

---

17. Ibid., 3.

decision to support Karzai, a petition, signed by more than half the jirga delegates, was being circulated calling for the return of the king to power.) Subjects such as religion, the role of parliament, stability, and economic development dominated the *loya jirga* debates. This easing of ethnic suspicions and rivalry, however, proved short-lived.

As suggested by table 13.1, Karzai increased Pashtun representation in his new transitional administration. Pashtun membership rose from the eleven members in the interim administration to sixteen members, while representation of the remaining ethnic groups stayed fairly constant relative to their total representation in the transitional administration.[18] This increase in Pashtun representation was certainly an attempt by Karzai to shore up support with his Pashtun brethren and to respond to Lakhdar Brahimi, the special representative of the UN secretary-general, and others who suggested that the ELJ should correct the imbalances resulting from Bonn and more closely reflect the Afghan demographics. Nonetheless, many of the most important and powerful ministries remained with the Panjshiri Tajik Shura-e Nezar who were in control of the security apparatus dominating Kabul.

Karzai signaled his acceptance of the Panjshiris as necessary partners in his militarily weak government. He renamed as defense minister Mohammed Fahim, leader of the Northern Alliance forces based in the Panjshir Valley and boss of a private militia of ten thousand. He also strengthened Fahim's position in the transitional government by appointing him one of his three vice presidents.[19] This move indicated the power of the Tajiks and the Northern Alliance.

For all practical purposes only one key removal from the cabinet resulted from the ELJ—the departure of interior minister Qanooni. Qanooni, a senior figure in Jamiat-e Islami, had represented Northern Alliance interests at Bonn and played a key role in initially securing support for Karzai's candidacy among the powerful Tajik-led political and military coalition. But the relationship between Karzai and Qanooni had become contentious, which led to his controversial dismissal. Panjshiri soldiers and policemen in the ministry initially resisted the change, staging roadblocks and work stoppages. Karzai then appointed Qanooni as adviser for internal security, a newly created post, as well as minister of education.[20] At the time of the ELJ, Fahim, Qanooni, and Ahmad Zia Masoud[21] were all vying for the leadership

---

18. Note that the total number of cabinet positions increased in the transitional government as compared to the interim administration.

19. Fahim controls a private militia of ten thousand, most of whom are loyal, well equipped, and well paid. In his Panjshir Valley base of operations, he controls a vast heavy-weapons arsenal, which includes BMPs (combat infantry vehicles), BTRs (another Soviet infantry ground vehicle), and Scud missiles.

20. "Karzai Swears in the New Afghan Cabinet," *Washington Post Foreign Service,* June 24, 2002.

21. Ahmad Zia Masoud is the younger brother of the slain Northern Alliance leader and Afghan national hero, Ahmad Shah Masoud.

of the Panjshiris (Shura-e Nezar), and relations among them reportedly became strained. Karzai was caught in the middle of this politicking among the Panjshiri clique.

The interim government did not hold a monopoly on the legitimate use of force in Afghanistan, as both ISAF and separate U.S. troops within the coalition forces continued operations throughout the country. Nor did the interim government control the use of force in general. One year after the agreement, Human Rights Watch noted that the problem of warlordism was not merely pervasive, it was seemingly permitted: "The U.S. and its coalition partners, as well as Iran and Pakistan, failed to back immediate efforts to centralize military authority. While the official policy of these countries was to work with President Karzai to help him strengthen his administration, the U.S., Iran, and Pakistan actively supported local warlords in various regions of the country."[22] The external powers that had pledged to support Karzai thus undermined his authority at the same time, given that he had stated an intention to reduce the influence of the warlords. Instead, Karzai continued to fight with them "for authority, money, and legitimacy."[23]

Loya Jirgas and Post-conflict Stability: Ethnic Dimensions

Questions of ethnicity are critical in assessing the implications of the *loya jirgas* to future Afghan political and social stability. Past attempts at modern state formation in Afghanistan that directly challenged local tribal and religious structures resulted in ethnic backlash and state failure. Critics argue that the former mujahideen parties manipulated the *loya jirga* and transitional administration. As one International Crisis Group report stated, Karzai's failure to ensure transparent and accountable procedures meant a missed "opportunity to establish new constituencies and develop support for the peace-building process."[24]

Afghanistan's diverse ethnic composition makes democracy and even state building difficult. The present boundaries were created to serve as a buffer between British and Russian empires as Afghanistan confronted modernity through its forced integration into a Eurocentric state.[25] As is

---

22. According to the report, this support includes cash, weapons, uniforms, and communications equipment from the United States as late as October 2002. Human Rights Watch, "Afghanistan's Bonn Agreement One Year Later: A Catalog of Missed Opportunities," December 5, 2002, www.hrw.org/backgrounder/asia/afghanistan/bonn1yr-bck.htm. See also Milan Vaishnav, "Afghanistan," in *Winning the Peace*, ed. Robert C. Orr et al. (Washington, D.C.: Center for Strategic and International Studies, 2004), 252.

23. Vaishnav, "Afghanistan," 252.

24. International Crisis Group, *Afghanistan's Flawed Constitutional Process*, ICG Asia Report no. 56 (June 12, 2003), 2.

25. Barnett R. Rubin, *The Fragmentation of Afghanistan* (New Haven and London: Yale University Press, 2002), 5.

often the case in Asia, Africa, and the Middle East, Afghanistan's boundaries were not drawn along ethnic, linguistic, or religious lines. The externally imposed "state" comprises a complicated mix of people, most of whom live in small, kin-based communities outside of the limited urban areas. Some of these groups are ethnically and linguistically distinct, but they are not necessarily different in terms of culture.[26] However, Afghanistan's governments have been unable to create a sense of genuine national unity in times other than during crisis.[27]

Not only do Afghans lack a sense of national identity, they also do not agree on what form of state Afghanistan should have. Afghanistan's Pashtuns would like a strong Pashtun-run central state, Tajiks focus on power sharing in the central state, and Uzbeks and Hazaras desire recognition of their identities and mechanisms of local government.[28] Historically, the more populous Pashtun tribes of the south ruled Afghanistan, and therefore the early Pashtun dominance of Karzai's interim government created an atmosphere of tension between them and the remaining ethnic groups in Afghanistan. Unlike other ethnic groups, the Pashtuns emphasize tribal structures and codes at the expense of the state. Other ethnic groups did not truly establish themselves as a political and military force until the Soviet Union's invasion of Afghanistan in 1979. Before the Soviet incursion, fighting for control of the state had occurred primarily among Pashtun groups (for example, Durranis versus Ghilzais). As other ethnic groups rose in importance and sought to rule, civil war destroyed the Afghan state structure.

Afghan rulers have commonly attempted to manipulate ethnic groups in their efforts to control the state. For example, as Barnett R. Rubin writes, "to weaken the Barakzais, Ahmad Shah Masoud, the 'father' of modern Afghanistan, appointed a separate khan for the Achakzais, making the clan into a separate tribe, a status that they retain today."[29] Successful Afghan ruling authorities have been artful in underscoring and exploiting the differences among groups, often encouraging conflict among them in order to maintain control. Further complicating the dynamics of Afghan society are the relationships among the tribes themselves and among the varying ethnic groups that compose the nation-state. Simply put, the relationships among tribes are

---

26. The Pashtuns, representing 42 percent of the population, are the largest ethnic group in Afghanistan. Ethnic Tajiks represent 27 percent of the population. The Hazaras represent another 9 percent. Groups such as the Aimaks, Turkmen, Baluch, Uzbek, among others, comprise the remaining 22 percent. The country is almost totally Muslim, with the Sunnis representing 80 percent of the population and the Shi'as representing 19 percent. See "Afghanistan," *The World Factbook 2004* (Washington, D.C.: Central Intelligence Agency, 2004), www.cia.gov/cia/publications/factbook/geos/af.html.

27. John C. Griffiths, *Afghanistan: Key to a Continent* (Boulder, Colo.: Westview Press, 1981), 78.

28. Rubin, *The Fragmentation of Afghanistan*, 11.

29. Ibid., 46.

generally marked by "competition and outright animosity."[30] Unfortunately, many past Afghan regimes have failed to bridge the gap among these competing groups and have played different groups against each other in order to consolidate their power.[31]

Karzai's choice of cabinet members for the transitional government did not favor a balanced and professional cabinet. Karzai had not been able to remove faction leaders and install members with professional qualifications, as the Pashtun community had anticipated, because the Northern Alliance was reluctant to cede the considerable power it received from the Bonn Conference. In his cabinet, Karzai recognized the importance of balance between the Pashtuns and the Tajiks. He also recognized the extremely difficult task of assembling an administration that would satisfy all major ethnic groups while meeting the country's desperate need for professional governance after years of ruinous conflict.

Although the United States and other international actors viewed the outcome of the ELJ as legitimate, fellow Pashtuns were skeptical about Karzai's transitional government. The continued power of the Tajiks alienated Karzai's Pashtun power base. Many Pashtuns were dismayed and angered that none of the king's aides had been given senior posts.[32] In July 2002, a *Washington Post* article titled "Pashtuns Losing Faith in Karzai" posited that the Pashtuns were "becoming rapidly disillusioned by a series of developments that have reinforced the power of rival ethnic Tajiks and militia leaders, left the former king politically sidelined and a Pashtun vice president assassinated, and subjected Pashtun villages to lethal U.S. air attacks."[33] Padsha Khan Zadran, a powerful Pashtun warlord who reportedly controlled the three southeastern provinces of Khost, Paktia, and Paktika, in the spring and summer of 2002 summed up the sentiments of many Pashtuns when he asked, "Why are they humiliating Pashtuns? We're the majority. They placed Hamid Karzai at the top as a representative of Pashtuns. But in reality he's no longer a Pashtun. He's sold himself out. He's a traitor. Pashtuns cannot sit around waiting. They will react and will claim their rights."[34]

---

30. Kenneth Christie, *Ethnic Conflict, Tribal Politics: A Global Perspective* (Richmond, Surrey, UK: Curzon Press, 1998), 5.

31. Rubin, *The Fragmentation of Afghanistan*, 47.

32. Pamela Constable, "Cabinet Is Sworn in; Intense Negotiations Yield Greater Ethnic, Political Balance," *Washington Post Foreign Service*, June 25, 2002.

33. "Pashtuns Losing Faith in Karzai," *Washington Post*, July 13, 2002.

34. "Warlord Pushes for Control of a Corner of Afghanistan," *New York Times*, August 6, 2002.

The Constitution

While the constitution and the actual process employed for its ratification and adoption must be seen as positive steps for Afghanistan's future, the actual document and process surrounding it were not without flaws and have the potential to inhibit future stability. The Bonn Agreement called for a constitutional *loya jirga* (CLJ) to adopt a new Afghan constitution within eighteen months of the establishment of the transitional authority. In January 2003, Lakhdar Brahimi acknowledged at an open meeting of the UN Security Council that the "drafting and ratification of the new constitution . . . will also be a fundamental state building exercise." Brahimi stressed the need to "broaden the political base supporting the peace process" because "too many Afghans feel excluded from the government and political transformation which Afghanistan is undergoing."[35]

Brahimi's warnings were not heeded. The constitution was delayed and thus a rushed affair that provided few opportunities for participation by Afghan citizens. None of the bodies involved in the process of drafting, ratifying, and debating the constitution consulted or incorporated nonelites in the process. Three constitution-making organs—the Drafting Commission (DC), the Constitutional Review Commission (CRC), and the CLJ—played a role in the process.[36] Of the eighteen months originally envisaged in the Bonn Agreement for a constitution-making exercise, only thirteen remained when the DC began work—a limited amount of time in which to educate the Afghan people, who are largely illiterate, and to query them on subjects as complicated and foreign as many of those in the constitution.

The CRC, a thirty-five-member commission appointed by the president, also suffered delays. The jihadist group Shura-e Nezar dominated the commission, and therefore it was "never likely to yield individuals who could be viewed as legitimate national figures capable of transcending narrow, sectarian interests. . . . several experienced politicians from *jihadi* groups have been included but respected moderate leaders and members of democratic groups are conspicuously absent."[37] Like the drafting commission, this review body constituted "primarily factional bargaining at the cabinet level without significant consideration of the public interest."[38]

---

35. Open Meeting of the United Nations Security Council, Briefing of Special Representative of the Secretary-General Lakhdar Brahimi, January 31, 2003, www.un.org/News/dh/latest/afghan/brahimi31jan03.htm.

36. The United Nations (especially the UN Assistance Mission, UNAMA, and the UN Development Programme, UNDP) heavily supported these organs. See "The Constitution-Making Process in Afghanistan," report prepared by the Secretariat of the Constitutional Commission of Afghanistan, March 10, 2003.

37. International Crisis Group, *Afghanistan's Flawed Constitutional Process*, 16–17.

38. Ibid., 16.

The 502-person CLJ, which was selected in UN-run caucuses, met to deliberate on the draft constitution from December 13, 2003, to January 4, 2004. This body, which could include no militia commanders or government officials, was meant to confer legitimacy on the constitution through review and adoption.[39]

The final version of the constitution established a strong presidential system in which the president served as both head of state and head of government.[40] The president would be elected by a majority of the popular vote and would be eligible to serve two five-year terms.[41] A proposal sponsored by the Northern Alliance to establish a prime minister as a check on the presidency was removed, probably owing to Karzai supporters' concerns that a prime minister might emerge as a rival to the president.

The constitution established a bicameral legislature and a supreme court with high courts and appeals courts. It established no separate religious courts, but powerful Islamists presently are in or have influence in the emerging Afghan judiciary. The legislative body of the Wolesi Jirga (lower house or House of People) would promulgate laws, ratify treaties, and approve budgets. The Meshrano Jirga (upper house or House of Elders), with the authority to approve proposed laws and the budget, would consist of a mixture of appointed and elected members.[42] The constitution explicitly stipulated that 50 percent of the appointees to the Meshrano Jirga must be women, meaning that one-sixth of upper house members were to be women. In the elected lower house, at least sixty-eight of those elected (two per each of the thirty-four provinces) "should" be women.[43] That gave women about 25 percent of the seats in the Wolesi Jirga. Aside from these quotas, the precise nature of the electoral system was left to legislation rather than enshrined in the constitution. The constitution also gave the legislature the ability to impeach the president.

Map drawing in Afghanistan has always been contentious and related to issues of power alignment between Kabul and the hinterlands. In order to create multiethnic local government representation and to respond to long-held perceptions by minority ethnic groups that the primarily Pashtun-dominated provinces were biased against the non-Pashtun regions, the

---

39. Ibid. UNAMA coordinated international technical and financial support; UNDP provided financial management and administrative and operational support.

40. For the entire text of the constitution, see www.afghangovernment.com/2004constitution.htm.

41. Two vice presidents would run on the same election ticket as the president, and one would succeed him in the event of the president's death. Vice presidents were to serve a single five-year term. If no presidential candidate received at least 50 percent of the vote on election day, a run-off was to be held within two weeks.

42. One-third of the seats were to be appointed by the president, one-third were to be selected by Provincial Councils, and one-third were to be selected by District Councils.

43. This goal of female representation was to be met through election rules that would give the top two women vote getters in each province a seat in the Wolesi Jirga.

constitution called for two new non-Pashtun–dominated provinces. There-fore, on March 28, 2004, a Hazara-dominated province, Diakondi, within the northern section of Oruzgan Province, came into being, and on April 13, 2004, the government created a Tajik-dominated province, Panjshir, within Parvan Province. The thirty-four provinces, total, are governed by a provin-cial council whose members are to be popularly elected to four-year terms.

The constitution was vague about political parties. It allowed for them to be established so long as their charters "do not contradict the principles of Islam" and they do not have affiliations with foreign countries. The political parties law that was later enacted by the Karzai government provided the procedures for the legal registration of political parties in accordance with the constitution. This law prohibits political parties whose charters are "opposed to the principles of the holy religion Islam," which is problematic since Islamic principles are open to interpretation. Furthermore, this dynamic affords influential Islamist groups an instrument to block parties they deem politically unacceptable.[44]

Security Sector Reform

The security environment in Afghanistan suffered from reinforcing flaws: the accommodation of warlords, the availability of narcotics to fund non-state forces, the slow development of the Afghan army, and the uneven footprint of external forces. In May 2005, the Afghan National Army, reported to have a strength of thirty thousand, was far from its authorized level of seventy thousand. A report by the Feinstein International Center identified three zones of perception among Afghans regarding external security forces: a "Kabul bubble," in which the ISAF are concentrated, "benign and well accepted"; a light footprint of ISAF Provincial Recon-struction Teams (PRTs) in the northeast, the north, and the west; and "men-acing and aggressive" coalition forces in the remaining areas fighting residual Taliban and al-Qaeda elements, as well as coalition PRTs engaged in nation building.[45] The general lack of security made public consultation and organization for elections very difficult for the interim regime.

Efforts to reorganize the Afghan National Army were beset with prob-lems, including recruitment shortages and infiltration issues. The domestic and international actors alike were many and inchoate. Disarmament, demo-bilization, and reintegration (DDR) of uniformed armies is challenging, and militias are even less easily brought into the fold. The lead nations assigned

---

44. International Crisis Group, *Political Parties in Afghanistan,* Asia Briefing no. 39 (June 2, 2005).
45. Antonio Donini, Larry Minear, Ian Smillie, Ted van Baarda, and Anthony C. Welch, *Map-ping the Security Environment"* (Medford, Mass.: Tufts University/Feinstein International Center, 2005).

at Bonn to address these issues had overlapping duties. Japan took the lead in DDR, but the United States led the process of training the Afghan National Army. The American Coalition Joint Task Force Phoenix—composed mainly of National Guard units as well as other U.S. and coalition elements—held overall responsibility for the Afghan National Army to the level of creating the Ministry of Defense. U.S. Embedded Training Teams provided coaching and mentoring for Afghan forces.[46] British Gurkhas taught the course for noncommissioned officers, while the French taught the Officer Basic Course and the Command and General Staff Course for senior officers. Meanwhile, Germany led in training the police forces and the United Kingdom in the counternarcotics effort. If coherent education and training are vital to army cohesion, the Afghan program was not promising.

Afghan Elections

According to the Bonn Agreement, free and fair elections had to be held no later than two years from the date of the convening of the ELJ.[47] Concurrent elections for the presidency, the National Assembly, and Provincial Councils were scheduled for the spring of 2004, a timetable that was repeatedly changed. A series of events—including electoral infrastructure delays, accelerating instability, and the apparent reemergence of the Taliban—led to the postponement and separation of those three types of elections. The presidential elections were moved from June to September, then to October 2004. National Assembly and Provincial Council elections were eventually scheduled for September 2005.

On May 25, 2004, Karzai passed an electoral law by presidential decree.[48] This law made the following provisions:

- The populace would vote for individual candidates rather than political parties in the parliamentary elections.
- Government officials, *except the president,* who sought office as candidates were required to resign from their government positions at least seventy-five days before the elections.
- To be eligible to run, presidential candidates were required to produce at least ten thousand copies of eligible voter registration cards as evidence of voters' support.

---

46. Coalition Joint Task Force Phoenix official Web site, tfphoenix.omd.state.ok.us/mission. htm; and Lt. Col. Susan Meisner, "Command and General Staff College Graduates 4th Class" (Kabul: OMC-A Press Release, January 26, 2005).

47. UN Security Council, Agreement on the Provincial Arrangements, 3.

48. "New Afghan Election Law Endorsed," *Kabul Radio,* FBIS No. IAP20040527000095, May 27, 2004; and "Afghan Leader Karzai Endorses Election Law," *Kabul Hindokosh News Agency,* FBIS No. IAP20040527000099, May 27, 2004.

The months leading up to June 2004, the date originally set for the elections, saw a significant rise in violence throughout the country, especially toward election workers.[49] While some of this violence could be attributed to the reemergence of the Taliban, there was also a significant acceleration of an insurgency (especially in the east and west of the country) against the Karzai regime and U.S. forces. Voter registration soared in anticipation of free and fair elections, with most eligible voters registering even under the cloud of Taliban threats to kill registrants.[50] Although 9 million of the eligible 9.8 million eligible voters registered, the registration process was marked by blatant irregularities, including 140 percent voter-registration rates in thirteen provinces.[51] The Organization for Security and Cooperation in Europe (OSCE) refused to send election monitors to Afghanistan because it believed that "conditions in Afghanistan [were] significantly below the minimum regarded by OSCE . . . as necessary for credible election observation."[52]

In December 2003, with the encouragement of the United States, Karzai tried to undercut support for the Taliban by inviting "moderate supporters" of the Taliban (who also happened to be mostly ethnic Pashtuns) to join the political process in exchange for their agreement to cease fighting the government.[53] Tajik leaders viewed this move with suspicion, thinking Karzai sought to promote his fellow Pashtuns within his government. Karzai received de facto endorsement by the U.S. and European governments and took advantage of U.S. assets during his campaigning. It was alleged that much of Karzai's campaign financing came directly from foreign countries, in violation of Afghan election laws.[54] Concerning foreign support for Karzai, as M. Nazif Shahrani notes, it was suggested that

Karzai was . . . the only candidate who enjoyed access to US military aircraft for campaign travel as well as round-the-clock protection by a private US security firm. The Afghanistan Research and Evaluation Unit (AREU) report also found ambient suspicion that the US had allocated $30 million for the registration of Afghan refugees in Pakistan, who are primarily Pashtun, to enhance Karzai's chances for reelection. The appearance of favoritism in the ethnically charged climate of Afghan politics makes it seem that the goal of the campaign is to elect a president at any cost, especially in the eyes of the often ignored and abused non-Pashtun "minorities."[55]

---

49. A total of 4,807 polling centers were eventually staffed by approximately 120,000 workers.
50. Craig Charney, "Afghan Success Story," *Washington Post*, July 30, 2004.
51. Scott Baldauf, "Afghans Vote, Ready or Not," *Christian Science Monitor*, October 8, 2004.
52. Ibid.
53. Nicholas Kralev, "U.S. Backs Intention to Work With Ex-Taliban," *Washington Times*, June 15, 2004.
54. See, for example, "Afghanistan: President Karzai Accused of Illegal Electioneering," FBIS No. IAP20040810000129, August 10, 2004.
55. M. Nazif Shahrani, "Afghanistan's Presidential Elections: Spreading Democracy or a Sham?" *Middle East Report Online*, October 8. 2004, www.merip.org/mero/mero100804.html.

Karzai needed to expand his influence beyond the city limits of Kabul. Therefore, as part of the election process, he took long-expected (and long-threatened) action to marginalize the warlords. On September 2004 Karzai removed Ismail Khan as governor of Herat Province.[56] A particularly bold move on July 26, 2004, was the dismissal of Mohammad Fahim, the powerful Tajik minister of defense and leader of the Northern Alliance, as one of his vice presidents. It is very interesting to note that July 26 was the last official date for the filing of presidential election candidacy forms, according to the rules adopted by Afghanistan's Joint Electoral Management Body.[57] It is reasonable to believe that Karzai waited to the very last moment before dumping Fahim because he probably expected that such a strategy would prohibit the Tajiks from regrouping and promoting a new candidate.

Karzai's strategy backfired; it provided the impetus for the emergence of overt ethnic politics. The Tajik and Northern Alliance leader Qanooni parted from Karzai to announce his own candidacy, taking the opportunity to suggest that Karzai's dismissal of Fahim had exacerbated "inter-ethnic tension."[58] On July 27, Karzai placed Kabul on a high security alert, probably because of rumors in the capital that armed forces loyal to Fahim might stage an uprising. In addition to being Afghanistan's defense minister, Fahim commanded the Afghan army's 8th Division, with an estimated five thousand loyal troops stationed in the Shomali Plain—the fertile land just north of Kabul—and in the capital itself. Fortunately, Fahim and his militia did not take any extra-legal actions. Qanooni's candidacy soon garnered the support of Fahim, Foreign Minister Abdullah, and all the core leaders of the Tajik-dominated Northern Alliance. It seemed that the election was going to revert to a question of renewed interethnic strife.

The Presidential Elections

On October 9, 2004, the presidential election took place, with eighteen eligible candidates on the Afghan presidential ballot.[59] As expected, Hamid Karzai was elected with 55.4 percent of the vote, garnering three times more votes than any other candidate. Karzai's main opponents—Qanooni, Haji Mohammed Mohaqiq, and Abdul Rashid Dostum—received, respectively, 16.3 percent, 11.7 percent, and 10 percent. Twelve candidates received

---

56. "Administrative Reforms or Settling Accounts with Herat?" *Kabul Arman-e Melli* in Dari, FBIS No. IAP20040912000048, September 12, 2004.

57. "Afghan Election Body Urges Presidential Candidates to Register by 26 July," *Kabul Radio Afghanistan* in Pashto 1330 GMT, FBIS No. IAP20040725000113, July 25, 2004.

58. Camelia Entekhabi-Fard, "Afghan President Karzai May Rue Dumping Fahim—Presidential Rival," *Eurasia Insight*, July 28, 2004, www.eurasianet.org/departments/insight/articles/eav072804a.shtml.

59. This section draws upon previous work. See Thomas H. Johnson, "Democratic Nation Building in the Arc of Crisis: The Case of the Presidential Election in Afghanistan," in *Critical Issues Facing the Middle East Security: Security, Politics, and Economics*, ed. James Russell, 125–146 (New York: Palgrave Macmillan, 2006).

less than 1 percent of the vote. The lone female candidate, Masooda Jalal, finished sixth, with ninety-one thousand votes, or 1.1 percent. While there were complaints about voter intimidation (especially in the Pashtun south and east) and voting procedures, along with allegations of multiple voting and irregularities in counting in some areas, an impartial panel of election experts concluded that the outcome had not been affected.[60]

The presidential election was a watershed event, but what do the results represent? A statistical analysis suggests that the election clearly reified traditional ethnic splits in the country and that traditional ethnicity remains at the forefront of Afghan politics.[61] Afghans tended to vote along ethnic lines. Karzai was elected with a majority of the vote, but not with a majority of the vote from any ethnic group outside his own dominant Pashtun base. His claim to represent a truly national candidate with support across ethnic lines is not borne. Qanooni received most of the Tajik vote, while veteran strongman Dostum garnered the votes of his fellow Uzbeks in the north; Mohaqiq received the vote of the Shi'a Hazaras from his stronghold of central Afghanistan.

The challenge now is to unite the Afghan people: to bolster national identity while respecting ethnic traditions and norms. Unification will be extremely difficult because each ethnic group is attempting, often at the expense of other groups, to gain a foothold in government. The fragmentation will continue until either one dominant ethnic group controls all of the governmental power or ethnic politics makes way for increased internal conflict.[62]

The Legislative Elections

The Afghan legislative elections (including district elections), initially planned to be held simultaneously with the presidential elections, were eventually rescheduled for September 18, 2005. These elections were expected to be a mandate concerning the political direction taken since the ouster of the Taliban and the subsequent Bonn Agreement. The Karzai administration had pushed vigorously for political reforms and governmental institutionalization, and the continuation of Karzai's agenda depended significantly on the government's ability to engender support of a National Assembly. These elections were also expected to establish political blocs that would eventually become actual political parties, a seemingly critical component for a lasting Afghan democracy. Finally, the voting patterns of these elections would "signal the extent to which

---

60. See International Crisis Group, "Political Parties" and "Final Report of the Impartial Panel Concerning Afghanistan Presidential Elections 2004," November 1, 2004, www.elections-afghanistan.org.af/.
61. Johnson, "Democratic Nation Building."
62. Ibid.

influence [would] be based on common political ground—rather than strictly ethnic, religious, or provincial divisions."[63]

Approximately six thousand candidates sought approximately 390 parliamentary (Wolesi Jirga) positions and 217 Provincial Council positions through direct elections in multimember constituencies, using the single nontransferable vote (SNTV) system.[64] Under SNTV, candidates run as individuals rather than as a party bloc; multiple candidates run in each constituency; each voter casts one vote, and the candidates with the most votes win the seats. The Joint Electoral Management Board determined the number of seats for each province based on population figures provided by the Central Statistics Office and a formula established in the 2005 electoral law. At a minimum, each province was guaranteed two seats. Larger provinces such as Kabul, Herat, and Nangarhar received thirty-three, seventeen, and fourteen seats, respectively, in the Wolesi Jirga, while smaller provinces such as Nimrus, Nurestan, and Panjshir received the minimum of two seats. A similar, but more complicated, apportionment of seats was decided for Provincial Councils (see table 13.2).[65]

Unlike the presidential election, which had suggested that Afghanistan remains deeply divided along multiple fault lines—ethnic, linguistic, and ideological—the legislative elections were thought to provide the opportunity for politics to move in a less factionalized direction. Unfortunately, the structure and procedures for these elections were typical of the more general personalistic political processes that have been employed since Bonn. In particular, the notion of political party development to articulate voter interests was thwarted in the early electoral sequence.

The electoral law severely weakened the new political parties because it prohibited them from running on the ballot, and candidates were not allowed to run under a party banner. Candidates could be independent—nominated or endorsed by a political party—but the actual political party symbols could not appear on the ballot. Meanwhile, "old *jihadi* networks continued to have access to power and resources."[66] So many candidates contended because the election rules played against political parties in favor of individuals. More-

---

63. For the official Afghan government views concerning the importance of these elections, see Afghanistan Votes, www.rferl.org/en/specials/elections/FAQs.asp.

64. Forty-five candidates were refused because of their connections with armed groups or for not giving up their government jobs, although an alleged 207 other militia leaders were legislative candidates. During March 2005 it was announced that the district elections were postponed until 2006 (exact date to be determined) because of complications in the determination of individual district boundaries. This postponement means that these District Councils cannot select their upper house representatives.

65. For complete election rules, see the Joint Electoral Board Management Body (JEMB), "Wolesi Jirga and Provincial Council Elections 2005: Background Briefing," September 15, 2005, www.jemb.org.

66. International Crisis Group, *Afghanistan Elections: Endgame or New Beginning?* Asia Report no. 101 (July 21, 2005): i.

Table 13.2 Afghan Legislative Election Voting by Province

Province	Population	Registered Voters	Registered as Percent of Population	Provincial Council Seats	Total Votes	Percent of Registered Voters	Wolesi Jirga Seats	Total Votes	Percent of Registered Population
Badakhshan	790,300	400,918	50.73%	15	243,250	60.67%	9	243,740	60.80%
Badghis	412,400	234,680	56.91%	9	136,676	58.24%	4	136,781	58.28%
Baghlan	748,000	386,713	51.70%	15	209,027	54.05%	8	209,165	54.09%
Balkh	1,052,500	600,893	57.09%	19	306,575	51.02%	11	307,115	51.11%
Bamiyan	371,900	176,008	47.33%	9	125,869	71.51%	4	126,296	71.76%
Daikondi	383,600	253,589	66.11%	9	156,713	61.80%	4	156,630	61.77%
Farah	420,600	192,614	45.80%	9	110,818	57.53%	5	110,828	57.54%
Faryab	824,600	410,716	49.81%	15	256,750	62.51%	9	256,797	62.52%
Ghazni	1,020,500	745,225	73.03%	19	379,260	50.89%	11	378,577	50.80%
Ghowr	574,800	320,374	55.74%	15	213,413	66.61%	6	213,293	66.58%
Helmand	767,300	528,124	68.83%	15	194,742	36.87%	8	194,162	36.76%
Herat	1,515,400	824,722	54.42%	19	517,217	62.71%	17	517,926	62.80%
Jowzjan	443,300	218,548	49.30%	9	138,084	63.18%	5	138,085	63.18%
Kabul	3,013,300	1,193,472	39.61%	29	396,130	33.19%	33	399,810	33.50%
Kandahar	971,500	744,952	76.68%	15	188,377	25.29%	11	188,677	25.33%
Kapisa	367,500	202,800	55.18%	9	84,519	41.68%	4	83,966	41.40%
Khost	478,100	336,125	70.30%	9	188,751	56.16%	5	188,473	56.07%
Konar	374,700	274,583	73.28%	9	126,076	45.92%	4	126,282	45.99%
Kondoz	817,500	402,195	49.20%	15	246,535	61.30%	9	246,758	61.35%
Laghman	371,000	230,948	62.25%	9	87,444	37.86%	4	87,484	37.88%

Table 13.2 (cont.)

Province	Population	Registered Voters	Registered as Percent of Population	Provincial Council Seats	Total Votes	Percent of Registered Voters	Wolesi Jirga Seats	Total Votes	Percent of Registered Population
Lowgar	326,200	197,380	60.51%	9	76,254	38.63%	4	76,270	38.64%
Nangarhar	1,237,800	804,515	65.00%	19	382,186	47.51%	14	383,170	47.63%
Nimruz	135,900	85,562	62.96%	9	37,724	44.09%	2	37,750	44.12%
Nurestan	123,300	124,583	101.04%	9	80,184	64.36%	2	79,865	64.11%
Oruzgan	291,500	150,865	51.75%	9	35,388	23.46%	3	35,363	23.44%
Paktia	458,600	394,504	86.02%	9	251,931	63.86%	5	251,489	63.75%
Paktika	362,100	500,719	138.28%	9	261,749	52.27%	4	264,858	52.90%
Panjshir	127,900	139,397	108.99%	9	49,422	35.45%	2	49,218	35.31%
Parvan	550,200	245,385	44.60%	15	86,647	35.31%	6	87,517	35.67%
Samangan	321,500	165,218	51.39%	9	109,890	66.51%	4	109,955	66.55%
Sar-e Pol	463,700	192,294	41.47%	9	120,968	62.91%	5	120,939	62.89%
Takhar	811,800	418,696	51.58%	15	279,181	66.68%	9	279,246	66.69%
Wardak	496,800	243,219	48.96%	9	100,764	41.43%	5	100,663	41.39%
Zabol	252,700	102,695	40.64%	9	20,695	20.15%	3	20,695	20.15%
TOTALS	21,678,800	12,443,231	57.40%	420	6,199,209	49.82%	239	6,207,843	49.89%
KUCHI election		534,105						409,644	76.70%

Source: Joint Election Management Body (JEMB), www.jemb.org/.

over, this rule portended to favor candidates appealing to regional or ethnic biases rather than political ideologies and programs such as would have accompanied an election that encouraged political party participation, because forcing individuals to operate within the ideological frameworks of larger political organizations often moderates their appeals.

The fact that this electoral system disempowered political parties was entirely intentional. As suggested by the Afghan government itself, Karzai's electoral law chose the SNTV voting system precisely to limit the potential influence of political parties.[67] The rationale was that many Afghans are leery of political parties because parties such as the Communist People's Democratic Party (both the Khalq and Parcham factions), the Taliban, and various mujahideen parties wreaked havoc on the country over the past three decades. [68] Despite Karzai's efforts, at the time of the elections, seventy-two political parties were registered in Afghanistan.[69] Nevertheless, all political parties confront a hostile climate.[70]

Karzai's decision to adopt the SNTV system and to reject proposals for a proportional representation, party-list electoral system was made against the advice of UN and international advisers—with the exception of his most powerful backer, U.S. ambassador Zalmay Khalilzad.[71] The critics of SNTV have been harsh, arguing that in a context like that of Afghanistan, SNTV creates a legislative body that does not reflect the political preferences of the citizens. First, as Rubin argues, SNTV "virtually guarantees the formation of an unrepresentative parliament of local leaders with no incentive to cooperate with one another or the government. It places a premium on vote buying and intimidation, since swinging even a small number of votes can easily affect the outcome."[72] Other experts argued that SNTV was particularly ill suited for Afghanistan precisely *because* the country lacks well-organized political parties. When SNTV operates in a context without strong political parties, voters will pool their votes behind a few strong candidates, leaving open room for many candidates without strong popular bases to win seats. When parties are strong, however, they can educate their supporters in each region as to how to apportion votes across candidates. A party could easily gain a very different number of parliamentary seats than its percentage of the

---

67. Afghanistan Votes, www.rferl.org/en/specials/elections/FAQs.asp.

68. In fact many Afghans associate the words *hizb* (party), *harakat* (movement), and *tehrik* (way) with the violent histories of former leftist and Islamist parties. See International Crisis Group, *Political Parties in Afghanistan*, Asia Briefing no. 39 (June 2, 2005): 11.

69. See JEMB, www.jemb.org/.

70. International Crisis Group, *Afghanistan Elections*, 3.

71. Ibid., 10.

72. Barnett Rubin, "Afghanistan: The Wrong Voting System," *International Herald Tribune*, March 16, 2005.

vote might suggest it deserved.[73] In the Afghan context, this meant that those with the ability to discipline their supporters were large ethnic and regional parties, leading to the disproportionate representation of some of those parties or, conversely, resulting in a fragmented legislature.

Fifty-seven percent of the Afghan population registered and were eligible to vote in the legislative elections. Three provinces had more than 100 percent voter registration.[74] These data suggest voter fraud in the primarily Tajik home province of Karzai's major opponent, Qanooni, and in the primarily Pashtun province of Paktika. The latter also had significant over-registration in the presidential election and overwhelmingly voted for Karzai (88.4 percent). The over-registration did not lead to additional votes in Panjshir. Only 35 percent of Panjshiri "registered" voters actually voted in the election. This would seem to suggest that the registration process in this Tajik province was of questionable integrity, but the ultimate implications proved negligible.

The national election voter turnout—49.8 percent—was substantially lower than in the October 2004 presidential election. Turnout was highest in the north—generally greater than 60 percent—and lowest (below 30 percent) in some of the Pashtun-speaking southeastern areas where the Taliban insurgency is strongest. Oruzgan (23 percent) and Kandahar (25 percent) have been Taliban strongholds—the former being the home of Mullah Omar and the latter being the spiritual capital of the Taliban (as well as Karzai's home base)—where remnants of the Taliban pursued campaigns of intimidation against prospective voters. Surprisingly low turnout (34.5 percent) in Kabul is especially troubling considering that this urban populace is the best educated and most politically sophisticated in the country.

Electoral rules created confusion in many voters as to whom they were voting for. Moreover, the sheer number of candidates running under ballot banner icons, such as cups, beds, lions, rings, leaves, footballs, and cars, was extremely confusing. Candidates were not able to choose the icons themselves; instead, the electoral committee selected them. Such icons were reportedly used because a sizable percentage of the Afghan population is illiterate. Illiteracy and lack of voting experience also had other influences on the actual act of voting. The *Economist,* for example, found that some provinces required ballots up to forty pages long. The journal suggested that some voters were confused simply by the notion of turning the pages of those ballots.[75]

---

73. Andrew Reynolds and Andrew Wilder, *Free, Fair or Flawed: Challenges for Legitimate Elections in Afghanistan* (Afghanistan Research and Evaluation Unit (AREU), September 2004), 12.

74. For the full electoral results, see JEMB, www.results.jemb.org/home.asp. Unless otherwise noted, all analyses of the electoral results are the author's own. For a more extended analysis of the results, see Thomas H. Johnson, "The Prospects for Post-Conflict Afghanistan: A Call of the Sirens to the Country's Troubled Past," *Strategic Insights* 5, no. 2 (February 2006), www.ccc.nps.navy.mil/si/2006/Feb/johnsonFeb06.asp.

75. "A Glass Half Full," *Economist,* September 15, 2005.

The final election results were delayed by accusations of fraud and were not declared until November 12, 2005. The results upheld the notion that the procedures used in this election would favor localized candidates and strong regional figures and groups. In particular, they represented a victory for Islamic conservatives and the mujahideen: nearly half the seats of Wolesi Jirga were captured by Islamist or conservative religious figures.[76] Most of the elected former mujahideen leaders, shut out of the Karzai administration, found their way into the legislature because they had electoral bases in ethnic groups and regions where they exercise considerable influence and control. Thus, the legislative elections gave the mujahideen an opportunity to reassert their influence.

The results represented a defeat for the Karzai government. While these results did not deliver a clear anti-Karzai parliamentary majority, neither did they represent a clear mandate for the Karzai administration.[77] The election results suggested that the 249-member Wolesi Jirga will consist of five broad, possibly overlapping groups: (1) former mujahideen, including approximately forty members of Hizb-e Islami;[78] (2) independents, technocrats, and those tribal or regional leaders who are not presently affiliated with any of the established Afghan political parties; (3) former communists and other leftists, many of whom have joined mujahideen parties or remnants of the Taliban; (4) former members of the Taliban establishment; and (5) former ministers and deputy ministers of the government, many of whom Karzai had dismissed as he attempted to consolidate power over the previous three years.[79]

Because of SNTV and the prohibition of meaningful political party participation, many candidates won almost by chance, and the legislature became populated with virtually unknown candidates. For example, in Wardak Province, where sixty-nine candidates competed for five Wolesi Jirga seats, the leading vote getter (Abdul Reza Rezaee) received 10 percent of the vote. The other winners, who included the former Taliban planning minister (Haji Mosa Hotak) and a Hizb-e Islami candidate (Roshanka Wardak), received from 6.6 percent to 3.9 percent of the votes, respectively. Numerous other

76. "A Place for Warlords to Meet," *Economist,* January 5, 2006.

77. A Congressional Research Service Report to Congress posited that "the new parliament . . . appears to have a slim majority of Karzai loyalists." Kenneth Katzman, *Afghanistan: Presidential and Parliamentary Elections,* CRS Report for Congress (Washington, D.C.: Congressional Research Service, November 16, 2005), 5.

78. The party was registered in August 2005 with the Justice Ministry by its new leader, Khaled Faruqi, a former commander of Hekmatyar. Faruqi won a seat in the Wolesi Jirga.

79. The most prominent member of the ousted Taliban regime, former foreign minister Mawlawi Wakil Ahmad Mutawakkil, fared very poorly in his candidacy in Kandahar Province. Abdul Rasul Sayyaf, an ethnic Pashtun and a Karzai supporter who is an extreme Islamist and alleged war criminal as well as terrorist supporter, also won a parliament seat from Kabul with a bare minimum of votes.

provinces experienced the same kind of results, where candidates were elected by chance.

Kabul is the most populous province in the country, with more than 3 million people; 1,193,472 registered voters cast only 399,810 valid votes (35 percent). Mohaqeq received the highest percentage of votes of any candidate in Kabul—13.2 percent.[80] Qanooni and Dostum were the next two largest voting percentages, with 7.8 and 7.7 percent, respectively. The other thirty winning candidates received from 2.5 to 0.4 percent of the vote. That thirty of the thirty-three representatives elected to the parliament from the country's capital individually received less than 3 percent of their constituents' votes is amazing. Fifty-six percent of the Kabuli electorate voted for losing candidates; this would not be surprising if only two or three candidates where running, but for Kabul representation in the legislature there were 387 candidates. The aggregate nationwide votes collected by all Wolesi Jirga winners represented only 35.8 percent of the total vote.[81] Put another way, 64.2 percent of the Afghan voters supported losing candidates.

It is evident that the SNTV and the lack of political party participation helped to skew the election results and produce a Wolesi Jirga that will be highly fragmented and potentially gridlocked. If the legislative body proves ineffectual, then the odds of groups pursuing their own parochial interests by other means are greatly increased. This is a dangerous possibility considering that Afghanistan, an ethnically, linguistically, religiously diverse and extremely complex country with no democratic tradition, has been in continual violent conflict since the 1970s. Faith in the democratic process could quickly wane, and discontent could ignite the many elements in the country that are already interested in pursuing power via extralegal ways. A legislative impasse in the Wolesi Jirga could also push Karzai to personalize the Afghan government to an even greater extent and, in the process, alienate his opponents.

The members of the legislature body were not elected with the support of the majority of Afghan citizens. Moreover, they comprise influential coalitions of former mujahideen and Taliban commanders, communists, tribal nationalists, royalists, warlords, and urban professionals who do not like one another. Two parliamentarians were murdered before the legislative body convened. Although Karzai backed Abdul Rasul Sayyaf, an Islamic extremist, for speaker in parliament, allegations about his war crimes hurt his candidacy, and Karzai's rival Yunus Qanooni won the post.[82]

---

80. The author calculated these Kabul electoral results based on data presented by the JEMB.
81. The aggregated vote of all Wolesi Jirga winners was 2,225,068; 6,207,843 total votes were cast.
82. "A Place for Warlords to Meet."

Conclusion

There is little doubt that substantial, indeed historic, achievements have taken place in Afghanistan since the fall of the Taliban, and many of these achievements are directly attributable to the Bonn process. Nevertheless, serious flaws bode ill for Afghanistan's prospects to become a democratic, peaceful, and secure country.

In an interesting twist on the theme of international interventions in transitional governance that unites this volume, it is possible that Afghanistan's transition would not have taken place were it not for the al-Qaeda attack on the United States on September 11, 2001, and the subsequent U.S. attack on the Taliban government. That is, internal processes were previously insufficient to unseat the Taliban nor, after the fall of 2001, to unify the nation.[83] Yet, echoing Manning's analysis in this volume, regime change through foreign invasion has not been able to radically change the power elite in Afghanistan. Some Taliban remnants and local warlords gained power in the Wolesi Jirga, while others have regrouped and are presently engaged in an intensifying insurgency that is beginning to mimic those in Iraq. In retrospect, Bonn should have attempted to draw in moderate Taliban elements and include them in the government. Just wishing the movement will go away is not enough.

The failure of Bonn to address the problem of regional warlords was a monumental mistake that has undermined the ability of the fledgling central state to impose order on the country and to become the genuine ruler of Afghanistan. Without first demobilizing the regional power holders and mujahideen, the interim and transitional governments became dependent on them, and in the process of creating a permanent government, they earned themselves some measure of formal legitimacy. While Karzai eventually moved, with considerable U.S. support, to co-opt these warlords, their power bases remain intact. The problem of regional militias and the influence of warlords, many fueled by lucrative drug production and trade, is a colossal one.

The Afghan constitution is an extremely important accomplishment of the Bonn process. But the lack of a full public debate before its ratification was a missed opportunity to address two divisive issues: the role of Islam and the specification of relations between Kabul and the regions. Divisions between the mujahideen and the central government could deepen factional conflict if improperly handled. Islam, in contrast, could become an umbrella issue that would facilitate a coalition among disparate regional commanders who are discontented with the Karzai administration or are searching for ways of

---

83. Barnett R. Rubin, "(Re)Building Afghanistan: The Folly of Stateless Democracy," *Current History* 103, no. 672 (April 2004): 165–170.

expanding their territorial influence. Yet this is not a panacea: there is a long-term risk that the incorporation of Islam into the constitution will empower extremist groups, such as Ittehad-e Islami Afghanistan and factions within Jamiat-e Islami, and weaken new democratic groups, thereby undermining the foundations of civil liberties, particularly for women and the Shi'a minority.[84]

Karzai's election was a reification of long-held ethnic biases and conflicts. He was not able to engender significant support beyond his Pashtun base, and he has not proven to wield much influence beyond the city limits of Kabul. The legislative election results were even more disappointing. The election rules backfired on the Karzai administration: rather than disempowering organized political formations, as intended, and providing space for politics to coalesce around new lines, the election allowed elements that were already strong and organized to gain representation. Moreover, the voting results suggested that the Wolesi Jirga does not have public legitimacy, being elected by a minority of the electorate. The fact that so many candidates could be elected to this important legislative body with less than 5 percent of their respective electorates' support does not suggest that democracy is flourishing in Afghanistan. These elections were tragically flawed, and their results have the potential to derail the ordinary Afghan's faith in the legislative process.

Karzai's fear of a multiparty system was extremely counterproductive. The numerous parties that have been formed since Bonn should be encouraged to participate in public debate. Afghanistan is and will remain a fragmented society. But diversity of opinions need not be manifested in conflict dynamics. Interchange and a viable Afghan multiparty system should be encouraged, not discouraged.

Another problem facing Afghanistan and its transition to a stable democratic country is its narcotics production and transport. Afghanistan's economy has been captured by opium production and trafficking. Approximately 87 percent of the world's heroin is now produced in Afghanistan.[85] Current estimates posit that opium accounts for 45 to 60 percent of the national economy. Quite simply, Afghanistan is on the verge of becoming a narco-state, according to the United Nations, with drug barons, narco-terrorists, and corruption overwhelming the society.[86] As suggested by President Karzai, "poppy, its cultivation and drugs are Afghanistan's major enemy."[87]

---

84. International Crisis Group, *Afghanistan's Flawed Constitutional Process*, 6.

85. See United Nations Office on Drugs and Crime and the Government of Afghanistan's Counter Narcotics Directorate, *Afghanistan Opium Survey, 2005* (United Nations, November 2005).

86. United Nations Office on Drugs and Crime, *2006 World Drug Report* (New York: United Nations, 2006).

87. Yousuf Azmiy, "Karzai Says World Is Not Doing Enough on Afghan Drugs," ABC News International and Reuters, August 22, 2006, abcnews.go.com/International/wireStory?id=2341232.

The opium economy and the influx of narco-money have contributed to the spread of corruption into all spheres of government. Narco-associated corruption permeates Afghan society, especially in the judiciary and police, according to Ahmad Fahim Hakim, deputy chairman of the Afghan Independent Human Rights Commission.[88] Abdul Latif Pedram, an Afghan opposition politician, states, "There has never been so much corruption in the country. We have a mafia economy and a drug economy."[89] According to the *Washington Post*, "The drug trade in Afghanistan is growing more pervasive, powerful and organized, its corrupting reach extending to all aspects of society."[90] Ali Jalali, a former interior minister who quit the job last summer, explicitly points to the extent of the problem. According to *Newsweek*, he has stated that he has a "list of more than 100 high-ranking Afghan officials he suspects of involvement in the drug trade. A source close to him, fearful of being killed if identified, says Jalali's unpublished list includes at least 13 former and present provincial governors and four past or present cabinet ministers."[91] Jalali's supposition is supported by others.

Many of the underground industry's most important figures are said to be senior government officials in Kabul and the provinces. Amanullah Paiman, a newly elected member of Parliament from the far northern province of Badakhshan, has studied the country's drug problem and says Afghan government officials are involved in at least 70 percent of the traffic. "The chain of narco-dollars goes from the districts to the highest levels of government," he says.[92]

Ultimately, the problem of opium production and trafficking will have a major impact on the success or failure of democratic development in Afghanistan. The U.S. State Department has recently stated that an increase in the production of illicit drugs in Afghanistan is "a problem for the integrity" of the Afghan government.[93]

Ultimately, the success or failure of Bonn will depend on conditions particular to Afghanistan—a legal state, but one that has been in conflict for nearly three decades. The essential condition for a state is to have an effective monopoly over the means of violence, and there is no escaping the fact that Afghanistan suffers from inefficient, dysfunctional political institutions, including its security services. Heavy reliance on the international community—particularly the United States—to fill the gap in both functional politi-

88. Carlotta Gall, "Nation Faltering, Afghans' Leader Draws Criticism," *New York Times*, August 23, 2006.

89. Ibid.

90. PBS Online NewsHour, "Combating Poppy Production," www.pbs.org/newshour/bb/asia/afghanistan/aug03/drugs.html.

91. Ron Moreau and Sami Yousafzai, "A Harvest of Treachery," *Newsweek*, January 9, 2006.

92. Ibid.

93. Tom Casey, "Daily Press Briefing," U.S. Department of State, August 17, 2006, www.state.gov/r/pa/prs/dpb/2006/70877.htm.

cal processes and security services has left Afghanistan without an effective revenue base and dependent on international donor aid for reconstruction. Bonn's results would likely be in question regardless, particularly due to the condition of the Afghan state and the underlying problems within the country, including extremist beliefs, patronage politics, highly available drug revenues, and tribal rivalries.

14

Is This Any Way to Run an Occupation?

Legitimacy, Governance, and Security in Post-conflict Iraq

Christina Caan, Beth Cole, Paul Hughes, and Daniel P. Serwer

Editors' Note

Writing on Iraq, Christina Caan, Beth Cole, Paul Hughes, and Daniel P. Serwer bring the insider's perspective to an analysis of interim government under insecure conditions, administered by an international coalition that was unprepared to run an occupation government. Rich in empirical detail and thoughtful analysis, their piece drives home one basic point: once you lose the ability to provide security for the people, almost all else is lost. Their analysis of Iraq continually brings out the theme of an "iron triad" of legitimacy, governance, and security. Interim governments must succeed in achieving all of these to create any form of government that can rule without major challenge.

Analyzing a series of international administrations that came to be through a process of foreign invasion and imposition, the authors show how the early legitimacy accorded to the coalition forces was quickly squandered when they lost control over the security situation in the wake of the fall of Baghdad. Every time the coalition forces made an improvement in legitimacy, governance, or service provision, the failing security situation would create problems for the continuance of those improvements. This dynamic plagued the occupation governments, the hybrid international-domestic interim government, and even the fully domestic interim regime that eventually took over from coalition forces. Within this theme, the chapter brings out strongly the idea that international legitimacy does not create domestic legitimacy and that domestic legitimacy is easily lost. On this point, the authors raise a strong challenge that would arise for any international administration: the international administrations in Iraq lost domestic legitimacy in part precisely because they were not elected from below, and the Iraqis felt no sense of ownership in the process. In this sense, the chapter brings the volume back full circle to Antonio Donini's insights that a failure to bring about positive peace can actually threaten even the minimalist concept of securing the negative peace.

Ultimately, this is a cautionary tale about what not to do in international interim governments: do not go in without a genuine plan, do not go in without a nuanced understanding of the situation, and do not believe everything that expatriates tell you. The authors tie in a strong analysis of prewar planning failures to their effects on the "postwar" period: the consequences for quelling resistance and ensuring stability, reconciling factions into participatory political processes, garnering legitimacy, and providing basic services. They close their chapter by posing a thoughtful counterfactual, speculating as to whether the United Nations or an immediate interim government composed of either exiles or locals would have been more effective agents of transition.

Introduction

On March 20, 2003, as dawn broke across Baghdad, the United States and its coalition partners began military operations against Iraq with the launch of more than forty Tomahawk cruise missiles and strikes fired from F-117 Nighthawks. The official objectives of the U.S.-led military campaign, Operation Iraqi Freedom, included securing Iraq's weapons of mass destruction, removing Saddam Hussein's Ba'athist regime, and providing humanitarian assistance to the Iraqi people, along with assisting in the transition to representative self-government.

By early April, Baghdad had fallen to coalition forces. Just a month later, speaking on board the USS *Abraham Lincoln,* U.S. president George W. Bush officially declared the end of major combat operations in Iraq. In less than two months, Operation Iraqi Freedom had achieved a decisive military victory and ended the reign of Saddam Hussein and the Iraqi Ba'ath party. With this military victory, the United States and its coalition partners began their new mission: "post-conflict" reconstruction and stabilization.

The post-conflict conditions in Iraq, a country of more than 25 million people who had lived under a dictatorship for more than thirty-five years, were dire. With the coalition victory, Iraq's national government disintegrated. Only in the Kurdish northeast, where two Kurdish political parties reached a peaceful modus vivendi in the early 1990s, was there anything resembling legitimate civil authority, although it was supported by party-based militias *(peshmerga).* In the southern, Shi'a-dominated areas, Iraqi religious authorities held sway; while in the Sunni-dominated west, scattered remnants of the old regime persisted. Baghdad, Iraq's proud though shabby capital, had no army, no police, no courts, no city government, no parliament, and virtually no ministries. Iraq's borders were unguarded, its customs posts unmanned, and its army essentially defeated.

By early 2006, the situation had changed significantly. Iraq had held national elections, installed a popularly elected parliament and government as well as provincial councils, and drafted a new constitution, which was approved in an October 2005 referendum. Ministries, courts, police, and army all existed, although they operated at far below full effectiveness. Borders and customs posts were at least partially manned. While improvements were evident, Iraq's fragile new institutions were struggling to prove themselves capable of developing effective local and national governing agencies that could unite the country, end a virulent insurgency, stem the rampant sectarian violence, gain widespread legitimacy, and be sustained without foreign protection. Whether these institutions will ever gain traction and become sustainable remains to be seen.

The international transitional administration format utilized in Iraq differs markedly from the form of international administration presented in the typology for interim governance provided by Yossi Shain and Juan Linz.[1] As Karen Guttieri and Jessica Piombo argue in the introduction to this volume, Shain and Linz's model of international interim government is not nearly as controlling and invasive as the international administrations in Iraq have been. Also, the models in *Between States* all indicate some level of sound planning, an aspect which, we will argue, was markedly absent in the Iraqi transition. Finally, Iraq has been ruled by several forms of transitional governments and not just by one form. Transitional regimes in Iraq evolved through a series of four ad hoc phases, each aimed at resolving immediate problems while trying to lay the basis for longer-term stability and democratic transition. This reactive, phased format is not depicted in any of the interim administration models identified by Shain and Linz or, indeed, in other post-conflict reconstruction and stabilization operations. The various phases of interim governance in Iraq each came about because of the failures of the previous form of rule. Throughout these transitions there emerges a complex relationship among government effectiveness, violence, and domestic legitimacy.

This chapter will present a critical analysis of each of the phases of transitional administration in Iraq, focusing mainly on their contributions to legitimate, effective, and sustainable governance. The four phases to be explored include the Office of Reconstruction and Humanitarian Assistance (January–May 2003); the Coalition Provisional Authority (May 2003–June 2004),

---

1. Yossi Shain and Juan Linz, eds., *Between States: Interim Governments and Democratic Transitions* (Cambridge: Cambridge University Press, 1995).

which includes the Interim Governing Council; the Interim Iraqi Government (June 2004–January 2005); and the Transitional National Assembly (January–December 2005).

While inadequately prepared in advance and ineffectively implemented at every stage, this phased transition generally led to improvements in governance, with increasing acceptance by the Iraqi population and markedly less political intervention by the coalition. But regardless of the relative improvements, the security environment ultimately dictates any government's ability to sustain itself and effectively fulfill its responsibilities. It is not clear at this writing whether the devastatingly deadly and inhumane insurgency and the sectarian violence that it has sparked—the single greatest threat to Iraq's political stability and national unity—will allow effective governance to develop or undo what progress has been made. Thus, while progress is evident, the exact shape, nature, and sustainability of Iraq's nascent democratic government remains unclear.

The Office of Reconstruction and Humanitarian Assistance

Post-conflict planning for Iraq got off to a late and inadequate start. Civilian planning for the post-conflict phase in Iraq officially began in late January 2003, just two months before the war began, when President Bush signed NSPD-24 creating the Office of Reconstruction and Humanitarian Assistance (ORHA). Placed under the purview of the Department of Defense, this new office was to both design the post-conflict plans for Iraq and lead the transitional administration. Yet, ORHA's name intentionally left out "transitional administration," as the civil administration pillar within ORHA was to have a light footprint. Led by Lt. Gen. Jay Garner, U.S. Army (Ret.), ORHA was a multiagency office, with people from the Departments of Defense, State, Treasury, Justice, Agriculture, Commerce, and Energy, the United States Agency for International Development, and the United Kingdom and Australia. Garner reported directly to Secretary of Defense Donald Rumsfeld and assumed a coordinating role with Gen. Tommy Franks, then-commander of the U.S. Central Command.

The plans devised by ORHA for post-conflict Iraq were based on four assumptions that were handed down mainly by the Department of Defense but also by the White House and the Office of the Vice President.[2] The first assumption was that there would be a widespread humanitarian disaster, including a massive refugee crisis, substantial environmental damage from the igniting of Iraq's oil fields, and possible contamination from the use of

---

2. Peter Slevin and Dana Priest, "Wolfowitz Concedes Iraq Errors," *Washington Post*, July 24, 2003.

weapons of mass destruction. Second, the Department of Defense assumed that Iraqi security forces would largely be responsible for providing law and order, while the U.S. and coalition soldiers would be welcomed into Iraq as liberators with limited responsibilities. Third, ORHA based its plans on the assumption that the provision of such basic services as electricity and water would be relatively easy to ensure in a short time. Finally, ORHA planned for an interim Iraqi administration, selected by several hundred Iraqi leaders, to be inaugurated within weeks of the end of major combat operations.[3] This temporary administration, mentored by coalition members' staff, would include Iraqi exiles and would be responsible for administering the country during what ORHA thought would be a brief transitional period. ORHA also assumed that the Iraqi ministries, including the police and the interior, would be intact and capable of immediately performing essential government functions, even if Saddam Hussein and his close supporters were removed. Given these assumptions, ORHA's governance team was initially composed of fewer than two dozen people.

Planning for the post-conflict phase was obviously far from robust, with significant assumptions about how the vacuum created by Saddam Hussein's regime collapse would be filled. Planners assumed that the Iraqi government could be decapitated and still operate if given guidance from the coalition. Legitimacy would not be an issue under continuing Iraqi management. Additionally, the Bush administration and the Pentagon assumed that the new Iraqi government would quickly become self-sustainable.

Once General Garner and his staff gained entry into Iraq in late April, it became clear that all four assumptions were wrong. No humanitarian or environmental crisis emerged. After a decade of sanctions and misappropriation of oil-for-food money, nearly all the basic services in Iraq were on the verge of collapse. Hospitals and schools were in shambles. Sewage flowed through the streets and directly into the Tigris River. The provision of electricity was erratic. Iraq lacked even the most basic building blocks of democratic governance. Political opponents to Saddam and NGOs had been driven into exile. Civil society had been silenced and replaced with an entrenched culture of corruption and fear. The police, the military, and intelligence assets mostly evaporated during the invasion; those that remained had little experience with the rule of law—they had all answered to Saddam Hussein. Given these unexpected realities, ORHA's plans immediately proved inadequate.

Moreover, as Baghdad fell, widespread lawlessness swept across the country. Rampant looting and criminality took hold, resulting in the gutting of government ministries, museums, schools, hospitals, and power plants. Seventeen of the twenty-three ministries were completely destroyed. Lacking

---

3. Celeste J. Ward, *The Coalition Provisional Authority's Experience with Governance in Iraq: Lessons Identified,* Special Report 139 (Washington, D.C.: The United States Institute of Peace Press, 2005).

the force structure and orders to impose martial law, coalition forces stood by and watched the rampage. Washington-based officials dismissed it as minor and understandable in a new state of freedom. Secretary of Defense Rumsfeld, in response to the looting, merely remarked, "Stuff happens."[4]

The impact of the looting and lawlessness was devastating. It compounded the already dilapidated state of Iraq's infrastructure, making it far more difficult to provide even the most basic services. The destruction of the ministries made it impossible to operate according to the "decapitation" plan ORHA had devised, and the looting and lawlessness undermined ORHA's standing in the eyes of the Iraqis. Impunity rather than accountability seemed to be the first product of liberation. While many in Baghdad and southern Iraq had hated Saddam Hussein, much of the goodwill that the coalition forces earned for defeating the Hussein regime quickly dissipated when the victors failed to deliver law and order, basic services, or even a clear plan for the future.

What the coalition needed in order to establish itself as a legitimate authority in the initial period was a broad mix of forces that included gendarmerie-type police forces and international police with executive authority, accompanied by international police advisers, police trainers, international jurists, and penal managers, as well as a military force structure sufficient to impose martial law, if that proved necessary.[5] Yet, the Defense Department rejected suggestions made before the war to recruit this force spectrum.[6] International judicial, penal, and police forces have been used with notable success in other post-conflict settings, such as in Haiti and Kosovo, and they could have been called upon for post-conflict Iraq. Most of the looting and lawlessness could have been prevented, spoilers could have been subjected to a judicial and penal system that dealt with impunity, and the initial damage to the ministries and other facilities of civilian authority might have been avoided.

In sum, initial planning failures led to serious obstacles to effective and legitimate governance. Proper planning would have ensured that the necessary capabilities were in place to implement the post-conflict plans. It would also have helped to ensure that local expectations about the post-conflict phase were better managed. Perceived practical effectiveness would have made the transitional administration more acceptable, even for those Iraqis who resented the international presence and doubted the transitional administration's claims to authority. Lack of proper planning, and the consequent

---

4. Sean Loughlin, CNN Washington Bureau, "Rumsfeld on Looting in Iraq: Stuff Happens," April 12, 2003, www.cnn.com/2003/US/04/11/sprj.irq.pentagon/.

5. Robert Perito, *Where Is the Lone Ranger When You Need Him? America's Search for a Postconflict Security Force* (Washington, D.C.: United States Institute of Peace Press, 2004).

6. Public Broadcasting Service, "Frontline: Truth, War, and Consequences," www.pbs.org/wgbh/pages/frontline/shows/truth/.

lack of capabilities, left ORHA prepared for events that did not occur and ill-prepared for those that did. This forced ORHA to come out of the gate stumbling in an already highly demanding environment.

Explaining the Planning Failures

Why weren't the proper plans developed? While a definitive answer to this question may be available only after classified files have been opened to public scrutiny, several factors that contributed to inadequate planning are evident: (1) the domestic U.S. political and military context; (2) unfounded assurances by Iraqi expatriates that Iraqis could handle the country so long as Saddam Hussein and his chief supporters were removed from power; (3) the short time frame; and (4) the location of ORHA within the Defense Department.

The Bush administration came into office highly critical of nation-building efforts by the Clinton administration (especially in the Balkans), and Secretary Rumsfeld was determined to transform the U.S. military into a smaller but more capable war-fighting force. The planning for postwar Iraq suffered as a result. If the administration thought President Clinton was wrong to attempt nation building in the Balkans, how could it accept the notion that it would be necessary in Iraq? Moreover, the war against the Taliban in Afghanistan at that point was being conducted without a major U.S. nation-building effort. Perhaps it would be unnecessary in Iraq as well. Likewise, keeping the military force in Iraq relatively small—as the United States had done in its aid to insurgents in Afghanistan—would demonstrate the potential of Secretary Rumsfeld's transformed military to do more with fewer people.

Iraqi expatriates reinforced this line of thinking within the administration. Convinced that Iraqis would welcome the coalition as liberators, they envisaged the removal of Saddam Hussein and his main lieutenants followed by a quick transition to a newly constituted Iraqi government, which some of the expatriates thought they could lead. This was an attractive proposition from the U.S. government's perspective: it would put Iraq into the hands of people who were at least well known, if not always well liked. The question of legitimacy would then have been posed in the first instance to Iraqis, not Americans.

Even if the Bush administration had wanted to plan more extensively, there was little time. The claim that Iraq posed an imminent threat first became public in the January 2002 State of the Union address delivered by President Bush.[7] Had the post-conflict planning begun immediately in 2002,

---

7. U.S. Office of the Press Secretary, "State of the Union Address," January 2002, www. whitehouse.gov/news/releases/2002/01/20020129-11.html.

there would still have been only just over one year to get it right. A year would have been better than a few months, but it most likely still would have fallen short. In essence, the hurried timetable made proper planning of the transitional administration impossible.

Ironically, something like planning had begun in the State Department in April 2002, with discussions centered on the likely issues and challenges that would arise in a post-Saddam Iraq. These discussions were part of the "Future of Iraq" project, which included a series of seventeen working groups that focused on a diverse set of topics, from media to governance. Hundreds of Iraqi expatriates and other Iraq experts participated. Even though the $5 million project was underfunded and understaffed, the working groups met for nearly ten months and produced numerous reports.[8] While the reports were of varying quality, and many were far from adequate as planning documents, some of their insights have proven applicable and accurate.[9] Instead of building on the State Department's discussions on post-conflict Iraq, however, General Garner was explicitly told to ignore them and to focus ORHA planning on the (faulty) assumptions of the Department of Defense.[10]

Normal interagency communication, cooperation, and coordination might well have mitigated this problem. Instead of placing ORHA under the purview of either the Department of Defense or State, President Bush could have appointed an interagency coordinator to oversee ORHA, operating under his authority and reporting to the National Security Council. This would at least have enabled the State Department to raise the issues with which it was concerned and to challenge the Defense Department's assumptions.

The Coalition Provisional Authority

While Garner had anticipated that "the nucleus of a temporary Iraqi government would be in place" by the second week of May 2003, actual conditions made that impossible.[11] With government buildings dismantled by looters and ORHA's planning clearly insufficient, the coalition changed its approach. Discarding the notion that transition to an Iraqi-led government would be rapid and that a light governance footprint would suffice, the coalition implemented an acknowledged, formal occupation on April 23,

8. David L. Phillips, *Losing Iraq: Inside the Postwar Reconstruction Fiasco* (Boulder, Colo.: Westview Press, 2005), 37.

9. Eric Schmitt and Joel Brinkley, "State Department Study Foresaw Trouble Now Plaguing Iraq," *New York Times*, October 19, 2003, http://www.nytimes.com/2003/10/19/international/worldspecial/19POST.html?pagewanted=1&ei=5007&en=8c9bed012fe42718&ex=1381896000&partner=USERLAND.

10. Col. Paul D. Hughes, U.S. Army (Ret.), Iraq Program Officer, Peace and Stability Operations, United States Institute of Peace, in discussion with Christina Caan, July 5, 2005.

11. Ward, *The Coalition Provisional Authority's Experience with Governance in Iraq.*

2003. On this date, Lt. Gen. David McKiernan, U.S. Army, stated that "the Coalition alone retains absolute authority within Iraq."[12] The shift from liberators to occupiers became official.

By May 8, 2003, just a week after President Bush had declared the end of major combat operations in Iraq, the permanent representatives of the United Kingdom and the United States sent a letter to the president of the UN Security Council stating that they had created the Coalition Provisional Authority (CPA) to administer the occupation. Subsuming ORHA and thus beginning the second phase of transitional administration, this new entity would "exercise powers of government temporarily, and, as necessary, especially to provide security, to allow the delivery of humanitarian aid."[13] On May 13, 2003, Presidential Envoy Ambassador L. Paul Bremer III was designated the administrator of the CPA, and by May 22, the CPA had been officially recognized by the United Nations under its Security Council Resolution 1483.[14] The CPA was vested with executive, legislative, and judicial authority "to restore conditions of security and stability, to create conditions in which the Iraqi people can freely determine their own political future, (including by advancing efforts to restore and establish national and local institutions for representative governance) and [to facilitate] economic recovery, sustainable reconstruction, and development."[15]

While the CPA's mission was clear, the question of how and under what authority it was established, and who within the U.S. government was responsible for establishing it, remained vague. According to a Congressional Research Service Report released in April 2004, "available information about [the CPA] found in materials produced by the Administration alternatively: (1) deny that it is a federal agency; (2) state that it is a U.S. government entity; (3) suggest that it was enacted under United Nations Security Council Resolution 1483; (4) refer to it, and OHRA, as 'civilian groups . . . reporting to the Secretary [of Defense]'; and (5) state that it was created by the United States and United Kingdom."[16]

This ambiguity had positive and negative implications. On the positive side, ambiguity enabled the CPA to enjoy the best of multiple worlds: it was able to draw more resources than if it were solely an international organization

12. Michael R. Gordon and John Kifner, "U.S. Warns Iraqis Against Claiming Authority in Void," *New York Times*, April 24, 2003.

13. United Nations Security Council, "Letter from the Permanent Representative of the UK and the US to the UN addressed to the President of the Security Council," May 8, 2003.

14. United Nations Security Council Resolution 1483 (May 22, 2003).

15. U.S. Office of Management and Budget, "Report to Congress Pursuant to Section 1506 of the Emergency Wartime Supplemental Appropriations Act, 2003 (Public Law 108-11)" (Washington, D.C., June 2003), 2; and David B. Rivkin Jr. and Darin R. Bartram, "Military Occupation: Legally Ensuring a Lasting Peace," *Washington Quarterly* 26, no. 3 (Summer 2003): 87–103.

16. L. Elaine Halchin, *The Coalition Provisional Authority (CPA): Origin, Characteristics, and Institutional Authorities* (Washington, D.C.: Congressional Research Service, April 29, 2004).

or a U.S. agency, and it was ultimately able to draw backing from those hesitant to support the CPA as a U.S. agency and from those hesitant to support it as merely an arm of the United Nations. Thus, ambiguity allowed the CPA "to perform multiple roles, each with its own chain of command, stakeholders or constituents, funding, and accountability policies and mechanisms."[17] On the negative side, this ambiguity blurred lines of authority, reduced transparency, and contributed to mistrust in the Iraqi population.

While there can be no doubt about the formal legality of the occupation from an international perspective, the CPA never gained full legitimacy with many Iraqis, who feared it would last for a long time. This problem was compounded by the lack of a formal surrender or cessation of hostilities. While it was clear that the coalition had won the conventional military struggle, it lacked public acknowledgment of incontestable defeat from Saddam Hussein. Had the coalition insisted on such an acknowledgment from whatever remained of the previous regime, several groups in the subsequent insurgency, particularly the Sunni and Ba'ath party components, might have had a more difficult time organizing and gaining support.

For the United States, the occupation was a temporary arrangement that could not be sustained; it was necessary only in order to lay the basis for a legitimate, constitutional government. The initial idea was for the CPA to preside over the writing of a permanent Iraqi constitution, followed by elections and the transfer of civilian authority to a democratically legitimized Iraqi government.

Yet, the CPA's tenure did not unfold as smoothly as many had hoped. On May 8, the same day the CPA was officially announced, twenty-three-year-old Pfc. Marlin T. Rockhold, U.S. Army, was shot and killed by a sniper as he directed traffic in Baghdad. His death marked the onset of what would become a widespread and sophisticated insurgency that may ultimately result in civil war. Over the coming months, not only would the insurgency take the lives of civilians and military personnel, Iraqis and non-Iraqis alike, it would also hinder progress on reconstruction projects, most notably in areas such as Sadr City, Falluja, and Najaf. Further, it would prevent Iraqis from working and cooperating with the coalition and cost the coalition dearly in security expenditures. While the coalition was slow to recognize its strength, the insurgency—along with the sectarian violence it sparked—would quickly become the single greatest threat to political stability and national unity, the CPA's authority, and effective, sustainable, democratic governance.

---

17. Ibid.

CPA Governance

The newly inaugurated CPA took two early steps that would have major impacts on governance: de-Ba'athification and cancellation of the first post-conflict local elections. Both moves were intended to use the occupation authority vested in the CPA to correct what had come to be regarded as an insufficiently decisive course pursued by General Garner's ORHA. As it turned out, neither helped the CPA to gain control of an ever-worsening situation.

The process for de-Ba'athification was implemented on May 23, 2003—under Order Number Two, titled "Dissolution of Entities"—just a day after the CPA had been officially recognized by the United Nations. This order, strongly supported by the Kurdish population, officially dissolved all former Iraqi military services, as well as the Republican Guard, the Special Republican Guard, the Al Quds Force, and the Iraqi paramilitary groups, among others.[18] While the CPA initially offered members of the dissolved groups below the rank of colonel a termination payment equal to one month's salary, this move left three hundred fifty thousand to four hundred thousand soldiers and some two thousand Information Ministry staff unemployed, with no alternative employment opportunities or strategies for reintegration.[19]

To many Iraqis, Order Number Two appeared to be unjust punishment for Ba'ath party membership, as many had joined the Ba'ath party merely to secure a government job or a place in the armed forces. Moreover, by disbanding Iraq's security services in an environment that lacked a functioning justice and penal system, the provision of law and order was left entirely up to coalition forces. Based on the Defense Department's initial assumptions about Iraq, there were no plans—other than a sixty-day assessment mission—to beef up the Iraqi police or other indigenous security forces.[20] Because coalition forces lacked the capacity to provide for public security themselves, "everyday law enforcement, of criminal infractions, just fell by the wayside."[21]

---

18. Coalition Provisional Authority, "Order Number 2: Dissolution of Entities," www.cpa-iraq. org/regulations/20030823_CPAORD_2_Dissolution_of_Entities_with_Annex_A.pdf. It is important to note that there was substantial disagreement between the State Department and the Pentagon on the dissolution of the Iraqi military and security apparatuses and their role in the post-conflict reconstruction, with the State Department vying largely for using the Iraqi armed forces to assist in the reconstruction and the Pentagon vying for their dissolution.

19. Jane Arraf, "U.S. Dissolves Iraqi Army, Defense and Information Ministries," *CNN*, May 23, 2003, www.cnn.com/2003/WORLD/meast/05/23/sprj.nitop.army.dissolve/.

20. Ibid. It is worth noting that Gen. Eric K. Shinseki, then-U.S. Army chief of staff, did believe that a larger force of several hundred thousand soldiers would be needed in the post-conflict phase to ensure security and stability. Various other civilian personnel also recommended planning rule-of-law programs, but they were dismissed by senior U.S. government officials.

21. Mark Yanaway, interview by Bernie Engel, United States Institute of Peace, Association for Diplomatic Studies and Training, Iraq Experience Project, July 14, 2004.

As crime and lawlessness increased in the anarchic environment, the local population blamed the primary bodies responsible for law and order: coalition forces and the CPA. Also, the de-Ba'athification process disproportionately affected the Sunni population, compounding their already heightened fear of being cast out of the new Iraq, given their minority status and ties to the Ba'ath party. When former Iraqi soldiers gathered in Baghdad to protest Order Number Two, coalition troops, unprepared for crowd control and policing activities, opened fire, killing two.[22] Thus de-Ba'athification, which was intended to fortify the dream of a new Iraq, instead reduced the acceptability of the CPA among an important part of the population and increased resistance to its authority.

In this manner, the de-Ba'athification process created a negative feedback loop that undermined the CPA in several ways. First, de-Ba'athification eradicated Iraqi security forces, which created a sense of injustice among those now unemployed. Not having the right composition of forces for providing basic security to Iraqi civilians, and now without help from Iraqis themselves, the CPA could not quell rising lawlessness. Increasing disorder then threatened other aspects of the CPA's programs, lowered the quality of life for Iraqis, and led to a further loss of credibility for the CPA. Finally, losing credibility compounded a mounting legitimacy crisis and further enshrined an emerging Iraqi view of the occupation as illegitimate.

The second action taken by the CPA that had a substantial impact on governance occurred in June 2003, when the CPA and coalition forces canceled local elections for mayors and city councils across Iraq. According to Ambassador Bremer, local elections were canceled because "in a postwar situation like this, if you start holding elections, the people who are rejectionists tend to win. . . . It's often the best-organized who win, and the best-organized right now are the former Ba'athists and to some extent the Islamists."[23] Many in the CPA thought this a wise decision, based on bad experiences with early elections in the Balkans conflicts of the 1990s. Therefore, U.S. military commanders instead installed their own handpicked local leaders. Unfortunately, while these selected leaders were not "rejectionists," many of these individuals were former Ba'ath military leaders or disreputable members of the community.

Postponing the elections further exacerbated the domestic legitimacy crisis for the CPA. By failing to properly communicate through a nationwide public diplomacy campaign why the elections were canceled, the CPA unintentionally conveyed a message to the Iraqi people that they were not to be in charge of their own destiny. Moreover, by installing former Ba'ath military leaders in positions of power, Iraqis began to feel control over their destiny

---

22. Arthur Max, "U.S. Troops Kill Two Iraqi Protestors," *Associated Press*, June 18, 2003.
23. William Booth and Rajiv Chandrasekaran, "Occupation Forces Halt Elections throughout Iraq," *Washington Post*, June 28, 2003.

slipping away and, more important, to see the dream of a new Iraq being threatened. In response, protests broke out around the country. In Najaf, crowds shouted, "Canceled elections are evidence of bad intentions" and "O America, where are promises of freedom, elections, and democracy?"[24] Because support for the coalition was largely based on the Iraqi people's desire for a new Iraq, marginalizing this dream was especially damaging to the CPA's acceptability.

The decision to cancel elections also encouraged Iraqis to look to the CPA to provide for their needs. But because Iraq was in such disrepair and because the CPA lacked the necessary personnel, it was unable to fulfill expectations. The difficulty the CPA experienced in providing basic services was so extreme that U.S. military commanders began to refer to it as "Can't Provide Anything." The inability to provide basic services, coupled with the inability to provide basic law and order, only further increased resentment and frustration in the local population.

While various other moments throughout the next year continued to undermine the legitimacy of the CPA and fanned the flames of violence, including the Abu Ghraib prison scandal that became public in April 2004, these two initial actions were especially problematic. In essence, although the CPA quickly gained some international legitimacy in UN Security Council Resolution 1483, it had lost legitimacy among the Iraqi population. Ba'athists and anti-Ba'athists, Sunnis and Shi'as, and those who welcomed the U.S. victory and those who resisted it all found themselves alienated from an authority that failed to deliver basic law and order, water, electricity, or democracy. The purely international transitional regime had lost so much legitimacy not because it was international in nature but because it failed to breathe life into a new Iraq by providing security, governance, and services on the ground. As a result, the coalition began to look for alternate ways to regain lost ground.

The Interim Governing Council

To address these legitimacy and governance crises, the CPA sought to put an Iraqi face on the administration. Faced with growing skepticism among Iraqis about how they were to be governed during the occupation, Bremer reacted by shifting gears on July 13, 2003. Responding to pressures to include more explicitly an Iraqi voice in the transitional administration of the country, the coalition created the Interim Governing Council (IGC). The IGC was established to appoint interim ministers and to draft an interim administrative law to govern the country until a permanent constitution

---

24. Ibid.

could be written. At the time, the plan was to turn over sovereignty and hold elections only after the writing of the permanent constitution. The IGC was composed of twenty-five members, including thirteen Shi'as, five Sunnis, five Kurds, one ethnic Turk, and one Assyrian Christian.[25] This composition more or less reflected the ethnic makeup of Iraq and was intended to make the IGC acceptable to all ethnic groups. The presidency of the IGC rotated on a monthly basis among nine of the twenty-five members.

The IGC faced serious challenges, and ultimately it had as much difficulty generating legitimacy and effective governance as had the CPA. The monthly rotation of the presidency, for one, was criticized for contributing to a lack of leadership on the IGC. Security also proved to be a seriously debilitating problem for the council. According to Col. Mark Yanaway, who served with the CPA, the coalition failed initially to provide the IGC with adequate security. The weapons provided to the security teams of the IGC members were "all junk . . . in some cases there was concrete in the barrels . . . some of them just did not work, period."[26] By not providing adequate security, the CPA undermined the IGC's standing with Iraqis. Moreover, because they lacked capable protection, two members of the IGC were assassinated: one was one of the three women serving on the IGC and the other was killed while he was acting president.

In addition, because the IGC had been appointed by the CPA, the Iraqi public tended to view it as a kind of puppet government. This perception was not entirely mistaken, because the CPA did hold veto power over IGC decisions. In addition, nine of the twenty-five IGC members were returned exiles, many relatively unknown to most Iraqis. A general suspicion of returned exiles and a sense that they were out of touch with the country prevented the population from supporting their involvement in the IGC. In all, the many challenges the IGC faced significantly depleted its ability to help foster much needed stability in the country, as the CPA had hoped it would.

Despite the challenges the IGC faced, over the next year it did accomplish its two main objectives. First, the IGC appointed twenty-five interim ministers—thus constituting the first postwar Iraqi government. Second, the IGC drafted the transitional administrative law (TAL), which is a revolutionary legal document for Iraq because it established such fundamental democratic rights as freedom of religion, freedom of speech, and freedom of the press, all of which had been long denied. Reflecting a consensus that "the system of government in Iraq shall be republican, federal, democratic, and pluralistic," the TAL also established the cultural equality and rights of the Kurds by

25. Council on Foreign Relations, "Iraq's Governing Council," www.cfr.org/publication. php?id=7665.
26. Yanaway interview.

recognizing the Kurdistan regional government and designating Kurdish an official language.[27]

While drafting the TAL was a major accomplishment, the process of obtaining its approval revealed a sharp increase in interethnic tensions. On the eve of its signature, the Shi'a members of the IGC decided—at the request of their religious leader, Grand Ayatollah Ali al-Sistani—to refuse to sign the TAL. Ayatollah al-Sistani and the Shi'a were specifically opposed to Article 61 (c) of the TAL, which effectively granted the Kurds veto power over the draft permanent constitution, and to the structure of the presidency. Article 61 (c) also granted the Sunni-majority provinces a veto, but this was not an issue at the time. The Shi'a members of the IGC preferred a rotating five-person presidency that would have included three Shi'a, one Sunni, and one Kurd. They argued that a five-member body was more representative of the Iraqi population and thus more democratic. Even more important, however, was Ayatollah al-Sistani's claim that the TAL was an illegitimate document because an unelected body wrote it. Arguing that the process used to devise the TAL was flawed, Ayatollah al-Sistani condemned it, calling for a more democratic and transparent process.

Despite the objections, all the members of the IGC signed an unaltered TAL days later, under substantial pressure from the CPA. But the lack of cohesion and the claims of illegitimacy damaged the public perception of the TAL and thus limited the impact of this critical document. What was needed was a united front that displayed confidence in the TAL and the democratic future of the country. What occurred instead was the use—more accurately the misuse—of the TAL for political posturing and political gain. This highlighted and heightened the lack of national unity and national identity in Iraq, sharpened ethnic differences, and decreased not only Iraqi but also coalition confidence in the IGC.

Planning the Transfer of Sovereignty

By the end of August 2003, just a month after the creation of the IGC, the torrent of security crises was creating ever-increasing obstacles for the transition. The United Nations had been the victim of a suicide truck bombing that took the life of its special representative, Sergio Vieira de Mello, and several of his colleagues. With this attack, the UN mission—along with dozens of NGOs—withdrew from Iraq, depriving the CPA of an on-the-ground ally that some believe might have helped it achieve greater legitimacy. The Green Zone, which housed CPA headquarters, quickly became a

---

27. Coalition Provisional Authority, "Law of Administration for the State of Iraq for the Transitional Period," www.cpa-iraq.org/government/TAL.html.

heavily fortified compound, defended with "coils of razor wire, chain-link fences, armed checkpoints, M1 Abrams tanks, Bradley fighting vehicles, and HUMVEEs with .50 caliber machine guns on top."[28] Thus, just four months after the creation of the CPA, occupation was proving far more difficult—and dangerous—than had been anticipated.

In October 2003, through Security Council Resolution 1511, the United Nations in New York tried to boost the coalition by bestowing international legitimacy to it. This resolution officially authorized the existence and operations of the coalition forces and renamed them "multinational forces."[29] This UN mandate does not appear to have helped the security situation, which continued to deteriorate rapidly. Then, on November 15, 2003, the coalition once again adjusted its plans for transitional administration in Iraq. Plans for a long-term occupation were scrapped, as Ambassador Bremer announced that sovereignty would be transferred to the Iraqis by June 30, 2004. The proposed plan for the transfer of sovereignty called for the selection of an Interim National Assembly to be chosen through a complicated "caucus" system, which would in turn select Iraq's new government. This new government was to be in place by the time sovereignty was transferred.

The November 15 plan quickly ran into problems. The system for choosing the assembly members was difficult to understand, but it seemed to leave a lot of power in the hands of IGC members and the CPA. By January 2004, Ayatollah al-Sistani had publicly condemned the plan and called for elections prior to the transfer of sovereignty. To deal with this challenge, the CPA turned to the newly appointed UN special envoy, Ambassador Lakhdar Brahimi, who was tasked with assisting in developing a plan for the transfer of sovereignty and the holding of elections that would be acceptable to all parties and actionable given the conditions in Iraq. By the end of February, Ambassador Brahimi concluded that holding elections prior to June 30 was not feasible.

The final process that was agreed upon was that the IGC would select an Interim Iraqi Government (IIG), to which sovereignty would be transferred before June 30, 2004. On June 8, 2004, the United Nations endorsed this plan by unanimously passing Security Council Resolution 1546.[30] This resolution also reaffirmed the UN mandate for the multinational forces, but it articulated that they would serve "at the request of the Interim Government of Iraq."[31] In addition, UN Security Council Resolution 1546 outlined the official

28.John Pike, "Military: Green Zone," www.globalsecurity.org/military/world/iraq/baghdad-green-zone.htm.

29. United Nations Security Council Resolution 1511 (October 16, 2003).

30. "U.N. Resolution on Iraq Passes Unanimously," CNN, June 8, 2004, www.cnn.com/2004/WORLD/meast/06/08/un.iraq/.

31. United Nations Security Council Resolution 1546 (June 8, 2004).

timetable for the full transition to democratic government, which included the following:

(a) Formation of the sovereign Interim Government of Iraq that will assume govern-ing responsibility and authority by 30 June 2004; (b) convening of a national confer-ence reflecting the diversity of Iraqi society; and (c) holding of direct democratic elections by 31 December 2004 if possible, and in no case later than 31 January 2005, to a Transitional National Assembly, which will, inter alia, have responsibility for forming a Transitional Government of Iraq and drafting a permanent constitution for Iraq leading to a constitutionally elected government by 31 December 2005.[32]

In preparation for this transition, between May 2003 and June 2004 the CPA pushed forward on reconstruction and governance issues in an effort to meet the high expectations its own rhetoric had helped to create. It intro-duced a new currency, established a central banking system, and lowered unemployment rates to between 30 and 40 percent.[33] Progress was also made in reconstructing schools, hospitals, and power plants and in ensuring the provision of various other basic services, although to varying degrees, throughout the country.

Even though progress was made, the quick fix, large-scale approach the CPA used too often left new schools without teachers and new hospitals without electricity.[34] Many projects also failed to hire local Iraqis, leaving the local population without income and without a sense of ownership in the reconstruction process. The CPA's preference for large-scale infrastructure projects, which take a great deal of time and expertise, left local people won-dering why they still lacked consistent services. Major infrastructure proj-ects also created targets for the insurgency, which found it could easily cause major delays. Although Iraq's economy and essential services began to improve, the near total state of disrepair, lack of security, focus on large-scale projects, lack of local ownership, and poor expectation management signifi-cantly limited the pace of progress, which in turn further eroded the CPA's legitimacy and credibility.

With regard to developing indigenous governance, the focus fell on build-ing national institutions, especially the ministries, court system, and police. The focus on national governance stemmed from the many security threats the CPA faced, as well as a lack of qualified international personnel. This focus, however, slighted the development of local governance. There was a lack of funding provided to local councils, as well as a lack of expertise pro-

32. Ibid.

33. Michael E. O'Hanlon and Adriana Lins de Albuquerque, "The Brookings Institution Iraq Index," www.brookings.edu/fp/saban/iraq/index.pdf.

34. Frederick Barton and Bathsheba Crocker, *Progress or Peril: Measuring Iraq's Reconstruction* (Washington, D.C.: Center for Strategic and International Studies Press, September 2004).

vided to assist in their development. One CPA provincial coordinator stated, "City council members were not being paid for months and months. We were trying to empower local government, but we couldn't pay them and they had no power."[35] Opportunities to build legitimacy at the grass roots were therefore missed, although some progress was made in political party development, the empowerment of civil society groups, and citizen education, which has supported democratization at the local level.

The Interim Iraqi Government

On June 28, 2004, two days ahead of schedule, the CPA transferred sovereignty to the Iraqis in a small private ceremony. While the multinational forces remained in the country, the CPA, along with the IGC, dissolved. Thus, after thirteen months, the occupation phase of the transitional administration in Iraq officially came to an end.

With the end of the occupation came the start of the IIG. Iyad Allawi, a former member of the IGC, was chosen to be prime minister, while Sheikh Ghazi al-Yawar was chosen to be president, a largely ceremonial post. The IIG would remain in place until elections were held, overseeing administration of the country during a period that included the greatest security crises since the fall of the Saddam Hussein government.

The IIG was the first phase of transitional administration in Iraq that proved to be capable of garnering noteworthy, but short-lived, acceptability among the Iraqi population. By July 2004, just a month after being inaugurated, polls showed that just over 30 percent of the population believed that Prime Minister Allawi had been effective since taking office, while only 9 percent believed he had been very ineffective.[36]

Maintaining even this basic level of acceptability in a rapidly deteriorating security environment was a challenging task for the inexperienced IIG. By August 2004, attacks on the multinational forces had reached their highest level since the start of the war, averaging nearly eighty a day.[37] Intensive fighting between the multinational forces and insurgents had broken out in the holy city of Najaf. Led by Shi'a religious cleric Muqtada al-Sadr, the al-Mahdi Army, which had previously staged a coordinated uprising in April–May 2004, fought the multinational forces for nearly three weeks. The Najaf insurgency was estimated to include at least twenty thousand Shi'a fighters,

---

35. Larry Diamond, *Squandered Victory: The American Occupation and the Bungled Effort to Bring Democracy to Iraq* (New York: Henry Holt and Company, 2005), 115–116.

36. International Republican Institute, "Survey of Iraqi Public Opinion," September 24–October 4, 2004, www.iri.org/10-22-04-iraq.asp.

37. O'Hanlon and de Albuquerque, "The Brookings Institution Iraq Index."

while just over one hundred sixty thousand international troops remained on the ground.[38]

The fighting in Najaf had an especially debilitating impact on the IIG. The Najaf battleground ultimately showed where power rested in Iraq, and it was not in the hands of Prime Minister Allawi. During the Najaf standoff, Allawi consistently and very publicly attempted to negotiate a settlement with al-Sadr, going as far as to offer limited amnesty for insurgents.[39] After weeks of effort, Ayatollah al-Sistani arrived in Najaf and within hours brokered a peace accord that not only stopped the fighting but also drew al-Sadr into the political process. This display of Ayatollah al-Sistani's power eroded support for Allawi, who came to be viewed as incapable of providing security.

While Ayatollah al-Sistani's negotiations damaged Allawi's credibility, his actions still had a positive impact on governance. Since al-Sadr was not defeated militarily or constrained from violence, it was critical that he be drawn into the political process. Otherwise, al-Sadr would have continued to challenge the interim government and to prevent progress in the reconstruction effort. Whether al-Sadr's participation in the political process can be sustained, however, remains uncertain. Ayatollah al-Sistani's role also sent a clear message to the religious Shi'a population that their leader supported the political process.

While the fighting raged in Najaf, the Iraqi National Conference was convened in Baghdad to select the Interim National Council (INC), which would exercise legislative powers until national elections could be held. The conference had already been delayed twice because of numerous problems, including security issues, threats of boycotts, poor preparation, lack of publicity, and difficulty choosing delegates. The third time proved the charm, and more than one thousand delegates to the national conference selected eighty-one individuals to serve in the INC. The IGC selected an additional nineteen members. Little heralded at the time and since forgotten, the INC represented a small but important step forward: it gave Iraq a body more representative than the IGC and began the process of engaging a wider circle of Iraqis in governance.

The selection of the INC was not without blemishes. Only 53 percent of the population even knew that the national conference was occurring or that the INC had been chosen.[40] This again demonstrates the failure of the coalition to promote effective public education campaigns to connect the general public to political developments—a problem that consistently plagued the coalition and damaged their ability to capitalize on and increase public support for representative governance. Moreover, there was widespread frustration that

---

38. Ibid.
39. Dean Yates, "Iraq Offers Amnesty to Insurgents," *Reuters*, August 8, 2004.
40. International Republican Institute, "Survey of Iraqi Public Opinion."

"six political parties, most of them made up of returned exiles, dominated the process and alienated exactly the kind of popular leaders the conference was supposed to attract."[41] The conference also failed to attract important Sunni organizations, such as the Association of Muslim Scholars, leaving them outside the political process. This further widened the divide between the Sunni population and the rest of the country.

Rampant security challenges proved to be a continuing problem from the inauguration of the INC through the winter. By September 2004, polling showed that Iraqi acceptance of Prime Minister Allawi had plummeted.[42] This was likely the result of his inability to control the substantial increase in violence that occurred during August and of the continuing lack of employment, enduring corruption, and unmet infrastructure needs. By November, fighting had broken out again in Falluja, where Sunni insurgents posed a major challenge to coalition forces, and by early January 2005 it appeared that security concerns might even delay the elections.

The Transitional National Assembly

In spite of the security situation, the January 30, 2005, elections for members of the 275-member Transitional National Assembly and governorate councils turned out to be a major governance milestone. Sanctioned by UN Security Council Resolution 1546 and organized by an independent Iraqi Election Commission that was supported by the United Nations, the success of the elections provided the assembly with far more democratic legitimacy than any previous transitional body. Voter turnout was nearly 60 percent. Those who did not participate were largely prevented from doing so by security conditions, threats, and intimidation by insurgents and by the failure of some polls to open. The United Iraqi Alliance won slightly more than 50 percent of the seats.

The January 30 election did in fact experience few breaches of security and proved that the majority of the Iraqi public demanded indigenous, representative rule. As Iraqis marked their fingers with purple ink to signify that they had voted, the country—and much of the world—celebrated this important moment in the birth of a democratic Iraq. While one election does not ensure sustainable peace, this was a major step in the right direction. Yet, a lack of Sunni participation in the elections—and their consequent weak representation in the assembly—posed a major problem for the

---

41. Annia Ciezadlo, "Deep Divides Halt Key Iraq Meeting," *Christian Science Monitor*, July 30, 2004, www.csmonitor.com/2004/0730/p06s01-woiq.html.

42. Nearly 30 percent of the population now claimed that Prime Minister Allawi had been very ineffective since taking office, while just over 13 percent still believed he had been very effective. See International Republican Institute, "Survey of Iraqi Public Opinion."

next stage in the long process of establishing legitimate authority and good governance in Iraq: constitution writing.

The final "transitional" phase got off to a slow start. The assembly did not meet until March 16, did not choose its speaker until April 3, did not choose the president and prime minister, Ibrahim al-Jaafari, until April 7, and did not swear in ministers until May 3.[43] Many more stable countries take this long to put a new government in place, but in the Iraqi context speed was of the essence. With a raging insurgency, continuing high levels of unemployment, and an inadequate provision of basic services, many Iraqis were looking for quick and decisive action from their democratically elected assembly and government. They did not get their wish.

In meeting its main responsibility to write a constitution, the assembly faced particular difficulty. Because of the single-district proportional system used in the elections, low Sunni turnout, and ethnically based voting, few Sunnis were elected to the assembly. In fact, the largest Sunni political party to participate in the elections, the Iraqis, won only five seats. Weeks of negotiation were therefore required to form the constitutional commission and weeks more to add fifteen unelected Sunnis to its de facto membership. Only on July 8 did the additional Sunnis attend their first meeting of the constitutional commission. By August 8, the main negotiations on the constitution had been moved from the commission into a "leadership council" (also known as "the kitchen") to which Sunnis were often not invited. The newly constituted U.S. embassy precipitated this change to meet the August 15 deadline for writing the constitution laid down in the TAL.

Although the August 15 deadline was missed, the rushed effort did enable the referendum on the proposed constitution to be held on the TAL-directed date of October 15. The constitution passed. While many Sunnis voted against it, they proved unable to garner the two-thirds rejection in three governorates required to block the measure.[44]

The approved constitution was essentially a federalist compromise between Shi'a and Kurds, as they held the overwhelming majority of seats in the assembly and made up the leadership council. Kurds and Shi'as in Iraq generally suffered under the Saddam Hussein regime, but they have many differences, most notably on the role of religion, secularism, the role of women, and attitudes toward Americans. The result was a constitution that leaves substantial scope for regional devolution of power—in the first instance to Kurdistan in the north but with the possibility of forming one

43. Council on Foreign Relations, "Iraq Timeline 2005," October 13, 2005, www.cfr.org/publication/8429/.

44. Independent Electoral Commission of Iraq, "Certification of the Constitutional Referendum Final Results," October 25, 2005, www.ieciraq.org/final%20cand/20051102%20Certified%20Referendum%20Results%20English.pdf.

or more Shi'a-dominated regions in the south. The difficult issue of oil was resolved by allowing local control over oil management but by also sharing oil wealth, at least from existing oil fields, on a national, per-capita basis.

On the face of it, the constitution is not bad from a Sunni perspective: the Sunnis too might form one or more regions with substantial self-governing authority, and even though there is little oil production in Sunni-majority areas, Sunnis are guaranteed a share of oil wealth. The main Sunni substantive objection to the constitution is that it leaves the door open for Iranian influence in Shi'a regions and even for the eventual dissolution of the country. The Sunnis prefer a strong central government, which they still hope to dominate, as they have since the 1920s. But more than the substance of the constitution, Sunnis objected to the process, which fell far short of the transparent, open process with strong public participation that was expected and mandated by the United Nations.

The Iraqi National Assembly

While Sunnis have concerns over the constitution, these concerns have not alienated them completely from the political process. Sunni candidates, political parties, and voters registered and participated in the December 15 elections for the Iraqi National Assembly in large numbers, despite the threats of disruption by Ba'athists and foreign jihadists. The December 2005 elections marked another major step forward in establishing an Iraqi government that is sovereign in deed and in word and that is recognized by most Iraqis as legitimate, effective, and sustainable.

While the Iraqi National Assembly and the government of Prime Minister Nouri al-Maliki that it installed in April through May 2006 may maintain more legitimacy than any of their predecessors, the continuing insurgency, the escalating ethnic and sectarian divisions and violence, and the unmet basic needs of vast segments of the Iraqi population demonstrate that there is still a long way to go. Moreover, the lack of a monopoly on the legitimate use of force will continue to undermine this government's effectiveness, just as it did for its predecessors. The continuing presence of multinational military forces, which is still necessary to counter both insurgency and sectarian violence, casts a shadow on Iraq's claim to sovereignty and legitimacy. Further, while the insurgency continues—Ba'athists who want to restore their supremacy and foreign jihadists remain active throughout the country—the new constitution allows regions to maintain their own armed forces. The *peshmerga*, the Badr Organization, the Mahdi Army, and other militias will therefore continue to pose a challenge to both local and national governance. This situation will warrant the continuing, although likely reduced, presence of multinational forces. It is not clear that U.S. willingness to devote virtually all of its ground combat forces to the effort in Iraq will outlast insurgency and sectarian reprisals.

Would Something Else Have Worked Better?

No one would claim that the twists and turns that took Iraq through a series of transitional administrations—ORHA, the CPA, the IGC, the IIG, and the Transitional National Assembly—were ideal. Certainly, other approaches could have been taken. Would any of them necessarily have worked better? Could a transitional administration made up of Iraqi exiles—or a UN-led transitional administration—have been more legitimate and better able to accelerate Iraq's transition and political stability?

An Iraqi government-in-exile, formed before the war by expatriates, was seriously considered as an option. The idea likely faltered less because of its merits than because of the difficulties of getting U.S. government agencies to agree on who would lead and staff it. While it is impossible to tell whether such a government would have been more effective, it is apparent from the role of the expatriates since the war that they had no great claim to being able to govern Iraq. Many have failed to gain much traction in an Iraq that has changed a great deal since their departure. Iraqis in general have little admiration for the expatriates, who face considerable resentment because they are viewed, at best, as out of touch with the country and, at worst, as people who had abandoned and thus betrayed their country. Thus, it is unlikely that an expatriate administration would have been more legitimate solely because of the nationality of its members. Had a transitional government of exiled Iraqis been installed to lead the post-conflict phase, it would likely have faced problems similar to those faced by the IGC, although arguably the additional time to prepare for a governing role would have been beneficial.

Assuming that opposition in the UN Security Council and the secretariat could have been overcome by a concerted U.S. diplomatic effort, a UN-led transitional administration would likewise have faced significant problems that would have hindered its legitimacy and effectiveness. At the end of the war, Iraqis were not well disposed toward the United Nations, which they blamed for crippling the country during the years of sanctions and for collaborating with Saddam Hussein's regime. Adding to this negative perception of the United Nations, the oil-for-food scandal would have seriously degraded its acceptability as an authority figure. The UN mandate that coalition forces received in October 2003 did nothing perceptible to increase their acceptability to most Iraqis.

Conclusion

The shortcomings of the coalition in Iraq do not necessarily demonstrate that some other model would have worked better. The effectiveness of the phased format that was implemented was ultimately limited not so much by the approach it followed as by the failure to plan and prepare adequately, to staff appropriately, and to use its considerable resources effectively. In other words, it was not the format for transitional administration in post-conflict Iraq that was flawed; it was the implementation that was problematic. ORHA lacked basic functioning communications systems, computers with Internet capabilities, office furniture and supplies, and security. Neither ORHA nor the CPA was fully staffed, and both were particularly lacking in Arabic speakers and governance experts. Coordination with the military was inadequate. Funds flowed slowly and then mainly to U.S. contractors, who failed to sufficiently engage Iraqis in their efforts. Security for civilian workers was seriously lacking. These are not problems necessarily derived from the format of transitional administration. In short, the mechanisms for governance in post-conflict Iraq could have functioned more effectively had sufficient plans and resources been provided.

More important, however, post-conflict Iraq demonstrates that the type of interim regime may not be the primary determinant of the political outcome. In fact, the most significant lesson from Iraq—which other experiences in interim governance corroborate—is that the political outcome is first and foremost contingent on the level of security throughout the country. The operation in Iraq has witnessed levels of violence largely unheard of in post-conflict reconstruction operations, with the possible exception of operations in Liberia, Cambodia, and Haiti. From May 2003 to December 2005, 42,500 Iraqi civilians were killed.[45] While peace processes and reconstruction efforts were able to proceed in those other cases, the failure to rapidly gain control over the security situation in Iraq squandered early legitimacy and decreased the local community's acceptance of the occupying authorities, undermining virtually all subsequent reconstruction and governance efforts.

The security environment sets the experience in Iraq apart from other operations, and it is this factor that played—and continues to play—the pre-eminent role in shaping the political outcome of the country. It is likely that the final political outcome in Iraq, which will not be clear for a number of years, will shape the willingness of the international community to intervene in the midst of violence again. Iraq has demonstrated that without a monopoly on the legitimate use of force, no form of interim governance can ensure full effectiveness and sustainability. A more robust planning process would have anticipated the breakdown of public order, provided for much

---

45. O'Hanlon and de Albuquerque, "The Brookings Institution Iraq Index."

closer coordination between military and civilians, and redoubled political efforts even while slowing the infusion of money for large projects and augmenting the flow of funds into local councils and smaller community projects. No plan survives encounter with the enemy, but some plans are better than others in anticipating where things can go wrong. Planning for Iraq was unnecessarily and fatally constrained to a single scenario. It was not a rosy one, but it was one that fit the predilections of top decision makers in Washington better than it fit the reality in Iraq.

In all, Iraq's transitional period demonstrated the unbreakable link among security, governance, and legitimacy. After the fall of Baghdad, the lack of security and the rule of law triggered serious obstacles to effective governance. From looted government buildings to assassinated political leaders, the security crises often impeded both local and national political bodies from successfully executing the most elementary governance tasks. This, in turn, led to a hemorrhaging of domestic legitimacy. With each drop in legitimacy, insecurity escalated and insurgent and sectarian conflict—directed at both the coalition and Iraqis—increased. In this way, the initial security crises, which could have been mitigated with proper prewar planning and an appropriate post-conflict force structure, propelled a downward spiral that tore at the fabric of national unity and that may have undermined the prospect of sustainable democratic governance in Iraq.

The coalition response to this spiral tended to focus on military solutions that aimed to resolve the immediate security crises. In a post-conflict environment, however, the focus must be on achieving political stability. Resolving political crises fundamentally requires bolstering the effectiveness of governance institutions by undertaking specific tasks, such as training local government officials, providing resources to build and support government institutions, and monitoring government bodies for corruption and other illegal behavior. If the coalition had devoted considerable resources to these tasks, it might have been able to enhance the effectiveness of Iraq's transitional governing bodies, thereby boosting the legitimacy of local and national democratic structures. By doing so, the coalition might have been able to prevent some of the violence that a lack of legitimacy fueled, particularly in the Sunni communities. Until the focus shifts toward achieving political stability, it is unclear if Iraq's new democratic institutions will be able to withstand the violence wreaking havoc on the country. What is clear is that the lack of legitimate governance is both a consequence and cause of the violence in Iraq, and it will take the presence of effective governance to end it.

Part Three

Conclusions

15

Conclusions and Policy Implications

Yes, It Makes a Difference

Daniel P. Serwer

This is a wonderful but complicated book. It starts in the academic realms of prior literature and political theory. It proceeds through many case studies, each challenging in their own right. It focuses on difficult concepts: sovereignty, governance, legitimacy, transition, and authority. My job in this brief coda is to boil its conclusions down to lessons learned to inform those who may undertake interim governance responsibilities and to improve not only their understanding but also their practice.

It is important first to view interim governments in context. They are only a small part of the puzzle and democratization is only one of the processes involved in societies emerging from conflict. The authors in this volume have paid a good deal of attention to some other parts, in particular to security and rule of law. They have occasionally touched on economic issues—particularly when they affect the security situation or political claims—and more rarely on social questions, such as feeding and sheltering the general population or developing mechanisms that will enable war-torn societies to understand and reconcile with their own pasts. But a lot has not been discussed, such as jobs, monetary policy, reconstruction, the organization of ministries and a civil service, the vetting of former combatants, the return of displaced people and refugees to their homes, and the development of intelligence services. There is a long list of things other than the issues focused on within this volume that ultimately determine success or failure. In order to work well, the governance piece of the puzzle has to fit in with the creation of a safe and secure environment, the establishment of the rule of law, the development of a sustainable economy, and the improvement of social well-being. While these other objectives are beyond the scope of this book, they should be kept in mind when thinking about interim governance.[1]

Fortunately, there is a remarkable consensus today on what the governance objective should be: democracy. Despite the incredible variety of cases and circumstances discussed in this book—and others not discussed here—the international community has come to regard some sort of representative democracy as the only legitimate long-term objective, however difficult and foreign to the particular circumstances it may seem. Today, interim governance means governance between whatever unsatisfactory situation a society emerging from conflict finds itself in and a democratic outcome. Such a consensus did not exist before the end of the Cold War, when the emergence of a dictatorship could sometimes satisfy at least some in the international community. The main preoccupation then was whether a society emerging from conflict would align itself on one side or the other, not how it was governed. Moreover, the democratic objective seems widely shared by local populations, who almost without exception welcome the opportunity to speak their minds freely and to vote once war is over (while often choosing as their representatives some of what the international community would regard as the worst elements of the wartime period). Certainly, there are local elites and even internationals who might prefer—in circumstances like those in Afghanistan or Iraq, for example—nondemocratic outcomes, but such outcomes would generally be regarded as failures according to contemporary norms.

That said, the challenges faced by those who lead a society emerging from conflict—whether locals or internationals—are formidable. In all-too-often chaotic conditions, they are called upon to develop and execute complex plans that require unity of purpose among various military groups (local and international), government authorities, international organizations, NGOs, and even the private sector. They need to garner the necessary financial and staff resources—without being sure what a rapidly evolving situation may require—in countries whose infrastructure and revenue-generating capacities, as well as qualified personnel, may have been all but zeroed out.

Even with a clear mandate, leadership in societies emerging from conflict will have to cultivate and maintain legitimacy, both with the local population and the international community. The local population will view legitimacy as closely connected to the delivery of services and human security: if you are unable to get the lights turned on or feed the popula-

---

1. These ideas are discussed in more detail in Daniel P. Serwer and Patricia Thomson, "A Framework for Success: International Intervention in Societies Emerging from Conflict," in *Leashing the Dogs of War: Conflict Management in a Divided World*, ed. Pamela Aall, Chester A. Crocker, and Fen Osler Hampson (Washington, D.C.: United States Institute of Peace Press, 2006).

tion, you are going to have a hard time convincing people to cooperate with you. The internationals will be far more concerned with whether you were cooperative at the negotiating table and delivered an important constituency to sign the peace agreement, or whether you can pose serious obstacles to its implementation. This is an odd basis on which to accord legitimacy, but it is also necessary in many situations in order to remove obstacles. Inclusion, at least of those who appear prepared to lay down arms, is generally to be preferred. But in some cases it may even be necessary to include those who still keep open the option of resorting to violence.

International legitimacy is important for an interim government. In addition to UN Security Council permanent members, neighbors and regional powers are particularly important, since it is clear that stabilizing a society emerging from conflict becomes far more difficult—perhaps even impossible—if neighboring or nearby states are uncooperative. Conversely, helpful neighbors can do a great deal to alleviate burdens and create favorable conditions for a successful transition.

It cannot be assumed that the local population will support either local or international leadership once a conflict subsides. Local elites often incorporate those who were previously responsible for abusing the population, and internationals are likely to be welcomed only by some. A real constituency in support of peace emerges slowly at best, while spoilers with a vested interest in continuing conflict are likely to persist for a long time. The drivers of conflict do not disappear automatically after a peace agreement, and new ones may emerge. Politics—even democratic politics—is war by other means.

In the immediate aftermath of conflict, power grows from the barrel of a gun—whether held by a local tribal chieftain or a blue-helmeted soldier. Democratization requires a transition to civilian control, which in turn entails building the institutions that the fighting has likely destroyed or rendered powerless. This is no easy task, but it will be harder if those institutions never existed or were completely destroyed. In such cases, internationals often take over, but they need to keep in mind from the start that, eventually, authority must be turned over to the locals.

With all these requirements, it is no wonder that brilliant, quick success is nowhere to be found in interim governments. Setbacks are frequent, steps that were intended to be final instead become phases, one-year timetables stretch into many-year timetables, fighting sometimes resumes, and, ultimately, something a good deal less than full success may have to suffice. There is no guarantee of linearity; in fact, there is a virtual guarantee that things will not go in a planned or logical sequence. Some things may happen on schedule, while others will lag. Asynchronicity is the rule, not the exception.

International involvement greatly complicates the analysis of interim governance. There is, of course, a fundamental contradiction when the "international community"—in the form of the United Nations, a coalition of the willing, or a regional organization—intervenes to push a society emerging from conflict in a democratic direction. The internationals are not directly accountable to the citizens, and imposing democracy is an obvious contradiction in terms. Moreover, the local leadership may welcome internationals who will take the tough decisions out of their hands, thus taking the rap for policies that the local population does not support. This "moral hazard" locks some societies into a cycle of dependency on the internationals and makes the transition to local control exceedingly difficult. Complaining about the internationals is virtually the national pastime in societies emerging from conflict.

International intervention—lighter as in the case studies toward the beginning of this volume or heavier as in those toward the end—has nevertheless become a common feature in societies emerging from conflict. While some would argue that wars should be fought to a definitive conclusion, the spillover from allowing them to persist has become objectionable, both morally and practically. There are few wars in which one or another part of the international community does not have an interest in finding a way to end the fighting well before victory, and even wars that end in victory can entail in the aftermath difficult governance problems requiring international attention.

So what lessons can we draw from both the theoretical part of this volume and the case studies about whether international intervention is advisable and, if so, whether it should be lighter or heavier?

The first lesson is a warning: no matter how compelling the case for international intervention, the difficulties and uncertainties of interim governance—whether of the more direct or less direct sort—are so great that any rational person should think twice before undertaking the effort. It will likely prove more difficult, cost more, and last longer than the advocates of international intervention estimate. There is no case in this book—indeed, no case in the past fifteen years—in which international intervention has proven easy, swift, or cheap. International interim governments last decades, not months or years. Although in general the interventions described here have improved the situation, the changes are not nearly as unequivocal or as dramatic as their advocates promised before the fact.

Planning and training for international intervention, in particular on the civilian side, is at best spotty. It is quite apparent that experienced personnel and organizations know their business, especially when it comes to organizing elections. It is far harder to find those needed to organize a parliament, an interior ministry, or a municipal government. For many interim governance tasks, ad hoc solutions prevail. Moreover, those who work on interim governance generally work in isolation from one another, and in isolation from those who work on rule of law or other issues, with little prior coordination and rarely with any in-depth planning with the international military forces to be deployed. "Peacefare"—the training and doctrine required for peace building—is far less advanced than warfare.

While undertaken these days always for the most enlightened reasons, the exigencies of interim governance will necessarily conflict with the high ideals that motivate it. The negative part is not so problematic: international intervention can remove a dictator or end a civil war, provided the situation is more or less ripe and the resources provided are adequate. But when the longer-term goals of democracy and freedom confront warlords and spoilers, the warlords and spoilers all too often come out on top, or close to it. Accountability for past abuses, which has often been the primary justification for the intervention, may be long in coming, even when the international interveners are completely in control.

Security is job one. Without it, nothing else will go well. Interveners generally rely on the military and police forces that accompany them—backed by UN Security Council or other international confirmations of legitimacy—to ensure primacy, and in many cases they succeed in establishing a safe and secure environment, or some semblance of it (Iraq, and increasingly Afghanistan, are exceptions). But even when backed by impeccably drafted UN Security Council resolutions and accepted by the warring parties, legitimacy in the eyes of the local population remains problematic, and as a consequence, establishing the rule of law is challenging.

Rule of law goes beyond a safe and secure environment. It is about the protection of individuals, the elimination of impunity, and the creation of institutions and procedures that can function fairly across the population, in the provinces as well as in the capital. Situations that precipitate international intervention often involve mass abuses against at least a part of the population. Establishing the rule of law takes longer than many other tasks, but it is vital if the interveners are ever to fulfill their ambition to leave. The effort therefore needs to be started early, not postponed until after many other tasks are completed. The pursuit of justice is not an idealistic option but a necessity.

Democracy is not just elections, and governance is not just convening a parliament or naming a prime minister. The milestones that interveners often set out on the path to democratic governance are just that—milestones, not to be mistaken for goals. Getting to democratic governance can be botched in many ways: elections too early or elections too late; spoilers in or spoilers out; too much focus on what is going on in the capital or too little; too many expats or too few. Deciding these issues requires deep knowledge of the local context, knowledge not acquired in weeks or months. And by the time the knowledge is acquired, the international interveners are likely to have already empowered—intentionally or unintentionally—elites who will have distinct advantages in the political competition to follow.

International interveners, whose primary relationship is most often with politicians and armed groups in the capital, too seldom search for legitimacy in the local population and build there a constituency for peace. This is surprising but not irremediable: interveners need to look beyond the power brokers who dominate the capital, seeking those who really want peace in the broader population and consulting them seriously and often. Interveners also need to understand what makes the power brokers powerful, including their sources of financing and their roles in the previous regime. Blindly treating everyone "fairly" will more likely than not end in empowering those who oppose the intervention's democratic objective.

How does one get rid of "bad actors," "spoilers," and abusers from the previous regime? Not easily. Sometimes it is possible to remove them from the scene directly, either by military means or by arrest and trial. Doing so quickly and decisively has facilitated a number of transitions. But once they or their erstwhile supporters become participants in an interim regime, it becomes more difficult. Elections are unlikely to do it. Sustained effort to undermine their hold on the economy may work, as may efforts to level the political playing field and ensure real competition. But an early commitment by interveners to depart will undermine both economic and political efforts to weaken the illicit networks that previous warring parties or nasty regimes leave behind.

Power sharing is a common feature of societies emerging from conflicts that have not been fought to victory and defeat but instead to a mutually hurting stalemate. The warring parties may then decide they are better off in a "mutually hurting balance of power," one that will almost certainly not correspond to a democratic outcome but at least gives the weaker party some confidence of being treated better than during wartime. Many interim governments pass through a power-sharing phase, and some power-sharing arrangements are even codified in constitutions and laws. But this will surely make getting to truly representative democracy more difficult—clarity about that purpose should trump the interests of former warring parties when it comes to the more permanent arrangements.

Some might conclude from these lessons that international intervention is hopeless, and that societies emerging from conflict should do it on their own, without international assistance. That would be a mistake. Despite the challenges—and the mistakes—many millions of people are a lot better off than they would have been without international intervention. This is true even in the dramatically difficult cases, such as Cambodia, Afghanistan, and Iraq, where the outcomes can certainly not be described as satisfactory. It is also clearly the case for El Salvador, Guatemala, and East Timor, and even for Burundi, the Democratic Republic of the Congo, and Liberia.

Full success has proven elusive—the lengthy interventions in Kosovo and Bosnia are not yet at the goal line. The impact of early mistakes is particularly notable; they seem to have a disproportionate effect on future prospects. The lighter interventions seem to allow for an easier transition to local control, because they interfere less with the legitimacy of local leaders. But in many situations heavier intervention at the beginning is required— for the security and the well-being of both the internationals and the local population. Whether light or heavy, the internationals need to be better prepared, better informed, more insightful, more careful, more transparent, more persistent, and more respectful. But they can and do make a difference, no matter how confused and problematic any particular moment may appear and no matter how elusive the ultimate goal proves to be.

Acknowledgments

This project began in late 2004 as the product of our research and teaching on post-conflict security building, comparative politics, ethnic conflict, and stability operations at the Naval Postgraduate School in Monterey, California. Many of our students, predominantly United States and international military officers, were fresh from conflictual or transitioning countries, or preparing to enter them, and our discussions often focused on the processes and difficulties of transitioning from conflict to a stable, democratic peace. We found few texts that dealt directly with such issues in an in-depth manner, so we developed the idea to organize a collection of theoretical works and case studies on interim governments for use in our classrooms and beyond. We began this project with our own students in mind, so we thank them for their service and commitment.

The International Programs Office of the United States Navy generously provided the support for us to put together a workshop on interim governments in July 2005, and this book is the outcome of the workshop's discussions. We would like to thank all the workshop participants who turned their papers into polished book chapters for adhering to our guidelines, timelines, and overall vision for the project. All collaborative efforts depend on the active participation of the contributors, so we hope that they are as pleased with this volume as we are.

We are also grateful to Ambassador Carlos Pascual, then newly appointed Coordinator for Reconstruction and Stabilization at the Department of State, who encouraged this project at its conception. Our intention to foster a scholar-practitioner dialogue was well served by the policymakers, diplomats, and scholars contributing to the project. We owe particular thanks to the following who read and commented upon drafts and offered valuable insight and advice during our workshop: Hamid Abdeljaber, Jason Aplon, Jan Black, Tom Bruneau, Anne Clunan, Sarah Farnsworth, Scott Feil, Fen Hampson, Jeff Larsen, Leslie Lebl, Thomas Montgomery, Andy Morrison, Robert Ogilvie, James Russell, Judy Van Rest and Susan Woodward.

The project owes an intellectual debt to a 1995 volume on interim regimes, *Between States*, edited by Yossi Shain and Juan Linz. We were very fortunate that Yossi was able to attend the conference and bring his valuable insights to the project. He contributed tremendously to the workshop and this volume.

Jennifer Hambleton provided excellent research and administrative support throughout the project, and the workshop would not have been a success without her dedicated work. Thanks also go to Barry Zellen, our conference recorder, and to Izumi Wakugawa for assisting with the workshop.

The United States Institute of Peace Press has an excellent record of producing policy-relevant scholarly work. We offer many thanks to our editor,

Kurt Volkan, for taking on this project with an open mind and enthusiastic approach. We are also grateful to the anonymous reviewers of this work for their constructive criticism and helpful suggestions.

Finally, heartfelt thanks are due to our own teachers and mentors. In particular, we remember our wonderful colleague Donald Rothchild, professor of political science emeritus at the University of California at Davis. Sadly, as we prepared this manuscript to go to press, Don lost his battle with cancer. True to himself and his extraordinary work ethic, he completed his final chapter edits just weeks before his passing, all while undergoing arduous treatments and without saying a word about his condition. Don expressed keen consideration for people and ideas, and we were lucky to have had him on the project. While his work dealt with some of the darker sides of human conduct, he himself possessed an innocence and spirit of humanity that shines through all of his works. His scholarship always resisted facile caricature and brought us a deep and nuanced understanding of our complicated world. Thank you, Don.

Contributors

Mark Baskin is a political scientist, author, scholar, and field practitioner with particular interests and expertise in conflict and post-conflict administration, peacekeeping strategies, rule of law, local government, and conflict mitigation. His geographic area of emphasis has been the Balkans.

He spent nearly a decade working for UN peacekeeping operations in the field and at mission headquarters in Zagreb, Vukovar, and Sarajevo. He served as the United Nations' deputy regional administrator in Prizren, Kosovo, and as Prizren's municipal administrator from 1999 to 2000. His research has focused on ethnicity and nationalism in socialist Yugoslavia, economic and political transitions in the Balkans, and the establishment of rule of law and governance in conflict zones. He has taught at the University of Michigan, Manhattanville College, and the University of North Carolina–Greensboro. He is the author of numerous scholarly publications, book reviews, and journal articles on his experiences and is frequently invited to give public presentations.

He holds a doctorate in political science from the University of Michigan. In 2003–2004, he was a public policy scholar at the Woodrow Wilson International Center for Scholars in Washington, D.C. He speaks fluent Serbo-Croatian and Russian.

Christina Caan is a former research assistant at the United States Institute of Peace where she coauthored several papers on transitional governance. She is currently a PhD student in the Political Science Department at George Washington University.

Lenard J. Cohen is a professor of political science at Simon Fraser University. He specializes in Russian and East European politics, with a focus on the Balkans. During the last decade, he has also been working on questions of regional security in Southeastern Europe, international relations, and both Canadian and U.S. foreign policy toward Eastern Europe. His authored and coedited books include *Communist Systems in Comparative Perspective* (1974), *Political Cohesion in a Fragile Mosaic: The Yugoslav Experience* (1983), *The Vision and the Game: Making the Canadian Constitution* (1987), *The Socialist Pyramid: Elites and Power in Yugoslavia* (1989), *Broken Bonds: Yugoslavia's Disintegration and Balkan Politics in Transition* (1993; 2nd edition, 1995), and *"Serpent in the Bosom": The Rise and Fall of Slobodan Milosevic* (2000; 2nd edition, 2002). His most recent books, both published in 2003, are *NATO and European Security: Alliance Politics from the End of the Cold War to the Age of Terrorism* and *Foreign Policy Realignment in the Age of Terror*. He has also published widely in political science journals and edited collections, and he is currently working on a study of democratization in Southeastern Europe titled "Embracing Democracy: Political Change in Southeastern Europe."

Beth Cole is a senior program officer in the Center for Post-Conflict Peace and Stability Operations at the United States Institute of Peace. She leads USIP's Civilian Peacefare Initiative that began in 2007 and co-chairs the Working Group on Civil-Military Relations in Non-Permissive Environments. Cole coauthored *The Beginner's Guide to Nation-Building* and a number of USIP Special Reports including "Transitional Governance: From Bullets to Ballots" (2006) and "Building Civilian Capacity for U.S. Stability Operations: The Rule of Law Component" (2004).

Aurel Croissant is professor of political science at the Ruprecht Karl University of Heidelberg. From 2004 to 2006 he was assistant professor in the Department of National Security Affairs at the Naval Postgraduate School. He has published more than fifty articles and book chapters on politics in Southeast and East Asia, political theory, political institutions, civil society and democratization.

Devon Curtis is a college lecturer in the Department of Politics at Cambridge University. Her research analyzes the incentives and limits of power-sharing arrangements following ethnic conflict and the transition from rebel movements to political parties in Africa. She is currently completing a book manuscript about the peace process in Burundi. Previously, she was a postdoctoral research fellow at the Saltzman Institute of War and Peace Studies at Columbia University and an adjunct assistant professor at the School of International and Public Affairs, where she taught a course on the politics of peace building and post-conflict reconstruction. Before that, she was a predoctoral fellow at Stanford University's Center for International Security and Cooperation. She has also worked for the Canadian government, the United Nations Staff College, and the Overseas Development Institute. She received her PhD in international relations from the London School of Economics and both her BA and her MA from McGill University.

Antonio Donini is a senior researcher at the Feinstein International Center at Tufts University's Friedman School of Nutrition Science and Policy, where he is working on issues relating to the future of humanitarian action. From 2002 to 2004 he was visiting senior fellow at the Watson Institute for International Studies at Brown University. He has worked for twenty-six years in the United Nations in research, evaluation, and humanitarian capacities. His last post was as director of the UN Office for the Coordination of Humanitarian Assistance (OCHA) to Afghanistan (1999–2002). Before going to Afghanistan, he was chief of the Lessons Learned Unit at OCHA, where he managed a program of independent studies on the effectiveness of relief efforts in complex emergencies. He has published widely on evaluation, humanitarian, and UN reform issues. He is coediter of a volume titled *Nation-Building Unraveled? Aid, Peace and Justice in Afghanistan* (2004) and has written several articles exploring the implications of the crises in Afghanistan and Iraq for the future of humanitarian action.

Andrew J. Enterline is associate professor of political science at the University of North Texas. His research focuses on imposed polities and national/regional outcomes, third-party intervention in civil war, and dynamic models of interstate conflict and occupation. He has written numerous book chapters and has published articles in such journals as the *Journal of Politics, International Studies Quarterly,* the *Journal of Peace Research,* and the *Journal of Conflict Resolution.* He received his PhD in political science from the State University of New York at Binghamton.

J. Michael Greig is assistant professor of political science at the University of North Texas. His primary research interests are in the areas of conflict management, international conflict, and computer simulation. Currently, he is researching ripeness for international mediation as well as how peace diffuses between states. He has published articles in the *Journal of Conflict Resolution* and *International Interactions.* He received his PhD in political science from the University of Illinois–Urbana-Champaign.

Karen Guttieri is a member of the Cebrowski Institute for Innovation and the faculty of the Naval Postgraduate School (NPS) in Monterey, California. Her research on military operations in civilian environments addresses issues of effectiveness, organizational learning, and civil-military relations. Her publications on these topics include "Unlearning War: U.S. Military Experience with Stability Operations," in *Organizational Learning in the Global Context* (2006); and "Professional Military Education in Democracies," in *Who Guards the Guardians and How* (2006). She completed the Civil-Military Cooperation course at the Lester B. Pearson International Peacekeeping Training Centre; the Joint Civil-Military Operations Course at the Joint Special Operations University; and World Vision's Level II Security Management Training Course. She earned her doctorate at the University of British Columbia in Vancouver, Canada, and conducted postdoctoral research at Stanford University's Center for International Security and Cooperation before joining the NPS faculty in 2001.

Paul Hughes is a senior program officer in the Center for Post-Conflict Peace and Stability Operations at the United States Institute of Peace. Prior to joining the Institute, he served as an active duty Army colonel and as the Army's senior military fellow to the Institute for National Security Studies of the National Defense University. As the director of national security policy on the Army staff, he developed and provided policy guidance for the Army in numerous areas, such as arms control, weapons of mass destruction, missile defense, information operations, emerging nontraditional security issues, and crisis prediction.

Thomas H. Johnson was appointed to the faculty of the Naval Postgraduate School's National Security Affairs Department in December 2003, where he teaches courses on Afghanistan, Central Asian crises, politics, terrorism, and security. For two decades, he has conducted research and written on Afghanistan and South Asia. He has directed major research efforts for the U.S. government on Afghanistan and U.S. policy toward that country. He has published numerous studies on Afghanistan and its politics, culture, and anthropology. He is a member of the Afghanistan Editorial Board of the National Security Archive. He has also published in the areas of Central Asia and Afghanistan, insurgencies, foreign policy analysis, peace research/conflict resolution, and political and defense economics modeling and simulation. His most recent publications include "Democratic Nation Building in the Arc of Crisis: The Case of the Presidential Election in Afghanistan," in *Critical Issues in Middle East Security: Stability after Saddam?* (2006); "The Origins and Financing of Afghan Terrorism: Thugs, Guns, Drugs, Interlopers, and Creative Movements of Money," in *Terrorist Financing and State Responses: Comparative Perspective* (2006); and "A Hard Day's Night? The United States and the Global War on Terror," with James A. Russell, *Comparative Strategy* (2005). His earlier work has appeared in such journals as the *American Political Science Review*, the *Journal of Politics*, the *Brown Journal of World Affairs*, *Strategic Review, Politikon: South African Journal of Political Science, Journal of Modern African Studies*, and in numerous edited volumes and scholarly texts.

Michael S. Malley is an assistant professor of comparative politics in the Department of National Security Affairs at the Naval Postgraduate School. His research focuses on issues of state formation, state failure and survival, and regime change in Southeast Asia. He has particular expertise in the area of center-local relations, decentralization policy, and provincial politics and political economy in Indonesia. His research has been supported by grants from the Social Science Research Council, the National Security Education Program, the Institute for the Study of World Politics, the US-Indonesian Society, and Fulbright. His recent publications include several book chapters and articles: "Regions: Centralization and Resistance" (1999); "Beyond Democratic Elections: Indonesia Embarks on a Protracted Transition" (2000); "Class, Region, and Culture: The Sources of Social Conflict in Indonesia" (2001); "Indonesia: Violence and Reform beyond Jakarta" (2001); "State Institutions and Ethnic Conflict in Indonesia" (2002); and "New Rules, Old Structures, and the Limits of Indonesia's Democratic Decentralization" (2003). He earned his doctorate in political science at the University of Wisconsin–Madison, after receiving an MA in Southeast Asian studies from Cornell University and a BA from Georgetown University's School of Foreign Service. As part of these academic programs, he also studied at the National University of Singapore and two Indonesian universities—Gadjah Mada University in Yogyakarta and IKIP in Malang. He speaks Indonesian fluently and has lived, worked, and traveled extensively in Indonesia since the late 1980s.

Carrie Manning is an associate professor and the director of graduate studies in the Department of Political Science at Georgia State University–Atlanta. She is the author of *The Politics of Peace in Mozambique* (2002) and more than a dozen articles on post-conflict democratization and state building. Her work has appeared in *Comparative Politics, Journal of Democracy, Democratization, Studies in Comparative International Development, International Peacekeeping*, and *Party Politics*, among other journals. She has received nationally competitive grants to conduct field research in Africa and the Balkans. She was country director for the National Democratic Institute in Angola in 1996–97 and continues to consult periodically on a range of democratization issues in Africa. She was a visiting professor at the Naval Postgraduate School in 2004 and has conducted civil-military relations programs in Africa and Latin America for the Center for Civil-Military Relations. Her current research focuses on the role of elections in state building and political party development. She holds an MA in public and international affairs from the Woodrow Wilson School at Princeton University and a PhD in political science from the University of California–Berkeley.

E. Philip Morgan is a professor at the Monterey Institute of International Studies, specializing in public administration, public organizations, and institutional development. He has worked, inter alia, with the World Bank, the United States Agency for International Development, and the United Nations Development Programme on diagnostic studies, technical assistance, and training in the areas of organization and management improvement; human resource development; program evaluation; and trade capacity building. He has published widely in the areas of program and project management, comparative civil service systems and reforms, and the linkages between development policymaking and the instruments of policy action. He also serves on the editorial advisory boards of several journals and publishing firms specializing in international development policy and management. He earned his doctorate at Syracuse University's Maxwell School of Citizenship and Public Affairs. After serving many years as a professor and administrator at the School of Public and Environmental Affairs of Indiana University–Bloomington, he became dean of the Graduate School of International Policy Studies at the Monterey Institute of International Studies in California in 1997. In 2003, he returned to teaching, research, and consulting.

Jessica Piombo is an assistant professor and regional coordinator for Sub-Saharan Africa in the Department of National Security Affairs at the Naval Postgraduate School, where she teaches courses on African politics, comparative politics, and ethnic politics and conflicts. She is also a visiting scholar at Stanford's Center for African Studies. In the past, she has been a research associate at the Centre for Social Science Research and the African Studies Centre of the University of Cape Town. Her research focuses on democratization and electoral politics, ethnic and political mobilization, and mechanisms to manage ethnic conflict. She joined the NPS in 2003 after completing her PhD in the Department of Political Science at the Massachusetts Institute of Technology. She is the editor of *Electoral Politics in South Africa: Assessing the First Democratic Decade*, and she has authored or coauthored several book chapters and numerous articles, including "Political Institutions, Social Demographics and the Decline of Ethnic Mobilization in South Africa, 1994–1999," *Party Politics* (July 2005) and "Opposition Parties and the Voters In South Africa's 1999 Election," with Robert Mattes, *Democratization* (Autumn 2001). She has conducted extensive research in South Africa, having lived there between 1999 and 2001, and she has worked with the University of Cape Town, the Institute for Democracy in South Africa, and the University of Durban–Westville, and as an election monitor and member of the Steering Committee of the Peace Monitoring Forum of the Western Cape.

Donald Rothchild is a professor of political science at the University of California, Davis. He is the author of numerous books and articles on African politics, ethnic conflict and conflict management, and civil war termination. His recent books include *Managing Ethnic Conflict in Africa: Pressures and Incentives for Cooperation; Sovereignty as Responsibility: Conflict Management in Africa; The International Spread of Ethnic Conflict: Fear, Diffusion, and Escalation;* and *Africa in the New International Order: Rethinking State Sovereignty and Regional Security.* He recently completed a coedited volume with Philip G. Roeder titled *Powersharing and Peacemaking.*

Daniel P. Serwer is the vice president and director of Peace and Stability Operations and the Balkans Initiative at the United States Institute of Peace. He coordinates the Institute's on-the-ground efforts in conflict zones, including nonviolent conflict strategies, facilitated dialogue, and post-conflict reconstruction. He has worked on preventing interethnic and interreligious conflict in Iraq and has been deeply engaged in facilitating dialogue between Kosovo Serbs and Albanians. He was a senior fellow at the Institute working on Balkan regional security in 1998–99, and before that he was a minister-counselor at the U.S. Department of State, where he won six performance awards. As State Department director of European and Canadian analysis in 1996–97, he supervised the analysts who tracked Bosnia and implementation of the Dayton Peace Agreement as well as the deterioration of the security situation in Albania and Kosovo. He served from 1994 to 1996 as U.S. special envoy and coordinator for the Bosnian Federation, mediating between Croats and Muslims and negotiating the first agreement reached at the Dayton peace talks. From 1990 to 1993 he was deputy chief of mission and chargé d'affaires at the U.S. embassy in Rome; as such, he led a major diplomatic mission through the end of the Cold War and the entire course of the Gulf War. He has previously coauthored Institute publications on Iraq as well as Croatia, Kosovo, Montenegro, and Serbia. He received his PhD in history from Princeton University.

William D. Stanley is associate professor of political science at the University of New Mexico (UNM). His research focuses on political violence and conflict resolution in Central America, with an emphasis on the impact of military, police, and judicial institutions. He is the author of *The Protection Racket State: Elite Politics, Military Extortion, and Civil War in El Salvador* and articles in *International Organization, Global Governance, International Peacekeeping, Studies in Comparative International Development,* Journal of International Affairs, *Latin American Research Review,* and in several edited volumes. His recent work includes articles and chapters on peacekeeping mission strategy; civil war resolution; policing, public safety, and justice reform in post-conflict societies; and the role of factional politics in episodes of extreme violence by states. He is currently writing a comparative book on civil war settlements in Central America, and his research has focused on political violence by states, military politics, police and judicial reform, and peacekeeping and democracy promotion in cases of internal conflict. From 2001 to 2004 he directed the Latin American and Iberian Institute at UNM, a Title-VI–funded national resource center. The United States Institute of Peace, the John D. and Catherine T. MacArthur Foundation, and the Institute for the Study of World Politics have also funded his research. He earned his PhD from the Massachusetts Institute of Technology. He received the UNM Regents' Lecturer Award, 2004–2007.

Index

AAK (Alliance for the Future of Kosovo), 245
Abacha, Sani, 205
Abdullah, Abdullah, 292, 305
Abu Ghraib prison scandal, 331
Abusive practices
  international intervention and ending of, 352
  of local community power holders, 44, 49
Academic area specialists, on the Balkans and Bosnia, 265
Accountability
  citizen conceptions of positive peace and, 46
  construction of political elites through interim governments, lessons learned on, 70
  in democracies, international interim governments and, 221
  government, elections in state undergoing transition and, 23
  international intervention and, 351
  nation-building and levels of, 43
  for past abuses, peace process in Afghanistan and, 44
  of president in Indonesia to legislature, 157–158
  of UNMIK in Kosovo, 17
Accra Comprehensive Peace Agreement, 83, 206–207, 209–210
Aceh, Indonesia
  Megawati's relations with military and conflict in, 166–167
  military and mass graves in, 159
  separatist movement in, 160, 161
  separatist movement in East Timor and separatists in, 226
  Wahid's weak control of military and conflict in, 166
Ad Hoc Commission, El Salvador, 134, 138
Adebajo, Adekeye, 202
Adim, Abdel Aziz, 84

Administrative transitional authority. *See also* International interim government model
  Doyle on, 219–220
  interim government in Cambodia as, 227
Afghan National Army, 302, 303, 305
Afghanistan
  benefits of international intervention in, 352
  Bonn Agreement and political reconstruction in, 289–291
  civic education by Tribal Liaison Office in, 50
  constitution of, 300–302
  elections and distribution of power sharing in, 64–65
  elections under Bonn Agreement in, 303
  ethnic dimensions of *loya jirgas,* post-conflict stability and, 297–299
  expatriate presence in, 38
  external actors and sovereign authority of interim regime in, 66–67
  forecast for imposed nondemocracy in, 117–118
  imposed democratic regime in, 96, 100
  insurgency as political challenge in, 103
  interim administration administrators/ministers, 293–295 (table)
  interim and transitional authorities in, 291–292, 295–297
  interim government after foreign invasion in, 29n, 30
  interim power-sharing arrangements in, 67, 68
  internal rivals to Karzai's central government in, 25
  as international administration model of interim government, 11, 31

365

Interim Governments

This book is set in Palatino; the display type is Optima. Hasten Design Studio designed the book's cover; Katharine Moore designed the interior. Typesetting, proofreading, and indexing was done by EEI Communications. The text was edited by Kurt Volkan.